Multinational Marketing Management

CASES AND READINGS

▲▼ Addison-Wesley Publishing Company

Reading, Massachusetts ▪ Menlo Park, California ▪ New York
Don Mills, Ontario ▪ Wokingham, England ▪ Amsterdam ▪ Bonn
Sydney ▪ Singapore ▪ Tokyo ▪ Madrid ▪ Bogotá ▪ Santiago ▪ San Juan

Library of Congress Cataloging-in-Publication Data

Buzzell, Robert D. (Robert Dow), 1933–
    Multinational marketing management.

    Bibliography: p.
    Includes index.
    1. Export marketing—Management.   I. Quelch, John A.
II. Title.
HF1009.5.B89 1988   658.8'48   87-12599
ISBN 0-201-07996-8

Many of the designations used by manufacturers and sellers to distinguish their products are claimed as trademarks. Where those designations appear in this book, and Addison-Wesley was aware of a trademark claim, the designations have been printed in initial caps or all caps.

PREFACE

There is no doubt that the international dimensions of marketing have become more important during the 1970s and 1980s. A generation ago, multinational marketing was largely the province of a few large corporations. Some of these companies were in industries such as oil and copper where the location of raw materials made multinational operations imperative. Others, such as Singer, Eastman Kodak, and IBM, had proprietary products or processes that could readily be exploited in overseas markets. A few, like Nestlé and Unilever, were pioneers in utilizing their marketing capabilities on a worldwide scale.

Companies in each of these three groups are still active in multinational business in the late 1980s, but they have lately been joined by a host of companies following other patterns of international competition, even in industries where rivalry has traditionally been confined within national boundaries. Consider just a few examples of some new patterns that have evolved:

- Commercial banking is becoming a "global industry." Branches of banking organizations based in dozens of home countries can be found in every major city around the world.

- Telecommunications has traditionally been a government-protected industry within each major country. By the mid-1980s, large multinational competitors were competing directly with each other in most areas.
- Automobile producers must design their new models for world markets to achieve the volumes needed for competitive costs.
- Even in retailing, the most locally oriented of industries, multinational companies are emerging.

As these examples suggest, there are few lines of business that are not affected in important ways by multinational influences. Companies that don't sell their products or services outside their home countries may nevertheless compete with multinationals, buy goods overseas, borrow from foreign banks, and have foreign shareholders. The trend toward international integration of all phases of business activity is natural in an era of ever-improving transportation and communication. All things considered, we believe that this trend is a healthy one, in that it benefits consumers and promotes international understanding.

The growing internationalization of business is also creating new challenges for managers, government regulators, and students of business. It is for the men and women in these groups that we have prepared and assembled the materials in this volume. We hope that reading and discussing the cases and readings will help managers, managers-to-be, and others to understand the issues involved in multinational marketing.

The book is organized into three parts. In the first, we explore the linkages between marketing and basic questions of multinational competitive strategies. The underlying theme is that the best foundation for effective multinational marketing is a clearly defined overall strategy.

The second part deals with the design and execution of multinational marketing programs. The cases and readings in this section illustrate the pros and cons of "standardizing" major marketing program elements such as product lines, prices, distribution, and communications. They also raise questions about how marketing activities in different countries can be "harmonized" to achieve the full benefits of operating multinationally.

The cases and readings in the third part deal with the organization and coordination of multinational marketing operations. Here we raise questions about the proper degree of centralization in multinational organizations and provide examples of the difficult process of changing a long-established structure.

All of the materials included in the book have been used in Harvard

Business School MBA courses and executive programs. The structure of the book, and most of the cases and readings, are based on a week-long executive program in Multinational Marketing Management, first offered in 1985. This program, which has been held in Italy and Switzerland, was designed for experienced multinational company executives. Participants in 1985 and 1986 came from 16 countries, representing such companies as Eastman Kodak, Nestlé, IBM, Bayer, Procter & Gamble, Sandoz, Corning Glass, Volkswagen, and Deutsche Bank. We and our colleagues in the program faculty have learned a great deal from the participants about the realities of managing in multinational enterprises.

We are grateful to several of our Harvard Business School colleagues for allowing us to include their case studies: Christopher Bartlett, Robert Dolan, James Heskett (in collaboration with Sergio Signorelli), Rowland Moriarty, and Michael Yoshino, all of whom graciously consented to contribute cases that cover important topics in the field of multinational marketing and general management.

Special thanks go to Ulrich Wiechmann, a former HBS colleague, for his three cases. We also appreciate being able to include as readings *Harvard Business Review* articles by Thomas Hout, Michael Porter, and Eileen Rudden; Gary Hamel and C.K. Prahalad; Theodore Levitt; and Christopher Bartlett. Edward Hoff, currently enrolled in Harvard's Doctoral Program in Business Economics, helped to prepare the Nestlé case and also coauthored the reading on "Customizing Global Marketing."

Shirley Spence, formerly a Research Associate at HBS, did much of the work involved in preparing the Instructor's Manual for the book. We appreciate her contributions and also the proofreading work of Thelma Prince. We also appreciate the efforts of Susan Blackman and Phyllis Sexton who typed the manuscript.

The Harvard Business School Division of Research supported the original development work represented in the materials included here. Our thanks to the Division, and to Dean John McArthur, for providing a working environment that encourages and makes possible the development of up-to-date teaching materials.

Stephen Mautner of Addison-Wesley worked closely with us from the beginning in the planning and preparation of this volume. We appreciate Steve's interest and help.

While many people have helped us, we remain responsible for the shortcomings of this book. In spite of these shortcomings, we hope it will be a useful contribution to learning about multinational marketing.

Boston   R.D.B.
                                                                                                              J.A.Q.

CONTENTS

PART 1

Designing Strategies for Multinational Competition

Introduction **2**

READINGS

How Global Companies Win Out by Thomas Hout, Michael E. Porter, and Eileen Rudden **9**

Do You Really Have a Global Strategy? by Gary Hamel and C.K. Prahalad **29**

CASES

Benetton by James L. Heskett and Sergio Signorelli **47**

The World Pharmaceutical Industry: Prospects for the 1980s by Robert D. Buzzell **77**

Ciba-Geigy Pharmaceuticals Division: Multinational Strategic Planning by Robert D. Buzzell **92**

Henkel Group: Umbrella Branding and Globalization Decisions by Robert J. Dolan **112**

Mövenpick Unternehmungen by Ulrich Wiechmann and Kate Gillespie **130**

ix

PART 2
Multinational Marketing Programs

Introduction   **156**

READINGS
Can You Standardize Multinational Marketing? by Robert D. Buzzell   **164**
The Globalization of Markets by Theodore Levitt   **186**

CASES
Hoover: Multinational Product Planning by Robert D. Buzzell and Jean-Louis LeCocq   **206**
Computervision Japan by Rowland T. Moriarty   **230**
Fisher-Price Benelux by Robert D. Buzzell, Carlos del Nero and Stephen Muirhead   **259**
Minolta Camera Co., Ltd. by Ulrich Wiechmann   **279**
British Airways by John A. Quelch   **291**

PART 3
Organizing and Controlling Multinational Operations

Introduction   **322**

READINGS
Customizing Global Marketing by John A. Quelch and Edward J. Hoff   **329**
MNCs: Get Off the Reorganization Merry-Go-Round by Christopher A. Bartlett   **348**

CASES
Nestlé S.A.: International Marketing by John A. Quelch and Edward J. Hoff   **363**
Chandler Home Products by Michael Y. Yoshino and Yaakov Keren   **396**
Procter & Gamble Europe: Vizir Launch by Christopher A. Bartlett   **423**
Yoshida Kogyo K.K. by Ulrich Wiechmann   **448**
Citibank: Marketing to Multinational Customers by Robert D. Buzzell   **469**

SELECTED BIBLIOGRAPHY   **499**

Multinational Marketing Management
CASES AND READINGS

PART 1
Designing Strategies for Multinational Competition

Introduction

Readings

1.1. How Global Companies Win Out by Thomas Hout, Michael E. Porter, and Eileen Rudden

1.2. Do You Really Have a Global Strategy? by Gary Hamel and C.K. Prahalad

Cases

1.3. Benetton by James L. Heskett and Sergio Signorelli

1.4. The World Pharmaceutical Industry: Prospects for the 1980s by Robert D. Buzzell

1.5. Ciba-Geigy Pharmaceuticals Division: Multinational Strategic Planning by Robert D. Buzzell

1.6. Henkel Group: Umbrella Branding and Globalization Decisions by Robert J. Dolan

1.7. Mövenpick Unternehmungen by Ulrich Wiechmann and Kate Gillespie

In a multinational company, the primary role of marketing management is to design and implement marketing programs in each of several — perhaps many — countries. This task, which is complex enough in a single marketplace, is much more so when companies must accommodate the needs and preferences of customers that have different levels of purchasing power as well as different climates, languages, and customs. Moreover, patterns of competition and methods of doing business differ among nations, and sometimes the differences are extreme. For example, producers of razor blades must be able to sell their product through self-service displays in supermarkets in major industrial countries and at the same time distribute single blades in less-developed economies by means of street vendors.

In a large multibusiness corporation, multinational marketing management involves hundreds or thousands of decisions about specific aspects of marketing programs: new product or service development, pricing, distribution channels, advertising and sales promotion, and so on. Often these decisions appear to have little or nothing to do with each other: for example, is there a connection between granting additional trade promotion allowances to, say, a retailer in France and introducing a new product in Canada? In a multinational environment, these aspects of marketing *are* interrelated, and effective performance requires that they be coordinated as well. In the example just given, promotional allowances granted a customer in France might lead to transshipments of a product to the French-speaking areas of Canada at below-normal prices. This, in turn, might damage the manufacturer's ability to secure distribution for a new product in Canada. Thus, it is essential that the marketing policies and programs of a multinational enterprise be *harmonized*. To accomplish this, successful multinational marketers employ three principal mechanisms:

- They develop, and periodically modify, a coherent, overall *competitive strategy* for multinational operations;
- They utilize the same basic *approach to marketing program design* for each country or region in which they operate; and
- They adopt systems for *organizing and controlling* multinational operations that ensure an adequate flow of information and clear assignment of responsibilities to individual managers.

These are the "building blocks" that make up the framework for this book. The cases and readings in Part 1 deal with basic issues of competitive strategy: How much emphasis should a company put on multinational sales? What products should it sell in which markets? How should financial and human resources be allocated among products and markets? Should a company establish foreign subsidiaries, license its products or trademarks to others, or form joint ventures?

In Part 2, we turn to the problems of designing multinational marketing programs. These include the familiar questions of developing an appropriate "marketing mix" for each country and the additional issue of coordinating program elements on a multinational, or even global, scale.

The materials in Part 3 deal with organization and control systems for multinational operations. Here, we explore such topics as headquarters-subsidiary relationships, transfer pricing, and coordinating relationships with multinational customer organizations.

MULTINATIONAL COMPETITIVE STRATEGY

Ideally, the starting point for any analysis or discussion of multinational marketing should be a company's underlying *competitive strategy*. The primary elements of competitive strategy, for a company overall or for a division or group within a diversified firm, are

- The *scope* of the business: what products or services it produces, sells, and/or distributes. In a multinational setting, scope must also be defined in geographic terms — in which countries will the enterprise locate each of the activities in what Michael Porter calls its "value chain."[1] (The value chain comprises all of a company's value-creating activities, including procurement, operations, technology development, physical distribution, and marketing.)
- The long-term *objectives* that are set for each component of the enterprise. These typically include goals for growth, profitability, and market share. In a multinational enterprise, they are established for each line of products or services in each country, and serve as guides to the allocation of resources within an organization. To illustrate: beginning in 1978, U.K.-based International Thomson Organization Ltd. made a series of acquisitions of book and magazine publishing companies in the

---

[1]Applications of the value chain concept to multinational strategy analysis are explored in Michael E. Porter (ed.), *Competition in Global Industries* (Boston: Harvard Business School Press, 1986), especially Chapter 1.

United States. By the end of 1986, the company's sales in the U.S. reached $850 million, or about one-third of its worldwide total. All of the acquisitions were guided by a clearly defined strategic objective: according to W. Michael Brown, Thomson's president, "Our goal is to get 80 percent of our income from our businesses here (in the U.S.)."[2]

■ The major *functional policies* that are adopted for an enterprise. These cover such matters as the extent of a business unit's vertical integration; whether it supplies branded products, private brands, or both; and whether it seeks to be a technological leader or a follower.

Every enterprise, whether or not it operates on a multinational scale, must resolve the strategic issues of product/market scope, long-term objectives, and functional policies. What distinguishes the problem of multinational competitive strategy formulation is its greater complexity — typically, there are many more possibilities for each element of strategy when multiple products/services *and* countries are involved. As a result, it is much more likely that conflicts in priorities will arise or that decisions in one area will be incompatible with those made elsewhere.

Must every enterprise *have* a competitive strategy? Some executives resist the idea, or at least resist the twin notions that strategies should be formulated by some structured planning process and should be explicitly stated ("put in writing"). One reason is their belief that a formal strategy will stifle creativity and destroy a company's flexibility. There is some merit to this view, but we believe that to rely completely on an informal, intuitive approach can be just as dangerous, especially in the multinational sphere, where too many companies have succumbed to the seductive lure of a "foreign affair" — without carefully analyzing the consequences or considering any alternatives. All too often what happens is that a company becomes too heavily committed to international operations by reacting to opportunities as they arise — a distributor here, a joint venture there, a license somewhere else. This process of reactions to what appears to be a simple series of opportunities can in fact result in an incoherent, ineffective network of activities that are difficult and costly to modify. Many companies suffer operating losses and painful write-offs of foreign investments.

A clearly defined multinational competitive strategy, then, is one on which subsequent decisions on marketing programs, organization structure, and control systems can be based.

---

[2]"Thomson's American Quest," *New York Times*, December 4, 1986, p. D–1.

EXHIBIT 1. Legal and organizational formats for participation in international markets

Organizational format	Key features
Exporting	Sell through distributors or importers
	Minimizes investment requirements and fixed-cost commitments
	Often used in early stages of international expansion
Licensing and franchising	May be used to exploit patents or specialized expertise
	In some countries, only way to participate in the market
	Limited commitment, but also limited control over licensees
Joint ventures/ coalitions	Co-ownership of a foreign operation with a local partner
	Required in some countries
	May reduce political risks
	Disputes among partners often arise
	May require disclosure of proprietary knowledge
Wholly owned subsidiaries	Maximum commitment to market participation
	Maximum control by parent company
	May be acquired or newly established

FORMS OF MARKET PARTICIPATION

In multinational operations, there are a number of legal and organizational formats to choose from, the principal ones being summarized in *Exhibit 1*.[3] Selecting the right format for each national market is an especially important dimension of competitive strategy. In some instances, a mixture of formats is used for participation in a single market. Often it is not a matter of free choice. The governments of many developing countries, and those of many centrally planned national economies, require local participation in any operations established within their territories. Thus, in many cases, the strategic alternatives may be reduced to say, licensing, or joint venture, or staying out of that particular market.

Within these limits, then, multinational enterprises can choose the form of market participation at the time they first enter each market. Later, as markets develop, they can elect to *change* their modes of oper-

---

[3]For further discussion of legal and organizational forms of market participation, see Philip R. Cateora, *Strategic International Marketing* (Homewood, IL: Dow Jones-Irwin, 1985), Chapter 14; and Subhash C. Jain, *International Marketing Management* (Boston: Kent Publishing, 1984), Chapter 1.

ation. A common pattern of evolution is from exporting (or licensing) to the operation of wholly owned subsidiaries. The latter involves maximum commitment to a market in terms of capital investment, ongoing costs, exposure to exchange rate risks, and potential costs of withdrawal. Acquiring or establishing subsidiaries is, therefore, appropriate only when a company is reasonably confident of a sufficiently large, continuing volume of business in a country.

MULTINATIONAL VERSUS GLOBAL STRATEGIC VIEWPOINTS

The term "multinational corporation" was first used in the 1960s to designate companies that had substantial operations and a significant share of their sales and profits in each of several countries. While some firms (such as Unilever, Nestlé, and N.V. Phillips) had operated on a multinational scale much earlier, it was not until the post-World War II years that multinationals emerged as a major force in the world economy.[4]

Competitive strategy formulation in multinational corporations has traditionally involved a balancing of local responsiveness and autonomy against the benefits of cross-country integration. Thus, top managers of many multinationals — perhaps most — have not thought in terms of an integral, overall competitive strategy for worldwide operations. Instead, they have conceived their role as one of reviewing and providing resources for the strategies of a collection of subsidiaries or divisions, each developed more or less independently. Some integration of national strategies takes place within this kind of multinational corporate system, but its extent is limited by the vested interests and conflicting goals of the component units.

The traditional view of multinational strategy has come under attack in the 1980s. In a steadily growing number of industries, it is claimed, the pattern of competition is shifting from "multidomestic" to "global." As Porter defines it, a global industry is one in which "a firm's competitive position in one country is significantly affected by its position in other countries and vice-versa."[5] This definition fits more and more industries for several reasons:

- Scale economies are of increasing importance. In such industries as aircraft manufacturing, automobiles, and electronics, the volume of operation needed to support a competitive level of R&D and/or

---

[4]See John M. Stopford and Louis T. Wells, Jr., *Managing the Multinational Enterprise* (New York: Basic Books, 1972).

[5]Porter, *op. cit.*, p. 18.

manufacturing requires multinational marketing of *reasonably* standardized products.

- Barriers to international trade — notably, tariffs and transportation costs — have steadily diminished.

- Customer needs and preferences are becoming more similar, due to increasing international travel, communication, and converging standards of living. This trend is especially important for high-technology products, products used by the professions, and products bought by high-income consumers.

- For many firms, a growing number of their customers operate multinationally. This factor has been of particular importance for providers of business services, such as banks and advertising agencies.

An industry's pattern of competition usually does not evolve from multidomestic to global in a gradual fashion. Rather, one or a few competitors within the industry see an opportunity for market growth and so adopt a so-called global strategy to take advantage of it. They may design products/services to appeal to reasonably large market segments in some (or all) major national markets; mechanize their manufacturing or operations activities; set prices based on an expectation of rapid growth in output; and promote their offerings aggressively. This was the pattern of Japanese producers in a variety of industries during the 1970s and 1980s, including automobiles, motorcycles, microwave ovens, VCRs, cameras, television sets, and machine tools.

In industries that shift from multidomestic to global, the established competitors usually find it difficult to respond to the challenge presented by the new competitive pattern. Often their response is a pattern of de facto withdrawal from the market, one segment at a time, typically beginning with the "low end" — small cars, small-screen TVs, small-volume copiers, and so on. This process of "segment retreat" is vividly illustrated in the history of the motorcycle industry in North America and Europe during the 1960s and 1970s. Honda and later other Japanese producers first penetrated these markets with small machines; then they gradually moved into mid-sized and eventually big bikes. By the early 1980s, the original British producers, having merged in a desperate effort to survive, had gone out of business. Harley-Davidson, the only remaining American manufacturer, was losing money and (in 1983) was reorganized via a leveraged buy-out.[6]

Multinationals threatened by the global strategies of competitors

---

[6]See Robert D. Buzzell, "Note on the Motorcycle Industry-1975," in John F. Cady and Robert D. Buzzell, *Strategic Marketing* (Boston: Little, Brown, 1986), pp. 17–44.

must eventually modify their strategies. Depending on the characteristics of the specific market involved, their strategic options may include:

- *Conversion to a global strategy:* This usually requires major changes in virtually all aspects of an enterprise's strategy. As Frederick W. Gluck of McKinsey & Company puts it:

  . . . companies in global industries have had to reshape their strategies in fundamental ways. In order to compete profitably, they have been obliged to redesign their whole system of doing business to take advantage of global markets. . . . If scale is important to product economics, they design a marketing system that gives them the broadest coverage and quickest penetration of world markets.[7]

- *Formation of a coalition with other companies:* Coalitions may take the form of joint ventures, cross-licensing agreements, long-term supply or distribution agreements, or other linkages. The object is to achieve global scope and scale within the coalition. This approach is illustrated by the agreements formed between AT&T and Olivetti in electronics and Honda and British Leyland in automobile production.[8]

- *Focusing on protected market segments:* If a company is unable or unwilling to pursue a truly global strategy, it may be possible for it to maintain a domestic or multidomestic strategy by serving a protected segment(s) in one or more countries. Segments may be protected by government regulations or buying practices, by nationalistic influences, or by customer concern about the risks or delays involved in distant sources of supply.[9]

Not every marketplace is characterized by global competition — some never will be. But even industries that have traditionally been purely domestic are being increasingly affected by global influences. Examples include telecommunications, commercial banking, and retailing (see the Benetton case below). As a result, virtually every enterprise, in developing their competitive strategy for the years ahead, should adopt, at minimum, a global perspective. This requires an awareness of new products, processes, and distribution methods in major markets around the world, as well as a sensitivity to the activities of potential new competitors.

---

[7] Frederick W. Gluck, "Meeting the Challenge of Global Competition," *The McKinsey Quarterly*, Autumn 1982.

[8] See Michael E. Porter and Mark B. Fuller, "Coalitions and Global Strategy," in Michael E. Porter (ed.), *Competition in Global Industries, op. cit.*, Chapter 10.

[9] For examples of these and other strategies, see M. R. Cvar, "Case Studies in Global Competition: Patterns of Success and Failure," *ibid.*, Chapter 15.

1.1 *READING*

How Global Companies Win Out

*Thomas Hout, Michael E.
Porter, and Eileen Rudden*

Hold that obituary on American manufacturers. Some not only refuse to die but even dominate their businesses worldwide. At the same time Ford struggles to keep up with Toyota, Caterpillar thrives in competition with another Japanese powerhouse, Komatsu. Though Zenith has been hurt in consumer electronics, Hewlett-Packard and Tektronix together profitably control 50% of the world's industrial test and measurement instrument market. American forklift truck producers may retreat under Japanese pressure, but two U.S. chemical companies — Du Pont and Dow — dramatically outperform their competitors.

Authors' note: We acknowledge that this article is based in part on a paper coauthored by Eric Vogt.

How do these American producers hold and even increase profitability against international competitors? By forging integrated, global strategies to exploit their potential; and by having a long-term outlook, investing aggressively, and managing factories carefully.

The main reason is that today's international competition in many industries is very different from what it has been. To succeed, an international company may need to change from a multidomestic competitor, which allows individual subsidiaries to compete independently in different domestic markets, to a global organization, which pits its entire worldwide system of product and market position against the competition. (For a more complete discussion of this distinction, see the boxed insert.)

The global company — whatever its nationality — tries to control leverage points, from cross-national production scale economies to the foreign competitors' sources of cash flow. By taking unconventional action, such as lowering prices of an important product or in key markets, the company makes the competitor's response more expensive and difficult. Its main objective is to improve its own effectiveness while eroding that of its competitors.

Not all companies can or should forge a global strategy. While the rewards of competing globally are great, so are the risks. Major policy and operating changes are required. Competing globally demands a number of unconventional approaches to managing a multinational business to sometimes allow

> Major investment projects with zero or even negative ROI.
> Financial performance targets that vary widely among foreign subsidiaries.
> Product lines deliberately overdesigned or underpriced in some markets.
> A view of country-by-country market positions as interdependent and not as independent elements of a worldwide portfolio to be increased or decreased depending on profitability.
> Construction of production facilities in both high and low labor-cost countries.

Not all international businesses lend themselves to global competition. Many are multidomestic in nature and are likely to remain so, competing on a domestic-market-by-domestic-market basis. Typically these businesses have products that differ greatly among country markets and have high transportation costs, or their industries lack sufficient scale economies to yield the global competitors a significant competitive edge.

Before entering the global arena, you must first decide whether your company's industry has the right characteristics to favor a global competitor. A careful examination of the economies of the business will highlight its ripeness for global competition.[1] Simply put, the potential for global competition is greatest when significant benefits are gained from a worldwide volume — in terms of either reduced unit costs or superior reputation or service — and are greater than the additional costs of serving that volume.

Identifying potential economies of scale requires considerable insight. Advantages to increased volume may come not only from larger production plants or runs but also from more efficient logistics networks or higher volume distribution networks. Worldwide volume is also particularly advantageous in supporting high levels of investment in research and development; many industries requiring high levels of R&D, such as pharmaceuticals or jet aircraft, are global. The level of transport or importing costs will also influence the business's tendency to become global. Transport is a relatively small portion of highly traded optical goods, for example, while it is a barrier in trading steel reinforcing bars.

Many businesses will not be able to take the global step precisely because their industries lack these characteristics. Economies of scale may be too modest or R&D spending too closely tied to particular markets. Products may differ significantly across country boundaries, or the industry may emphasize distribution, installation, and other local activities. Lead times may be short, as in fashion-oriented businesses and in many service businesses, including printing. Also, transportation costs and government barriers to trade may be high, and distribution may be fragmented and hard to penetrate. Many consumer nondurable businesses or low-technology assembly companies fall into this category, as do many heavy raw-material processing industries and wholesaling and service businesses.

Our investigation into the strategies of successful global companies leads us to believe that a large group of international companies have global potential, even though they may not know it. Almost every industry that is now global — automobiles and TV sets, for example — was not at one time. A company must see the potential for changing competitive interaction in its favor to trigger a shift from multidomestic to global competition. And because there is no guarantee that the business can become global, the company must be willing to risk the heavy investment that global competition requires.

A company that recognizes its business as potentially global but not yet so must ask itself whether it can innovate effectively and must understand its impact on the competition, to find the best answers to these three questions:

---

[1]For a more detailed look at globalization, see Michael E. Porter, *Competitive Strategy* (New York: Free Press, 1980).

1. What kind of strategic innovation might trigger global competition?
2. Is it in the best position among all competitors to establish and defend the advantages of global strategy?
3. What kind of resources — over how long a period — will be required to establish the leading position?

THE SUCCESSFUL GLOBAL COMPETITOR

If your industry profile fits the picture we've drawn, you can better judge your ability to make these kinds of unconventional decisions by looking at the way three global companies have succeeded. These organizations (American, European, and Japanese) exemplify the global competitor. They all perceive competition as global and formulate strategy on an integrated, worldwide basis. Each has developed a strategic innovation to change the rules of the competitive game in its particular industry. The innovation acts as a lever to support the development of an integrated global system but demands a market position strong enough to implement it.

Finally, the three companies have executed their strategies more aggressively and effectively than their competitors. They have built barriers to competitive responses based on careful assessment of competitors' behavior. All three have the financial resources and commitment needed to compete unconventionally and the organizational structure to manage an integrated system.

We will take a careful look at each of these three and how they developed the strategic innovation that led, on the one hand, to the globalization of their industries and, on the other, to their own phenomenal success. The first company's innovation was in manufacturing; the second, in technology; and the third, in marketing.

THE CATERPILLAR CASE: WARRING WITH KOMATSU

Caterpillar Tractor Company turned large-scale construction equipment into a global business and achieved world leadership in that business even when faced with an able Japanese competitor. This accomplishment was difficult for a variety of reasons. For one thing, specifications of construction equipment varied widely across countries. Also, machines are expensive to transport, and field distribution — including user financing, spare parts inventories, and repair facilities — is demanding and best managed locally.

Navy Seabees who left their Caterpillar equipment in other countries following World War II planted the seeds of globalization. The company established independent dealerships to service these fleets, and this base of units provided a highly profitable flow of revenue from spare parts, which paid for inventorying new units. The Caterpillar dealers quickly became self-sustaining and to this day are larger, better financed, and do a more profitable parts business then their competitors. This global distribution system is one of Cat's two major barriers against competition.

The company used its worldwide production scale to create its other barrier. Two-thirds of the total product cost of construction equipment is in heavy components — engines, axles, transmissions, and hydraulics — whose manufacturing costs are capital intensive and highly sensitive to economies of scale. Caterpillar turned its network of sales in different countries into a cost advantage by designing product lines that use identical components and by investing heavily in a few large-scale, state-of-the-art component manufacturing facilities to fill worldwide demand.

The company then augmented the centralized production with assembly plants in each of its major markets — Europe, Japan, Brazil, Australia, and so on. At these plants Cat added local product features, avoiding the high transportation cost of end products. Most important, Cat became a direct participant in local economies. The company achieved lower costs without sacrificing local product flexibility and became a friend rather than a threat to local governments. No single "world model" was forced on the customer, yet no competitor could match Caterpillar's production and distribution cost.

Not that they haven't tried. The most recent — and greatest — challenge to Caterpillar has come from Komatsu (see *Exhibit 1* for a financial comparison). Japan's leading construction equipment producer forged its own global strategy based on exporting high-quality products from centralized facilities with labor and steel cost advantages. Over the last decade Komatsu has gained some 15% of the world construction-equipment market, with a significant share of sales in nearly every product line in competition with Cat.

Caterpillar has maintained its position against Komatsu and gained world share. The two companies increasingly dominate the market vis-à-vis their competitors, who compete on a domestic or regional basis. What makes Caterpillar's strategy so potent? The company has fostered

EXHIBIT 1. Financial comparison of Caterpillar and Komatsu

	Caterpillar	Komatsu
1980 estimated sales of construction equipment	$7.2 billion	$2.0 billion
1974–1979 averages:		
Return on capital employed	13.6%	4.0%
Debt/equity	0.4 times	2.1 times
Return on equity	19.1%	12.2%
Percent of earnings retained	69%	65%
Spare parts as percentage of total revenue (estimated)	30% to 35%	15% to 20%
Cash flow available from operations	$681 million	$140 million

Source: Financial statements.

the development of four characteristics essential to defending a leading world position against a determined competitor:

1. **A global strategy of its own.** Caterpillar's integrated global strategy yields a competitive advantage in cost and effectiveness. Komatsu simply plays catch-up ball rather than pulling ahead. Facing a competitor that has consciously devised a global strategy, Komatsu is in a much weaker position than were Japanese TV and automobile manufacturers when they took off.

2. **Willingness to invest in manufacturing.** Caterpillar's top management appears committed to the kind of flexible automated manufacturing systems that allow full exploitation of the economies of scale from its worldwide sales volume.

3. **Willingness to commit financial resources.** Caterpillar is the only Western company that matches Komatsu in capital spending per employee; in fact, its overall capital spending is more than three times that of the Japanese company. Caterpillar does not divert resources into other businesses or dissipate the financial advantage against Komatsu by paying out excessive dividends. Because Komatsu's profitability is lower than Caterpillar's, it must exhaust debt capacity in trying to match Cat's high investment rates.

4. **Blocking position in the Japanese market.** In 1963, Caterpillar formed a joint venture in Japan with Komatsu's long-standing but weaker competitor, Mitsubishi. Operationally, the venture services

the Japanese market. Strategically, it acts as a check on the market share and cash flow of Komatsu. Japan accounts for less than 20% of the world market but yields over 80% of Komatsu's worldwide cash flow. The joint venture is number two in market position, serving to limit Komatsu's profits. Japanese tax records indicate that the Cat-Mitsubishi joint venture has earned only modest profits, but it is of great strategic value to Caterpillar.[2]

L.M. ERICSSON: CAN SMALL BE BEAUTIFUL?

L.M. Ericsson of Sweden has become a successful global competitor by developing and exploiting a technological niche. Most major international telephone-equipment producers operated first in large, protected home markets that allowed the most efficient economies of scale. The additional profits helped underwrite R&D and provided good competitive leverage. Sweden's home market is relatively small, yet Ericsson translated the advent of electronic switching technology into a powerful global lever that befuddled competitors in its international market niche. In the electromechanical era of the 1960s, the telephone switching equipment business was hardly global. Switching systems combine hardware and software. In the electromechanical stage, 70% of total installed costs lay in hardware and 70% of hardware cost was direct labor, manufacturing overhead, and installation of the equipment.

Each country's telephone system was unique, economies of scale were low, and the wage rate was more important than the impact of volume on costs. In the late 1960s, major international companies (including Ericsson) responded by moving electroswitching production to LDCs not only to take advantage of cheaper labor but also to respond to the desire of government telephone companies to source locally.

Eventually, each parent company centrally sourced only the core software and critical components and competed on a domestic-market-by-domestic-market basis. For its part, Ericsson concentrated investment in developing countries without colonial ties to Europe and in smaller European markets that lacked national suppliers and that used the same switching systems as the Swedish market.

---

[2]For more on this subject, see Craig M. Watson, "Counter-Competition Abroad to Protect Home Markets," *Harvard Business Review*, January-February 1982, p. 40.

The telecommunications industry became global when, in the 1970s, electronic switching technology emerged, radically shifting cost structures and threatening the market position Ericsson had carved for itself. Software is now 60% of total cost; 55% of hardware cost is in sophisticated electronic components whose production is highly scale sensitive. The initial R&D investment required to develop a system has jumped to more than $100 million, which major international companies could have amortized more easily than Ericsson. In addition, the move to electronics promised to destroy the long-standing relationships Ericsson enjoyed with smaller government telephone companies. And it appeared that individual electronic switching systems would require a large fixed-cost software investment for each country, making the new technology too expensive for the smaller telephone systems, on which Ericsson thrived.

Ericsson knew that the electronic technology would eventually be adapted to small systems. In the meantime, it faced the possibility of losing its position in smaller markets because of its inability to meet the ante for the new global competition.

The company responded with a preemptive strategic innovation — a modular technology that introduced electronics to small telephone systems. The company developed a series of modular software packages that could be used in different combinations to meet the needs of diverse telephone systems at an acceptable cost. Moreover, each successive system required fewer new modules. As *Exhibit 2* shows, the first system — Södertalje in Sweden — required all new modules, but by the third year, the Åbo system in Finland required none at all. Thus the company rapidly amortized development costs and enjoyed economies of scale that steepened as the number of software systems sold increased. As a result, Ericsson was able to compete globally in small systems.

Ericsson's growth is accelerating as small telephone systems convert

EXHIBIT 2. Ericsson's technology lever: reduction of software cost through modular design

	Representative systems	New modules required	Existing modules used
Year 1	Södertalje, Sweden	57	0
Year 2	Orleans, France	22	57
Year 3	Åbo, Finland	0	77

Source: Boston Consulting Group, *A Framework for Swedish Industrial Policy* (Uberforlag, Stockholm, 1978).

to electronics. The company now enjoys an advantage in software cost and variety that continually reinforces itself. Through this technology Ericsson has raised a significant entry barrier against other companies in the small-system market.

HONDA'S MARKETING GENIUS

Before Honda became a global company, two distinct motorcycle industries existed in the world. In Asia and other developing countries, large numbers of people rode small, simple motorcycles to work. In Europe and America, smaller numbers of people drove big, elaborate machines for play. Since the Asian motorcycle was popular as an inexpensive means of transportation, companies competed on the basis of price. In the West, manufacturers used styling and brand image to differentiate their products. No Western market exceeded 100,000 units; wide product lines and small volumes meant slight opportunities for economies of scale. Major motorcycle producers such as Harley-Davidson of the United States, BMW of West Germany, and Triumph and BSA of the United Kingdom traded internationally but in only modest volumes.

Honda made its industry global by convincing middle-class Americans that riding motorcycles could be fun. Because of the company's marketing innovations, Honda's annual growth rate was greater than 20% from the late 1950s to the late 1960s. The company then turned its attention to Europe, with a similar outcome. Honda invested for seven full years before sustaining profitability in Europe, financing this global effort with cash flows earned from a leading market position at home and in the United States.

Three crucial steps were decisive in Honda's achievement. First, Honda turned market preference around to the characteristics of its own products and away from those of American and European competitors. Honda targeted new consumers and used advertising, promotions, and trade shows to convince them that its motorbikes were inexpensive, reliable, and easy to use. A large investment in the distribution network — 2,000 dealerships, retail missionaries, generous warranty and service support, and quick spare-parts availability — backed up the marketing message.

Second, Honda sustained growth by enticing customers with the upper levels of its product line. Nearly half of new bike owners purchased larger, more expensive models within 12 months. Brand loyalty proved very high. Honda exploited these trends by expanding from its line of a few small motorcycles to one covering the full range of size and features by 1975. The result: self-sustaining growth in dollar volume and

EXHIBIT 3. The effect of volume on manufacturing approaches to motorcycle production

Cost element	Low volume	High volume
Machine tools	Manual, general purpose	Numerical control, special purpose
Changeover time	Manual, slow (hours)	Automatic positioning, fast (minutes)
Work-in-process inventory	High (days of production)	Low (hours of production)
Materials handling	Forklift trucks	Automated
Assembly	Bay assembly	Motorized assembly line
Machine tool design	Designed outside the company, available throughout industry	Designed in-house, proprietary
Rework	More	Less

Source: *Strategy Alternatives for the British Motorcycle Industry,* a report prepared for the British Secretary of State for Industry by the Boston Consulting Group, July 30, 1975.

a model mix that allowed higher margins. The higher volume reduced marketing and distribution costs and improved the position of Honda and other Japanese producers who invaded the 750cc "super bike" portion of the market traditionally reserved for American and European companies. Here Honda beat the competition with a bike that was better engineered, lower priced, and whose development cost was shared over the company's wide product line.

The third step Honda took was to exploit economies of scale through both centralized manufacturing and logistics. The increasing volume of engines and bike assemblies sold (50,000 units per month and up) enabled the company to use less costly manufacturing techniques unavailable to motorcycle producers with lower volumes (see *Exhibit 3*). Over a decade, Honda's factory productivity rose at an average annual rate of 13.1% — several times higher than European and American producers. Combined with lower transportation cost, Honda's increased output gave it a landed cost per unit far lower than the competition's. In turn, the lower production cost helped fund Honda's heavy marketing and distribution investment. Finally, economies of scale in marketing and distribution, combined with low production cost, led to the high profits that financed Honda's move into automobiles.

WHAT IS A GLOBAL INDUSTRY?

The nature of international competition among multinationals
has shifted in a number of industries. *Multinational* generally
denotes a company with significant operations and market interests outside its home country. The universe of these companies is large and varied, encompassing different kinds of
organizations operating in different types of industries. From a
strategic point of view, however, there are two types of industries in which multinationals compete: *multidomestic* and *global*.
They differ in their economics and requirements for success.

In *multidomestic* industries a company pursues separate
strategies in each of its foreign markets while viewing the competitive challenge independently from market to market. Each
overseas subsidiary is strategically independent, with essentially autonomous operations. The multinational headquarters will
coordinate financial controls and marketing (including brand-
name) policies worldwide and may centralize some R&D and
component production. But strategy and operations are decentralized. Each subsidiary is a profit center and expected to contribute earnings and growth commensurate with market
opportunity.

In a multidomestic industry, a company's management tries
to operate effectively across a series of worldwide positions,
with diverse product requirements, growth rates, competitive
environments, and political risks. The company prefers that local managers do whatever is necessary to succeed in R&D, production, marketing, and distribution but holds them responsible
for results. In short, the company competes with other multinationals and local competitors on a market-by-market basis. A
large number of successful U.S. companies are in multidomestic
industries, including Procter & Gamble in household products,
Honeywell in controls, Alcoa in aluminum, and General Foods
in branded foods.

A *global* industry, in contrast, pits one multinational's entire
worldwide system of product and market positions against another's. Various country subsidiaries are highly interdependent
in terms of operations and strategy. A country subsidiary may
specialize in manufacturing only part of its product line, ex-
changing products with others in the system. Country profit targets vary, depending on individual impact on the cost position

or effectiveness of the entire worldwide system — or on the subsidiary's position relative to a key global competitor. A company may set prices in one country to have an intended effect in another.

In a global business, management competes worldwide against a small number of other multinationals in the world market. Strategy is centralized, and various aspects of operations are decentralized or centralized as economics and effectiveness dictate. The company seeks to respond to particular local market needs, while avoiding a compromise of efficiency of the overall global system.

A large number of U.S. multinationals are in global industries. Among them, along with their principal competitors, are: Caterpillar and Komatsu in large construction equipment; Timex, Seiko, and Citizen in watches; General Electric, Siemens, and Mitsubishi in heavy electrical equipment.

The multidomestic and global labels apply to distinct industries and industry segments, not necessarily to whole industry groups. For example, within the electrical equipment industry, heavy apparatus such as steam turbine generators and large electric motors is typically global while low-voltage building controls and electrical fittings are multidomestic in nature.

WHAT CAN WE LEARN?

Each of these successful global players changed the dynamics of its industry and pulled away from its major competitors. By achieving economies of scale through commonality of design, Caterpillar exploited both its worldwide sales volume and its existing market for parts revenues. Competitors could not match its costs or profits and therefore could not make the investment necessary to catch up. Ericsson created a cost advantage by developing a unique modular technology perfectly adapted to its segment of the market. Its global strategy turned electronics from a threat to Ericsson into a barrier to its competitors. Honda used marketing to homogenize worldwide demand and unlock the potential for economies of scale in production, marketing, and distribution. The competition's only refuge was the highly brand-conscious, small-volume specialty market.

In each case, the industry had the potential for a worldwide system of products and markets that a company with a global strategy could exploit. Construction equipment offered large economies of scale in component manufacture, allowing Caterpillar to neutralize high transportation costs and government barriers through local assembly. Ericsson unlocked scale economies in software development for electronic switches. The modular technology accommodated local product differences and governments' desire to use local suppliers. Once Honda's marketing techniques raised demand in major markets for products with similar characteristics, the industry's economies of scale in production combined with low transportation costs and low tariff barriers to turn it into a global game.

In none of the cases did success result from a "world product." The companies accommodated local differences without sacrificing production costs. The global player's position in one major market strengthened its position in others. Caterpillar's design similarities and central component facilities allowed each market to contribute to its already favorable cost structure. Ericsson's shared modules led to falling costs each time a system was sold in a new country. Honda drew on scale economies from the centralized production of units sold in each market and used its U.S. marketing and distribution experience to succeed in Europe.

In addition to superior effectiveness and cost advantages, a winning global strategy always requires abilities in two other dimensions. The first is timing. The successful global competitor uses a production cost or distribution advantage as a leverage point to make it more difficult or expensive for the competitor to respond. The second is financial. The global innovator commits itself to major investment before anyone else, whether in technology, facilities, or distribution. If successful, it then reaps the benefits from increased cash flows from either higher volume (Honda and Ericsson) or lower costs (all three companies). The longer the competitor takes to respond, the larger the innovator's cash flows. The global company can then deploy funds either to increase investment or lower prices, creating barriers to new market entrants.

A global player should decide against which of its major competitors it must succeed first in order to generate broad-based success in the future. Caterpillar located in the Far East not only to source products locally but also to track Komatsu. (Cat increasingly sources product and manufacturing technology from Japan.) Ericsson's radical departure in technology was aimed squarely at ITT and Siemens, whose large original market shares would ordinarily have given them an advantage in the smaller European and African markets. Honda created new markets in the United States and Europe because its most powerful competitors, Yamaha and Kawasaki, were Japanese. By exploiting the global opportunity first, Honda got a head start, and it remained strong even when competitors' own international ambitions came to light.

PLAYING THE GLOBAL CHESS GAME

Global competition forces top management to change the way it thinks about and operates its businesses. Policies that made sense when the company was multidomestic may now be counterproductive. The most powerful moves are those that improve the company's worldwide cost position or ability to differentiate itself and weaken key worldwide competitors. Let us consider two potential moves.

The first is preempting the leading positions in major newly industrializing countries (NICs). Rapid growth in, for example, Mexico, Brazil, and Indonesia has made them an important part of the worldwide market for many capital goods. If its industry has the potential to become global, the company that takes a leading position in these markets will have made a decisive move to bar its competitors. Trade barriers are often prohibitively high in these places, and a company that tries to penetrate the market through a *self-contained* local subsidiary is likely to fall into a trap.

The astute global competitor will exploit the situation, however, by building a specialized component manufacturing facility in an NIC which will become an integral part of a global sourcing network. The company exports output of the specialized facility to offset importing complementary components. Final assembly for the domestic and smaller, neighboring markets can be done locally. (Having dual sources for key items can minimize the risk of disruption to the global sourcing network.)

A good illustration of this strategy is Siemens's circuit breaker operation in Brazil. When the company outgrew its West German capacity for some key components, it seized the opportunity presented by Brazilian authorities seeking capital investments in the heavy electrical equipment industry. Siemens now builds a large portion of its common components there, swaps them for other components made in Europe, and is the lowest-cost and leading supplier of finished product in Brazil.

Another move that can be decisive in a global industry is to establish a solid position with your largest customers to block competitors. Many businesses have a few customers that dominate the global market. The global competitor recognizes their importance and prevents current or prospective competitors from generating any sales.

A good example is a British company, BSR, the world's largest producer of automatic record changers. In the 1970s, when Japanese exports of audio equipment were growing rapidly, BSR recognized that it could lose its market base in the United States and Europe if the Japanese began marketing record changers. BSR redesigned its product to Japanese specifications and offered distributors aggressive price discounts and inventory support. The Japanese could not justify expanding their own capacity. BSR not only stalled the entry of the Japanese into the record-changer market but it also moved ahead of its existing competitor, Garrard.

A global company can apply similar principles to block the competition's access to key distributors or retailers. Many American companies have failed to seize this opportunity in their unwillingness to serve large, private-label customers (e.g., Sears, Roebuck) or by neglecting the less expensive end of their product line and effectively allowing competitors access to their distributors. Japanese manufacturers in particular could then establish a toehold in industries like TV sets and farm equipment.

The decision on prices for pivotal customers must not be made solely on considerations of ROI. Equally important in global competition is the impact of these prices on prospective entrants and the cost of failing to protect and expand the business base. One way to control the worldwide chess game in your favor is to differentiate prices among countries.

MANAGE INTERDEPENDENTLY

The successful global competitor manages its business in various countries as a single system, not a portfolio of independent positions. In the view of portfolio planning theory, a market's attractiveness and the strength of a company's position within it determine the extent of corporate resources devoted to it. A company should defend strong positions and try to turn weak ones around or abandon them. It will pursue high-profit and/or high-growth markets more aggressively than lower-profit or lower-growth ones, and it will decide on a stand-alone basis whether to compete in a market.

Accepting this portfolio view of international competition can be disastrous in a global industry. The global competitor focuses instead on its ability to leverage positions in one country market against those in other markets. In the global system, the ability to leverage is as important as market attractiveness; the company need not turn around weak positions for them to be useful.

The most obvious leverage a company obtains from a country market is the volume it contributes to the company's overall cost or effectiveness. DuPont and Texas Instruments have patiently won a large sales volume in the sophisticated Japanese market, for example, which supports their efforts elsewhere. Winning a share of a market that consistently supports product innovation ahead of other markets — like the United States in long-haul jet aircraft — is another leverage point. The competitor with a high share of such a market can always justify a new product investment. Or a market can contribute leverage if it supports an efficient scale manufacturing facility for a region — like Brazil for Siemens. Finally, a market can contribute leverage if a position in it can be used to affect a competitor's cash flow.

ORGANIZATION: THE ACHILLES' HEEL

Organizational structure and reporting relationships present subtle problems for a global strategy. Effective strategic control argues for a central product-line organization; effective local responsiveness, for a geographic organization with local autonomy. A global strategy demands that the product-line organization have the *ultimate* authority, because without it the company cannot gain systemwide benefits. Nevertheless, the company still must balance product and area needs. In short, there is no simple solution. But there are some guidelines to help.

No one organization structure applies to all of a company's international businesses. It may be unnecessarily cumbersome, for example, to impose a matrix structure on all business. Organizational reporting lines should probably differ by country market depending on that market's role. An important market that offers high leverage, as in the foregoing examples, must work closely with the global business-unit managers at headquarters. Coordination is crucial to success. But the manager of a market outside the global system will require only sets of objectives under a regional reporting system.

Another guideline is that organizational reporting lines and structures should change as the nature of the international business changes. When a business becomes global, the emphasis should shift toward centralization. As countries increase in importance, they must be brought within the global manager's reach. Over time, if the business becomes less global, the company's organization may emphasize local autonomy.

The common tendency to apply one organizational structure to all operations is bound to be a disadvantage to some of them. In some U.S. companies, this approach inhibited development of the global strategy their industries required.

MATCH FINANCIAL POLICIES TO COMPETITIVE REALITIES

If top management is not careful, adherence to conventional financial management and practices may constrain a good competitive response in global businesses. While capital budgeters use such standard financial tools as DCF return analysis or risk profiles to judge investments and creditors and stock analysts prefer stable debt and dividend policies, a global company must chart a different course.

ALLOCATING CAPITAL

In a global strategy, investments are usually a long-term, interdependent series of capital commitments, which are not easily associated with returns or risks. The company has to be aware of the size and timing of the total expenditures because they will greatly influence competitors' new investment response. Most troublesome, however, is that revenues from investments in several countries may have to build up to a certain point before the company earns *any* return on investment.

A global strategy goes against the traditional tests for capital allocation: project-oriented DCF risk-return analysis and the country manager's record of credibility. Global competition requires a less mechanical approach to project evaluation. The successful global competitor develops at least two levels of financial control. One level is a profit and cost center for self-contained projects; the other is a strategy center for tracking interdependent efforts and competitors' performance and reactions. Global competitors operate with a short time frame when monitoring the execution of global strategy investments and a long time frame when evaluating such investments and their expected returns.

DEBT & DIVIDENDS

Debt and dividend policies should vary with the requirements of the integrated investment program of the whole company. In the initial stages, a company with a strong competitive position should retain earnings to build and defend its global position. When the industry has become global and growth slows or the returns exceed the reinvestment needed to retain position, the company should distribute earnings to the rest of the corporation and use debt capacity elsewhere, perhaps in funding another nascent global strategy.

Honda's use of debt over the last 30 years illustrates this logic (see *Exhibit 4*). In the mid-1950s, when Honda held a distant second place in a rapidly growing Japanese motorcycle industry, the company had to

EXHIBIT 4. Honda Motor Company's financial policy from 1954 to 1980

Period	Interest-bearing debt-to-equity ratio	Strategic phase
1954–55	3.5 times	Rapid growth in domestic motorcycle market; Honda is low-margin, number two producer
1959–60	0.5	Domestic motorcycle market matured; Honda is dominant, high-margin producer
1964–65	0.7	Honda makes major penetration of U.S. motorcycle market
1969–70	1.6	Honda begins major move in domestic auto market
1974–75	1.3	Investment pause due to worldwide recession; motorcycle is major cash generator
1978–80	1.0	Auto exports are highly profitable, as are motorcycles

Source: Annual reports.

leverage its equity 3.5 times to finance growth. By 1960, the Japanese market had matured and Honda emerged dominant. The debt-equity ratio receded to 0.5 times but rose again with the company's international expansion in motorcycles. In the late 1960s, Honda made a major move to the automobile market, requiring heavy debt. At that time, motorcycle cash flows funded the move.

WHICH STRATEGIC ROAD TO TAKE?

There is no safe formula for success in international business. Industry structures continuously evolve. The Caterpillar, Ericsson, and Honda approaches will probably not work forever. Competitors will try to push industrial trends away from the strengths of the industry leaders, and technological or political changes may force the leading companies to operate in a multidomestic fashion once again.

Strategy is a powerful force in determining competitive outcomes, whether in international or domestic business. And although adopting a global strategy is risky, many companies can dramatically improve their positions by fundamentally changing the way they plan, control, and operate their businesses. But a global strategy requires that managers think in new ways. Otherwise the company will not be able to

THE MERCHANT ADVENTURER

Years ago, as a college professor, I used to walk downtown for lunch with a fellow intellectual. On the corner was a livery stable run by a man named Warren. As an adjunct to the livery business the old man conducted a hay and feed store. I can remember our satirical and superior comments on Mr. Warren's profession. "What a job, selling hay and feed! What interest can life hold for such a man?"

Later a bad physical breakdown forced me into outdoor work. . . . So it was that in the space of ten years, by a process of involution, I had fetched a circuit and come round to the despised profession of Mr. Warren. And the curious thing was that I had come to like the hay and feed business and to find more real interest in it than in trying to teach college students something about Attila, the Hun, and Theodoric, the Ostrogoth.

If one's own little business teems with interest, the complex business of international trade fairly boils with it. Somebody has yet to write the epic of romance in business. The inventive genius, the passionate endeavor, the venturesome courage of the race are built into the unfolding drama of world trade. . . .

We know something about the mighty influences which have shaped world trade in the past . . . Singularly enough, we understand less clearly what is going on in the world trade of our own day. If a man had the mental grasp and an amplified vision, he could write a five-pound book about the changes which are taking place beneath our eyes, changes of which we are only dimly and vaguely aware. . . .

The charm of life is mystery. Mystery is romantic. The romance of world trade! That which lies ahead of the explorer, the merchant adventurer in all ages, the lure of the unknown, romance, mystery — mystery that ends in either peace and plenty or failure and defeat.

From Alfred Pearce Dennis, *The Romance of World Trade* (New York: Henry Holt and Company, 1926).

recognize the nature of competition, justify the required investments, or sustain the change in everyday behavior needed.

If the company can successfully execute a global strategy, it may find itself joining the ranks of the truly successful international companies. Whether they be Japanese, American, European, or otherwise, the strategic thread that ties together companies like IBM, Matsushita, K. Hattori (Seiko), Du Pont, and Michelin clearly shows that the rules of the international competitive game have changed.

1.2 READING

Do You Really Have a Global Strategy?

Gary Hamel and
C.K. Prahalad

The threat of foreign competition preoccupies managers in industries from tele-communications to commercial banking and from machine tools to consumer electronics. Corporate response to the threat is often misdirected and ill timed — in part because many executives don't fully understand what global competition is.

They haven't received much help from the latest analysis of this trend. One argument simply emphasizes the scale and learning effects that transcend national boundaries and provide cost advantages to companies selling to the world market.[1] Another holds that world products offer customers the twin benefits

---

[1]See Reading 1.1: "How Global Companies Win Out."

of the low-cost and high-quality incentives for foreign customers to lay aside culture-bound product preferences.[2]

According to both of these arguments, U.S. organizations should "go global" when they can no longer get the minimum volume needed for cost efficiency at home and when international markets permit standardized marketing approaches. If, on the other hand, they can fully exploit scale benefits at home and their international export markets are dissimilar, U.S. executives can safely adopt the traditional, country-by-country, multinational approach. So while Caterpillar views its battle with Komatsu in global terms, CPC International and Unilever may safely consider their foreign operations multidomestic.

After studying the experiences of some of the most successful global competitors, we have become convinced that the current perspective on global competition and the globalization of markets is incomplete and misleading. Analysts are long on exhortation — "go international" — but short on practical guidance. Combine these shortcomings with the prevailing notion that global success demands a national industrial policy, a docile work force, debt-heavy financing, and forbearing investors, and you can easily understand why many executives feel they are only treading water in the rising tide of global competition.

World-scale manufacturing may provide the necessary armament, and government support may be a tactical advantage, but winning the war against global competition requires a broader view of global strategy. We will present a new framework for assessing the nature of the worldwide challenge, use it to analyze one particular industry, and offer our own practical guidelines for success.

THRUST & PARRY

As a starting point, let's take a look at what drives global competition. It begins with a sequence of competitive action and reaction:

- An aggressive competitor decides to use the cash flow generated in its home market to subsidize an attack on markets of domestically oriented foreign competitors.

---

[2]See Reading 2.2: "The Globalization of Markets."

■ The defensive competitor then retaliates — not in its home market where that attack was staged — but in the foreign markets where the aggressor company is most vulnerable.[3]

As an example, consider the contest between Goodyear and Michelin. By today's definitions, the tire industry is not global. Most tire companies manufacture in and distribute for the local market. Yet Michelin, Goodyear, and Firestone are locked in a fiercely competitive — and very global — battle.

In the early 1970s, Michelin used its strong European profit base to attack Goodyear's American home market. Goodyear could fight back in the United States by reducing prices, increasing advertising, or offering dealers better margins. But because Michelin would expose only a small amount of its worldwide business in the United States, it has little to lose and much to gain. Goodyear, on the other hand, would sacrifice margins in its largest market.

Goodyear ultimately struck back in Europe, throwing a wrench in Michelin's money machine. Goodyear was proposing a hostage trade. Michelin's long-term goals and resources allowed it to push ahead in the United States. But at least Goodyear slowed the pace of Michelin's attack and forced it to recalculate the cost of market share gains in the United States. Goodyear's strategy recognized the international scope of competition and parried Michelin's thrust.

Manufacturers have played out this pattern of cross-subsidization and international retaliation in the chemical, audio, aircraft engine, and computer industries. In each case international cash flows, rather than international product flows, scale economies, or homogeneous markets, finally determined whether competition was global or national. (For a detailed explanation, see the box insert on cross-subsidization.)

The Goodyear vs. Michelin case helps to distinguish among

■ Global competition, which occurs when companies cross-subsidize national market share battles in pursuit of global brand and distribution positions.

■ Global businesses, in which the minimum volume required for cost efficiency is not available in the company's home market.

---

[3]See Craig M. Watson, "Counter-Competition Abroad to Protect Home Markets," *Harvard Business Review,* January-February 1982, p. 40.

■ Global companies, which have distribution systems in key foreign markets that enable cross-subsidization, international retaliation, and world-scale volume.

Making a distinction between global competition and a global business is important. In traditionally global businesses, protectionism and flexible manufacturing technologies are encouraging a shift back to local manufacturing. Yet competition remains global. Companies must distinguish between the cost effectiveness based on off-shore sourcing and world-scale plants and the competitive effectiveness based on the ability to retaliate in competitors' key markets.

IDENTIFYING THE TARGET

Understanding how the global game is played is only the first step in challenging the foreign competitor. While the pattern of cross-subsidization and retaliation describes the battle, world brand dominance is what the global war is all about. And the Japanese have been winning it.

In less than 20 years, Canon, Hitachi, Seiko, and Honda have established worldwide reputations equal to those of Ford, Kodak, and Nestlé. In consumer electronics alone, the Japanese are present in or dominate most product categories.

Like the novice duck hunter who either aims at the wrong kind of bird or shoots behind his prey, many companies have failed to develop a well-targeted response to the new global competition. Those who define international competitiveness as no more than low-cost manufacturing are aiming at the wrong target. Those who fail to identify the strategic intentions of their global competitors cannot anticipate competitive moves and so often shoot behind the target.

To help managers respond more effectively to challenges by foreign companies, we have developed a framework that summarizes the various global competitive strategies (see *Exhibit 1*). The competitive advantages to be gained from location, world-scale volume, or global brand distribution are arrayed against the three kinds of strategic intent we have found to be most prevalent among global competitors: (1) building a global presence, (2) defending a domestic position, and (3) overcoming national fragmentation.

Using this framework to analyze the world television industry, we find Japanese competitors building a global presence, RCA, GE, and Zenith of the United States defending domestic dominance, and Philips

EXHIBIT 1. A global competitive framework

	Build global presence	Defend domestic dominance	Overcome national fragmentation
1965	Access volume		
		Response lag	Response lag
1970	Redefine cost-volume relationships		
		Match costs	
1975	Cross-subsidize to win the world		Reduce costs at national subsidiary
		Amortize world-scale investments	
1980	Contiguous segment expansion		Rationalize manufacturing
		Gain retaliatory capability	
1985			Shift locus of strategic responsibility
1990			

of the Netherlands and CSF Thomson of France overcoming national fragmentation. Each one uses a different complement of competitive weapons and pursues its own strategic objectives. As a result, each reaps a different harvest from its international activities.

LOOSE BRICKS

By the late 1960s, Japanese television manufacturers had built up a large U.S. volume base by selling private-label TV sets. They had also established brand and distribution positions in small-screen and portable televisions — a market segment ignored by U.S. producers in favor of higher margin console sets.

In 1967, Japan became the largest producer of black-and-white TVs; by 1970, it had closed the gap in color sets. While the Japanese first used their cost advantages, primarily from low labor costs, they then moved quickly to invest in new process technologies, from which came the advantages of scale and quality.

Japanese companies recognized the vulnerability of competitive positions based solely on labor and scale advantages. Labor costs change as economies develop or as exchange rates fluctuate. The world's low-cost manufacturing location is constantly shifting: from Japan to Korea, then to Singapore and Taiwan. Scale-based cost advantages are also vulnerable, particularly to radical changes in manufacturing technology and creeping protectionism in export markets. Throughout the 1970s, Japanese TV makers invested heavily to create the strong distribution positions and brand franchises that would add another layer of competitive advantage.

Making a global distribution investment pay off demands a high level of channel utilization. Japanese companies force-fed distribution channels by rapidly accelerating product life cycles and expanding across contiguous product segments. Predictably, single-line competitors have often been blind-sided, and sleepy product-development departments have been caught short in the face of this onslaught. Global distribution is the new barrier to entry.

By the end of the decade, the Japanese competitive advantage had evolved from low-cost sourcing to world-scale volume and worldwide brand positions across the spectrum of consumer electronic products.

RCA AT HOME

Most American television producers believed the Japanese did well in their market simply because of their low-cost, high-quality manufacturing systems. When they finally responded, U.S. companies drove down costs, began catching up on the technology front, and lobbied heavily for government protection.[4] They thought that was all they had to do.

Some could not even do that; the massive investment needed to regain cost competitiveness proved too much for them and they left the television industry. Stronger foreign companies purchased others.

Those that remained transferred labor-intensive manufacturing offshore and rationalized manufacturing at home and abroad. Even with costs under control, these companies (RCA, GE, and Zenith) are still vulnerable because they do not understand the changing nature of Japanese competitive advantage. Even as American producers patted themselves on the back for closing the cost gap, the Japanese were cementing future profit foundations through investment in global brand positions. Having conceived of global competition on a product-by-product basis, U.S. companies could not justify a similar investment.

Having conceded non-U.S. markets, American TV manufacturers were powerless to dislodge the Japanese even from the United States.

While Zenith and RCA dominated the color TV business in the United States, neither had a strong presence elsewhere. With no choice of competitive venue, American companies had to fight every market share battle in the United States. When U.S. companies reduced prices at home, they subjected 100% of their sales volume to margin pressure. Matsushita could force this price action, but only a fraction of it would be similarly exposed.

We do not argue that American TV manufacturers will inevitably succumb to global competition. Trade policy or public opinion may limit foreign penetration. Faced with the threat of more onerous trade sanctions or charges of predatory trade tactics, global competitors may forgo a fight to the finish, especially when the business in question is mature and no longer occupies center stage in the company's product plans. Likewise, domestic manufacturers, despite dwindling margins, may support the threatened business if it has important interdependencies with other businesses (as, for example, in the case of Zenith's TV and data systems business). Or senior management may consider the business important to the company's image (possible motivation for GE) for continuing television production.

The hope that foreign companies may never take over the U.S. market, however, should hardly console Western companies. TVs were no

---

[4]See John J. Nevin, "Can U.S. Business Survive Our Japanese Trade Policy?" *Harvard Business Review*, September-October 1978, p. 165.

more than one loose brick in the American consumer electronics market. The Japanese wanted to knock down the whole wall. For example, with margins under pressure in the TV business, no American manufacturer had the stomach to develop its own videocassette recorder. Today, VCRs are the profitability mainstay for many Japanese companies. Companies defending domestic positions are often shortsighted about the strategic intentions of their competitors. They will never understand their own vulnerability until they understand the intentions of their rivals and then reason back to potential tactics. With no appreciation of strategic intent, defensive-minded competitors are doomed to a perpetual game of catch-up.

LOOSE BRICKS IN EUROPE, TOO

Philips of the Netherlands has become well known virtually everywhere in the world. Like other long-standing MNCs, Philips has always benefited from the kind of international distribution system that U.S. companies lack. Yet our evidence suggests that this advantage alone is not enough. Philips has its own set of problems in responding to the Japanese challenge.

Japanese color TV exports to Europe didn't begin until 1970. Under the terms of their licensing arrangements with European set makers, the Japanese could export only small-screen TVs. No such size limitation existed for Japanese companies willing to manufacture in Europe, but no more than half the output could be exported to the rest of Europe. Furthermore, because laws prohibited Japanese producers from supplying finished sets for private-label sale, they supplied picture tubes. So in 1979, although Europe ran a net trade deficit of only 2 million color televisions, the deficit in color tubes was 2.7 million units. By concentrating on such volume-sensitive manufacturing, Japanese manufacturers skirted protectionist sentiment while exploiting economies of scale gained from U.S. and Japanese experience.

Yet just as they had not been content to remain private-label suppliers in the United States, Japanese companies were not content to remain component suppliers in Europe. They wanted to establish their own brand positions. Sony, Matsushita, and Mitsubishi set up local manufacturing operations in the United Kingdom. When, in response, the British began to fear a Japanese takeover of the local industry, Toshiba and Hitachi simply found U.K. partners. In moving assembly from the Far East to Europe, Japanese manufacturers incurred cost and quality penalties. Yet they regarded such penalties as an acceptable price for establishing strong European distribution and brand positions.

If we contrast Japanese entry strategies in the United States and Europe, it is clear that the tactics and timetables differed. Yet the long-term strategic intentions were the same and the competitive advantage of Japanese producers evolved similarly in both markets. In both Europe and the United States, Japanese companies found a loose brick in the bottom half of the market structure — small-screen portables. And then two other loose bricks were found — the private-label business in the United States and picture tubes in Europe.

From these loose bricks, the Japanese built the sales volume necessary for investment in world-scale manufacturing and state-of-the-art product development; they gained access to local producers, who were an essential source of market knowledge. In Europe, as in the United States, Japanese manufacturers captured a significant share of total industry profitability with a low-risk, low-profile supplier strategy; in so doing, they established a platform from which to launch their drive to global brand dominance.

REGAINING COST COMPETITIVENESS

Philips tried to compete on cost but had more difficulties than RCA and Zenith. First, the European TV industry was more fragmented than that of the United States. When the Japanese entered Europe, twice as many European as American TV makers fought for positions in national markets that were smaller than those in the United States.

Second, European governments frustrated the attempts of companies to use offshore sources or to rationalize production through plant closings, layoffs, and capacity reassignments. European TV makers turned to political solutions to solve competitive difficulties. In theory, the resulting protectionism gave them breathing space as they sought to redress the cost imbalance with Japanese producers. Because they were still confined to marginal, plant-level improvements, however, their cost and quality gap continued to widen. Protectionism reduced the incentive to invest in cost competitiveness; at the same time, the Japanese producers were merging with Europe's smaller manufacturers.

With nearly 3 million units of total European production in 1976, Philips was the only European manufacturer whose volume could fund the automation of manufacturing and the rationalization of product lines and components. Even though its volume was sufficient, however, Philip's tube manufacturing was spread across seven European countries. So it had to demonstrate (country by country, minister by minister, union by union) that the only alternative to protectionism was to support the development of a Pan-European competitor. Philips also had to

WHAT IS CROSS-SUBSIDIZATION?

When a global company uses financial resources accumulated in one part of the world to fight a competitive battle in another, it is pursuing a strategy we call "cross-subsidization." Contrary to tried-and-true MNC policy, a subsidiary should not always be required to stand on its own two feet financially. When a company faces a large competitor in a key foreign market, it may make sense for it to funnel global resources into the local market share battle, especially when the competitor lacks the international reach to strike back.

Money does not always move across borders, though this may happen. For a number of reasons (taxation, foreign exchange risk, regulation) the subsidiary may choose to raise funds locally. Looking to the worldwide strength of the parent, local financial institutions may be willing to provide long-term financing in amounts and at rates that would not be justified on the basis of the subsidiary's short-term prospects. One note of caution: If competitors learn of your subsidiary's borrowing needs, you may reveal strategic intentions by raising local funds and lose an element of competitive surprise.

Cross-subsidization is not dumping. When a company cross-subsidizes it does not sell at less than the domestic market price. Rather than risk trade sanctions, the intelligent global company will squeeze its competitor's margins just enough to dry up its development spending and force corporate officers to reassess their commitment to the business.

With deteriorating margins and no way of retaliating internationally, the company will have little choice but to sell market share. If the competitor uses simple portfolio management techniques, you may even be able to predict how much market share you will have to buy to turn the business into a "dog" and precipitate a sell-off. In one such case a beleaguered business unit manager, facing an aggressive global competitor, lobbied hard for international retaliation. The corporate response: "If you can't make money at home, there's no way we're going to let you go international!" Eventually, the business was sold.

wrestle with independent subsidiaries not eager to surrender their autonomy over manufacturing, product development, and capital investment. By 1982, it was the world's largest color TV maker and had almost closed the cost gap with Japanese producers. Even so — after more than ten years — rationalization plans are still incomplete.

Philips remains vulnerable to global competition because of the difficulties inherent in weaving disparate national subsidiaries into a coherent global competitive team. Low-cost manufacturing and international distribution give Philips two of the critical elements needed for global competition. Still needed is the coordination of national business strategies.

Philip's country managers are jealous of their autonomy in marketing and strategy. With their horizon of competition often limited to a single market, country managers are poorly placed to assess their global vulnerability. They can neither understand nor adequately analyze the strategic intentions and market entry tactics of global competitors. Nor can they estimate the total resources available to foreign competitors for local market share battles.

Under such management pressure, companies like Philips risk responding on a local basis to global competition. The Japanese can "cherry pick" attractive national markets with little fear that their multinational rival will retaliate.

THE STRATEGIC IMPERATIVE

International companies like General Motors and Philips prospered in the fragmented and politicized European market by adopting the "local face" of a good multinational citizen. Today Philips and other MNCs need a global strategic perspective and a corresponding shift in the locus of strategic responsibility away from country organizations. That need conflicts with escalating demands by host governments for national responsiveness. The resulting organizational problems are complex.

Nevertheless, companies must move beyond simplistic organizational views that polarize alternatives between world-product divisions and country-based structures. Headquarters will have to take strategic responsibility in some decision areas; subsidiaries must dominate in others. Managers cannot resolve organizational ambiguity simply by rearranging lines and boxes on the organization chart. They must adopt fundamentally new roles.

National subsidiaries can provide headquarters with more competitive intelligence and learn about world competitors from the experiences of other subsidiaries. They must fight retaliatory battles on behalf of a larger strategy and develop information systems, decision protocols, and performance measurement systems to weave global and local perspectives into tactical decisions. Rather than surrender control over manufacturing, national subsidiaries must interact with the organization in new and complex ways.

Such a realignment of strategic responsibility takes three steps:

1. Analyze precisely the danger of national fragmentation.
2. Create systems to track global competitive developments and to support effective responses.
3. Educate national and headquarters executives in the results of analysis and chosen organization design.

This reorientation may take as long as five years. Managing it is the hardest challenge in the drive to compete successfully.

A NEW ANALYSIS

Managers must cultivate a mind-set based on concepts and tools different from those normally used to assess competitors and competitive advantage.

For example, the television industry case makes clear that the competitive advantage from global distribution is distinct from that due to lower manufacturing costs. Even when they don't have a cost advantage, competitors with a global reach may have the means and motivation for an attack on nationally focused companies. If the global competitor enjoys a high price level at home and suffers no cost disadvantage, it has the means to cross-subsidize the battle for global market share.

Price level differences can exist because of explicit or implicit collusion that limits competitive rivalry, government restrictions barring the entry of new companies to the industry, or differences in the price sensitivity of customers.

The cash flow available to a global competitor is a function of both total costs and realized prices. Cost advantages alone do not indicate whether a company can sustain a global fight. Price level differences, for example, may provide not only the means but also the motivation for cross-subsidization.

If a global competitor sees a more favorable industry growth rate in a foreign market populated by contented and lazy competitors, who are unable or unwilling to fight back, and with customers that are less price sensitive than those at home, it will target that market on its global road. Domestic competitors will be caught unaware.

The implications for these strictly domestic companies are clear. First, they must fight for access to their competitors' market. If such access is unavailable, a fundamental asymmetry results. If no one challenges a global competitor in its home market, the competitor faces a reduced level of rivalry, its profitability rises, and the day when it can attack the home markets of its rivals is hastened. That IBM shares this view is evident from its pitched battle with Fujitsu and Hitachi in Japan.

Global competitors are not battling simply for world volume but also for the cash flow to support new product development, investment in core technologies, and world distribution. Companies that nestle safely in their home beds will be at an increasing resource (if not at a cost) disadvantage. They will be unable to marshal the forces required for a defense of the home market.

Not surprisingly, Japanese MNCs have invested massively in newly industrializing countries (NICs). Only there can European and American companies challenge Japanese rivals on a fairly equal footing without sacrificing domestic profitability or facing market entry restrictions. The failure of Western organizations to compete in the NICs will give the Japanese another uncontested profit source, leaving U.S. and European companies more vulnerable at home.

NEW CONCEPTS

Usually, a company's decision whether to compete for a market depends on the potential profitability of a particular level of market share in that country. But the new global competition requires novel ways of valuing market share; for example:

- Worldwide cost competitiveness, which refers to the minimum world market share a company must capture to underwrite the appropriate manufacturing-scale and product-development effort.
- Retaliation, which refers to the minimum market share the company needs in a particular country to be able to influence the behavior of key global competitors. For example, with only a 2% or 3% share of the foreign market, a company may be too weak to influence the pricing behavior of its foreign rival.
- Home country vulnerability, which refers to the competitive risks of national market share leadership if not accompanied by international distribution. Market leadership at home can create a

false sense of security. Instead of granting invincibility, high market share may have the opposite effect. To the extent that a company uses its market power to support high price levels, foreign competitors — confident that the local company has little freedom for retaliation — may be encouraged to come in under the price umbrella and compete away the organization's profitability.

CRITICAL NATIONAL MARKETS

Most MNCs look at foreign markets as strategically important only when they can yield profits in their own right. Yet different markets may offer very different competitive opportunities. As part of its global strategy, an organization must distinguish between objectives of (1) low-cost sourcing, (2) minimum scale, (3) a national profit base, (4) retaliation against a global competitor, and (5) benchmarking products and technology in a state-of-the-art market. At the same time, the company will need to vary the ways in which it measures subsidiary performance, rewards managers, and makes capital appropriations.

PRODUCT FAMILIES

Global competition requires a broader corporate concept of a product line. In redefining a relevant product family — one that is contiguous in distribution channels and shares a global brand franchise — an organization can, for example, scrutinize all products moving through distribution channels in which its products are sold.

In a corollary effort, all competitors in the channels can be mapped against their product offerings. This effort would include a calculation of the extent of a competitor's investment in the distribution channel, including investment in brand awareness, to understand its motivation to move across segments. Such an analysis would reveal the potential for segment expansion by competitors presently outside the company's strategic horizon.

SCOPE OF OPERATIONS

Where extranational-scale economies exist, the risks in establishing world-scale manufacturing will be very different for the company that sells abroad only under license or through private labels, compared with the company that controls its own worldwide distribution network. Cost advantages are less durable than brand and distribution advantages. An investment in world-scale manufacturing, when not linked to an investment in global distribution, presents untenable risks.

In turn, investments in worldwide distribution and global brand franchises are often economical only if the company has a wide range of products that can benefit from the same distribution and brand investment. Only a company that develops a continuous stream of new products can justify the distribution investment.

A company also needs a broad product portfolio to support investments in key technologies that cut across products and businesses. Competitors with global distribution coverage and wide product lines are best able to justify investments in new core technologies. Witness Honda's leadership in engine technology, a capability it exploits in automobiles, motorcycles, power tillers, snowmobiles, lawnmowers, power generators, and so forth.

Power over distribution channels may depend on a full line. In some cases, even access to a channel (other than on a private-label basis) depends on having a "complete" line of products. A full line may also allow the company to cross-subsidize products in order to displace competitors who are weak in some segments.

Investments in world-scale production and distribution, product-line width, new product development, and core technologies are interrelated. A company's ability to fully exploit an investment made in one area may require support of investments in others.

RESOURCE ALLOCATION

Perhaps the most difficult problem a company faces in global competition is how to allocate resources. Typically, large companies allocate capital to strategic business units (SBUs). In that view, an SBU is a self-contained entity encompassing product development, manufacturing, marketing, and technology. Companies as diverse as General Electric, 3M, and Hewlett-Packard embrace the concept. They point to clear channels of management accountability, visibility of business results, and innovation as the main benefits of SBU management. But an SBU does not provide an appropriate frame of reference to deal with the new competitive milieu.

In pursuing complex global strategies, a company will find different ways to evaluate the geographic scope of individual business subsystems — manufacturing, distribution, marketing, and so on. The authority for resource allocation, then, needs to reside at particular points in the organization for different subsystems, applying different criteria and time horizons to investments in those subsystems.

Global competition may threaten the integrity of the SBU organization for several reasons. A strong SBU-type organization may not facilitate investments in international distribution. To justify such investments, especially in country markets new to the company, it may have to gain the commitment of several businesses who may not share the same set of international priorities.

Even if individual SBUs have developed their own foreign distribution capability, the strategic independence of the various businesses at the country level may make it difficult to cross-subsidize business segments or undertake joint promotion. The company loses some of the benefits of a shared brand franchise.

Companies may have to separate manufacturing and marketing subsystems to rationalize manufacturing on a local-for-global or local-for-regional basis. Economic and political factors will determine which subsidiaries produce which components for the system. In such a case, a company may coordinate manufacturing globally even though marketing may still be based locally.

Companies might also separate the responsibility for global competitive strategy from that for local marketing strategy. While national organizations may be charged with developing some aspects of the marketing mix, headquarters will take the lead role in determining the strategic mission for the local operation, the timing of new product launches, the targeted level of market share, and the appropriate level of investment or expected cash flow.

GEOGRAPHY-BASED ORGANIZATIONS

For the company organized on a national subsidiary basis, there is a corollary problem. It may be difficult to gain commitment to global business initiatives when resource allocation authority lies with the local subsidiary. In this case, the company must ensure that it makes national investments in support of global competitive positions despite spending limits, strategic myopia, or the veto of individual subsidiaries.

Finally, the time limit for investments in global distribution and brand awareness may be quite different from that required for manufacturing-cost take-out investments. Distribution investments usually reflect a long-term commitment and are not susceptible to the same analysis used to justify "brick and mortar" investments.

NEW STRATEGIC THOUGHT

Global competitors must have the capacity to think and act in complex ways. In other words, they may slice the company in one way for distribution investments, in another for technology, and in still another for manufacturing. In addition, global competitors will develop varied criteria and analytical tools to justify these investments.

In our experience, few companies have distinguished between the intermediate tactics and long-run strategic intentions of global competitors. In a world of forward-thinking competitors that change the rules of the game in support of ultimate strategic goals, historical patterns of competition provide little guidance. Executives must anticipate competitive moves by starting from new strategic intentions rather than from precooked generic strategies.

It is more difficult to respond to the new global competition than we often assume. A company must be sensitive to the potential of global competitive interaction even when its manufacturing is not on a global scale. Executives need to understand the way in which competitors use cross-subsidization to undermine seemingly strong domestic market share positions. To build organizations capable of conceiving and executing complex global strategies, top managers must develop the new analytic approaches and organizational arrangements on which our competitive future rests.

MARRIAGE: AN ACCEPTABLE SOLUTION

. . . the White House . . . should investigate a simpler supply side solution to the nation's monetary and fiscal problems — merger between the U.S. and Japan.

. . . an American-Nippon union would vastly increase the supply of savings in the U.S. financial markets.

Marriage has long been an acceptable solution to the microeconomic problems of individuals. . . .

Like all insecure nations, modern Japan has a great propensity to work and save. Like all imperial powers in transition to humbler status, the U.S. has a great compulsion to borrow and spend in order to maintain a lifestyle which it can no longer really afford. . . .

It was once fashionable to argue that capitalist countries had to pursue expansionary foreign policies in order to find new markets. But Japan and the U.S. have turned traditional theories about imperialism upside down.

The U.S. has solved the old problem of under-consumption by creating a welfare state and military industrial complex. It no longer needs a reserve army of consumers, but a reserve army of savers.

In Japan, by contrast, the financial system discourages consumption and the constitution prohibits rearmament. Japan has thus evolved into a natural saver of last resort for the U.S.

Why solemnise this relationship in a formal union when the current dalliance is so satisfactory? . . .

First, the U.S. economic boom is maturing. As inflationary wrinkles appear in 1985, even the Japanese will begin to wonder if they should recycle their dollars as freely as they have so far. . . .

Secondly, . . . If the U.S. would eliminate the fiction of having a financial system autonomous from Japan's, dollar interest rates could collapse and alleviate Latin American's [sic] debt servicing problem.

Third, union with Japan will permit the U.S. to continue looking after the defence needs of its older relatives in Europe. . . .

The final argument . . . is that the U.S. Treasury may accidentally destroy the unique trans-Pacific financial equilibrium now sustaining U.S. recovery and rearmament.

From David Hale "A Modest Proposal for Marriage," *Financial Times* October 17, 1984. Reprinted by permission of the publisher.

1.3 CASE

Benetton

James L. Heskett and
Sergio Signorelli

Luciano Benetton leaned across his desk in an office decorated with frescoes carefully restored to their original beauty in the splendid eighteenth-century Villa Minelli in Ponzano Veneto near Treviso, the soft light of the early winter Italian sun providing a contrast to the forcefulness of his voice:

> When speaking of the "second generation" Benetton, I am thinking of a new business reality which is extra-European in scope. But we have to take into account the diverse requirements of the markets we are planning to enter.

In particular, decisions were being made in late 1982 about how the Benetton Group should best carry out its plans to enter the U.S. and Japanese markets for casual wear garments. In addition to questions as to how best to present its

Note: Portions of this case are based on a case, Benetton, prepared by Professor Signorelli. Selected data in the case were based on estimates or are disguised.

products to consumers in such markets, Benetton's management was reviewing alternative methods of providing production and logistical support for new markets. It was hoped that some or all of the unique features of the company's marketing and operating strategies could be preserved to provide it with the advantages it would need in these new, highly competitive markets.

COMPANY BACKGROUND

The Benetton[1] Group was one of several entities comprising the INVEP Group, an organization that encompassed all of the business activities controlled equally by three brothers, Luciano, Gilberto, and Carlo Benetton, and their sister, Giuliana. By specializing in the production and retailing of casual wear clothing items, particularly woolen sweaters, cotton T-shirts, and jeans, Benetton had, by 1982, become the world leader in the field of knitwear. In that year it had sold 26.9 million units of clothing, of which nearly half were for export from Italy. It supplied more than 1,900 shops, nearly all of which were operated with the understanding that the shops would stock only Benetton products. As a result, Benetton was thought to be the largest consumer of wool in the world, purchasing nearly nine million pounds in 1982. About 60% of all garments sold through Benetton stores were of wool.

The Benettons had developed their business from rather meager beginnings. Their father, a truck driver in Treviso, a town situated north of Venice, had died just after World War II when the eldest, Luciano, was 10 years old, requiring that he and his siblings find work at an early age. Nineteen years later, in 1965, they formed their company when Luciano and Giuliana decided that their complementary skills could provide the basis for a venture. At the time, Giuliana was sewing woolen sweaters of traditional somber colors and scratchy wool for one of the region's many textile artisans while developing much more colorful and fashionable designs in her own time. Luciano, a wholesaler who sold the output of a number of artisans to department stores, remarked: "I saw Giuliana's designs and I was sure I could sell them."[2]

Soon the pair had their first success with a violet pullover made of

---

[1]Pronounced be–net–ón. Many people mistakenly pronounced the name as if it were spelled b–e–n–e–l–t–o–n. Names ending in consonants, while not typical of Italy in general, were quite common in the region of Treviso.

[2]Kenneth Labich, "Benetton Takes on the World," *Fortune*, June 13, 1983, p. 114.

a soft blend of wool, angora, and cashmere. Other colorful sweaters achieved similar success, and the two youngest Benetton brothers joined the partnership. Gilberto, formerly employed by the Crafts Association of Treviso, was put in charge of administration, and Carlo, the youngest and a draftsman in a small local engineering company, assumed responsibility for production.

The Benettons initially sold their products through leading Italian department stores. But in 1968, as soon as their product line was sufficiently extensive to permit it, they opened their first shop in Belluno. It occupied only about 400 square feet, in part because of the limited Benetton product line at the time. But it set the pattern for the stores to follow. By 1975 they owned or franchised some 200 shops throughout Italy.

In 1978, the company realized $78 million in sales, 98% of it in Italy. The decision to launch a major export program to the rest of Europe at that time provided the basis for even more significant growth. By 1982, Benetton's sales had grown to roughly $311 million,[3] or about two-thirds of that for the INVEP Group. The latter included revenues from Benetton Cotone (cotton) (20%), as well as three manufacturing operations.

Financial statements for the Benetton Group are presented in *Exhibits 1* and *2*.

THE KNITWEAR INDUSTRY

The knitwear industry generally was considered to comprise basic categories of knitted underwear, hosiery, and knitted overwear. Its development in Italy and the United States had followed distinctly different paths.

In Italy, knitted overwear represented about two-thirds of the industry production. In general, knitted overwear production involved more steps, more labor, less expensive equipment, and lower levels of technology than either underwear or hosiery production.

Starting with low-level industrialization of knitting between 1870 and 1890, the industry extended from the Biella area across northern Italy. It was concentrated in areas in which small subcontractors, specializing in one or more of the several steps in production shown in *Exhibit 3*, were located. This "externally decentralized" system of pro-

---

[3]Actual sales figures for Benetton were 404 billion lire and for INVEP 624 billion lire. An approximate average exchange rate of $1 = 1,300 lire has been assumed throughout the case for 1982.

EXHIBIT 1. Income statements for the Benetton Group, 1981 and 1982

	1981[a]		1982	
	In billions of lire	*As % of adjusted billings*	*In billions of lire*	*As % of adjusted billings*
Net consolidated billings	373.7	92.9%	404.1	100.6%
= adjusted	+28.4	+7.1%	−2.4	−.6
Adjusted billings	402.1	100.0	401.7	100.0
Expenses:				
Purchases	(157.4)	(39.1)	(134.5)	(33.5)
Labor costs	(21.1)	(5.2)	(26.4)	(6.6)
Other costs[b]	148.0	(36.7)	(175.4)	(43.7)
Balance	75.9	19.0	65.5	16.3
Less financial charges	(15.1)	(3.8)	(20.7)	(5.2)
Plus interest income	2.4	.6	3.5	.9
Less miscellaneous charges	(5.2)	(1.3)	(6.3)	(1.6)
Plus miscellaneous income	6.5	1.6	7.4	1.8
Less depreciation of multiannual charges[c]	(9.1)	(2.3)	(6.3)	(1.6)
Less equipment and plant write-offs	(10.4)	(2.6)	(12.6)	(3.1)
Gross profit before reserves and transfers	45.1	11.2%	30.4	7.6%
Less various reserves	(9.8)[d]	(2.4)	(1.7)[e]	(.4)
Less losses on transfers of assets	(.1)	—	(.1)	—
Plus gains on transfers of assets	.7	.2	.3	.1
Plus capitalized financial charges	—	—	—	—
Gross profit before taxes	35.9	8.9%	29.0	7.2%
Less taxes	(16.3)	(4.1)	(12.6)	(3.1)
Net profit	19.6[f]	4.8%	16.4[f]	4.2%

[a]In evaluating 1981 data, please note that they cover 18 months for the main operating company (Benetton SpA).

[b]Of which royalties of 10.0 billion in 1981 and 13.0 billion lire in 1982 were paid to INVEP. Roughly 80% of these costs represented payments to Benetton's manufacturer-contractors.

[c]Including depreciation of start-up costs.

[d]Of which 4.0 billion lire was placed in reserves for future risks and 4.0 billion lire was placed in reserves for reinvestment funds (according to Law No. 675-1977).

[e]Of which 1.4 billion lire of exchange fluctuation reserves were increased by Benetton and Benetton Lana.

[f]For purposes of rough calculations, the average exchange rate for the dollar against the lira was about $1 = 1,150 lire in 1981 and $1 = 1,300 lire in 1982.

EXHIBIT 2. Consolidated balance sheets of the Benetton Group, December 31, 1981 and 1982 (in billions of lire)*

Account	December 31, 1981	December 31, 1982
Cash	12.8	3.4
Net commercial credits	85.5	140.1
Remainders of the period	52.0	49.6
Financial credits to the Holding Society	9.7	6.7
Other current active accounts	11.5	25.6
Gross current assets (1)	171.6	225.4
Suppliers (accounts payable)	65.3	72.6
Negative balances with banks	23.2	47.3
Financial debits to the Holding Society	1.7	—
Other current debits	18.8	16.9
Current debits (2)	109.0	136.8
Current net assets (1 − 2) = (3)	62.6	88.6
Gross technical investments	57.8	71.9
Less depreciation	(10.4)	(22.6)
Net technical investments	47.5	49.3
Preemptions for investments	.4	8.4
Financing for third parties	—	—
Net investments (4)	47.9	57.7
Multiannual charges (5)	1.2	2.5
Start-up charges (6)	16.3	10.5
Medium- and long-term passive funds:		
Guaranteed loans	5.1	4.6
Nonguaranteed loans	.1	47.7
Employees' pension fund	2.8	3.7
Tax fund	16.2	.3
Currency fluctuation fund	1.1	2.0
Total, medium- and long-term passive funds (7)	25.3	58.3
Net capital (3) + (4) + (5) + (6) − (7)	102.6	100.9

*Exchange rates were $1 = 1,212 lire, December 31, 1981 and $1 = 1,382 lire, December 31, 1982.

EXHIBIT 3. Diagram showing the flow of work through Benetton's factories and subcontractors

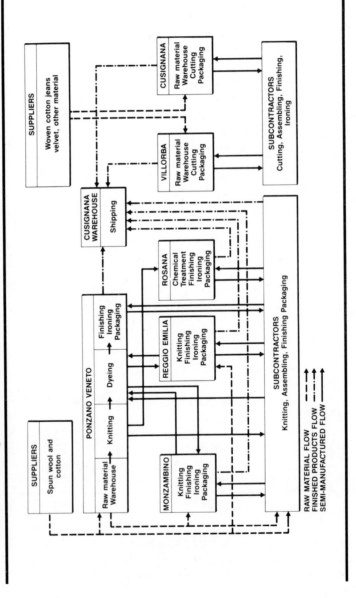

duction had evolved from the original system based on homework that prevailed into the 1950s.

Reliance on homework offered significant labor cost savings, often involving low wages and no responsibility for fringe benefits. It limited investment in fixed assets to that required for relatively simple knitting machines. It allowed a company to smooth its workload while passing fluctuations on to individual homeworkers. And it provided surprisingly high productivity.

In the 1950s, institutions called "groupers" began to appear. They were owned by artisans who acted as intermediaries between a company and homeworkers, collecting orders and in some cases material from contracting companies, organizing work by distributing it to various individuals paid directly by the grouper, and guaranteeing the final product. Relationships between companies, groupers, and homeworkers seldom were exclusive.

By the 1970s, the small artisanal subcontractor companies had replaced many of the homeworkers. Among factors accounting for this were: growth in the sector requiring subcontractors with greater production capability; more complex products; the passage of a new law on homework introducing standards and making use of homework more expensive and less flexible; and the introduction of tax reform in 1973 to discourage the hiding of income. As a result, the importance of the grouper had declined.

Nevertheless, in 1981, according to an estimate by Databank, the knitted overwear sector of Italy consisted of approximately 17,500 companies (consisting in turn of 27,000 local units) employing a total of 130,000 people, other than homeworkers. There were thought to be only 17 companies with 250 employees or more. Among these, Benetton was dominant, with more than three times the sales volume of the next largest manufacturer in the industry.

As a nation, Italy had become the largest producer of knitted overwear in Europe, producing 60% of all European Economic Community output in 1977 followed by the U.K. with 16%. Of its production, 47% was for export, with Germany (38.5% of Italian exports) representing by far the largest market followed by France and the Benelux countries. In total, EEC countries took 80% of Italy's exports. In contrast to major exporters in the Far East, most Italian exports of knitted overwear were marketed abroad under the trademarks of the producing companies.

Imports of knitted overwear garments in the EEC had been restricted by a series of so-called Multifibre Agreements which imposed strict limits on the growth of imports of such items from non-EEC countries. The most recent agreement extended such controls to 1986. By 1982, only 19% of the 810 million items of knitted overwear sold in the EEC originated from outside the community. Twenty-seven percent originated from EEC countries other than Italy, with Italian firms commanding a 54% share of total sales.

In contrast, the knitwear industry in the United States had become concentrated in its early stages of development on the production of knitted underwear and hosiery. The need for high productivity in these sectors had resulted in relatively high investments, factories employing hundreds of persons, and vertically integrated companies engaged in many stages between the spinning of yarn to the production of finished garments. The largest of these firms was Burlington Industries, with 1982 sales of more than $2.5 billion. The strong promotion of, and preference for, garments of synthetic yarns had, if anything, accentuated the trend toward investment and industry consolidation. Manufacturers of knitted overwear, in contrast, had steadily declined in importance. The proportion of the total of nearly one billion knitted overwear garments sold in the U.S. in 1982 that were imported, primarily from the Far East, had climbed to roughly 40% in 1982 and was significantly higher in lower-priced categories.

MANUFACTURING

The basic process for the production of knitted overwear garments from wool and cotton is shown in *Exhibit 3*. Traditionally, it had involved the spinning or purchase and dyeing of yarn, the warehousing of spun material in finished or unfinished form, finishing operations such as mercerizing (immersion in caustic soda to produce a shinier material), waxing (to improve gliding properties and reduce friction during manufacturing and cleaning), and the removal of residual oil.

For women's garments, for example, first a prototype and sample collection was prepared. At Benetton, this generally was done four times per year under the direction of Giuliana Benetton, twice for the major spring/summer and fall/winter collections and twice for "integrative" collections for Christmas and for sport. Including woolen and other garments, a major collection contained typically 450 items, while the "integrative" collection following it featured perhaps 50 fashion-oriented items. The same line was created for all countries. It was estimated that about half of the items contained in the two main collections represented about 90% of sales.

Once designed, garments were then manufactured by machines producing parts of garments in their correct shapes or woven materials that had to be shaped. The next stage, assembly, involved joining the basic parts of each garment, such as front, back, and sleeves for sweaters. This could be accomplished in a visible manner with the edges of two parts sewn together, or a remeshing process associated with higher-quality garments that produced an invisible seam. The latter was used for most Benetton garments. Finishing operations included those of making buttonholes, sewing buttons, ironing, labeling, and final inspection prior to packaging for shipment.

In contrast to operations required for knitted products of natural materials, those made from synthetic fibers which dominated the U.S. market could be shaped and assembled with highly machine-intensive operations. This ranged from hosiery, which could be produced nearly totally by machine in several operations, to knitted underwear, for which finishing operations often were simple and performed in the least expensive manner.

PUTTING FASHION ON AN INDUSTRIAL LEVEL

Benetton had, over the years, been an innovator in the production of knitted overwear products. Ten years before the development of machinery for making hard and rough wool soft and pliable, for example, Luciano Benetton had improved on a crude process that he had observed in Scotland for achieving the effect produced by rudimentary machines with wooden arms that battered the raw knitwear in water. Similarly, in order to avoid the use of centrifugal dryers that shrank the wet knitwear, at Benetton a process was developed by which it was placed in a bag on a stick and rotated vertically in the air.

At a time when women's seamless stockings became popular, hosiery knitting machines that could only produce seamed stockings were made obsolete. One of Benetton's employees had recommended buying and converting the equipment for the production of overwear. Machines providing 90% of Benetton's knitting capacity in its early years were thus purchased for approximately $1,000 per machine, converted for an additional $4,000 each at the time and performing the work of machines valued at much more. They since had been replaced by more modern knitting machines, some of them driven by magnetic tape programmed to provide intricate knitted designs.

But perhaps the most significant development in Benetton's operations occurred when the company began dyeing assembled garments rather than yarn in 1972. It required that garments first be treated in a strong chemical solution for about 20 minutes to soften them and increase their receptiveness to dye. Next, garments were "cooked" for 40 minutes and then stirred in dye-filled vats. Including time for softening, the vat time required for the entire process was about two hours.

The dyeing rooms at the Ponzano plant contained ten smaller vats in which batches with an average size of about 300 garments were processed. They required careful loading and checking of dyes to insure desired colors. The room also contained four newer dyeing machines with automatic dye control and water extracting capability with capacities of 530 garments each per batch.

Dyeing represented a bottleneck at the Ponzano factory. As a result, for much of the year the dyeing machines were operated on a three-shift basis. Even though the process was critical to product quality, Benetton was able to dye only about 35% of its total production at the Ponzano factory and an additional 20% at other company plants. The remaining 45% was dyed by contractors, with more than half of it dyed by two large contractors owned by the Benetton family.

It was estimated that labor and production overhead costs for garments dyed after manufacture were 10% higher than those for garments knitted from dyed thread. Benetton, it was thought, was the only manufacturer of woolen garments that dyed them from grey stock.

The garment-dyeing capability allowed more popular items in Benetton's line to be produced in response to requests for changes in pre-season orders from agents serving retail outlets. As a result of this development, it was estimated that Benetton's inventory turnover for cotton and woolen items at the factory and warehouse was no more than the typical industry figure of 4.5 times per year in spite of the fact that its product line for knitted wear contained nearly 500 different color and style combinations.

As Luciano Benetton had remarked in an interview with an American business journalist:

> . . . *we have kept the same strategy all along — to put fashion on an industrial level. Most of the rest of Italian fashion is still on an artisan level.*[4]

MANUFACTURING ORGANIZATION

The company relied heavily both on internally and externally decentralized operations in the language of the industry. Its internal decentrali-

---

[4]Labich, "Benetton Takes on the World," p. 116.

zation involved nine Benetton facilities, seven in Italy, one in France, and one in Scotland, employing about 1,700 people. Operations performed at the seven Italian locations, along with the associated flow of material, are shown in *Exhibit 3*.

All thread was received at the Cusignana warehouse (about 12 miles from Ponzano) and subsequently shipped to various factories. Textile fabrics were shipped by suppliers directly to Benetton's plants, including those of two of its contractors. Each factory in the group differed in size and functions performed.

For example, some woolen knitwear was produced in Ponzano (all processes), some in Rosana (chemical treatment and finishing), and some in Reggio Emilia and Mozambino (knitting and finishing). Some manufactured items (those in "tintura d'al greggio" or undyed form) were then returned to Ponzano for dyeing and reshipment to the warehouse in Cusignana.

Ready-made material for cotton garments was shipped to the Cusignana factory, assembled there, and stocked in the central warehouse. Summer cotton shirts, however, were produced in Fontane, where only a part of the manufacturing was done internally.

Jeans were the only product category manufactured nearly totally outside Benetton's factories. However, final stages providing necessary controls were centralized in the Cusignana factory.

Functions performed and products made at Benetton's foreign factories differed as well. For example, the plant in Scotland manufactured only items knitted of cashmere for distribution through some twenty shops operated under the name Casa di Hogg, in Italy, with no association with Benetton's name. Another plant at Troyes, France, produced only woolen garments for distribution to a portion of the French retail stores. Constituting only about 5% of Benetton's total sales, none of these garments required dyeing.

Selected data on Benetton's factories is contained in *Exhibit 4*.

In addition, Benetton utilized a network of about 220 production units, either subcontractors or groupers, employing a total of about 10,000 people. These were located mostly near Benetton's production facilities in northeast Italy at Ponzano Veneto, Cusignana, and Fontane, but increasingly were being developed near other plants as well. Subcontractors and groupers performed about 40% of the company's knitting of wool, 60% of the work of assembling garments and 20% of the finishing operations. Typically, the more complex garments were produced internally in Benetton's factories. Cutting and dyeing of nearly all wool was performed in Benetton's plants.

EXHIBIT 4. Selected data for Benetton's facilities, December 1982

Company name	Location	Land and building surface in square meters[a]		Number of employees	Product (processes)
Benetton Lana	Ponzano Veneto	39,720[b]	(19,901)[b]	346	Wool knitwear
Benetton Lana	Rosana	20,440	(3,233)	138	Wool knitwear
Benetton Lana	Mozambino	6,500	(4,751)	180	Wool knitwear
Benetton Lana	Quattro Castella	23,542	(3,523)	77	Wool knitwear
Benetton Cotone	Fontane	16,852	(5,794)	94	Cotton overwear
Benetton Cotone	Villorba	13,865	(14,100)	130	Cotton overwear
Benetton Jeans	Cusignana	65,665[c]	(40,417)[c]	274	Trousers, jeans
Benetton[d]	Castrette	—	—[e]	—	
Benetton	Ponzano Veneto	—	—	247[f]	Control, management
Benetton	Cusignana	—	—	51	Control, management
Totals		186,584	(91,719)	1,537	

[a]One square meter = approximately 10 square feet.
[b]Includes the area of the technical offices in Ponzano Veneto rented by Benetton.
[c]Includes the area of the factory rented by Benetton.
[d]The company also owned the Villa Minelli located in Ponzano Veneto. This was an historical building used for management offices situated on 37,935 square meters of land with a floor space of 5,049 square meters.
[e]This was a piece of land on which the building of an industrial complex was started in 1982. Warehousing for finished products now located at Cusignana in the factory owned by Benetton Jeans was to be moved here.
[f]Including the employees at Villa Minelli.

The contracting network on which Benetton relied represented a kind of "parallel empire" to the company itself. Many of the contractors were owned in whole or in part by managers of Benetton. According to one trade article:

> *The system is now established, and one can say that there is no head or manager from Benetton who is not at the same time owner, president, or director of a leading contracting company in the whole Lombardia-Veneto area (northern Italy).*[5]

According to the head of the textile section of the trade union, the production rates among contractors were superior to those of Benetton's factories for comparable jobs. There was a second tier to this system of external decentralization as well, consisting of subcontractors. It was alleged by one trade unionist that trade union minima and working hours were adhered to only at the first level of decentralization. There was no doubt that subcontractor costs included lower employment tax payments to the state than those incurred by Benetton. In addition to other benefits, the contracting network provided Benetton with a flexible production capacity that absorbed most of the fluctuations in demand. It provided work for many relatives of the company's full-time employees as well.

However, the production processes required a constant shuttling of work in process from one location to another, a function performed largely by subcontractors. While this reduced cost savings from external decentralization, it resulted in total production costs for woolen items that were perhaps 85% of those producers of garments of comparable quality in Europe and on a par with those in the Far East. More important, it reduced Benetton's risk from business fluctuations.

Still other functions were centralized at the company's headquarters. Technical research and planning, for example, were carried out at Ponzano Veneto. Under the supervision of Giuliana Benetton, product planning and design as well as the acquisition and exploitation of necessary patents and rights was managed.

All purchasing was done at Ponzano Veneto. Wool was purchased in spools from Italian producers. Material for newer items in the product line was purchased in more nearly finished form. Cotton was purchased already woven. Velvet arrived already dyed and ready for cutting. And the predyed cloth for jeans, introduced by the company first in 1972,

---

[5]Giuseppe Cosentino, "The Benetton Case — The Top of the Iceberg," *Panorama*, December 15, 1982.

was totally imported from the United States. Cutting was done on the basis of layouts produced by computer at Ponzano.

THE SUPPLY CYCLE

The large volume of business done by the company required that production planning for woven cotton and woolen items be begun far in advance of shipment to the stores. For example, for the spring-summer major line to be introduced in the stores early in January, final designs were prepared in February and early March, as shown in *Exhibit 5*. Samples of each of the 600 items in the total collection were assembled. In April about a fourth of the items were eliminated in a "pre-presentation" meeting between Giuliana Benetton, Benetton's product and manufacturing managers, and several of the company's 70 agents. The remaining were then produced in small quantities for presentation by area managers to agents and by agents to their individual clients (store owners) in a process that extended from mid-May to mid-July. Within two weeks after the collection of the first orders from franchisees by agents in early June, a rough production plan for the season, by fabrics and styles, was "exploded" from the first 5% to 10% of total orders. This allowed time for the placement of final orders for purchased threads and garments as well as negotiations with subcontractors for necessary increases or decreases in subcontracted volumes prior to the start of production of "basic" retail stocks early in July in advance of the company's three- to four-week vacation in August.

As orders for basic stocks were received from agents, they were assigned reserved slots in the rough production plan by fabric, style, color, and individual store. These orders were produced for delivery to stores from early November through late May for a sales season beginning early in January in the stores. They were scheduled so that each store could present 80% to 90% of all items (fabrics, styles, and colors) in its basic collection to its customers at the outset of the selling season. Other items and remaining quantities ordered arrived at the stores during the selling season.

Because Benetton required its clients to commit themselves to specific orders seven months in advance of the start of the selling season, it provided several opportunities to franchisees to adjust the actual items presented to their customers. From August through early December, as they gathered more information about color preferences, clients and agents were allowed to specify colors for woven items held in "greggio" up to that point, with a limit of 30% of the total orders for woolen items on such orders. During this period, Benetton's product managers

EXHIBIT 5. Operating cycle, Benetton Group

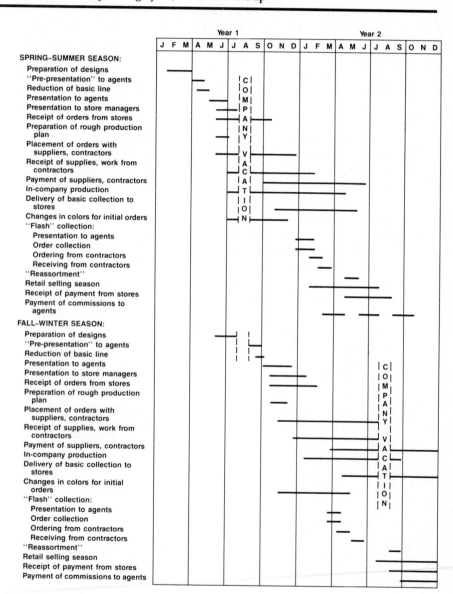

negotiated with agents to encourage them to concentrate their orders on items achieving the highest order popularity.

A second process, called the "flash collection," involved the addition of about 50 items to each season's product line based on early customer requests for fabric-style-color combinations not found in the store. This occurred for the spring-summer collection in January, and required the analysis of requests by Benetton's product and manufacturing managers and a subset of agents prior to the presentation of the flash collection by agents to the stores.

A third process, "reassortment," involved the acceptance of additional orders for rapid delivery later in the selling season, approximately March for the spring-summer collection. Fill-in reassortment orders were processed for store delivery roughly five weeks from the date of their receipt at Benetton. It was made available only for a small number of items determined through a process of negotiation between Benetton's product managers and agents. Because of its process of dyeing "grey" garments, Benetton's plant at Ponzano had the capability to fill an order within seven days of its receipt from an agent. This practice, occasionally requested by agents through Luciano Benetton and product managers, was not encouraged, because it often resulted in dye batches smaller than vat capacity and interfered with long-standing production plans.

Major collections were planned so that about 80% of a season's total sales volume was represented by the basic collection, less than 10% by the flash collection, and less than 10% by reassortment. The remaining sales were realized from a small "cruise" collection presented in the spring and a small "Christmas" collection presented in the fall. In total, sales of the fall-winter collection approximated 60% of a typical year's sales volume.

Production of the basic spring-summer collection ended in late April for final deliveries to stores by late May, by which time production for the following season's fall-winter collection was well underway.

Payments to subcontractors, representing a major cash outflow, were made 70 days after the end of the month in which production occurred or, in the case of the spring-summer collection, in October. Collections from retail franchisees were based on a season beginning date of March 30 for the spring-summer season, with one-third of payment due 30, 60, and 90 days after that date or the date of actual receipt of merchandise. This was designed to minimize retailers' investment in inventories.

The construction of a company-owned wool-spinning mill which could supply about 20% of Benetton's needs was in the planning stage.

MARKETING

From the beginning, Benetton's marketing strategy had been based on the development of fashionable, but casual knitted garments featuring bright colors, in contrast to much of the available product in European stores at the time. Colors such as pink and turquoise were staples at the time only in Benetton's product line and continued to be popular items.

PRODUCT DEVELOPMENT

The basic philosophy behind the design of products had varied little over the years. According to one recent report:

> The company has no plans to vary the design philosophy behind its product line. Though Giuliana has hired designers from top firms all over the world and follows major fashion trends, she contends that she has merely enlarged on her original insight that young, free-spending customers will always be attracted to brilliant reds and greens and a variety of pastels. "You never discover a new design," she says. "You merely make small changes in the old ones."[6]

The number of product lines had, however, been expanded in conjunction with efforts to retail Benetton products under different labels and store names. Thus, a "012 Benetton" line of children's wear had been developed for presentation in shops decorated with stuffed animals and rainbows carrying the same name. "Jeans West" shops carried Benetton knitwear and trousers targeted to the youth market. Stores carrying Benetton knitwear and trousers with higher fashion content for men and women were named "My Market." A line of items was produced for the "Sisley" label, directed to sophisticated men and presented in stores carrying that name. Although there was no direct equivalent to Sisley for women, shops with the "Mercerie" name stocked some items aimed at a similar market segment, but bearing the Benetton label. Shops under all of these names were intended for center city locations in European cities. In addition, recently a number of shops named "Tomato" had been opened in outlying urban areas to carry knitwear and trousers aimed at the youth market. They featured flashing lights and rock music.

In fact, for each trade name, the appropriate style of furniture and equipment, color of lighting, type of music, and appropriate sex, age, and dress style for salespeople was studied and selected to attract the targeted clientele.

---

[6]Labich, "Benetton Takes on the World," p. 115.

Overall, Benetton shops were identified by more than 10 different names, most of which were not known outside Italy. In spite of the multiplicity of names for stores, it was estimated that during 1982, 70% of total sales were made under the Benetton label and 25% under the 012 Benetton label. However, in total, the Benetton catalogue listed more than 2,000 different item-label combinations.

PRICING

The median retail price of Benetton garments in 1982 was about $20. Prices ranged from under $10 for a pair of socks to $120 for a high-fashion denim jacket. While opinions differed, prices generally were considered lower than competition for the quality of product, nearly always offered in natural wool or cotton. The price-quality combination, high-fashion content, and the multiplicity of bright colors were at the core of the company's retailing strategy.

DISTRIBUTION

Concurrent with the development of their product line, Benetton began searching for ways of gaining control over their channels of distribution.

Benetton had achieved its retail distribution through an unusual arrangement with "agents" in Italy and other countries of Europe. According to one company marketing executive, the use of the term "franchising" in describing Benetton was a misnomer. Largely through verbal agreement, agents of the company were assigned large territories in which to encourage the development of Benetton retail outlets. They would in turn find smaller investors and store operators with the "Benetton mentality" (according to Benetton's director of communications) with whom they established individual partnerships at the level of the individual outlet. An individual agent might thus supervise and hold an interest in a number of stores. Late in 1982, Benetton conducted its business with 70 such agents. Agents were compensated by Benetton on the basis of a commission of about 4% of the factory sales of goods sold through their retail outlets, in addition to their share of the profits of the stores in which they held ownership.

For their part, agents found and helped train individual store operators, displayed the Benetton collection to store operators in their regions, assembled orders for the initial stock and stock reordered during each season, and generally supervised the merchandising and pricing at the stores.

Store owners were required to pay Benetton neither a fee for use of its name nor a royalty based on a percentage of sales or profits. Among other things, they were required to carry only Benetton merchandise, maintain a minimum sales level (equivalent to orders for about 3,500 garments per year), adhere to suggested mark-ups of about 80% from cost, pay for their orders according to a preset schedule,[7] and, in the words of one Benetton manager, develop "an understanding of Benetton's way of doing business."

In a recent interview, Luciano Benetton had provided some insight into the company's strategy for developing shopowners:

> We have caused a (new) type of retailer to become important, who until the day before was perhaps a florist or a hairdresser. His prior career was of no importance, but he had to have the right spirit to work in a Benetton shop.

The ideal Benetton retailer was relatively young and thought to have good potential for "growing with Benetton."

All Benetton outlets were required to use Benetton fixtures and follow basic merchandising concepts, the most important among them being that all merchandise was to be displayed on open shelves accessible to customers who could touch it and try it on. The open displays in an otherwise undecorated space created an impression of great color and fashion to the window-shopping customer. This was thought to be especially effective with the 19-to-25-year-old market toward which Benetton had directed its European marketing efforts.

Benetton clients were expected to maintain storage facilities which, in combination with their store shelves, could accommodate 30% to 40% of a season's sales in addition to merchandise still being sold from the preceding season. Typically, such storage consisted of small basement rooms under the retail outlets. However, the company's written agreement with a client when it existed, typically was limited to the use and protection of Benetton's trademark.

Benetton's relationship with agents was managed largely on a verbal basis of trust. Agents rarely had to be replaced for failure to meet expectations.

Benetton had given a great deal of attention to store location, emphasizing areas of high traffic for young adults. Most important, European locations had been selected by Luciano Benetton and his assis-

---

[7]Payment terms calling for one-third of payment within 30, 60, and 90 days each of the beginning date of the season (for goods received prior to that time) could result in payments on average being made to Benetton in about 80 days, depending on the relation between the date the merchandise actually was received and the date set for determining payment dates.

tants, according to a pattern of market development in which the first store in a given market often was sited in a high-prestige location. According to one legend in the company, it had taken Mr. Benetton six years to find the proper location for one shop in Turin. Once the site for a lead store had been selected and developed, an effort was made rapidly to blanket the area around it with shops offering Benetton's merchandise.

As many as six different shops, of which no more than two might be called Benetton, could be located within several city blocks of one another. The company had 46 shops in Milan, Italy alone. While they were adapted in layout to fit desirable sites, all were much smaller and had several characteristics that set them apart from other young women's casual apparel shops, as suggested by the comparative profiles shown in *Exhibit 6*. The layout of a typical Benetton shop is shown in *Exhibit 7*.

By the end of 1982, shops were being opened in Europe at the rate of one every working day. Of the more than 1,800 shops in operation at the time in Europe, 1,165 were located in Italy alone. (See *Exhibit 8* for a tabulation of shops by type and by location.) According to one company executive, while many shops had been moved, "none had been closed."

While Benetton retail shops differed, depending on available real estate, they all had one thing in common. They carried only Benetton products, in spite of the fact that only 20 of Benetton's stores outside Italy were owned by the company.

Retailers were expected to follow guidelines for offering sale merchandise. These were established and managed by agents in each region, who also moved merchandise among shops as sales patterns developed. As a result, the typical level of mark-downs as a percentage of sales for a Benetton retail outlet was relatively low, approximating seven percentage points of a retailer's prescribed initial margin. The "model" for Benetton retail store operations was that a store would have no more or less than 15% of a season's merchandise as it entered the last two weeks of a season. This could then be sold at cost to allow the retailer to present a newly merchandised store to the customer at the outset of the new season. Benetton did not accept merchandise returns from its agents or retailers.

PROMOTION

Benetton relied on location and bright, inviting store appearance as a cornerstone for its promotional effort. Window displays often were spare and allowed a clear view of the open shelves of colorful merchan-

EXHIBIT 6. Comparative profits for typical Benneton store, European young women's apparel store, and American specialty chain store for young women's apparel

Item	Typical Benetton store[a]	Store of European competition	American specialty chain store[a]
Annual sales, in $	$305,000	$150,000	$400,000
Selling space, in sq. ft.	500	1,200	2,700
Storage space, in sq. ft.	200	300	300
Type of location	Downtown street	Downtown street	Suburban shopping mall
Initial margins, as % of sales price	44%	50%	57%
Realized margins, as % of sales price	37%	45%	45%
Median sales price per unit, in $	18	40	23[b]
Average size per transaction, in $	26	50	35[b]
Employee hours per week	90	200	230
Selling hours per week	45	45	76
Average store inventory, at cost[c]	$ 40,000	$ 30,000	$ 50,000
Expense categories, as a % of sales:			
Cost of goods sold:	61%	55%	55%
Labor	7	29	13
Occupancy (rent and utilities)	5	7	10
Other (including overhead)	8	6	10
Net profit before tax	19%	3%	12%

[a]Based on casewriters' estimates.

[b]These figures had risen with the introduction of designers' clothing for casual wear. Stores not carrying such clothing realized average prices of perhaps $18 per garment. Stores featuring such clothing averaged as much as $55 per item for lines of clothing comparable to those sold by Benetton.

[c]Estimated on the basis of a store capacity of 2,000 pieces plus a back-up stock varying between 500 pieces toward the end of one season and 2,500 pieces at the beginning of the next.

dise from the street. In addition, it used mainly three media in Europe to advertise its name: television, press, and the sponsoring of sports events.

On television, spots were placed that concentrated on the "sport" and "youth" image of the Benetton name. Magazine advertising was used for institutional campaigns and emphasized color and the Benetton "lifestyle."

EXHIBIT 7. Typical layout of a Benetton retail store*

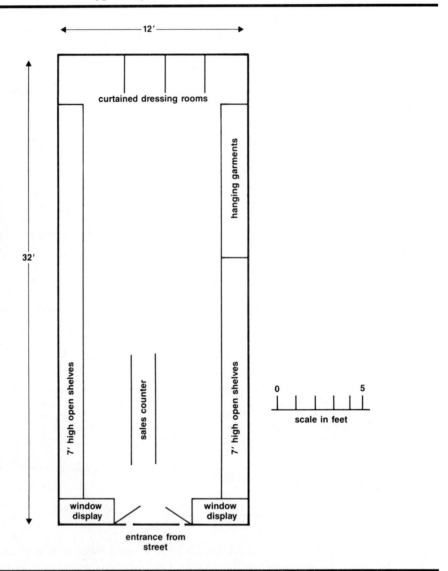

*In cases where a Benetton and Benetton 012 store were located next to one another, they might be connected by an interior doorway.

EXHIBIT 8. Location of Benetton stores, by country and product line, December 1982

Country	Benetton[a]	Number of stores, by product line		Total
		012[b]	Sisley[c]	
Italy[d]	659	380	126	1,165
France	198	80	5	283
Germany	138	30	—	168
Switzerland	53	10	3	66
United Kingdom	35	8	1	44
Austria	28	8	—	36
Belgium	12	2	—	14
Ireland	8	5	1	14
Sweden	9	4	—	13
Holland	8	3	—	11
Spain	9	—	—	9
Other	79	15	—	94
	1,236	545	136	1,917

[a]Figures for Benetton in Italy only included stores operated under the names of Tomato, Mercerie, My Market, Fantomex, Jeans West, Pulloveria, and several others.

[b]The 012 stores carried children's clothing.

[c]The Sisley stores specialized in fashion-oriented casual wear for men.

[d]Figures for Italy included "franchised affiliates," store sites developed and supervised by agents in the manner described in the case, and "third party shops," which, although not bound by agreements, adopted the same sales formula as the affiliates. Many of the latter had been converted to franchised affiliates, leaving only about 400 third-party shops by the end of 1982. At its peak in 1978, the number of company-owned shops reached 58. By 1982, there were none in Italy.

Benetton management had invested in the sponsoring of sports events throughout much of the company's existence, reflecting the interests of the Benettons themselves. Thus the company sponsored a rugby team which had moved into the top league in Italy, later adding the sponsorship of a handball team as well. It had already committed what was estimated to be well over $2 million for the sponsorship of a race car for the 1983 season of World F-1 auto racing.

All of these efforts were put forth on behalf of the Benetton name, the only Benetton trade name with enough volume and outlets to support a multinational campaign, and were intended to support the image of a product line aimed at the active, young adult or child. Benetton had spent over twice as much for advertising in Italy as its nearest European competitor, Maglificio Piave, manufacturer of the Stefanel brand of clothing. Over two-thirds of Benetton's 1981 advertising budget for Italy, 955 million lire, was spent for magazine advertising.

LOGISTICS

Logistics played an important role in the Benetton strategy. Starting at the retail level, stores carrying Benetton products were designed with limited storage space for back-up stocks. Upon arrival at the store direct from Benetton, merchandise often was checked and placed directly on the display shelves. This required that shipments to stores be planned and executed according to a carefully prepared schedule.

Agents managed the replenishment process by collecting and assembling orders from individual stores and relaying them electronically to Villorba, where directions were given for orders to be manufactured to order. In principle, Benetton did not manufacture anything without an order in hand. From receipt of a replenishment order, the company could have merchandise at the retail site in Europe no more than five weeks from the transmission of an order from an agent. (This contrasted with the shipment of a season's initial assortment, for which production began six months and ended 40 days in advance of the display of merchandise in the stores.)

All merchandise was premarked in the currency of the country of destination with tickets coded to be processed electronically at the time of the sale. To facilitate replenishment, Benetton had under design two major improvements in the logistics system. An elaborate new information network, relying on automatic cash registers in clusters of 10 shops each hooked into Benetton's three large Siemen's 7865 computing units in Italy and an Olivetti 5330 unit in Paris, recently had been proposed by Elio Aluffi, managing director of internal operations. It would be capable of instantly recording individual sales in Benetton's European shops. Its cost was estimated to be roughly $7.5 million. Although proposed for possible implementation by the summer of 1983, there was some question about its acceptance by agents, several of whom had indicated that the new system was not needed.

In addition, Luciano Benetton had on his desk a proposal for the construction of a new 200,000-square-foot central warehousing facility at Castrette, about 12 miles from the Ponzano headquarters, at a cost of about $20 million. The core of this facility would be 10 robot stacker cranes capable of stowing and picking cartons from its stocking capacity of nearly 250,000 boxes of merchandise. Its daily total handling capacity was estimated to be 15,000 boxes (either in or out of the warehouse). With the new warehouse operating by the end of 1984, plans called for a reduction in minimum lead time required for the distribution of orders for each collection from 40 to 35 days.

The number of items per box to be handled at Castrette would vary, but it was thought to average 28. It depended on the size of the order directed to an individual factory where the items would be boxed and shipped to Castrette. No boxes would be opened while at the Castrette warehouse. All were labeled at the factory for use with optical scanners which routed the merchandise through the warehouse. Prices to retailers did not vary on the basis of the number of items shipped per box.

In addition to service improvements, the new warehouse offered the possibility of savings of perhaps 20% on transport costs for finished products. Not only could orders be consolidated for an individual store at Castrette but they could be loaded in sequence for store delivery by truck. (All orders were sold at a "store delivered" price. This price did not vary by destination.) While a detailed analysis of current transportation costs had not been completed, the casewriters estimated that they could be as high as 5% of sales.

With the opening of the Castrette facility, the current warehouse at Cusignana would be closed and all items produced in Italy moved through Castrette.

EUROPEAN COMPETITION

Benetton had experienced increasing competition in Italy and Europe, primarily from firms emulating elements of its strategy. For example, other Italian manufacturers recently had instituted programs of direct selling by franchising local retailers. Both had had to abandon gradually their wholesale customers and launch new trademarks.

One, Maglificio Torinese, had, since 1980, been opening shops for the exclusive sales of the Kappa Sport product line specializing in casual sportswear. It now had more than 100 outlets in Italy with plans to extend its sales network to other countries. Maglificio Piave, launching its "Stefanel" trademark in 1979 to replace the Sigma brand formerly sold to wholesalers, already sold through 150 exclusive outlets in Italy and some 30 others throughout Europe.

It was apparent to Benetton's management that its current product lines were reaching the saturation point in the Italian market. As a result of this as well as increasing competition from emulators, a growing amount of competitive imported merchandise, and a stagnant economy, Benetton's billings in Italy had leveled out in real terms.

There had been some debate about the importance of other European markets in Benetton's future strategy. As Elio Aluffi, a long-time Benetton employee recently moved to his new post as head of internal operations, had said: "We haven't completed our work yet in Europe. We have to consolidate that market."[8]

But while there still appeared to be significant potential for Benetton in the rest of Europe, with expected annual increases in sales of 15% resulting from expanded efforts in England, Belgium, and the Netherlands, it was generally concluded that potential margins to be obtained from incremental sales in Europe were lower than those that might be realized in totally new markets like Japan and the United States. As a result, the Benettons and their senior managers were studying alternatives for developing the U.S. market, where it was felt there might be a potential for 1,000 or more retail outlets.

THE U.S. STRATEGY

Many issues had been raised at Benetton in the process of developing alternatives for serving the U.S. market. They reflected questions among managers whether the formula so successful in Italy could be applied in the U.S., and if it couldn't, whether Benetton would enjoy the competitive advantage that was responsible for its success in Europe.

Several elements of the U.S. market were particularly worrisome. First was its sheer size and the ability of Benetton to accommodate the volumes of potential sales it might enjoy. Second, the Benetton name and its associated labels were unknown except among those who had traveled in Europe. There was already formidable U.S. competition, primarily in the form of well-established manufacturers and retailers of casual wear. Several of these manufacturers carried on their own extensive consumer advertising program. Levi Strauss, with 1982 sales of about $2.3 billion, not only manufactured jeans and related items, but also operated retail stores, budgeting more than $100 million each year for advertising and promotion. In addition, several large retail chains

---

[8]Labich, "Benetton Takes on the World," p. 118.

carried a great deal of merchandise aimed at Benetton's prime markets, including The Limited (with approximately 750 retail stores), Charming Shops (260 stores), Petrie (nearly 800 stores), and Miller-Wohl (nearly 300 stores). While none of these competitors manufactured garments, many offered products produced with their labels. And several had engaged relatively heavily in media advertising to solidify their position; The Limited alone was thought to have an annual advertising budget of $20 million. All owned and controlled their own stores, mostly in modern shopping malls (largely nonexistent in many parts of Europe), with a size and sales volume per store considerably larger than Benetton's.

Nevertheless, it was thought that Benetton could capitalize on the strong image of Italian design and the upsurge of popularity of Italian fashion in the United States. And its nontraditional (for the U.S.) approach to retailing might provide advantages in finding good store locations that competitors couldn't utilize.

A debate had arisen concerning the product line and its presentation. Basic among the issues discussed was whether the product mix should be altered significantly. For example, there was some support for upgrading the target market, average sales points, and dollar margins per item for a U.S. strategy. This could be centered around the Sisley and Mercerie merchandise lines for men and women. Consistent with this long-term target, the INVEP Group recently had acquired a 50% interest in an Italian fashion house, Fiorucci. While the company was not highly profitable, the acquisition gave the Benettons entry into higher fashion markets, with potential benefits for the image of other of the group's labels.

On the other hand, it was argued that the company could gain maximum penetration by maintaining its European price points, adjusted only for U.S. import tariffs of 35% of manufactured cost. If this were done, however, little or no additional budget could be devoted to the development of designs especially for the U.S. market.

American preference for easy-to-care-for garments raised questions about the potential attraction of Benetton's natural fibers. Also, tastes seemed to be changing more rapidly than in the past. New products made of "plush" (velvet) and heavy knitted cotton had replaced wool among some consumers' preferences. As Luciano Benetton pointed out, however: "Heavy knitted cotton items have played an important part in all our recent collections. In cases such as this a company must be adaptable and ready to respond to the demands of the market."

In the process of developing an appropriate retailing strategy for the U.S., several questions had been raised. Should Benetton develop markets as they had in Europe, relying on agents to develop and control a retailing network? Twenty regions for U.S. development had been identified on the basis of population and per capita clothing purchase data. In addition, the question had been posed as to whether Benetton should rely on existing or new agents. Nearly all of its current agents were from Europe or the Middle East. But they knew the company and its policies and were trusted by Benetton's management. In addition, an opportunity to participate in the development of the U.S. market could increase their loyalty to the company. On the other hand, many of the existing agents did not know the U.S. market well. Several were thought already to be getting overloaded with work.

Whether agents were used or not, a decision had to be made whether "lead" stores displaying the Benetton name at prestigious addresses should be opened prior to blanketing a metropolitan area with numerous outlets. Or whether Benetton could rely on department stores to provide space for Benetton products until the name could become better known in the U.S. At least two leading U.S. department store organizations, Macy's and Associated Dry Goods, had approached Benetton with proposals to open small Benetton boutiques in their department stores, if necessary under the agent arrangement. However, both had desired an exclusive agreement with Benetton or its agents. Or should a new type of retailing outlet be designed altogether? In addressing this last question, Luciano Benetton commented:

> The idea we are looking for would represent a new era in the point-of-sale development. For instance, instead of small structures, we would have larger retail areas in which we would present more diverse merchandise. . . . Small shops like our conventional points of sale cannot serve as points of reference where people meet or listen to music. Today the necessity is felt, abroad as in Italy, for large spaces where consumers can meet.

Even Benetton's small shops required an investment estimated to average about $70,000 each for the U.S. This assumed pre-work to condition the space for Benetton's fixtures of $15,000 to $20,000, about $40,000 for the fixtures, and from $5,000 to $15,000 for transportation of the fixtures from Italy, depending on whether surface or air transport were used. It assumed no investment, for well-run stores, in inventory and the payment of no "key money" to obtain desirable retail locations.

It was clear to everyone concerned that it would be impossible to launch a full-scale advertising program for the Benetton name in the U.S. similar to that already existing in Europe. But it was thought that some promotional effort would be expected by Benetton's retailers. One estimate of the minimum annual advertising budget required just to achieve visibility and begin to build awareness for the name in the U.S.

was $2 million. Questions remained, however, as to how a budget of that size should be allocated to various media.

How would a new U.S. market be supported operationally? Alternatives under consideration were: (1) the development of a new plant with dyeing facilities and a warehouse in the U.S.; (2) the opening only of a new warehouse to stock finished product shipped from the Ponzano factory; or (3) direct distribution to U.S. retail sites from Europe, either using conventional forms of communication or an extended computer linked up with product shipment by air.

The first of these would require a capital investment of perhaps $10 million and labor costs perhaps 50% higher than at the Ponzano plant. Of more importance would be the difficulty of managing the crucial dyeing operation at a foreign site. Regardless of whether a new dyeing facility were opened in the U.S., it was assumed that the company could not afford to source "grey" garments in the U.S. at anywhere near the cost it experienced in Italy. Thus, added costs of shipping such garments by surface or air would be incurred anyway, with the difference in total transit time for the two methods being about three weeks. It was estimated that delivery by air to the U.S. in semifinished or finished form would add perhaps 50% to the current average of transportation costs for garments shipped in Europe or by surface means across the Atlantic Ocean.

The second alternative would make an investment in U.S. plant capacity unnecessary for the time being. But Benetton would lose inventory savings of the kind enjoyed in Europe, and its new warehouse at Castrette already could provide sufficient capacity to serve both the U.S. and European markets.

The third alternative would allow Benetton to delay significant commitments of capital to either plant or inventory but would require increased transportation costs even if no computer link-up were attempted. The latter would, it was thought, pay for itself in perhaps three years by providing more timely information.

Nor was entry into the U.S. market the only new venture confronting Benetton's management. Plans were underway to develop the Japanese market as well. And in one move apparently aimed at enhancing Benetton's image further, the family was reported to be considering a joint venture with a French manufacturer of perfumes to produce a new line of Benetton perfumes and cosmetics.

Benetton was reported to be having difficulties with its recent acquisition of an Italian shoe manufacturer, Calza Turificio di Varese, manufacturing one million pairs of shoes per year with 86 retail shops and 1982 sales of about $40 million. Benetton had bought a 70% interest in it for $12 million in June 1982. While this had not dimmed management's enthusiasm for adding Benetton shoes to its retail lines, Luciano Benetton commented that "as an experience, it has been quite interesting. But the factory is old and there have been many problems."[9]

In response to an interviewer who had questioned the acquisition of the shoe manufacturer, Luciano Benetton replied:

> *I don't agree, because there are too many logical relationships. We are known for woolen knitwear. And when we started making trousers, we thought this already might be a different sector. Instead, it was coordinated exactly as we can coordinate the shoes. . . . If the common denominator is clothing, we will also have to produce evening dresses. But we don't because ours is the "casual" market segment comprising clothing without too much elegance for specific hours of the day.*

By the end of 1982, action had been taken on a number of the issues concerning the development of the U.S. market. But others remained, several of which could greatly affect the company's U.S. strategy.

---

[9]Labich, "Benetton Takes on the World," p. 119.

1.4 *CASE*

The World Pharmaceutical Industry: Prospects for the 1980s

Robert D. Buzzell

During the 1980s, new challenges and opportunities have been emerging for pharmaceutical manufacturers throughout the world. Among the trends predicted by consulting firms, industry research organizations, and planners in the major companies are:

- A lower rate of industry growth, with real volume increases averaging around 7% annually rather than 10–12% as in the 1970s.
- Increased pressure on prices from regulatory agencies in most countries.
- Greater competition from "generic" (unbranded) drugs, because of both regulatory pressures and the expiration of patents on major products.

- More direct rivalry among firms based in different countries, and a possible increase in worldwide industry concentration.
- Growing importance of new technologies, especially "genetic engineering," as a source of new products.
- A continuing need for heavy spending on research and development.
- Growth in the number of practicing physicians at a rate significantly greater than that of the population in most countries.
- More self-medication, and generally greater involvement by patients in the choice of therapies.

Summing up these and other expected shifts, one leading consulting firm stated that the industry ". . . faces continuing changes in the regulation, technology, economics, and demographics of health care . . . companies are turning to strategies emphasizing marketing and manufacturing as well as research to maintain high returns and provide growth opportunities for the future."[1]

THE INDUSTRY

In its broadest sense, the term "pharmaceuticals" includes all kinds of medicinal substances, even medicinal herbs used as folk remedies. Substances produced and distributed commercially, however, are generally classified into one of two broad groups:

- *Ethical pharmaceuticals,* available only through a physician's prescription; and
- *Over-the-counter (OTC) and proprietary drugs,* sold without prescription. Within this category a further distinction is sometimes made between proprietaries (promoted, often very heavily, to the general public) and OTC products (promoted primarily to physicians and pharmacists).

In 1980, world sales of ethical pharmaceuticals were estimated at $70 to $75 billion, and sales of nonprescription drugs at $9 to $10 billion. It was difficult to draw an exact boundary between the two categories, because drugs that were sold only on physicians' prescriptions in one

---

[1]Arthur D. Little Decision Resources, Inc., *Outlook for the Pharmaceutical Industry to 1990,* Cambridge, Mass. January 1982.

country were available as OTC products in other countries. In addition, many products that had formerly been classed as ethical drugs had, over time, evolved into OTC products. Moreover, the technology, manufacturing, and distribution skills and facilities required to produce drugs were basically the same whether or not they were restricted to prescription-only sales. As a result, most large pharmaceutical firms produced OTC and/or proprietary products as well as ethicals. (Often these companies used different brand names and separate sales organizations for OTC or proprietary products, however, to avoid possible damage to their reputations among physicians.)

The remainder of this case deals with the *ethical* sector of the pharmaceutical industry, with only incidental mention of OTC and proprietary products.

INDUSTRY GROWTH

The industry had enjoyed steady growth from 1970 to 1980, on account of both rising standards of health care throughout the world and continuing product innovation by producers. From 1970 to 1980 worldwide demand grew, in real volume, at an average annual rate of 10–12%. Slower growth was, however, expected during the 1980s and early 1990s. Various consultants' forecasts for real growth rates during this period ranged from 5% to 8% annually.

Within the world market, growth rates varied considerably among countries and product categories. An estimated breakdown of worldwide ethical sales by countries/regions, along with past and projected growth rates, is given in *Exhibit 1*. During the 1980s, the most rapid growth was expected in the developing countries, primarily because of rising income levels. In 1980, total health care expenditures (including pharmaceuticals) averaged over 9% of GNP in developed countries compared with about 3% in developing countries.

Exhibit 2 summarizes estimated sales and projected growth rates for ethical drugs by therapeutic category. The definitions of categories used by different industry research sources and consultants varied considerably. As a result, it was impossible to determine how much consensus there was about estimates of market size or likely future growth. *Exhibit 3* shows three different systems that have been used to group ethical drugs into "markets."

COMPETITORS

Compared to other industries of its size, the pharma industry is relatively unconcentrated. Hundreds of companies produce ethical drugs,

EXHIBIT 1. Estimated sales and growth rates by region

Region	1980 sales[a] Billions of dollars	% of total	Growth rate[b] 1970–1980	1980–1990
North America	$14.5	20%	11%	6%
Western Europe	25.4	35	13	6
Japan	9.4	13	12	7–8
Latin America	2.9	4	12–14	10–12
Rest of world	21.3	28	10–12	8–10
Total	$72.5	100	11%	6–8%

[a]Sales in various regions converted to equivalent in U.S. dollars at 1980 exchange rates.
[b]Projected growth rates in real terms.
Source: Casewriter's estimates, based on several industry studies.

ranging from highly specialized firms operating in only one country up to highly diversified, multinational corporations. The latter, however, accounted for an increasing proportion of total world volume during the 1960s and 1970s.

  Exhibit 4 lists the 20 largest companies in the industry in 1980, ranked in order of estimated pharma turnover. Differences in company definitions of product classes and in reporting practices made it impossible to obtain precise sales data. For example, some firms reported no

EXHIBIT 2. Estimated worldwide sales and growth rates by therapeutic category

Category	Sales—billion $ 1980	1990	Growth rate*
Anti-infectives	$12.5	$23.5	6–7%
Antiarthritics/analgesics	8.9	18.3	7–8
Cardiovascular	10.9	24.6	8–9
Central nervous system/mental health	5.3	9.1	5–6
Dermatologicals	3.1	4.8	4–5
Respiratory	4.0	6.8	5–6
Others	27.8	47.5	5–6

*Projected growth rates in real terms.
Source: Casewriter's estimates, based on several industry studies.

EXHIBIT 3. Alternative systems for grouping pharmaceutical products into "markets"

Cocks & Virts (1974)	Vernon (1971)	A.T. Kearney (1971)
Analgesics and anti-inflammatories	Anesthetics	Anorexics
Anti-infectives	Antiarthritics	Antihematinics
Anticholinergics & antispasmodics	Antibiotics	Antibiotics
Antihypertensives	Antispasmodics	Anticonvulsants
Antiobesity drugs	Ataractics	Ataractics
Cough and cold	Bronchial dilators	Bronchial dilators
Diabetic therapy	Cardiovascular hypotensives	Coronary vasodilators
Oral contraceptives	Coronary-peripheral vasodilators	Diuretics
Psychopharmaceuticals	Diabetic therapy	Oral contraceptives
Vitamins & hematinics	Diuretics	Penicillins
	Enzymes-digestants	Psychostimulants
	Hematinics	Sedatives & hypnotics
	Sex hormones	Sulfonamides
	Corticoids	Thyroid preparations
	Muscle relaxants	Trichomonacides
	Psychostimulants	
	Sulfonamides	
	Thyroid therapy	

Sources: Douglas L. Cocks and John R. Virts, "Pricing Behavior of the Ethical Pharmaceutical Industry," *Journal of Business* 47 (July 1974), pp. 349–362.

John M. Vernon, "Concentration, Promotion, and Market Share Stability in the Pharmaceutical Industry," *Journal of Industrial Economics* 19 (July 1971), pp. 246–259.

A.T. Kearney, *A Study of Administration Costs Associated with Federal Drug Formulary Legislation,* consulting report (Chicago, 1971).

breakdowns of total corporate volume, while others combined ethical drug sales with those of OTC/proprietary medicines and/or animal health products.

Even among the top 20, pharma producers varied widely in size and diversity. As shown in *Exhibit 4*, total corporate sales in 1980 ranged from $1 billion to $16 billion. Sales of pharma products varied from 15–16% of corporate volume to 80–90%. In terms of market share, no one firm accounted for more than 3½% of world pharma sales. Within specific product categories, of course, market structures were considerably

EXHIBIT 4. Approximate sales and world market shares of leading pharmaceutical firms, 1980 (amounts in millions of dollars)

Company	Home country	Corporate sales	Worldwide pharmaceutical sales		
			Amount	*% of co. total*	*Market share*
Hoechst	Ger.	$16,000	$2,500	16%	3.4%
Bayer	Ger.	15,500	2,300	15	3.2
American Home	USA	3,800	2,100	55	2.9
Merck	USA	2,700	1,900	70	2.6
Warner-Lambert	USA	3,500	1,900	54	2.6
Ciba-Geigy	Switz.	6,100	1,700	28	2.3
Pfizer	USA	3,000	1,650	55	2.3
Hoffman-LaRoche	Switz.	3,000	1,350	45	1.9
Smith-Kline	USA	1,800	1,300	72	1.8
Sandoz	Switz.	2,500	1,300	54	1.8
Abbott	USA	2,050	1,200	58	1.7
Rhone-Poulenc	Fr.	5,800	1,100	19	1.5
Bristol-Myers	USA	3,200	1,100	34	1.5
Upjohn	USA	1,750	1,100	63	1.5
B. Ingelheim	Ger.	1,450	1,050	72	1.5
Lilly	USA	2,550	1,050	41	1.5
Squibb	USA	1,350	1,000	74	1.4
Takeda	Jap.	1,800	950	53	1.3
J&J	USA	4,800	900	19	1.3
Glaxo	UK	1,000	900	90	1.3

Source: Casewriter's estimates based on various industry sources. The figures should be regarded as *approximations*. More precise data are not available due to (1) difference in fiscal years of companies; (2) variations in data provided by financial reports, including different definitions of "pharmaceutical sales"; and (3) ambiguity as to the boundaries of the pharmaceutical market itself, as noted in *Exhibit 1*.

more concentrated, with the top four competitors typically sharing 40 to 70% of total sales in any one country.

During the 1970s, most of the major pharma companies had expanded their activities outside their home markets considerably. *Exhibit 5* summarizes estimates of 1980 geographic sales breakdowns for selected pharma producers. In almost every case, firms' sales outside their home countries had increased during the 1970s.

EXHIBIT 5. Approximate distribution of pharma sales by region, selected companies, 1980

	Percent of sales in ———				
Company	Home country	Europe	North America	Japan	Other
Takeda	95%	2%	1%	95%	2%
American Home	65	20	70	2	8
Upjohn	65	20	72	3	5
Pfizer	45	30	50	10	10
Hoechst	30	65	12	6	17
Bayer	28	60	15	7	18
Sandoz	6	50	25	10	15
Hoffman-LaRoche	5	45	30	7	18
Ciba-Geigy	3	50	25	7	17

Source: Casewriter's estimates based on company annual reports and industry studies.

INDUSTRY ECONOMICS

The ethical drug industry is often called a "two-tiered" industry. The major producers of branded products, such as those listed in *Exhibit 4,* comprise the first tier, while smaller companies with limited geographic markets and product lines comprise a second tier. Many of the latter group of firms concentrate on "generic" drugs that are chemically equivalent to branded products but sold either with *no* brand name or on a branded but unpromoted basis. These generic drugs were priced much lower than major brands, often 50% less, and had grown in importance during the 1960s and 1970s.

Typical price/cost/profit relationships for major pharma companies are quite different from those for the smaller firms who spent little on R&D or marketing. *Exhibit 6* contrasts the differences between the two groups.

MARKETING

As noted earlier, ethical drugs by definition can be purchased only on prescription by a physician. Consequently, pharma manufacturers' selling and promotional efforts are directed almost entirely toward physicians, including those in private practice and those working in clinics

EXHIBIT 6. Estimates of typical cost and profit ratios: major
pharmaceutical companies vs. smaller companies

	Major producer of branded drugs	Small generic drug producer
Manufacturer's selling price	100%	100%
Cost of goods sold (raw materials & mfg.)	30–35	55–60
Operating expenses:		
General & administrative	10–12	15
Marketing	20–30	
R&D	8–12	2–3
Pre-tax profit	20–25	25

Source: For major producers, based on figures reported in government
investigations in the U.S. (late 1950s–early 1960s) and the U.K. (early 1970s)
and in company annual reports. For small generic producers, based on annual
reports of one firm, which may not be representative.

and hospitals. Medical representatives ("detailers") call on doctors and
present information about new products and new dosage forms, as well
as distribute free samples. Advertising in medical media and direct mail
promotion is also aimed at prescribing physicians.

Upon receiving a prescription, a patient obtains pharmaceuticals
either by purchasing them from a pharmacy or via dispensing in a
hospital or clinic. Pharma products are distributed to drug stores
through independent wholesale distributors or manufacturers' wholesale branches. Combined retail and wholesale margins amount to 40–
50% of retail pharmacy prices.

In most countries, the national government and/or private insurers
reimbursed patients for all or part of the cost of prescription drugs under
some kind of health insurance scheme. Government agencies are also
major direct purchasers of drugs for use in hospitals. Because health
care costs represent a large and growing element of the national budget
in almost every country, there had been strong pressures from government agencies during the 1970s to reduce drug prices and to avoid excess prescribing.

Pharma manufacturers' marketing costs, on average, were considerably higher than those of most other industries. For example, data
compiled by the U.S. Federal Trade Commission showed that for ethical

drug divisions of major American corporations, total selling costs averaged 20.6% of sales in 1976.[2] Of the total, 4.2% was for media advertising and 16.4% for field selling, marketing administration, and miscellaneous items. Overall, the pharmaceuticals ranked 17th out of 275 industries in terms of marketing costs in relation to sales. Higher marketing cost ratios were reported for proprietary drugs (33.7%), toiletries (29.5%), liquor (24.2%), and jewelry (20.8%), among others. The average for all manufacturing industries was 6.6%. According to industry executives, high pharma marketing costs reflected the need to use highly educated sales representatives, the continuous flow of new products, and the intensity of competition among products that could be used for a given illness.

RESEARCH AND DEVELOPMENT

Besides being a "marketing-intensive" industry, pharmaceuticals is also "R&D-intensive." Major producers of branded products spend from 8% to 12% of sales on R&D. These budgets cover basic research, developmental research, and extensive clinical testing that are required before new drugs can be approved for sale.

Pharma R&D is characterized as costly, time-consuming, and uncertain in terms of end results. The time required to develop a "New Chemical Entity," including clinical testing, was typically around 10 years in the late 1970s. A significant part of this time was required for the clinical testing and appraisal mandated by government authorities before a new product could be approved for sale (see below).

PROFITABILITY

Profits, in relation to both sales and investment, are generally higher in pharmaceuticals than in most other industries. One compilation by a financial analyst, based on published data, showed leading firms' pre-tax profit margins on pharma sales ranging from 15 to 30% of sales in 1980 with an average of 22–25%. Average after-tax return on shareholders' equity (for U.S.-based producers) was stable at nearly 20% through

---

[2]Thayer C. Taylor, "How Do Your Sales Costs Rate?," *Sales & Marketing Management,* September 13, 1982, p. 60.

the 1970s, considerably above the average ROE for any other major manufacturing industry.

The pharma industry's high profit levels, along with its heavy expenditures on marketing, make it a frequent target for attack by politicians and consumer activists. According to one observer,

> . . . *practically all of the attacks on the drug industry stem from feelings about profits. That includes safety, efficacy, the brand name issue, molecular modifications, and others.*[3]

Controversy over allegedly "excessive" profits in the industry was reflected in a series of legislative hearings and special investigations in the U.S.A., the U.K., and elsewhere. In one celebrated case in the mid-1970s, the U.K. regulatory authorities forced Hoffman-LaRoche to make substantial reductions in the prices of its highly successful drugs Valium and Librium. A central part of the government's argument was that the company was charging excessive prices in relation to direct manufacturing costs and that profits were consequently too high.

Industry executives and trade associations denied that profits were excessive. They argued that [4]

1. "Accounting profit," as reported in company financial statements, is an inappropriate yardstick. According to some economists, heavy expenditures on R&D and marketing should be treated as investments and evaluated in relation to their (discounted) future effects. Although there was heated debate among economists about the proper method for adjusting reported profit, costs, and investment figures, one study showed that the U.S. pharma industry's "corrected" average ROE for the period of 1959–1973 was a third lower than its "accounting" rate of return.[5]

2. The riskiness of investments in R&D makes it appropriate for companies in the industry to earn a "risk premium."

---

[3]Joseph D. Cooper, "The Economics of Drug Innovation," in J.D. Cooper (ed.), *Proceedings of the Second Seminar on Economics of Pharmaceutical Innovation* (Washington, D.C.: The American University, 1976), p. 16.

[4]Numerous articles and books have been published on the subject of profitability in the pharma industry. For a recent summary, see John W. Egan, Harlow N. Higginbotham, and J. Fred Weston, *Economics of the Pharmaceutical Industry* (New York: Praeger Publishers, 1982).

[5]Kenneth Clarkson, *Intangible Capital and Rates of Return* (Washington, D.C.: American Enterprise Institute for Public Policy Research, 1977), p. 64.

3. Inter-industry comparisons of rates of return on investment are of limited use, in any case. The pharma industry is "knowledge-intensive," not capital-intensive, and high ROI is typical in such industries because physical assets, especially plant and equipment, are not of critical importance. (Industries with similar characteristics included minicomputers, computer software, and management consulting.)

REGULATION

The pharmaceutical industry is subject to extensive governmental regulation in almost every country in the world. In addition, in many nations the government (through national health care systems) is a direct buyer of drugs, a provider of insurance to patients, or both.

Almost all developed countries provide patent protection to companies that develop new pharmaceutical products. Some require an innovating firm to license competitors, but most permit exclusivity until the expiration of the patent.

As patents expire, innovating companies inevitably experience increased competition from producers of lower-priced generics. Direct competition is not unknown even before patent expiration: Frequently competitors are able to develop products very similar, but not identical, to a given compound. In addition, close substitutes are often supplied by producers located in countries where patent protection is ineffective, such as Italy.

In every major market, government agencies regulate the introduction of new drugs. The Food & Drug Administration (FDA) is responsible for this function in the U.S.A. In 1962, legislation was enacted (the "Kefauver amendments") to require more stringent criteria for approval of new drugs. The effect of this was a substantial reduction in the rate of new product introduction. Data compiled by an industry source on the total number of new products and the number of new "single chemicals" introduced before and after the adoption of the new rules showed the following:[6]

---

[6]Jerome Schnee and Erol Caglarcan, "The Changing Pharmaceutical R&D Environment," *Business Economics* 11 (May 1976), pp. 31–38.

	Average per year		
	1958–62	*1962–67*	*1968–72*
Total new products	300	126	80
New single chemicals	45	19	12

During the 1960s and 1970s the FDA process for testing and evaluating new drugs also became more complex and time-consuming. By the mid-1970s, it was estimated that for a "typical" new chemical entity the time interval from conception to final approval for full-scale marketing was 10 years. Of this period, only the first three years preceded the initial filing of a request for authorization to conduct tests on humans. Moreover, only a fraction (estimated at 10–15%) of all drugs approved for testing were subsequently approved for marketing.

Other countries, notably the U.K., had significantly less stringent new product approval standards than the U.S.A. As a result, many U.S.-based companies had moved during the 1970s to a pattern of introducing new drugs first in overseas markets. (A compilation of new chemical entities introduced in 1980 showed that fewer than one-tenth were first launched in the U.S.A.)

Even after approval for marketing, pharmaceuticals were subject to later recall if undesirable side effects showed up. A widely publicized case was that of Benoxaprofen, a anti-inflammatory drug introduced by Eli Lilly in the U.K. in 1980 under the name Opren and later in the U.S.A. as Oraflex.[7] Some patients who were treated with the drug developed jaundice, and several died. Eventually the U.K. authorities suspended sales of the product, and Lilly then voluntarily withdrew the product from the market worldwide.

In many countries government regulation extends to pharmaceutical pricing. Selling price, or changes in prices, are subject to review by government agencies or are effectively controlled by national health service agencies negotiating their own buying prices. According to industry executives, the impact of governmental price controls is especially severe in France, Spain, and the U.K.

---

[7]"Benoxaprofen Analyzed," *SCRIP-World Pharmaceutical News*, Nos. 755–756, December 20–22, 1982, pp. 16–17.

PROSPECTS FOR THE FUTURE

As indicated by the projections in *Exhibit 1,* pharmaceutical industry experts anticipate slower growth in the 1980s than in the 1960s and 1970s. Major new products, which had fueled the industry's expansion for three decades, have seemingly become few and far between. Reduced growth, it is thought, would lead to more intense competition for market share and perhaps to consolidation in the industry via mergers and acquisitions. One indication of intensified competition was an estimated increase of some 5% in the number of sales reps employed by the 20 largest U.S. companies. Since physicians had become less willing (or able) to see sales reps, the effective increase in selling effort was actually much greater than 5%.

Exhibit 2 shows that forecasted growth rates vary considerably among therapeutic categories. Products designed for cardiovascular disease and rheumatism are expected to have above-average growth prospects, primarily because of the increasing numbers of older persons in the developed countries. The high growth rates predicted for the developing countries (see *Exhibit 1*) also implies that there may be attractive opportunities for products effective in treating enteritis, malaria, leprosy, cholera, and diseases resulting from nutritional deficiency. Actual growth rates in the 1980s and beyond would, of course, depend on how successful pharma producers are in developing effective, safe, new chemicals.

Partly as a result of slower overall industry growth, it is expected that competition will become increasingly "global" during the 1980s and 1990s. Foreign sales by U.S.-based firms, for example, had increased steadily from around 25% in 1965 to over 40% by 1980. During the same period, the U.S. market share of foreign-based competitors had increased from 10% to 20%. One question that concerns U.S. and European companies is the possibility that some of the major Japanese producers will eventually move aggressively into international markets; up to 1980, none of them had done so.

TECHNOLOGY

During the 1980s and 1990s major developments are expected to take place in new health care technologies, including genetic engineering, ultrasonics, lasers, and electronic devices. One consulting firm predicted that sales of a group of health care products based on "emerging technologies," including bioprosthetic implants, clinical ultrasound, transdermal drug delivery, and digital radiography, would grow from $800 million in 1980 to $5.7 billion in 1990.[8] Another study projected sales of biotechnology-based pharmaceuticals at $11.7 billion by 1995.

While many of the "emerging health care technologies" are being developed outside the pharma industry, some of the major firms in the industry are participating in the area through joint ventures and/or acquisitions.

CONSUMERS

Pharmaceutical companies expected consumers (patients) to become better informed about health care, more critical of "the system," and more interested in self-medication and preventive medicine. The "do-it-yourself" trend is already in evidence in the growing use of home testing devices for blood pressure, pregnancy, and diabetes. Some observers believe that increasing patient involvement in the choice of therapies will lead pharma companies to promote their ethical products directly to end users. Most of the major companies are very cautious about any moves in this direction, however. Such advertising could, for one thing, increase product liability risks beyond their already high levels. Following the withdrawal of Benoxaprofen, Lilly was criticized for having publicized the drug in general media as well as medical journals, which allegedly had stimulated some patients to ask their doctors to prescribe it.

REGULATION

The prospects for changes in governmental regulation during the 1980s were mixed. On one hand, in the U.S., the FDA had announced its intention to streamline new drug approval procedures. It was not clear how much change could be expected, however, or when it would materialize.

In most other countries it seems likely that regulatory pressures will intensify. An area of particular concern is that of physicians' prescribing prerogatives. Most physicians prescribe drugs by brand name, and

---

[8]Stanford Research Institute, "Emerging Health Care Technology Markets," Report No. 82/665, 1982.

pharmacies are bound to fill the prescriptions accordingly. A possible change in regulations would permit pharmacists to substitute lower-priced generic equivalents. A more extreme variant would *require* the use of generics in situations where a national health service reimbursed the patient.

1.5 *CASE*

Ciba-Geigy Pharmaceuticals Division: Multinational Strategic Planning

Robert D. Buzzell

In the fall of 1981 the Strategy Guidance Committee of the Pharmaceuticals Division of Ciba-Geigy Ltd. was considering a proposed strategic plan for the company's dermatologicals business. The plan called for a major increase in research and development efforts for dermatologicals, which represented a small part of Ciba-Geigy's pharmaceuticals sales in most countries. The committee was comprised of Product Group heads for Ciba-Geigy's five major product groups, the heads of the five geographic regions into which the division divided its worldwide operations, and representatives of various headquarters departments. In evaluating the dermatologicals proposal, the committee members were concerned about the potential costs and benefits of the plan in its own right and about alternative uses of the resources required. The review was also considered to be a "test case" for the division's recently developed portfolio planning system, in which products were grouped into strategic business units on a worldwide basis.

CIBA-GEIGY LTD.

Ciba-Geigy, headquartered in Basel, Switzerland, was a diversified multinational corporation with affiliated companies in 60 countries. The company was formed via the October 1970 merger of two long-established Basel firms, Ciba and J.R. Geigy. Both Ciba and Geigy had been engaged in the production of fine chemicals, dyestuffs, and pharmaceuticals. Following the merger, Ciba-Geigy acquired Ilford, a British producer of photographic products; Airwick Industries, a U.S.-based household products company; and several small companies in the electronics field. The distribution of corporate sales in 1980 and in the first half of 1981 is shown below.

	1980 sales		First half 1981 sales	
	Millions of Swiss francs	*% change vs. 1979*	*Millions of Swiss francs*	*% change vs. 1980*
Dyestuffs and additives	2,007	+ 8%	1,137	+ 7%
Pharmaceuticals	3,213	+18	1,937	+25
Agricultural chemicals	2,683	+20	2,342	+30
Plastics and additives	2,345	+18	1,380	+12
Airwick	617	+32	355	+20
Ilford	619	+31	254	−21
Electronic equipment	430	—	230	+ 7
Totals	11,914	+20*	7,635	+18*

*+20 and +18 represent weighted averages.

The geographic distribution of Ciba-Geigy's 1980 sales was: Europe, 48%; North America, 26%; Latin America, 11%; Asia, 9%; other countries, 6%. Sales in Switzerland itself represented only about 2% of the total, but a substantial portion of the products sold in other countries were manufactured in Switzerland.

The structure of Ciba-Geigy's headquarters organization reflected the diversity of the company's activities: executives of the product divisions were responsible for worldwide strategies in their respective sectors and for reviewing the strategies of affiliated companies for their product lines. (Of these, two were based outside Basel — Ilford in the U.K. and Airwick in the U.S. and France.) Each of the affiliated companies was responsible for operations in a single country. These country affiliates were grouped into regions, and the regional organizations in Basel were responsible for reviewing the subsidiaries' plans and for coordinating them with those of the product divisions. Also based in Basel were corporate functional departments responsible for research, finance, personnel, control, legal, and other headquarters activities.

Altogether, Ciba-Geigy employed 81,000 persons worldwide, of whom about 20,000 were in Switzerland.

THE PHARMA DIVISION

The Pharmaceuticals Division (usually abbreviated to "Pharma") was the largest of Ciba-Geigy's divisions. With 1980 sales of 3.2 billion Swiss francs, its share of the worldwide pharmaceuticals business was between 2.5% and 3%, placing it among the leading companies in the industry.[1] Two other Basel-based companies, Sandoz and Hoffman-LaRoche, were also among the 10 leading worldwide pharmaceuticals producers.

The Pharma Division's strategy, as defined formally in planning documents prepared in 1976 and revised in 1981, was

> . . . to maintain and improve . . . our leading position in the health care industry. . . . We intend to concentrate on the pharmaceuticals business . . . [but] to extend the scope of our activities and to develop from a Pharmaceuticals Division to a Health Care Division.

Within ethical pharmaceuticals, the division produced and marketed nearly 300 different products in one or more countries. Many of these products were of relatively little importance, however, The top 15 products accounted for around 50% of total sales in 1980. (A single "product" typically was offered in several different dosages and/or "galenical

---

[1]There was some uncertainty about Ciba-Geigy's exact ranking, depending on what products were included as pharmaceuticals and on which countries were used as a basis for compiling "worldwide" statistics. According to one approach, the company was the third largest pharmaceuticals producer, while another set of estimates showed it sixth. (See section below on the dermatologicals market.)

forms," e.g., capsules, syrup, injectables. Consequently the product line included thousands of different items or stockkeeping units.) The pattern of high concentration of sales among a few highly successful products was typical of other major pharmaceutical companies as well as Ciba-Geigy.

Just as a few products accounted for the bulk of Pharma sales, a few major countries also represented most of worldwide volume. Ciba-Geigy's top seven markets made up almost 60% of total sales in 1980. Here again the pattern was similar for other multinational competitors. For firms based in the U.S. or Japan, sales were typically even more concentrated geographically because their home markets were so much larger than Switzerland.

An abbreviated organization chart for the Pharma Division is given in *Exhibit 1*. As shown here, the structure of the divisional organization mirrored that of the parent company in that it was based on a combination of central *product* management and decentralized *geographic* divisions (countries, grouped into regions).

The affiliated companies' Pharma Division activities were coordinated at headquarters through regional directors, who reported to the head of International Operations and Marketing (IOM). The function of IOM was to represent the interests of the operating companies at Basel and to provide a two-way channel of communication between the field and the parent company.

Within each affiliated company's Pharma Division, a general manager was responsible for overall operations. In some major countries these included manufacturing and/or R&D activities. In all 60 affiliated companies there were medical and marketing departments. Usually the bulk of local expenditures were accounted for by marketing, including the field force (primarily contacting physicians and hospitals) and advertising and sales promotion. After the merger, Ciba-Geigy had maintained both the Ciba and Geigy field forces, which overall were about equal in size and sales volume. Although the products handled by the two field forces overlapped to some extent, they were to some extent specialized by therapeutic areas. Thus, Ciba was seen as emphasizing cardiovascular drugs, while Geigy had a strong association with products for rheumatic conditions and diseases of the central nervous system.

The field force accounted for one-quarter of all employees in the Pharma Division. Selling effort was regarded as one of the most important scarce resources available to implement a strategy. Medical representatives could present, at most, three products to a doctor during a call, and in most countries could visit a physician only two or three

EXHIBIT 1. Partial organizational chart

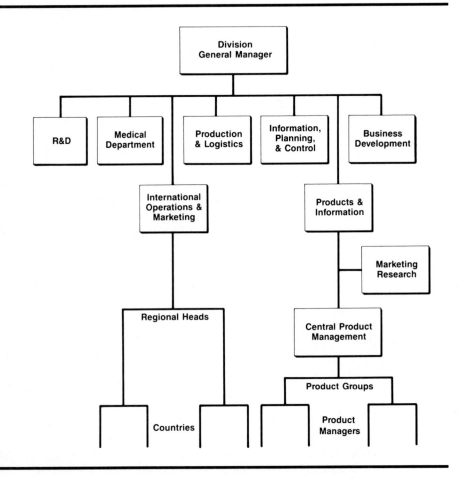

times per year. On average, each country had around 60 active products in the Ciba and Geigy lines combined and could expect to have two to four new products to introduce annually.[2] For major new products, "full power" programs were used in which both Ciba and Geigy sales forces were temporarily assigned to making introductory calls, thus covering a maximum number of physicians quickly.

---

[2]Most new products were developed by Ciba-Geigy in Basel, but some were licensed or acquired from other companies, or "co-marketed" with other companies.

STRATEGIC PLANNING

During the early 1970s, the management of Ciba-Geigy, including those of the Pharma Division, devoted much of their energies to integrating the two organizations. Ciba and Geigy product lines overlapped considerably, and there were many problems in deciding how the overall range should be structured.[3] By 1976, these problems had been resolved and the division was ready to develop a strategic plan. This plan included an explicit mission statement for the division, as quoted above. It also established two other key points:

1. Increasing market share, worldwide, was set as a strategic objective.
2. A philosophy was adopted under which the affiliated companies (country subsidiaries) were encouraged to act as "independent, entrepreneurial units." Affiliated company performance was measured primarily in terms of market share and contribution to parent company expenses and profits. Major decisions remained subject to headquarters approval. But, within broad guidelines established by Basel management, each affiliated company had considerable latitude in developing its own strategies and programs.

At the same time the strategic plan was adopted in 1976, it was decided that Pharma should become more "marketing oriented." To achieve this, the central product management structure (see *Exhibit 1*) was set up. The Central Product Management (CPM) group did not have line authority over the activities of affiliated companies. CPM's role was defined as follows:[4]

1. To define and help build the division's product range . . . in such a way that it meets the needs of the market and is consistent with divisional goals.
2. To develop marketing strategies for products and product groups so as to accomplish maximum market penetration and profitability.
3. To insure that local organizations throughout the world receive a regular flow of relevant information on products and competitive activity.

---

[3]In the U.S., some overlapping product lines had to be divested under the terms of a consent decree with the Department of Justice.

[4]Paraphrased from company documents.

CPM was assigned shared responsibility, along with International Operations and Marketing, for the growth and profitability of the division worldwide.

Another dimension of the effort to increase marketing orientation was the allocation of more resources to marketing research and to marketing management development. By late 1981 many of the marketing personnel in Basel had attended marketing seminars conducted by business school faculty members. Also, two week-long conferences had been held for the marketing directors of the affiliated companies, one in early 1979 and one in early 1981.

In 1980 changes were made in the Pharma Division R&D organization. A staff unit, "Strategy and Worldwide Research," was created and given responsibility for setting guidelines for R&D strategy, proposing R&D objectives, and coordinating worldwide research activities.

PORTFOLIO PLANNING

Following the adoption of the strategic plan and the strengthening of the central product management function, the Pharma Division grouped its products into primary therapeutic groups. Product group managers were assigned to each of four main therapeutic areas: Cardiovascular (CVS), Central Nervous System (CNS), Rheuma and Pain (RhP), and Infectious Diseases (ID). All other products, including Dermatologicals, were assigned to the Other Therapeutic Areas (OTA) product group.

Within each product group, product managers were assigned to more specific product lines. Thus, for example, one of the major lines within CVS was beta-blockers, a relatively new type of product in which Ciba-Geigy had a strong market position. Altogether there were 20 product managers in the five product groups.

The concept underlying the product group structure was that each of them should serve as a strategic business unit (SBU) for planning purposes. In 1979 one of the central product management groups prepared the first "strategic planning platform." By mid-1981 similar platforms had been prepared by all of the other product groups. In each case, information was collected from R&D, from the medical department, and from the affiliated companies via interviews, meetings, and correspondence. After review by the Strategy Guidance Committee, the planning platforms were circulated to the affiliated companies and to the Strategy and Worldwide Research unit.

Some Ciba-Geigy Pharma executives expressed doubts about the treatment of therapeutic areas as SBUs. The portfolio approach to strategic planning, they pointed out, had been developed primarily in industrial manufacturing companies where product divisions were often relatively independent of one another. At the corporate level in Ciba-Geigy, they argued, it might be reasonable to think in terms of a portfolio in which Pharma, Agrochemicals, Airwick, etc., were the SBUs. But within Pharma, there were many interdependencies among therapeutic categories. The same medical representatives handled a wide variety of products, and the bulk of both local country and Basel administrative costs were shared by all of the division's products. Also, most of the production facilities were not product or therapeutic area-specific but multipurpose. Even in R&D, the dividing lines among therapeutic areas were somewhat blurred.

Another criticism of the use of therapeutic areas as strategic business units was that each of the groupings included a variety of more specific subcategories which in some cases differed significantly in terms of market position, growth rate, etc. For example, CVS included beta-blockers, antihypertensives, and other preparations, which varied in age, technical maturity, and expected growth potential. OTA categories were even more varied, ranging from nasal decongestants to oral contraceptives.

Despite these criticisms, Mr. Cattila, the head of Central Product Management (CPM), believed that it made sense to develop strategies around therapeutic area groupings. For one thing, he thought physicians tended to regard pharmaceuticals producers as having specialized capabilities in particular fields of therapy. This perception probably reflected past successes (or lack thereof) in developing products. In addition, he said, medical representatives could not be experts in all areas of medicine. Based on their training and experience, they tended to develop specialized expertise in particular therapeutic areas. Mr. Cattila also felt that there were potential synergies in product management if effort could be focused on a few important therapeutic fields. Apart from major breakthroughs, many new products were developed through a process of modifying and refining existing products. An example cited was that of a product in the RhP category, which had originally been sold only in the form of 25 mg. tablets. Between 1978 and 1981, additional galenical forms had been added: a 100 mg. suppository, a 50 mg. tablet, and then a 75 mg. ampule. In one major country, 1981 sales were expected to be triple the 1978 level, with less than 20% coming from the 25 mg. tablets. Discovering opportunities for product modifications like this, Mr. Cattila believed, required careful and focused attention to physician and patient needs and preferences at the level of a therapeutic area. Finally, he argued that R&D productivity could also best be achieved by concentrating resources and specializing along the same therapeutic lines, even though research projects sometimes cut across therapeutic fields.

THE PORTFOLIO IN 1981

Using therapeutic areas and, to some extent, subdivisions of these areas as units of analysis, CPM had prepared a study of Ciba-Geigy's portfolio using a variation of the widely accepted growth-share matrix. The result is depicted in *Exhibit 2*. The sales and market share data used in preparing this analysis were for 1980, while the growth rates were those forecasted for 1980–1985.[5]

CPM's review of the divisional portfolio also involved a comparison of contribution margins for the various product groups. This analysis showed that CVS and RhP had contribution margins, as percentages of sales, approximately equal to the overall division average. ID's contribution was considerably below average, probably reflecting the fact that Ciba-Geigy had only recently entered this field. CNS and Dermatologicals, on the other hand, had above-average contribution margins.

Contribution margin, in the Ciba-Geigy accounting system, was defined as sales revenue *minus* direct variable costs of manufacturing, packaging, etc.; direct promotional expenses; field force costs (allocated on the basis of time devoted to each product); and certain allocated headquarters costs. The contribution for each product, thus defined, had to cover unallocated costs including R&D, fixed manufacturing costs, and general overheads, which amounted in total to about 25% of sales, as well as profits.

Variable costs for the major product groups differed significantly:

	CVS	RhP	CNS	ID	Derm.	Others
Variable costs	low	average	low	high	average	high
Promotion	high	low	average	high	low	low
Field force	high	average	average	high	low	high

Another factor affecting CPM's strategic planning was the expected flow of new products based on R&D projects already in progress. Phar-

---

[5]The growth rates shown in *Exhibit 2* and *Exhibit 3* are expressed in *current* monetary terms, i.e., including inflation, rather than in real terms. Inflation was forecasted at about 5% per annum.

EXHIBIT 2. Ciba-Geigy market position (market segments worldwide in 1980)

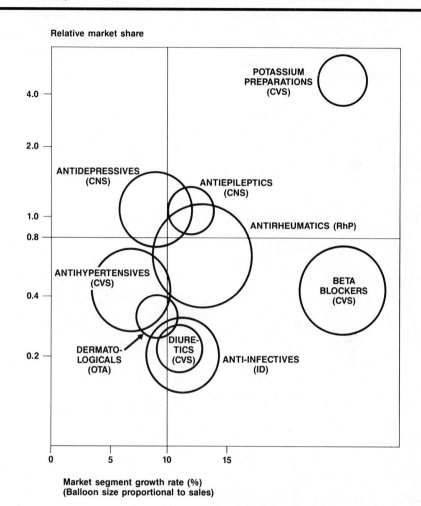

maceutical research was characterized by both long lead times and considerable uncertainty regarding technical success. R&D's best estimates of the number of new products to be available for introduction in each area up to 1990 are shown below.

Expected year of introduction	Number of products				
	CVS	CNS	RhP	ID	Dermatologicals
1981		1	1		1
1982	3			1	
1983	1	1	1		
1984				1	
1985	1	2			1
1986	1				
1987	2		2		
1988	1	4	1	2	1
1989	1	4			1
1990	1	1	1		

CPM had prepared sales forecasts for each therapeutic area which included estimates of volume for the new products projected by R&D. For each area, 1990 sales objectives were compared with the forecasts of sales for existing products plus sales of anticipated new products. For most of the therapeutic areas, the forecasts fell short of objectives; these shortfalls were referred to as "planning gaps." For the division overall, the planning gap was about 14% of the total sales goal. According to CPM, "to close these gaps the division will have to get more out of existing products and try to acquire additional products through licensing."

DERMATOLOGICALS

Dermatological products are used to treat skin diseases. Various product categories are available to physicians and patients. For Ciba-Geigy, areas of specific interest were topical corticosteroids (TCs) and nonsteroidal topical products (NS).

The TCs had some side effects related to properties of the excipients (e.g., irritation, burning) or to the steroidal component (e.g., skin atrophy, systemic effects). A nonsteroidal topical product (NS) was expected to have significantly fewer side effects.

Dermatologicals was a field of special concern to Ciba-Geigy: It was a relatively small but profitable business in which Ciba-Geigy had been present for a long time. A few countries accounted for the major share of worldwide sales. Many affiliated companies no longer promoted actively their dermatological product range. Worldwide, market share had dropped considerably during the 1970s. Guided by Central Product Management, a working group had studied the actual and future situation very carefully and elaborated three alternative strategies (see below).

THE DERMATOLOGICALS MARKET

Total world sales of TCs in 1981 were forecasted to be SF (Swiss francs) 1.7 billion. Sales of NS amounted to less than SF 500 million but were growing faster than TC sales.

The dermatologicals market was forecasted to grow somewhat less rapidly in the 1980s than the total pharmaceuticals market. Average annual real growth rates were estimated at 3% to 5% for dermatologicals versus 6% to 7% for the pharmaceuticals market as a whole.

Some important characteristics of the dermatologicals market were:

1. The life cycle of leading dermatologicals was generally long. The leading TCs, for example, were almost 20 years old.
2. Promotional expenditure on dermatologicals was as a rule comparatively high. The two main reasons for this were as follows:
   (a) The number of doctors confronted with skin diseases was large and included many types of physicians. In addition to dermatologists, general practitioners, internists, and pediatricians were all important as target groups owing to their considerable prescription potential.
   (b) Treatment of skin diseases generally took the form of short-course therapy, and here doctors displayed greater tendency to switch from one drug to another than was the case in the classic long-term therapy customary in hypertension, rheuma, etc. With skin diseases, moreover, there was an inherent tendency for relapses to occur, a further incentive to drug switching.
3. Product liability risks were low, relative to other therapeutic areas.

In a recent presentation to international Pharma Division managers, the head of Central Product Management had summarized the two dermatologicals subsegments as follows:

Nonsteroidal topical products (NS)
Market at present relatively small
Definite medical need
Competitive activities (R&D, marketing) were limited

Topical corticosteroids (TC)
Mature market
Medium size
Moderate growth
Highly competitive
Moderate price sensitivity
Geographical distribution of the total TC market is: U.S. 25%, Japan 20% of total

Only six major international companies had a significant presence in TC. Ciba-Geigy's five competitors all had higher recent growth rates in this segment, thanks on the one hand to their launching of new products (Diprosone/Schering Corporation, Dermovate/Glaxo) and, on the other, to vigorous marketing of their established TCs. The importance of the TC sector to each of these six companies is shown below.

The leading TC products were relatively old. Betnovate (Glaxo) had been introduced in 1964; Celestoderm (Schering) in 1968; Synclar (Syntex) in 1960; Topsyn (Syntex) in 1971; and Kenacort (Squibb) in 1960. These five products accounted for an estimated 40% of total worldwide TC sales.

Company	TC sales as % of total pharmaceutical sales
Glaxo	28%
Squibb	18
Syntex	32
Schering Corp.	12
Schering AG	11
Ciba-Geigy	<5

CIBA-GEIGY'S POSITION IN DERMATOLOGICALS

Dermatologicals represented less than 5% of Ciba-Geigy's pharmaceutical sales worldwide, and, as shown in *Exhibit 2*, the company's market share was smaller than it was for most other therapeutic areas. The situation differed considerably among countries, however, as shown in *Exhibit 3*. Differences in Ciba-Geigy's market position among countries

EXHIBIT 3. Dermatologicals (market segment by country, 1980)

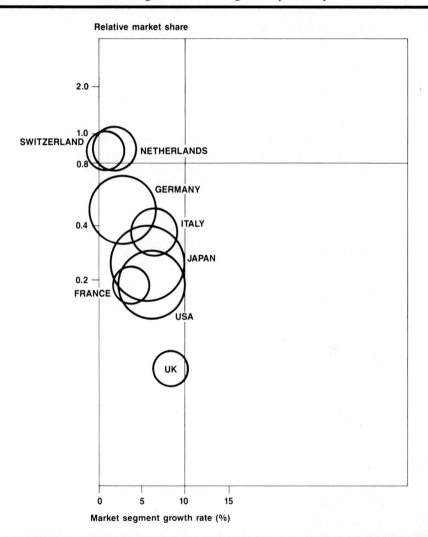

were attributed to several factors. For dermatologicals as for other products, the most important consideration was usually the timing of introduction into the various markets. Because of delays in obtaining approval from government agencies, the time lag between the time a product was first introduced in one country and its introduction into the last (of a series of countries) could be as much as three to four years. In the meantime, competitors offering similar products often established strong positions in particular markets. Beyond the matter of delays in approvals, there were also significant differences in competition and in the way the Ciba-Geigy affiliated companies allocated their field force and promotional resources. One country might push dermatologicals aggressively while another gave the products only nominal support.

Ciba-Geigy marketed nine TC products in 1981. Four of these, Locacorten-Vioform, Locasalen, Locacorten, and Vioform-Hydrocortisone, accounted for the bulk of sales. Another "classical TC" was scheduled for introduction during 1981.

As noted earlier, there were several TC and NS products in the R&D pipeline. Estimated probabilities of technical success for these products ranged from 10% to 20%.

ALTERNATIVE STRATEGIES

A task force working under the direction of Mr. Kline, the OTA product group manager, proposed three alternative strategies for dermatologicals. These ranged from a "milking" strategy to one based on aggressive development and marketing of new nonsteroidal products. Forecasts of sales, contribution, and expenses for these strategies are shown in *Exhibit 4,* and a brief summary of each is given below.

STRATEGY 1: MILKING OF EXISTING BUSINESS. This strategy was based upon existing TCs including the product to be launched in 1981. Pipeline products would not be launched but be licensed out or their development stopped.

R&D efforts could not be abandoned completely because some minimum capacity is needed for the development of new products in other therapeutic areas (which require skin tests).

Marketing expenses under this strategy would be at the minimum levels required to maintain a presence in the marketplace.

STRATEGY 2: EXPANSION OF EXISTING BUSINESS. This strategy was the same as strategy 1 except that the TC products in the pipeline would be launched. The objective was to improve Ciba-Geigy's present situa-

EXHIBIT 4. Projected sales, expenses, and contribution for alternative strategies (millions of SF—disguised data)

	Strategy 1	Strategy 2	TCs	NSs	Totals
				Strategy 3	
Dermatologicals market					
1990	3,500	3,500	3,500	400	3,900
1995	4,500	4,500	4,100	1,000	5,100
2000	5,700	5,700	4,700	2,500	7,200
Ciba-Geigy sales (market share)					
1987	185 (6.5%)	200 (7.0%)	200	—	200 (7.0%)
1990	220 (6.2)	250 (7.1)	240	100	340 (8.7)
1995	210 (4.7)	440 (9.8)	390	390	780 (15.2)
2000	180 (3.2)	510 (8.9)	400	650	1,050 (14.6)
Marketing expenses					
1987	20	22			22
1990	10	45			102
1995	12	27			84
2000	12	31			84
*Contribution**					
1987	90	95			95
1990	108	99			128
1995	103	194			310
2000	88	230			462
Research and development expenses					
1980–85 (6-year total)	14	27	27	18	45
1986–90 (5-year total)	14	26	26	14	40
2000 (annual)	4	8	8	4	12

*Contribution earned on all Pharma products covered unallocated expenses (including R&D) amounting to around 25% of divisional sales, as well as yielding pretax profits.

tion in the existing TC business, which required a maintenance of the R&D effort.

STRATEGY 3: EXPANSION OF EXISTING BUSINESS AND CREATION OF A NEW MARKET. Strategy 3 was strategy 2, plus the development and launching of nonsteroidal topical products. This strategy required a major increase in R&D spending and, when the new products were ready, substantially higher marketing expenses.

All of the estimates for strategies 2 and 3 in *Exhibit 4* were based on the assumption that the new products *would* be successfully developed, with introductions beginning in 1985.

In comparing the three strategies, the working group concluded that there were no significant differences in terms of required investments in fixed assets. The sales volumes projected for any of the three approaches could be handled with existing manufacturing and packaging facilities. An increase in sales would, however, imply greater working capital requirements to support inventory and receivables. As a rule of thumb, net working capital usually amounted to around 20% of sales in the industry.

The study of the working group was presented by the group product manager for OTA, Mr. Kline, to the Strategy Guidance Committee. He introduced the subject as follows:

> *Ladies and gentlemen! Today we shall discuss the significance of our dermatologicals business to the future of our company. We have basically three options: to give up a line of business that historically has meant a lot to us; to allow ourselves a moderate expansion in existing markets; or third, to grasp an opportunity which will be important to us in some 10 to 15 years' time. Let us show some foresight today and base our decision on the pros and cons as you can see them on this transparency. I am certain you will realize that the pros both qualitatively and quantitatively outweigh the cons and that your decision can only be strategy 3!*
>
> *As you see, the pros are*
>
> - *Ciba-Geigy has two NSs in the pipeline which are unique products.*
> - *The future of the NS market looks bright. A study conducted in 1979 in four major markets indicates that more than 80% of GPs and dermatologists perceive a need, and therefore a future, for NSs.*
> - *If Ciba-Geigy succeeds in being a pioneer in this business, it can achieve a strong market position by 1995.*
> - *R&D expenses would be relatively low as compared to the other product groups. We have to continue R&D activities anyhow, and to maintain a dermatologicals specialist team in our company.*
> - *We have a history and have a good image in the field. Our products are well accepted by both physicians and patients.*
> - *We have a lot of "dermatological" know-how available in research and development, production, medicine, and marketing.*
> - *Morbidity is high and will be increasing in the future.*

- *There are relatively moderate pricing problems.*
- *Product liability issues are minimal.*
- *Our future product range will be related to the expressed needs of the physicians.*

Compared to the list of pros, the list of cons is short:

- *The dermatological market is highly competitive (as others are, too).*
- *It requires a high level of promotional spending. However, thanks to our efforts to segment customers and thanks to the fact that we will launch unique products, the marketing expenses for our company will be moderate.*
- *The growth rate of the dermatologicals market is moderate compared to the growth rates forecasted for other markets.*

Mr. Kline concluded:

> *This, ladies and gentlemen, is my introduction to the discussion of a subject which, according to our working team, seems to be rather clear.*

Mr. Hamma, the SGC Chairman, invited discussion, which went on as follows:

Mr. Tall (group product manager): Mr. Chairman! Let us not be seduced by the eloquence of Mr. Kline. It is clearly not in our interest to split our resources: Let us concentrate in order to dominate. Let us concentrate on important products and markets! You are well aware that studies in various group companies have shown that we underpromote our drugs just because we do not concentrate.

Mr. Kline: I must object to Mr. Tall's statement. We have, for example, a very clear planning gap in his field and we do not know how to fill that gap. In dermatologicals we have unique products coming up, representing very good opportunities!

Mr. Bassett (group product manager): But is it not also true that the probabilities of technical success are only from 5 to 20% for these four products?

Mr. Drake (R&D coordinating manager): You have to realize that of course there are many more products in the pipeline for the other therapeutic areas. Let me just show you this slide.[6]

Mr. Kline: The probabilities of technical success are no different for those other products. Theoretically, it is as uncertain as it is for the

---

[6]At this point, Mr. Drake showed a slide of the R&D new product estimates through 1990, as tabulated above under "The Portfolio in 1981."

products in my area whether they will make it to the market or not. But the experts on our team have expressed very high confidence that our new dermatologicals will make it to the market if they get the right priorities.

Mr. Bassett: Your experts may have a vested interest and could therefore be biased.

Mr. French (head of a region): Did you include my countries in those sales figures you presented?

Mr. Kline: They are all in. We have calculated worldwide sales figures, assuming worldwide introductions.

Mr. French: With the situation in these countries, that calculation doesn't hold. Your figures are too optimistic. Given the priorities of Ciba and Geigy lines in those countries, it will be impossible to launch, at least within the present line set-up. Why not license it out?

Another regional manager nodded approvingly.

Mr. Redding (of Registration): You know how important it is for registration to show advantages for our new products. Can we be sure, Mr. Kline, that our nonsteroids are unique? Will the competition not have anything by the time we file the registration documents? If we are unique, i.e., the first, I agree with you, but if not . . .

Mr. Kline: We have recently done a patent search in the databanks. No recent patents of competitors were found. And even if we should be number two, the potential remains big. Sometimes it's an advantage to be second, considering the innovative characteristics of the pipeline products.

Mr. French: That would make the figures even more optimistic.

Mr. Kline: But, Mr. French, if the products are unique, won't your countries play along?

Mr. French: Yes, probably, *if* . . .

Mr. Cardinal (Controller): I have a problem, here, Mr. Kline. You say that it is a promotion-intensive market segment, and then you allocate very little money to promotion. Could you explain that, please?

Mr. Kline: Think about all the free publicity and word-of-mouth we will get on these truly unique products. Also, it isn't a critical issue with all that potential open to us. Furthermore, I mentioned already in my introduction the use of market segmentation.[7]

---

[7]"Market segmentation" referred to a system of focusing sales representatives' calls and promotional efforts on physicians with high prescription potentials for a particular type of product.

Mr. Cardinal: But market segmentation systems are not yet used at such a sophisticated level in many countries.

Mr. Hamma (the SGC Chairman): Ladies, gentlemen! This has been a very interesting discussion, but time is running short and I should like to come to a decision. Let me just restate the problem: Do we go for strategy 1, i.e., *do nothing,* or strategy 2, *expand the existing business* with the two traditional products now under preparation, or strategy 3, *expand the existing business and create a new market?*

Mr. Kline: May I just add that doing nothing still means keeping a certain R&D effort going — why not then take advantage of our know-how? Let's go the whole way and exploit our opportunities! Let's close the planning gap we have identified in the other areas!

1.6 *CASE*

Henkel Group: Umbrella Branding and Globalization Decisions

Robert J. Dolan

At Henkel Group, headquartered in Dusseldorf, West Germany, brand names were a highly valued asset. For example, the company's Persil brand detergent, introduced in 1907, was one of the most widely known and respected brand names in Europe. As marketing director of Henkel's Chemical Technical Products for Craftsmen and Do-It-Yourselfers (HD/BC), Gunther von Briskorn was custodian of two of Henkel's most important brands: Pritt and Pattex. In early 1981, von Briskorn was concerned about the performance of these household adhesives on an international basis. He was considering a radical change in brand strategy. As he discussed with Wolfgang Heck, his group product manager for Craftsman/DIY/Household Adhesives, and Mr. Heck's assistant for Household Adhesives, Herbert Tossing:

> *Mr. Heck, if we are to be successful in Germany and the rest of the world, we must find an innovative approach. These adhesive markets are small to begin with and*

now we are seeing increased fragmentation and specialization. Our friends in the detergent group do not face the same issues. Every country market they go into has a large, not strongly segmented detergent market. They can afford a policy of one brand for one product. The brand philosophy which has been successful for them has not been successful for us — we must develop greater coordination between the individual products we sell and the individual country markets we sell them in. Please get together with Mr. Printz (the HD/BC advertising manager assigned to von Briskorn's group) to develop some ideas on how we can move in the direction of greater coordination across products and markets.

In July 1981, six months of work researching and thinking about the problem had resulted in a proposed strategy which would fundamentally change HD/BC marketing practices. The strategy embodied two major concepts: umbrella branding (i.e., developing an integrated strategy for the marketing of a variety of products under each of the two brand names) and global standardization of the umbrella. As von Briskorn considered the proposal he had developed, he recognized that both concepts underlying the strategy were counter to the traditional "each product/each country profit center on its own" philosophy of the Henkel Group. Second, Dr. Roman Dohr, head of the Adhesives and Chemical Auxiliaries Division, had expressed concern about the umbrella branding aspects. In his own mind, von Briskorn knew the strategy was not without risk. Both Tossing (who became product manager when Heck was given a U.S. assignment in connection with Henkel's acquisition of Ross Chemical in Detroit) and Printz had raised quite valid concerns in laying out the "pros and cons" of the strategy. In view of the importance of the decision, von Briskorn resolved to consider all the evidence once again in resolving the issues he faced:

- Does the umbrella branding concept make sense for the household adhesives markets?
- Does it make sense specifically for the two brand names? Which products could be put under each umbrella?
- Is it possible to globalize an umbrella strategy?
- How could a global/umbrella strategy be implemented?
- What are the alternatives if we decide not to follow this strategy?

HENKEL GROUP

In 1980, the over 8,000 products sold by the Henkel Group yielded sales revenues of DM 6.9 billion. The family-owned company, founded by Fritz Henkel as a bleaching powder company in 1876, had grown to over

100 operating companies in more than 40 countries. The international scope of the company resulted in 60% of sales being outside Germany.

The diverse product line was sold by eight groups:

1. Detergents and cleaning agents
2. Personal care products and cosmetics
3. Household care products
4. Adhesives
5. Inorganic chemicals
6. Organic chemicals
7. Foodstuffs
8. Packaging

The common element through the groups was a reliance on "chemistry in production." Top management considered Henkel to be "specialists in applying chemistry to the needs of the consumer, of institutions, of industry, and of craftsmen."

Adhesives represented a major growth opportunity for Henkel. In 1980, the adhesives product line contained over 800 products and generated sales of approximately DM 1.2 billion. As shown in *Exhibit 1*, the Adhesives Division had three groups:

1. Industrial Adhesives
2. Leather and Textile Auxiliaries
3. HD/BC: Chemical Technical Products for Craftsmen and Do-It-Yourself markets/Building Chemical (in German, Handwerk/DIY/Bauchemie, hence the HD/BC abbreviation)

The pattern of new product development in the Adhesives group was typically to develop a product for industrial and craftsman use and then adapt it to the household market if possible. Despite the focus on industrial sectors for new product development, the HD/BC group accounted for 57% of Henkel's adhesives sales. The 15 items in the HD/BC product line are shown in *Exhibit 2*. These products were targeted to a variety of users, representing very different levels of product performance requirements and product knowledge. Main target groups included:

Craftsmen	**Households**	**Other**
Painter	DIY-ers	Office
Decorator	Hobbyists	School
Paperhanger	"Moonlighters"	Kindergartens

Craftsmen	**Households**	**Other**
Carpenter		
Shoemaker		
Floor coverer		
Bricklayer		
Metalworker		
Plumber		

As a consequence, HD/BC employed a broad array of distribution channels (see *Exhibit 3*) ranging from lumberyards to supermarkets.

Gunther von Briskorn explained the major marketing problems facing HD/BC:

As you can see from the number of products we sell and the channels we use, we face selling into very deeply segmented markets. Some of our users are very sophisticated — the craftsman usually has a very specific need, so we have to have the product out there to meet that need. For example, take our SISTA sealants product line. We have four different types of sealant: bathtub, glass, joints and cracks, and "multipurpose" because of differing needs. Then, you need different colors and package sizes — all told, we have 47 different type/color/package combinations. So, the craftsman coming into the store knows what he's looking for and we have it. But look what this does to our other market — households. This poor fellow probably buys sealants once a year, does not know anything about sealants. He comes into the store knowing he needs something to fix a drafty window — but he doesn't know if he should use tape or an adhesive or what. He may not even know what sealants are. And we give him four different types to choose from! So, first we have to educate him what to buy and then how to apply it — and all this on a small communications budget because it's a low expenditure per capita item.

Of course, our international strategy adds a second dimension to the problem. We sell the Pritt line in 15 European countries and 50 outside Europe. So, the "small markets" problem we see due to the low purchase frequency and deep segmentation in Germany is really compounded when we go into a market like Finland, where there just are not that many people. That's why I think we have to get multiple use out of our own resources by umbrella branding and global standardization where possible.

We face strong competition from Uhu, now owned by Beecham. Historically, there were two main segments of the craftsman/DIY market: contact adhesives for heavy jobs and "all-purpose" adhesives for jobs not requiring great bonding strength. We dominated the contact adhesive segment with our Pattex brand originally oriented to the craftsman and Uhu dominated the all-purpose segment with its more consumer-oriented products. In 1969, we attacked their light duty market by offering the Pritt Glue Stick. Uhu was not yet offering a contact adhesive although they did come after us in that segment four years

EXHIBIT 1. Organization chart

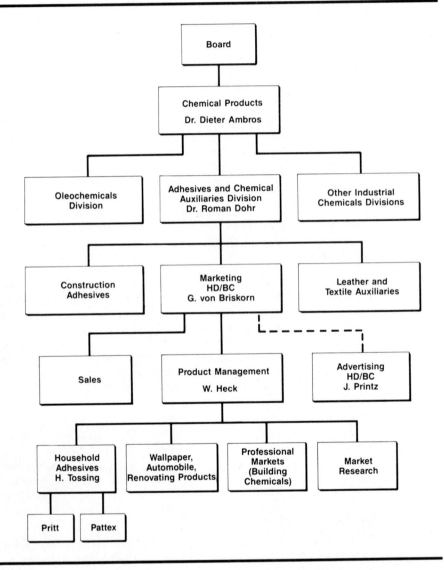

EXHIBIT 2. HD/BC product line

HD/BC Product Line

Henkel

Pattex contact cement

Ponal wood glue

Metylan wallpaper paste

Pritt stick/all purpose glue

Saxit tile adhesives

Polifac car care products

Assil structural adhesives

Thomsit floorlaying adhesives

Ovalit wallcovering adhesives

Tangit pvc pipe adhesives

Dufix home decorating products

Gori wood preservatives

Sista sealants + PU foam (Insulating foam)

Kieselit silicate paints

Randamit construction products

---

later with Uhu Greenit adhesive. Ever since then there has been brand proliferation and greater segmentation of the market.

PATTEX BRAND

Pattex held the "strength adhesive" positioning within HD/BC. Launched in 1956 as a contact adhesive for the professional, Pattex penetrated the household and DIY segments as well and became the leading contact adhesive in West Germany. The bonding strength required for the professional market, e.g., furniture and leather workers, necessitated a somewhat messy, drippy-with-strings formulation. By 1973, HD/BC was able to serve the DIY market better with a nondripping formulation, which sacrificed bonding strength to convenience. Pattex Compact, as the brand was called, was positioned as "The Clean and Powerful Adhesive." It was supported by an introductory advertising campaign of DM 2 million on television. It proved to be a good extension to the line, allowing Henkel to penetrate new segments rather than cannibalizing the original Pattex.

EXHIBIT 3. HD/BC distribution channels

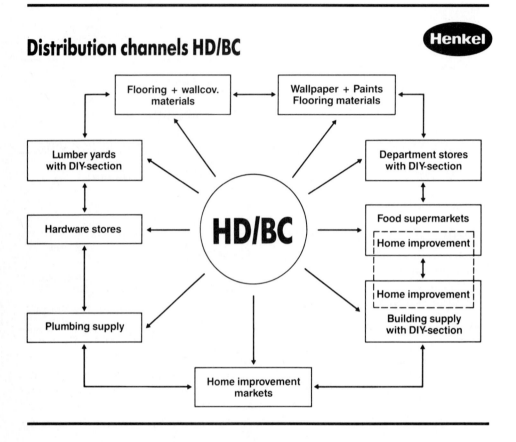

In 1980, Henkel held 80% of the contact adhesive market in West Germany (with sales split equally between Pattex and Pattex Compact). Brand awareness in West Germany topped 80% and trade support was excellent. Over 65% of Pattex sales came from outside Germany as Pattex was distributed in more than 50 countries worldwide. Total Pattex sales were approximately DM 66 million worldwide.

While worldwide sales increased during the late 1970s, sales in the West German market had stagnated (see *Exhibit 4*). Since Pattex was probably the secondmost important brand name within Henkel (next to Persil), Gunther von Briskorn was concerned about the performance as he assumed the HD/BC marketing director position in April 1979. Von Briskorn explained the situation:

EXHIBIT 4. Sales and advertising in Germany

	Pritt		Pattex	
Year	*Sales (DM millions)*	*Advertising (DM millions)*	*Sales (DM millions)*	*Advertising (DM millions)*
1970	4.0	1.0	16.0	0.3
1973	7.0	0.5	22.0	2.0
1976	9.0	2.0	22.0	1.0
1980	8.5	0.5	21.0	1.5
1981 (est.)	8.0	0.5	24.0	1.5

> *We were basically experiencing product life cycle problems. We had a pretty traditional technology — while we were holding our share of the contact adhesive market based on the Pattex technology, we were being attacked by alternative technologies. Probably the most important of these was the cyanoacrylates or CAs, the "Superglues" as people called them. In some respects they were super — offering a one-minute curing time as compared to Pattex's ten minutes, plus they were being offered by strong companies like Uhu and Loctite. At this time, we were selling lots of CAs to industrial users, but we were really concerned about offering it as a consumer product for health reasons. Anyway, these more modern technologies really hurt us — we had a great brand name in Pattex, but the product/technology attached to it was weakening.*

During 1980, Henkel responded to Uhu and Loctite's CA progress by introducing their own CA brand: Stabilit Rasant. However, the brand was given very little advertising support since it was a late entrant and some health concerns still remained within Henkel. Von Briskorn described the situation in early 1981:

> *It was pretty clear where the contact adhesive market was going — there were new, innovative growth segments popping up and attacking the "general purpose" contact adhesives like Pattex. First there were the Superglues, then the Two Component Glues. Also, we saw some potential for moving the hot melt technology from the industrial sphere to the consumer end. We already saw this occur in the U.S. and some small companies were offering it in Europe — but with no clear brand profile yet emerging.*

PRITT BRAND

Through the 1960s, the dominant company in the consumer adhesive market in Germany was Uhu. Introduced in 1932, Uhu's "Alleskleber" (i.e., all-purpose glue), held 80% market share and had easily fended off several competitive "all-purpose" strategies. The Pritt Glue Stick was an innovation developed as a segmentation strategy in the market. In 1969, Henkel introduced the Glue Stick to serve a special purpose: paper-sticking. This segment represented roughly 40% of the total consumer "all-purpose" adhesive market. The nationwide launch in 1969 (managed by von Briskorn as his first assignment with Henkel Corporation) was supported by a DM 3 million television, print, promotion, and point-of-purchase campaign.

The Pritt Glue Stick was a patentable innovation in formulation and convenience-oriented packaging. The density of the glue stick allowed it to be packaged in a twist-up tube, similar to lipstick. The user simply took off the top, twisted the bottom of the tube to push up the glue stick, and then applied a small amount of glue on the paper — the same way one would write with a crayon. Main user groups were households, offices, and schools. Schools were important because research in the adhesive market had shown that adults tended to use the brand they used as children. Thus, having the "no-mess" Pritt stick in kindergartens was important for future Pritt sales, as well as current revenues.

Henkel licensed the Glue Stick technology to a few selected licensees including Uhu. However, because of cannibalization problems and its commitment to the "general purpose" concept, Uhu did not aggressively pursue the stick market. The introduction of the Glue Stick was not easy for Henkel. Positioned as the "clean, easy-to-use paper glue," the primary markets would be schools and offices. Serving these markets effectively required stationery store distribution rather than the wallpaper and paint stores where Henkel was established selling the contact adhesive. Pelikan was the market share leader in products such as carbon paper, ink, stamps, etc. in the stationery story channel. Henkel and Pelikan reached an agreement for Pelikan to handle Pritt Glue Stick distribution in the paper/office/stationery (PBS) sector in Germany. The price of the Pritt Glue Stick was DM 1.2 for the German introduction. Production capacity for 1969 was strained at this price level.

In 1970, the international expansion of Pritt Glue Stick began. The introduction was standardized globally and by 1980, the Pritt Glue Stick was Henkel's most successful brand internationally. Distributed in 15 countries in Europe and 50 outside of Europe, annual sales totaled more than 50 million units with sales revenue of DM 80 million.

From 1972 to 1981, five additional products were introduced under the Pritt brand name. As shown in *Exhibit 5*, these products were:

1. **Pritt Alleskleber.** The Pritt All-Purpose Adhesive was introduced in 1972 with DM 2 million advertising support. Essentially a "me-

EXHIBIT 5. The Pritt product line

too" product to Uhu's all-purpose product, it received good sell-in to the trade because of the Pritt name and advertising support, but poor customer takeaway because of lack of any advantage over Uhu. Reformulated to have a "no-drip" feature, the product was relaunched in 1975, but was unable to achieve even sell-in to the trade because of the 1972 failure. These two failures led to adoption of a "no more me-too's" policy within HD/BC.

2. **Pritt Allesklebe Creme.** The Pritt All-Purpose Creme glue was launched in 1976 with a unique selling proposition. Other adhesives were solvent-based, which created health issues and concern about "glue sniffing." The All-Purpose Creme glue was not solvent-based and was therefore harmless. Supported by a DM 3 million advertising budget, the product received good sell-in but, as with the first Pritt all-purpose product, poor takeaway. Reasons for the lackluster performance seemed to be two: (1) the product performance was not very good on paper and cardboard, and (2) this was the first time an adhesive product used "creme" in the product name. The brand positioning was "strong bonding" and

there was some concern about the compatibility of the positioning and the name. "Creme" did not seem to imply strength.

3. **Pritt Hafties.** Pritt Buddies (as they were referred to in English) were introduced in 1976. Small wads of adhesive, these Buddies were to be used to stick notes on a door temporarily, hold an item in place on a desk, and hopefully a wide variety of other uses which consumers would discover. Initially supported by a DM 2 million advertising budget, the Buddies did well but sales dropped quickly as soon as the advertising support was dropped.

4. **Pritt Alleskleber (bottle).** In 1977, the Pritt all-purpose adhesive was put out in bottle form. Sales were poor due to inferiority in dispensing technology as compared to the Uhu bottled adhesive, the Uhu Flinke Flasche, introduced in 1976.

5. **Pritt Klebepads.** Introduced in 1978, Pritt Adhesive Pads (double-sided foam pads) were very similar in concept to the Pritt Buddies; the physical difference was that the adhesive pads were flat and used for permanent sticking. Not given any special support, the product never did very well. Consumers never seemed to figure out the best applications for these pads or Buddies.

Von Briskorn had been product manager for the Pritt Glue Stick launch in 1969, but had not presided over the product line extension activities of the 1970s, having left Dusseldorf for Henkel assignments in Italy and France. In April 1979, he returned to Dusseldorf to assume the role of marketing director HD/BC, responsible for 15 brands including his first assigned brand, Pritt. In early 1981, he addressed Wolfgang Heck, the present group product manager for Craftsman/DIY Products:

> *The Pritt Glue Stick has been great. It was a real innovation and allowed us to capture the clean, easy-bonding positioning. It is an international success story. But these flankers, the all-purpose product and the creme product and so on — they have really hurt us. We have created so many flops; we are losing money on them and everybody is mad at us. The retail trade is not giving us the sell-in and Pelikan, our key distributor, is angry too. We jeopardized our relationship with Kokuyo in Japan — the all-purpose products and the Buddies flopped there too. Maybe it's the products, they are really average in performance. There has been no real significant innovation since the Glue Stick. But we have not really developed any coordinated marketing strategy for these products either — the product line has no visual harmony (see Exhibit 5), all advertising has been for a single brand at a time. We face a real challenge in a few years when the Glue Stick formula patent expires. By that time, we have to be executing a coordinated strategy for the Pritt family or have cleared the scenery of these products which are pulling us down.*

UMBRELLA BRANDING POSSIBILITIES

With Wolfgang Heck's departure from Dusseldorf to a Henkel assignment in the United States, Herbert Tossing assumed the position of product manager Household Adhesives. Along with Joachim Printz, advertising manager, Tossing had the primary responsibility of developing the marketing strategy responsive to von Briskorn's declaration that "if we are to be successful in Germany and the rest of the world, we must find an innovative approach." *Exhibit 6* gives the HD/BC organizational structure through which Herbert Tossing would have to work in developing and implementing the strategy. Basically, HD/BC integrated sales and product management in the same organization. As shown in *Exhibit 6*, profit center responsibility was given to the three sales organizations serving Germany, and the affiliated companies in Europe and the affiliated companies overseas. Product management had no regional profit center responsibility, but rather global consolidated responsibility. It had an international role developing the central brand strategy, coordinating the individual market strategies and monitoring progress. The advertising function was similar in its international orientation. Printz would be responsible for developing the basic advertising concept and then coordinating with advertising agencies across the markets to ensure international implementation of the advertising strategy. Regional autonomy and profit center responsibility for affiliated companies was a strong part of the Henkel culture. Tossing began his strategy formulation with the Pattex brand.

PATTEX UMBRELLA POTENTIAL

In the case of Pattex, the umbrella question was easy to state: Could a very highly regarded brand name (Pattex) tied to a product in a no-growth segment (contact adhesives) be transferred to new products to be positioned in higher growth segments of the market? In particular, Tossing saw three possibilities:

1. Remarket Stabilit Rasant, Henkel's recent but unsupported entry into the fast-growing CA market, under the name Pattex Super Glue.
2. Develop a Pattex entry into the emerging "hot melt" market.
3. Market a Pattex No-Mix product which would be a new generation two-component glue, a special purpose item.

The first step in assessing the viability of these steps was to determine consumers' current perception of the Pattex brand name. Research

EXHIBIT 6. HD/BC organization structure

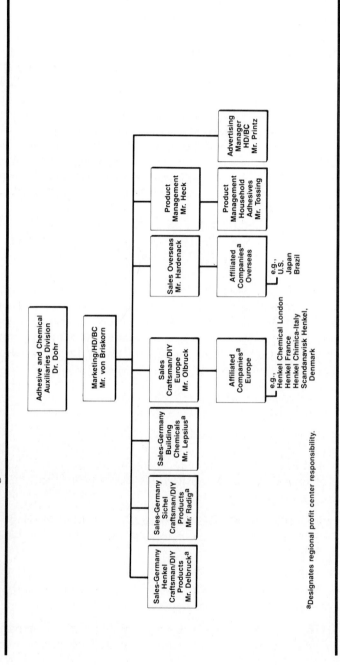

Adhesive and Chemical Auxiliaries Division
Dr. Dohr

Marketing/HD/BC
Mr. von Briskorn

Sales-Germany Henkel Craftsman/DIY Products
Mr. Delbruck[a]

Sales-Germany Sichel Craftsman/DIY Products
Mr. Radig[a]

Sales-Germany Building Chemicals
Mr. Lepsius[a]

Sales Craftsman/DIY Europe
Mr. Olbruck

Affiliated Companies[a] Europe

e.g.,
Henkel Chemical London
Henkel France
Henkel Chimica-Italy
Scandanavisk Henkel, Denmark

Sales Overseas
Mr. Hardenack

Affiliated Companies[a] Overseas

e.g.,
U.S.
Japan
Brazil

Product Management
Mr. Heck

Product Management Household Adhesives
Mr. Tossing

Advertising Manager HD/BC
Mr. Printz

[a]Designates regional profit center responsibility.

124

in West Germany, Benelux, and Austria showed the Pattex name to be associated with "strong bonding" and "technical uses." Researching the potential for stretching the Pattex name in the three directions noted above, Tossing found that

1. CAs had a very popular, not at all technical image. Consequently, the fit with Pattex's image on this dimension was not strong. However, Stabilit Rasant was not doing well because of its late entry into the market after Uhu and Loctite.

2. The *Hot Melt* market (with the dispensing guns) had a technical image. This could enhance the Pattex name. Henkel possessed the production know-how from industrial experience. Consequently, Henkel could probably produce a high-quality product for most applications. Consumer research showed that DIY-ers viewed Henkel as a credible source for hot melt products. Unlike other Pattex products, it would be a seasonal, gift-oriented item because of the cost of the dispensing gun. It was also felt that the market may be a price-oriented one.

3. Serving the *Two Compound Glue* segment with Pattex No Mix would definitely enhance the Pattex technical image as it required no dosing or mixing. The product would, however, be a niche product generating low turnover for the trade. Historically, Pattex had been viewed as a "fast mover" by the trade. A second problem with No Mix was consumers perceived it to smell very bad — would this "bad smell" perception hurt other Pattex brands if No Mix were brought under the Pattex umbrella?

In general, the research finding was that a line extension would not degrade consumers' perception of the Pattex name as long as the umbrella products were compatible with Pattex's high-bonding strength image. The research results in *Exhibit 7* show the mean score on a 1–10 scale of 100 respondents exposed to just the Pattex name (control group) and a test group exposed to the line extension through seeing product package mock-ups and product descriptions. The second research finding was that the new brands would benefit greatly from the power and authority of the Pattex name.

PRITT UMBRELLA POTENTIAL

The Pritt situation was quite different from Pattex. The Pattex name was currently positioned in a no-growth category and the extension under consideration was to new products or to a very recent introduction (Sta-

EXHIBIT 7. Research results—Pattex brand

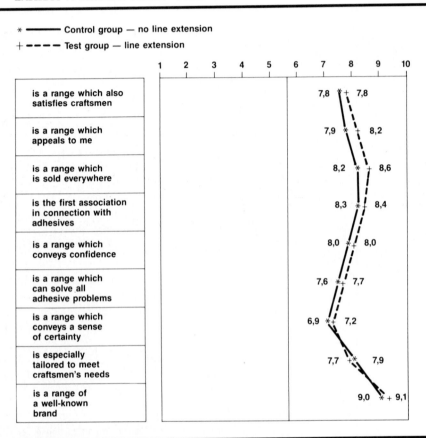

Note: One hundred people in each of the test and control groups were asked to indicate agreement/disagreement with the statement "Pattex is . . ." 1 indicates "strongly disagree" and 10 indicates "strongly agree."

bilit Rasant). The question for the Pattex situation was, can the new products save the brand? In Pritt, the question was, can the brand save the products (i.e., the flankers to the Glue Stick) if more actively promoted? Printz played a key role in reviewing packaging design, proposing a new line design, and testing the consumers' reaction to the new line.

The first step was to review the Glue Stick design for consumer acceptance and conveyance of a "modern image." Based on research in Benelux and West Germany, the red, white, and black Pritt stick design was deemed acceptable and "modern." Based on this, Printz proposed

EXHIBIT 8. Proposed visual harmonization of the Pritt product line

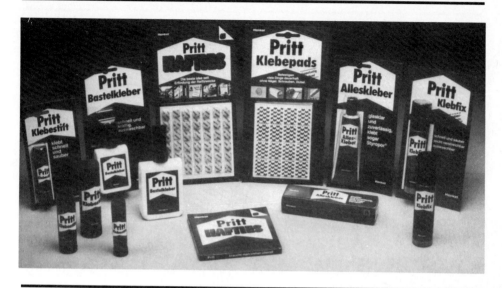

a visual harmonization of the line, all oriented toward the leader product. The proposed design is shown in *Exhibit 8.* This design introduced the chevron to all packages and extended the red background, black lettering on white color scheme of the Glue Stick to all elements in the line.

Printz proposed a similar visual harmonization as recently created for the Pattex line where the chevron was used but with yellow as the primary background color. Tests of the nonharmonized versus harmonized design for the Pritt product line were conducted. Results are shown in *Exhibit 9.* Respondents were exposed to either the harmonized or nonharmonized lines and asked to rate both Pritt and Uhu on the dimensions shown.

DECISIONS AND IMPLEMENTATION

Whatever strategy decisions he made, von Briskorn had to be concerned about how he could get the strategy sold within Henkel. He knew that Dr. Roman Dohr, head of Adhesives and Chemical Auxiliaries, would have questions on all aspects of the strategy. He had previously expressed concerns about the risks inherent in an umbrella strategy. The recent problems with the Pritt flankers and the declining fortunes of

EXHIBIT 9. Research results on perceptions of Pritt current line, Pritt harmonized line, and Uhu

	Pritt current (see *Exhibit 5*) N = 100		Pritt harmonized (see *Exhibit 8*) N = 100	
	Pritt	*Uhu*	*Pritt*	*Uhu*
Conveys confidence	6.8	8.5	7.5	8.3
Is of high quality	7.2	8.4	7.5	8.4
Is for special uses only	6.5	5.5	5.6	5.6
Is only for sticking paper	5.7	4.3	4.8	3.9
Is somehow likeable	6.4	7.2	6.6	7.2
Glues reliably	7.1	8.4	7.5	8.5
Is of great strength	6.9	8.3	7.1	8.4
Is a well-known brand	7.9	9.7	8.0	9.6
Is for general purposes	6.5	8.1	7.0	8.1
Is usually reasonably priced	6.5	6.7	5.9	6.4
Is sold everywhere	7.4	8.9	7.9	9.0
Offers all adhesives you need	7.1	8.3	7.2	7.9
Is more for children	4.9	4.5	4.9	4.6
Is more known from the office	6.3	5.6	5.9	5.5
Offers useful adhesives	8.0	8.7	8.1	8.7
Has a well-structured range	6.9	7.9	7.8	8.1
Is something for experts	2.4	3.0	3.3	3.5
Is clean in use	7.6	7.7	8.0	7.7

Note: One hundred people in each group were exposed to a simulated store setting showing either the current Pritt or proposed harmonized packaging design. They were then asked to indicate agreement/disagreement with the statements shown for Pritt and Uhu (1 = strongly disagree, 10 = strongly agree).

Pattex had made these two products highly visible in the Adhesives group. Von Briskorn and his product management team would also have to convince those with profit center responsibility in the affiliated foreign companies to implement the plan. His problems only began with the decision of which products to put under the umbrellas. He would have to make suggestions as well on Henkel advertising strategy, e.g., should they advertise the whole umbrella as a group, concentrate on one brand and hope others got pulled along somehow, or divide dollars and advertise each on its own? What should be the timing of the expansion of the strategy to worldwide markets — what kind of markets should be tried first? Should he advocate standardization of the strategy across markets or be yielding on individual adaptation? Last, he had to consider how to sell the ideas to the trade. Distributors and retailers were vital to Henkel success; however, with the recent record of HD/BC, trade receptivity to another HD/BC venture was not overwhelming.

Von Briskorn believed very strongly in the brand philosophy he had developed over the past few years — "Concentrate on a few, but really strong umbrellas and, as far as possible, have an internationally standardized strategy." In the abstract, the philosophy seemed to fit the adhesives market well, but now was the time to implement rather than philosophize.

1.7 CASE

Mövenpick Unternehmungen

Ulrich Wiechmann and
Kate Gillespie

In July 1977, Dr. Mario Wang and Herr Rudi Baur, both members of the executive board of Mövenpick Unternehmungen, met for a discussion of a matter of strategic importance to the firm. A group of investors had approached Mövenpick with a proposal involving the acquisition and management of five to ten established hotels in Europe. While no detailed plan or contract terms were included in the proposal, the general idea proposed by the investors was that Mövenpick would run the hotels to be acquired on a management contract basis.

"They are serious people and they mean business," said Herr Baur. "Of course, nothing is definite yet, but they want an answer from us whether we are, in principle, interested in such a deal. The details are up for negotiation. We certainly have experience in hotel and restaurant management, and the proposal could mean a big international expansion for us."

"It may be too big for us," Dr. Wang replied. "And I am not sure we want to expand in this way. In fact, I am not quite sure how all the international expansion projects we have undertaken in the past fit together. We have so many opportunities; there is a danger that we may be going into too many different directions."

COMPANY BACKGROUND

Mövenpick was a Swiss company, headquartered in Zürich, operating a chain of restaurants and hotels in Switzerland, Germany, and, most recently, Egypt. The company was founded in 1948 by Herr Ueli Prager, who in 1977 was still the president and the controlling shareholder of Mövenpick. Herr Prager's management style was described as a mixture of authoritative and participative. As one executive said:

> *Herr Prager is an entrepreneurial type who may break all management rules and accepted strategies. He always discusses major decisions with the key executives in the company, but he reserves the right to make the ultimate decision. He is very enthusiastic and it is at times difficult to convince him of a different course of action once he has made up his mind. There are occasionally breaks in his opinion and style from one meeting to the next. He is a charismatic type.*

In 1977, The Mövenpick group comprised 56 restaurants, operating under the names Mövenpick and Silberkugel, 7 hotels with restaurants, and 11 production and trading units. In its core trading area, Switzerland and Germany, Mövenpick was regarded as a very efficiently run company.

Restaurants operating under the Mövenpick trademark covered a wide variety of styles, price categories, and menus. Herr Baur explained:

> *Our Mövenpick restaurants differ greatly from each other. Common to all of them, however, is the efficient control and kitchen management system that we have developed over the years. Another common feature is that each Mövenpick in its own individual style tries to convey the image of being young, fresh, good, and giving the customer an interesting experience and excellent value for money.*

The Silberkugel restaurants, in contrast, were highly standardized fast-food outlets.

Mövenpick had entered the hotel business on a modest scale in the mid-1960s. Herr Prager's family background was in hotels, and he, therefore, had always looked at the hotel business as an interesting business activity for his company. A major investment in hotels was not made until 1973 when Mövenpick acquired a Holiday Inn franchise and began operations of two Holiday Inn hotels near Zurich Airport. In 1977, Mövenpick operated a total of seven hotels and motels, two of them were Holiday Inns, two were motels operated under the name of Jolie Ville, and three were small Swiss hotels run by Mövenpick on a management contract basis. In all their hotels and motels, Mövenpick aimed at providing "first-class accommodation at second-class rates; comfort instead of luxury."

The 11 production and trading companies were engaged in the manufacturing, purchasing, and marketing of products such as ice cream, salad dressing, bread and pastry, coffee, tea, and wines. The units had originally been set up to supply Mövenpick restaurants. By 1977, however, more than 50% of total turnover of these units went through grocery retail outlets to the final consumer. "Sales to the grocery trade just happened to evolve over time and had neither been pushed nor prohibited," said Herr Prager. The range of retail products was expanding, and the line, which was currently being sold only in Switzerland, was going to be introduced to the German market in 1978. Herr Prager also thought about supplying competing restaurants with these products.

In 1976 total consolidated sales of Mövenpick Unternehmungen amounted to Sfr. 249 million,[1] yielding a net profit after tax of Sfr. 5.9 million. (*Exhibits 1–4* show details of Mövenpick's financial position and development.)

The Mövenpick group had recently emerged from a major financial crisis. During fiscal year 1973/74 consolidated profits had dropped by roughly 55%. The reason for this unsatisfactory performance was that plans for the expansion in the hotel business had been made during years of growing demand for hotel rooms, and when construction of Mövenpick's new hotels was completed the market had seriously contracted. As a result of this recent crisis, top management of Mövenpick had adopted a very conservative attitude toward all new ventures that required capital expenditures and had stated as a priority objective to increase the proportion of equity as a percentage of total funds supplied.

Management felt that a conservative attitude should govern, in particular, projects of expansion outside of Mövenpick's core trading area;

---

[1]At year-end 1976 US$ 1.00 = Sfr. 2.44.

i.e., Switzerland and Germany. Herr Ueli Prager had made the following comments with regard to international expansion:

> *A healthy attitude of caution and restraint has to be combined with a pioneering spirit and willingness to take risks. The recipe for the right proportions in combining these elements has not yet been found. . . . We see our task in the planning and management of hotels and restaurants abroad and not in playing the role of investors in foreign countries.*

INTERNATIONAL ACTIVITIES

Mövenpick was currently involved in various overseas activities. Herr Baur, Manager of Mövenpick's Management and Product Planning Division, remarked:

> *We work in many parts of the world, in many different ways. For example: We are just starting a franchise system of Mövenpick restaurants in Japan. In Egypt we have constructed a hotel which opened this year. We are part-owners of the operating company and manage it under our Jolie Ville brand name. One of our architects just left for Nigeria to do a project feasibility study for a local client, and another man is doing a similar job in Venezuela. In several places we run restaurants for the account of the owners, on a management contract basis; we did that in London at the Swiss Center in Leicester Square for a long time. But we also act as restaurant and hotel consultants, for example, in Sierra Leone, Germany, and Holland. Furthermore, from time to time we are simply architects, doing design work according to the standard contracts of the Swiss association of architects.*

> *We do project studies, like those in Nigeria and Venezuela, in a wide geographical area. One reason is that we have to do a number of those studies in order to learn and to get a feel for several foreign markets before we can decide on any deeper involvement abroad. We want to have first-hand information on various countries and then sit down and evaluate where to focus our efforts.*

> *We have a fairly firm view that our own operations should be limited to certain geographical areas. We are thinking of Germany, France, the Middle East, the U.S.A., West Africa. Very roughly, we are looking for countries that in terms of their basic characteristics have a certain international traffic and economic growth. That's why Egypt was of interest to us. In fact, after our success with our Egyptian venture, we wouldn't mind investing a token 5–10% equity in a hotel company in order to show goodwill toward the local partner.*

> *One thing we do know is that we don't want a policy of "a little here, a little there." It would be too great a strain on management; shortage of qualified personnel is one of our biggest problems. There's a tendency in the international hotel business to build only one hotel per country. We can't afford to take on a*

EXHIBIT 1. Key financial and operations figures, 1971/72–1976

		1976	1974/75 15 months[a]	1974/75 12 months[b]	1973/74	1972/73	1971/72
Equity	Million Sfr.	57.8	54.4		54.9	36.8	25.1
Equity as percentage of total assets		32.9%	31.2%		28.4%	20.1%	18.6%
Consolidated sales	Million Sfr.	249.1	280.8	224.6	216.7	185.0	148.5
Percentage change		10.9%		3.6%	17.1%	24.6%	35.1%
Breakdown of total sales by country							
Switzerland		80.2%	83.6%	83.6%	84.8%	83.4%	82.3%
Germany[c]		19.6	16.4	16.4	15.2	16.6	17.7
Egypt[c]		0.2					
Total		100.0	100.0	100.0	100.0	100.0	100.0
Cash flow	Million Sfr.	26.6[d]	16.7	13.4	10.3	12.3	8.7
As percentage of equity		35.5%		24.6%	18.8%	33.4%	34.6%
As percentage of consolidated sales		7.1%	5.9%		4.8%	6.7%	5.9%
Consolidated net profit	Million Sfr.	5.9[d]	1.6	1.3	1.4	3.1	N.A.
Number of personnel							
Switzerland		2,620	2,650		2,820	2,470	2,350
Germany		940	780		760	790	650
Egypt		320					
Totals		3,880	3,430		3,580	3,260	3,000

Number of operating units by geography	Switzerland	57	56		54	49	42
	Germany	16	16		16	16	13
	Egypt	1					
	Totals	74	72		70	65	55
Number of operating units by type	Mövenpick restaurant	40	40		40	35	31
	Silberkugel	16	15		14	14	11
	Hotels with restaurant	7	6		5	5	3
	Production and trading	11	11		11	11	10
	Totals	74	72		70	65	55
Breakdown of total sales (including intra-company sales) by type of operating unit	Mövenpick restaurant	154.4	179.3	143.5	131.7	120.5	101.6
	Silberkugel	32.1	38.3	30.6	31.9	23.5	19.1
	Hotels with restaurant	33.2	32.5	26.0	25.1	11.4	5.9
	Production and trading	70.3	85.6	68.5	83.8	79.2	60.1
	Totals	290.0	335.7	268.6	272.5	234.6	186.7
Number of restaurant seats	Switzerland	8,244	8,149		7,827	7,118	5,696
	Germany	3,605	3,353		3,234	3,234	2,786
	Egypt	260					
	Totals	12,109	11,502		11,061	10,352	8,482
Hotels	Number of rooms	896	663		649	654	166
	Number of beds	1,622	1,116		1,095	1,121	284

[a] Fiscal year Oct. 1, 1974–Dec. 31, 1975. Before 1975, the fiscal year ended on Sept. 30. Starting in 1976, fiscal and calendar years were identical.

[b] Fiscal year converted to 12 months using the following formula:

$$\frac{(\text{Oct. 1, 1974–Dec., 31, 1975}) \times 12}{15}$$

[c] Rate of Exchange 1976: Sfr. 1.038 = DM 1.00; Sfr. 3.40 = 1 E£.

[d] Includes extraordinary profit resulting from a financial workout for the Mövenpick Hotel Optikon AG.

Source: Company records.

135

EXHIBIT 2. Performance figures for the first quarter 1977

	Budget Jan. 1–Apr. 30, 1977 (million Sfr.)	Actual Jan. 1–Apr. 30, 1977 (million Sfr.)	Previous year Jan. 1–Apr. 30, 1976 (million Sfr.)	Percentage change from previous year (%)
Sales				
Restaurants and hotels				
Switzerland	55.1	56.4	52.9	+ 6.6
Germany	21.4	23.8	15.5	+ 53.5
Egypt	2.9	3.0	—	+ 100.0
	79.4	83.2	68.4	+ 21.6
Production and trading companies	18.9	19.2	19.6	– 5.2
Total sales	98.3	102.4	88.0	+ 16.4
Cash flow				
Restaurants and hotels				
Switzerland	3.7	4.3	3.3	+ 30.3
Germany	1.1	2.0	1.1	+ 81.8
Egypt	0.3	0.4	—	+ 100.0
	5.1	6.7	4.4	+ 52.3
Production and trading companies	1.0	1.3	1.6	– 18.7
Total cash flow	6.1	8.0	6.0	+ 33.6

Exchange rates: DM 105.95 (1977), DM 99.50 (1976), E£ 3.40.
Source: Annual Report 1976/77.

EXHIBIT 3. Consolidated balance sheet (in million Sfr.)

	Dec. 31, 1976		Dec. 31, 1975			Dec. 31, 1976		Dec. 31, 1975	
Current assets					*Liabilities*				
Cash	6.15		5.93		Short- and medium-term liabilities				
Securities	3.86		1.31		Accounts payable	28.32		24.74	
Accounts receivable	12.28		11.17		Bank credit	21.21		6.37	
Other current assets	2.65		2.13		Other liabilities	10.50	60.03	3.80	34.91
Inventory	27.06	52.00	23.36	43.90	Long-term liabilities				
					Credits	7.15		12.40	
					Reserves	0.86		0.13	
					Mortgages	23.34		47.35	
					Debentures	8.65	40.00	8.66	68.54
					Total liabilities		100.03		103.45
					Investment of third parties in operations		17.84		16.78
Fixed assets					*Equity*				
Real estate	11.83		10.04		Common stock	11.00		11.00	
Buildings	60.43		63.48		Reserves	40.94		41.78	
Equipment	47.98		52.68		Consolidated net profit	5.90	57.84	1.62	54.40
Other fixed assets	3.47	123.71	4.53	130.73			175.71		174.63
		175.71		174.63					

Source: Annual Report 1976/77.

EXHIBIT 4. Consolidated statement of income (in million Sfr.)

		1976 (Jan. 1–Dec. 31, 1976)			1974/75 15 months (Oct. 1, 1974– Dec. 31, 1975)	
		Sfr.	%		Sfr.	%
Sales		249.13	100.0		280.84	100.0
Cost of goods sold		88.18	35.4		102.14	36.4
Gross margin		160.95	64.6		178.70	63.6
Personnel cost	89.01			99.05		
Other cost	52.76	141.77	56.9	61.58	160.63	57.2
Operating profit (before taxes and depreciation)		19.18	7.7		18.07	6.4
Extraordinary profit	6.33			2.15		
Extraordinary loss	3.18	3.15	1.3	2.07	0.08	0.1
		22.33	9.0		18.15	6.5
Taxes		1.77	0.7		1.48	0.5
Cash flow		20.56	8.3		16.67	6.0
Depreciation		12.17	4.9		17.69	6.3
		8.39	3.4		−1.02	−0.3
Share of third parties in profit or loss	Profit	2.49	1.0	Loss	2.64	0.9
Consolidated net profit		5.90	2.4		1.62	0.6

Source: Annual Report 1976/77.

major management task like that. Any new country or region we go into will have to have the potential to support several operations under one management. Of course, when we talk about a region, we mean more than just an area on the map. It must represent a unique market. As I mentioned, when we look for a region for expansion overseas, we look for an area with future potential to support several operations. This potential could be in the form of natural resources such as oil, or it could be a potential for tourism like in Egypt. One thing that is hard to predict is the political outlook for an area, and, after all, that can be the greatest determinant.

Politics in the world make us very reluctant to make big investments in the developing countries. Among the developed countries we are watching France and Belgium very closely. The Netherlands are not so attractive because of eating habits and the socialist government. Sweden we wouldn't touch because of the very difficult labor situation in that country. One of our project studies in Sweden helped us to reach this conclusion. We don't rule out North America and Canada, but there is a little bit of a distance problem. We are tempted but, frankly, we are also a bit scared of the North American market. We would have to be very careful and selective there.

In Western Europe we'll still concentrate on restaurants. For example, we believe France has a certain potential for a regional kitchen such as the Swiss Mövenpick. Also, France could be ready for fast-food restaurants. We look at politics in Europe just as we do overseas.

Dr. Wang explained that Mövenpick was not ambitious to become one of the biggest international restaurant and hotel chains. In fact, he described the company as being very cautious and reluctant to do something new which might turn out to be wrong. Mövenpick wanted growth, but not at any price. Instead, Mövenpick hoped to achieve a growth which did not sacrifice quality to quantity. Dr. Wang and Herr Baur both agreed that fast expansion would hurt Mövenpick's quality. Also, they believed that Mövenpick should avoid entering any business areas which were not easily reconciled with Mövenpick's current product line.

In a recent strategy meeting, Mövenpick's management had tried to arrive at some tentative guidelines for the company's international expansion. (Appendix A gives excerpts from a company document summarizing the tentative guidelines.) Herr Baur and Dr. Wang wondered whether these guidelines gave Mövenpick the sufficient and the right strategic direction. They decided to review some of Mövenpick's recent international ventures to see whether they might serve as models for the company's future expansion abroad.

MANAGEMENT CONTRACTS

Mövenpick gave priority to international ventures which required the construction and management of restaurants or hotels, since Mövenpick preferred to build projects as well as manage them. Herr Baur noted, however, that in Europe there was more opportunity to take over old hotels than to build new ones. Under a typical management contract, Mövenpick first designed and built the restaurant or hotel. Mövenpick also chose the management which, in turn, reported back to Mövenpick. As long as the contract was in operation, normally 15 years, the owners had the right to use the Mövenpick or Jolie Ville trademarks. For its management services, Mövenpick received between 3 and 5 percent of the operation's gross sales (excluding sales taxes) and 10 and 12 percent of the gross operating profit, defined as the difference between gross sales and all direct expenses related to operation, exclusive of interest, depreciation, taxes, etc. Mövenpick also charged a royalty (2% of sales) for the use of their trademark. Pre-opening arrangements such as the recruiting and training of staff, the setting of tariffs and prices, the development of promotional programs, and the preparation of the provisional operating budget were included in a separate fee. The owner alone supported any losses on the operation. One of Mövenpick's most famous management projects was the restaurant at the Swiss Center in London. The restaurant, built in the early 1960s, was under Mövenpick management for 15 years and was currently under a consulting contract with Mövenpick.

CONSULTING SERVICES

In exceptional cases Mövenpick acted as management consultants. A consulting contract might look attractive if it were financially rewarding while demanding little time, or if it were especially prestigious or offered Mövenpick a unique chance to expand its knowledge in a certain area. A consulting contract could require Mövenpick to help in such areas as sales and pricing policy, marketing programs, selection and training of management and personnel, advertising, purchasing, and control systems. A typical contract, such as one prepared for a restaurant in Vienna, earned Mövenpick 4 percent of sales (less sales taxes) with a minimum of Sfr. 10,000 a month for the first year. If the contract was continued beyond the first year, Mövenpick received 1 percent of sales and 10 percent of profit after tax. The restaurant could carry Mövenpick products but could not use the Mövenpick name. Mövenpick had rendered consulting services on a similar basis for a restaurant chain in Holland.

Mövenpick had recently undertaken a consulting job in Sierra Leone. The offer had come through a friend of Herr Prager. Mövenpick was originally reluctant to get involved and only accepted the job at a relatively high price. The consulting served as a form of "paid research," however, and allowed Mövenpick to get an insight into the local market. Mövenpick was currently considering a possible Jolie Ville project in Sierra Leone. Herr Baur believed that the project would require relatively little work and give Mövenpick more experience in the new market.

Mövenpick, however, did not want consulting contracts for operations which fell below Mövenpick's own standards or were unlike Mövenpick's operations. Management noted that Mövenpick would not accept consulting for resort operations; e.g., mountain or seaside hotels which were open a limited number of months a year. The company had been consulting for a resort hotel in Turkey but had recently terminated the contract.

ARCHITECTURAL SERVICES

Mövenpick considered the sale of architectural services as a possibility to keep the company's staff of architects busy during periods of slow business. At the moment, Mövenpick was only involved in one such project located in Montreux, Switzerland, and the company was largely hiring outside personnel to do the routine work. Furthermore, the project involved a one-year consulting agreement as well.

RESTAURANT FRANCHISING IN JAPAN

"Our first concern with entering the Japanese market was the question of increasing our foreign exposure," recalled Dr. Wang. "It took us a long time to decide to go to Japan. After all, we're reluctant to do things wrong."

After discussing possible markets abroad in which to expand, management at Mövenpick decided on Japan as one of the countries offering the most potential. In the early 1970s, the Japanese economy was rapidly expanding. The many Japanese tourists visiting Europe responded favorably to European cuisine and seemed willing to try Western concepts and innovations. As a result of management's interest, Dr. Wang and Herr Baur embarked on an exploratory trip to Japan.

Their first contact was a manufacturer in the fields of textiles and chemicals. This particular contact wished to expand into catering and food operations and had entered into negotiations with Mövenpick concerning a franchise relationship. The manufacturer suffered severe setbacks in late 1973, however, due to the phenomenal increase in the world price of petroleum following the Yom Kippur War; and the company was forced to pull out of the Mövenpick negotiations. In the end, Mövenpick management was relived by the outcome, realizing that they would likely be better off with a partner who already knew something about the business they were dealing in.

"We decided that we wanted a strong competent partner," remarked Herr Baur, "even with the risk that they would operate other restaurants. We began new negotiations with the Koizumi Group who own the successful chain of Totenko Chinese restaurants in Japan. There are now 22 Totenko restaurants with a total sales volume of roughly Sfr. 55 million."

Mövenpick and the Koizumi Group agreed to enter a franchisor-franchisee relationship. Mövenpick believed that it could offer the Koizumi Group considerable "know-how" and experience in European and fast-food preparation and marketing. After 28 years of operations, Mövenpick had developed a certain expertise in kitchen management and design as well as in the areas of menu choice and food preparation. Experts from Mövenpick would work with personnel from the Koizumi Group in the specific areas of forecasting statistics, menu design, food preparation, and the planning of special promotions. Koizumi would also receive guidance concerning standards, control, and choice of restaurant sites. Furthermore, all new ideas originating in Mövenpick would be transmitted to Japan, and a special Mövenpick team of inspectors and advisors would visit the Japanese operations four times in the first year and three times a year in the following years. Mövenpick, however, realized that setting up business in Japan would require the creation of certain new systems designed for the locality and not just a simple transferal of systems which worked in Western Europe. Moreover, new recipes would have to be formulated. Koizumi's experience in the Japanese market would be a critical input in designing a menu acceptable to Japanese consumers.

Some executives of Mövenpick foresaw certain risks with the venture in Japan. They felt an inherent danger of the franchise system was that the franchisee could learn what he wanted from the franchisor, then terminate the contract and go into business on his own. Mr. Prager disagreed: "I have complete trust in our Japanese partners; they are not going to cheat us."

Also, the initial investment of Mövenpick had exceeded the original plan. While Herr Baur had initially projected that Mövenpick would reach pay-back on their investment in Japan within two years, in 1977 it looked like the pay-back period would be closer to four years. Herr Baur explained: "We were dealing with a different culture and everything we did had to be done quite a bit differently."

The Mövenpick team working on the Japanese project found that "little details" were proving to be more time consuming than they had foreseen. Translation itself was a burdensome problem. Although the Koizumi Group paid any incurred expenses, they did not pay for the time of the Mövenpick team.

Another risk Mövenpick noted was the possibility that the restaurant in Tokyo would simply not be successful. Management considered this risk to be minor. After all, Tokyo was far away and could do negligible harm to their Western European operations and reputation.

Mövenpick had originally offered the Koizumi Group a contract stating the following terms: Koizumi would agree to open three restaurants within five years, paying an initial franchise fee of Sfr. 60,000 per unit. In addition, Mövenpick would receive 3 percent of total sales of all franchise operations. Koizumi would also send, at their expense, a pilot team to Zurich for training in order to create a nucleus of management talent for future development.

Herr Baur, recalling the negotiations, remarked:

> *The Koizumi Group wanted to involve Mövenpick more in the financing of the Japanese operations. At that time, however, we were having trouble with our hotels in Switzerland, and we needed all our resources there. We might consider a joint venture in the future — after the Koizumi Group proves itself. Another area of dispute was our reimbursement — 3 percent of total sales. The Koizumi Group originally wanted it to be a percentage of net profit, and they still want the percentage to be lower.*

Mr. Hirabayashi, manager of Koizumi's Totenko chain of Chinese restaurants, recounted the contract negotiations and development plans from the point of view of the Koizumi Group:

> *We first got interested in bringing the Mövenpick concept to Japan about five years ago. We dropped by Zurich on our way back from the U.S. and talked with Dr. Wang. At that time, we were told that Mövenpick already had other people in Japan. Three weeks later, however, they sent us a letter asking to continue discussion on the matter. In 1974, Dr. Wang and Herr Baur came to Japan at our expense. Then in spring of 1975, Herr Prager came over and things became active.*

> *We had just opened our first overseas restaurant in Dayton, Ohio, and we were looking for new opportunities for overseas expansion. Our original hope was to set up a joint venture with Mövenpick and perhaps use Mövenpick as a springboard for the expansion of the Totenko restaurants to Europe. Mövenpick, however, was only interested in a franchise agreement.*

> *Nevertheless, we believed the Mövenpick franchise was a good investment. Food consumption in restaurants in Japan totals about $30 billion annually, and a typical chain restaurant produces net profits of about 6 percent of sales. Japanese restaurants can be divided into three basic types — Japanese, Chinese, and Western food. Totenko is the second largest chain in the Chinese sector, but our sales increases there are leveling off. We wanted to expand into another sector. Japanese food consumption has become very Westernized over the last 100 years. The American influence has been the strongest, but French cuisine has*

been introduced by hotels. The Japanese have been becoming more knowledgeable and demanding with regard to European food. We analyzed that Mövenpick was a specialty restaurant offering the best of all European cuisines. Furthermore, there are enough competitors already in the American subsegment of the market. I'd say we do not have any direct competition to Mövenpick here.

In order to enter the Western food business, we needed a better management than we had in Japan. Mövenpick offered us good management. They have combined the concept of "fast food" with a unique, European menu; and they still have, despite all their rationalization, the kind of creativity and imagination needed in the restaurant business. Totenko has a very good control system, but Mövenpick offers us special expertise in the areas of product and recipe know-how and worldwide purchase control. We had previous experience with U.S. companies, but it didn't work out. This time we felt we had a better chance. We had extensive contact with the people from Mövenpick before we actually started the venture or signed a contract. There is mutual understanding between the two parties, and we especially value Herr Prager as a person. Without him there might not have been a contract.

The actual contract which we agreed upon is divided into three stages of development. First, Mövenpick prepares a market research study which we pay for. Second, we set up a pilot operation. This operation includes both a Mövenpick and a Silberkugel restaurant under one roof. We are obliged to pay for one year of the operation, then we can terminate the contract if we are not satisfied. Normally, Mövenpick requires a longer-term commitment than this, but we told them frankly what we thought, and they changed the standard contract. After all, we are the ones making the investment and taking the risks. Then finally, in the last stage — or "franchise" stage — we commit ourselves to opening 10 units over 10 years. Mövenpick has given us exclusive franchise rights to Japan, Hong Kong, and Korea. We pay a franchise fee for each outlet, including the pilot operation. We also pay a royalty to Mövenpick of 3 percent of sales; that's very high.

Right now, we're between stages one and two, and there is still uncertainty about the success of the venture. Mövenpick did a five-year study, projecting sales for our first outlet of a little over Sfr. 5 million for our first year of operations, with sales increases of 8 percent a year for the second and third years and a declining growth of about 5 percent in the fourth and fifth years. We've chosen a consumer segment, however, which lies between the high- and low-priced segments; and, therefore, we may be appealing to everybody or nobody. We are also concerned about the cost structure of a franchised restaurant. On the other hand, there is the question of opportunity loss — someone else might go in if we did not. There is also a great market potential. The Western food market in Japan is large and growing at a 40% annual rate. We're ambitious to grow in the restaurant area. If we are to reach our 1981 sales target, we need to develop several lines besides Chinese food. Despite the risks, Mövenpick fits into our plans.

HOTEL OPERATIONS IN EGYPT

In the mid-1970s, the Egyptian government agency for tourism and hotels asked Mövenpick to manage a bungalow-type hotel near the Pyramids outside Cairo. At the time of the request, the hotel had not yet been constructed, but the prefabricated aluminum bungalows had already been ordered from a Belgian supplier. Mövenpick agreed to accept the management contract only if they could control the architectural design and furnishing of the hotel. Although Mövenpick considered the Belgian bungalows to be beneath the company's usual standards, Mövenpick believed that the bungalows could be incorporated into an appropriate Mövenpick plan. The government agency agreed to the terms and granted Mövenpick an architectural and management contract.

The hotel was owned by the government and local businessmen. For managing the hotel, an operating company had been formed. Although Mövenpick had no interest in investing in the hotel's owning company, Mövenpick did agree to leave the fees it earned from its architectural services with the new hotel to serve as working capital. In exchange, Mövenpick acquired a 50% position in the hotel's operating company. Under the venture agreement, the operating company received 25% of gross operating profits (or losses) and the owning company received 75%. In addition, Mövenpick received 2% of total sales. Mövenpick was exempt from Egyptian taxes (about 40% of earnings) for the first five years of operations.

In a feasibility study done in October 1975, Mövenpick forecast the following sales and gross operating profits:

Annual operating forecast for the Jolie Ville Hotel, Cairo

At occupancy rate of:	75%	95%
Total sales Sfr.	7,312,800	9,191,600
Gross operating profit Sfr.	3,356,000	4,272,000

The Jolie Ville Hotel at the Pyramids opened in October 1976. In the fall of 1977, Herr Ammann, assistant manager of the hotel, commented on the success of the Mövenpick venture in Egypt:

We came into the market at just the right time. We have occupancy rates which are almost unheard of in the hotel business. This situation arises again and again in developing countries. A new market opens up and demand soars. Then everyone comes in and either builds new hotels or extends their current opera-

tions. The result is overcapacity. Right now hotel rooms are hard to get in Cairo. In five years, we'll be overbuilt.

Mövenpick's advantage is its ability to exploit this kind of situation. The big hotels, like the Hiltons and the Intercontinentals, have certain standards to live up to, and, therefore, they cannot afford to go "prefab."[2] Their type of hotel takes five or six years to build. Mövenpick, on the other hand, can put up a prefabricated hotel in eight months, reach pay-back in a couple of years, and have two or three very profitable years left before the competitors open their new hotels. When this happens and the industry enters overcapacity, we simply shut down our operations and start again in another developing market. We'll be able to catch the markets at the most profitable times.

The big risk and the big money is in developing countries. The way of doing business in these countries also varies. For one thing, it's impossible to insist on Swiss standards. You have to adapt to the local ones. Also, Mövenpick is constrained when it comes to management personnel; and, in order to expand in the developing countries, we will need more people with experience in these areas.

Herr Baur, however, disagreed with the strategy of leaving a new market after a short time. He believed that such actions would tend to give Mövenpick a bad name. Instead, Herr Baur considered Mövenpick in Egypt to be a long-term investment, and Mövenpick was currently planning to expand its operations in the country. Herr Baur foresaw Mövenpick's foreign expansion beginning with a pilot operation in a country or region. If the pilot operation proved successful, at least two other operations would be added in the locality and this local or regional base would become relatively autonomous in the long run. One of the main reasons for establishing several operations in the same area was the scarcity of available managerial personnel at Mövenpick. Under the current plan, several operations could be united under a single regional management.

Mövenpick had already completed a study concerning the building of another tourist hotel near the present Jolie Ville site. The total cost of the 272 guestroom project was approximately Sfr. 31 million, of which Sfr. 1.5 million would go to Mövenpick for architect and engineering fees and expenses. The hotel was expected to achieve an 80–90% occupancy rate over the next five years. Mövenpick was to receive a management fee of 15% of gross operating profits or approximately 6.5% of

---

[2]The colloquial term "prefab" referred to a building constructed from component parts manufactured prior to their assembly on a site.

total sales. Mövenpick projected a return on equity before taxes for the owning company of almost 30%.

Mövenpick was also negotiating to build and manage another Jolie Ville-type motel on the road between Cairo and Luxor and another in Luxor itself. Because of their locations, these motels would be almost completely for tourist use. Furthermore, Mövenpick was considering building the same style of prefabricated motel in other Arab countries.

ORGANIZATION FOR INTERNATIONAL EXPANSION

Mövenpick was organized into nine line divisions and six staff divisions. (See *Exhibit 5* for an abbreviated organization chart.) The managers of the line divisions met once a month with Herr Prager and his General Secretary, Dr. Wang, to discuss company strategy. Dr. Wang commented on these executive board meetings:

> At these meetings we discuss ideas for new ventures. Anyone can bring up a new idea or introduce a new lead. Then we decide which division the venture would fall under. The manager of that division then has the responsibility to pursue the idea. If a division is overloaded, however, the manager simply refuses to take on a new venture.

All international projects were currently handled by the Mövenpick Planning and Management Division (MPM), headed by Herr Baur. The Division performed a number of very different functions within Mövenpick:

1. The MPM was responsible for the planning and implementation of all architectural, technical, and construction activities necessary for the establishment and maintenance of Mövenpick restaurants and hotels. The Division included 39 managers and professionals in the areas of architecture, kitchen design, product planning, and operations. Aside from working on expansion projects for Mövenpick, the MPM also carried out architectural design work for third parties. In this function MPM competed with regular architectural bureaus.

2. The MPM had responsibility for exploiting foreign market opportunities through marketing Mövenpick's accumulated know-how in the fields of establishing and managing restaurant and hotel operations. All outside management contracts, franchising, and consulting were handled by MPM.

3. The MPM was responsible for all hotel operations of Mövenpick.

EXHIBIT 5. Abbreviated organization chart

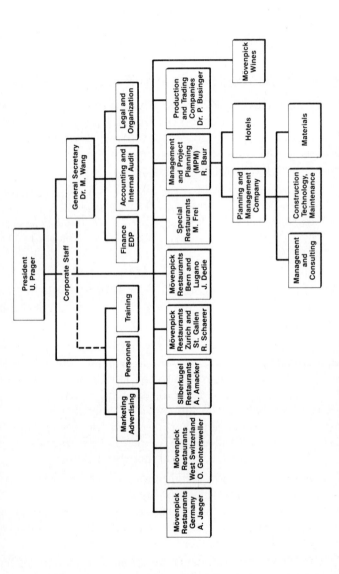

Herr Baur, commenting on the present and future role of MPM, remarked:

> *MPM should not be an operating company; that is, it should only be a temporary operating company. We want to set up regional companies which are able to operate independently. The role of MPM is to act as a service department for the other divisions of Mövenpick. We prepare consulting studies, and we plan and realize projects. Our responsibilities toward a project vary according to the division with whom we are working. The Swiss and German operations, with their relatively large staffs, only use us for pre-opening planning. The plans are actually implemented by the Swiss and German divisions. Within the next 18 months, we may establish an International subdivision with MPM, which would function similar to our present Hotels subdivision. International projects such as the Jolie Ville in Cairo would report to this International division instead of reporting directly to me. Once a regional operation becomes large enough — for example, three hotels in Egypt — it would leave International and MPM and become a regional division in itself.*

VIEWS OF MÖVENPICK'S PRESIDENT

The history and future of Mövenpick was heavily dependent on the personal beliefs, judgment, and management style of the company's founder and president, Herr Ueli Prager. Herr Prager had made the following comments on the evolution of Mövenpick:

Mövenpick's Concept of Operation

The critical step in my climb up the career ladder was my decision to join the Hoteltreuhandgesellschaft.[3] Immediately after the war (World War II), many large and small hotels developed financial difficulty as a result of the instantaneous cut back in travel and tourism. Those hotels then turned to the Hoteltreuhandgesellschaft with their troubles. It was my job to investigate the validity of the requests for support from distressed properties. The constant confrontation with marginal properties . . . developed in me, first unconsciously, a picture of the ideal operation. Although I realize today that my ideal in its pure sense cannot be converted to reality, it remains the basis upon which I developed my concepts. I dreamed of an operation without fluctuations during the year, during the 7-day week and during the 18-hour business day.

I perceived an operation which was neither affected by the moods of a specific class of people, the seasons, weather, nor political situations. I preferred to have a small profit daily, but then 365 days a year. If even later many mistakes and faulty performances occurred, I have tried never to lose this basic belief. For this

---

[3]Certified public accounting firm for the hotel and restaurant business in Switzerland.

reason, we stay away from pure resort locations which are highly seasonal. Egypt is somewhat of an exception, but we have no investment there. You need some flexibility in your concepts.

Mövenpick's International Expansion

There are certainly strategic decisions which are based on thorough analysis and planning. But there are also events which happen to you. Our international expansion falls into the latter category. You go through a process of maturing: You develop your business at home, you start playing with the idea "maybe we could also expand abroad," and then you are presented with an opportunity, and you grab it.

Our project in Egypt happened this way. There is a publishing house in Zurich, they print souvenir books with photos of Egyptian art treasures. They approached us with the proposal that it might be a good idea if the tourists in Egypt, tired from their visits to the museums, could rest in a Mövenpick restaurant. We were willing to entertain the idea, the Egyptians sent some plane tickets, and we went over to discuss the possibility of a restaurant in a museum. While we were there, I made a courtesy call to the Egyptian organization of tourism. The official in charge and I liked each other instantaneously, the way it sometimes happens when you meet somebody new. After a few minutes he posed the question: "Do you want to build a hotel near the Pyramids?" I was not prepared for this question, but it was the beginning of a very successful cooperation.

I had never planned to have a hotel at the Pyramids, but that's the way it goes, you open yourself gradually to such ideas and then comes the opportunity. Japan was similar. I had never had a long-range plan to expand in Japan; but then one day some Japanese businessman walked into our office with the idea of opening a chain of restaurants in Japan.

Mövenpick's Strengths and Weaknesses

Our strengths are flexibility, widespread knowledge of the restaurant and hotel business, the ability to feel what is the right formula for a restaurant, and being broadly rather than narrowly specialized.

Our weaknesses are having too many alternatives which occasionally lead us to inconsistent actions, and finding it difficult to define our corporate identity and the scope of our operations.

SUMMARY

It was against this background that Herr Baur and Dr. Wang investigated the current offer to manage five to ten major hotels across Europe. The hotels were quite different from one another but all of them were in excellent locations, and with proper management and efficient controls they could be turned into very lucrative ventures. Herr Baur was not sure, however, how these hotels would fit into the rest of Mövenpick's business. He commented:

> *If we accept this project, we will have to say no to other opportunities that may be closer to our existing skills. Those hotels seem very attractive, but even in the long run they could remain something that looks quite different from our other operations.*

While Mövenpick attributed much of its success to an entrepreneurial willingness to jump at new opportunities, Herr Baur worried that MPM's problem now was too many opportunities. As he reflected on Mövenpick's international expansion in the past, he contemplated how the company could better assess which opportunities to pursue.

Mövenpick Unternehmungen: Excerpts from a Company Document on Guidelines for Mövenpick's International Expansion

TASKS AND ACTIVITIES

It must be recognized that the availability of management capacity for international activities is limited. A careful and selective approach for international expansion is, therefore, necessary.

International projects should have a long-term attractiveness and allow the strengthening of Mövenpick's identity in the market.

We should concentrate on activities for which we have already developed strengths and which further the goodwill and the international reputation of Mövenpick Unternehmungen. In particular, we are thinking of international expansion with the following proven types of operation:

> Mövenpick restaurants
>
> Silberkugel restaurants
>
> Hotels of the Jolie Ville class

In terms of geographical spread, the following guidelines apply:

on the one hand, geographical clustering to facilitate regional management and control

on the other hand geographical dispersion with respect to

- growth potential
- markets
- spread of political risk

What activities do we engage in?

- Concept and feasibility studies
- Planning and implementation of construction projects
- Assistance in getting and keeping operations ready
- Management of third party operations
- Franchising
- Own operations
- Consulting in exceptional cases

What activities do we *not* engage in?

- General contracting beyond our range of operations
- Planning without plan implementation

- Projects without chances of economic success
- Management of operations without the possibility to implement our concepts of restaurant and hotel management
- Growth "at any cost"

OBJECTIVES

As a matter of principle, the following guidelines apply for investments in distant foreign countries:

Capital investments in a foreign country shall only be made if concept planning jobs and architectural services rendered in that country generate sufficient revenues to adequately cover the proposed investment, or if the funds necessary for the investment have already been earned in that particular country.

All such investments should reach the following target rate of return: annual net profits minus a management charge of 2% of sales should amount to at least 50% of total invested capital.

For pure management contracts coupled with the use of the Mövenpick trademark, a minimum remuneration of 2% of sales plus adequate participation in profits should be negotiated (rough rule: profit share should equal royalty income computed on the basis of sales volume).

NEW PROJECTS

As a matter of principle, the Mövenpick Planning and Management Division (MPM) engages only in "paid acquisition" of new projects; i.e. possible new ventures will be evaluated through paid feasibility studies.

The only exceptions from this principle are projects that appear particularly interesting from a strategic point of view.

For the entry into new markets, MPM may form a joint venture with a local partner who has particular strengths in the market that Mövenpick is lacking.

The cooperation with a local partner should be based on the principle of division of labor. In all cases, however, Mövenpick will perform the following functions:

- project planning
- plan implementation
- management of operations.

Management of a new operation by Mövenpick is only possible if MPM was also responsible for the planning of the project.

USE OF THE MÖVENPICK TRADEMARK

Possible only if:

we planned the operation

we evaluate and approve the operation and if it was built and is managed according to Mövenpick business principles.

PART 2
Designing Multinational Marketing Programs

Introduction

Readings

2.1. Can You Standardize Multinational Marketing? by Robert D. Buzzell

2.2. The Globalization of Markets by Theodore Levitt

Cases

2.3. Hoover: Multinational Product Planning by Robert D. Buzzell and Jean-Louis LeCocq

2.4. Computervision Japan by Rowland Moriarty

2.5. Fisher-Price Benelux by Robert D. Buzzell, Carlos del Nero, and Stephen Muirhead

2.6. Minolta Camera Co., Ltd. by Ulrich Wiechmann

2.7. British Airways by John A. Quelch

Managers responsible for marketing in a multinational enterprise must design appropriate marketing programs for each national market. To some extent, each country must be treated as a separate marketplace, because each has its own currency, legal requirements, and methods of doing business. However, by coordinating operations on a regional or global scale, multinationals can gain important competitive advantages.

The cases and readings in Part 2 illustrate some of the major issues involved in the development of multinational marketing programs. Broadly speaking, development comprises two distinctive aspects: One is the extent to which marketing program elements are *standardized* across national markets, rather than being tailored, or customized, to each country's individual characteristics. The pros and cons of standardization are discussed in the readings by Buzzell and Levitt. The second distinctive feature is the need in multinational marketing to *harmonize* the programs that have been adopted for the different national markets, even when they are extremely diverse. It is vital to avoid doing things in one country that may adversely affect results in other markets.

Issues related to standardization versus customization and to harmonizing multinational programs arise in connection with each of the major elements of the "marketing mix" — product/service policies, pricing, communications, and distribution.

PRODUCT/SERVICE POLICIES

Companies typically evolve from strictly domestic to multinational operations by exploiting their product development and manufacturing capabilities. A traditional model of this evolutionary process suggests that there is a "product life cycle" that includes four stages:

- An initial stage, in which a new product is developed in the United States (or another large, highly developed market) and then exported to other markets;
- A second stage, during which production in foreign markets begins;
- A third stage, in which producers from the original home market compete with those in other locations for worldwide export markets; and
- A final stage, characterized by imports into the original home market.

Louis T. Wells found that this so-called international trade life cycle described the histories of numerous consumer and industrial products during the 1950s and 1960s.[1] More recently, it seems clear that the United States no longer has the dominance that it once did in originating new products. But it is still true that innovations are usually first introduced in large, highly developed nations like the United States and subsequently spread to other smaller nations.

The fact that a producer transfers a successful product from its home market to other countries implies that multinational products are bound to be standardized to some degree. What the multinational has to offer, in competition with domestic producers in the same industry, is a product or service that is distinctive in some ways — based on patents, proprietary processes, specialized design capabilities, or possibly lower production costs. Transferring any of these competitive advantages to other national markets requires that at least some major components of the product be held constant. It is not surprising, therefore, that most multinationals offer identical, or very similar, products in most of the markets they serve. A survey of multinational consumer products companies carried out in the mid-1970s showed, for instance, that product characteristics, brand names, and packaging were usually highly standardized among North American and European markets.[2]

The more similar markets are, in terms of income levels, climate, and other characteristics, the more likely it is that they can and will accept the same kinds of products. When multinationals enter less-developed countries (LDCs), however, considerably greater modifications in products are usually required. One study of 174 consumer products showed that "only about one item in ten is transferred into developing country markets without modification."[3] Examples of modifications for LDC markets include smaller package sizes, simplified usage instructions, substitution of local ingredients, and toned-down advertising claims.

Even when a company begins its multinational operations with an essentially standardized product line, its policy may evolve over time toward one of greater diversity among markets. The managers of subsidiaries are often allowed, or even encouraged, to add products or services to the original line to meet specific local needs. The extent of this

---

[1] Louis T. Wells, Jr., "A Product Life Cycle for International Trade?," *Journal of Marketing* 32 (July 1986), pp. 1–6.

[2] Ralph Z. Sorenson and Ulrich E. Wiechmann, "How Multinationals View Marketing Standardization," *Harvard Business Review* (May–June 1975), pp. 38ff.

[3] John S. Hill and Richard R. Still, "Adapting Products to LDC Tastes," *Harvard Business Review* (March–April 1984), pp. 92–101.

kind of "evolutionary adaptation" in product offerings is usually closely related to a company's management philosophy regarding decentralization of authority, as discussed in Part 3.

The trend toward "globalization" of markets during the 1970s and 1980s (see Reading 2.2 by Theodore Levitt) reflects the increasing pressures for product standardization. In fact, in many industries, the advantages of standardizing at least the major components of a product make globalization virtually mandatory. It would be inconceivable, for example, for Boeing or Airbus Industrie to supply different passenger aircraft to customers in each country. The increasing importance of scale economies is also forcing greater standardization in products that, traditionally, *did* vary among countries. A prime example is automobiles. James Leontiades has vividly documented the changes in automobile design in his description of the Ford Motor Company's "Fiesta" model (originally named the "Bobcat").[4]

> *Development of the Fiesta began in 1972. It was conceived from the outset as a standardized car for all of Western Europe, and all of Ford's European subsidiary managers supplied inputs into the design process. Prior to the Fiesta, Ford and competing manufacturers had been more sensitive to supposed differences in national tastes: Italian drivers were thought to have strong preferences for speed, for example, while the French were reputed to value riding comfort more highly. Notwithstanding these differences, according to a Ford executive quoted by Leontiades, "There has to be a global strategy because it is getting so incredibly expensive to create new car model lines."[5]*

While proponents of global strategies advocate designing products to meet the needs of multinational markets, not many companies appear to follow their advice. It is still much more common, we believe, for products to be developed initially for a single market (usually the home market) and offered later, perhaps with modifications, in other markets. An interesting exception was the Canon line of "Personal Copiers" developed in 1980. This Japanese product was designed to use paper sizes that are commonly used in the United States and Europe but not in Japan![6] Presumably the product's sales potential in the North American and European markets was thought to be large enough to compensate for reduced home market sales.

---

[4]James C. Leontiades, *Multinational Corporate Strategy* (Lexington, MA: Lexington Books, 1985), Chapter 3.

[5]*Ibid.*, p. 34.

[6]Yoko Ishikura, "Canon, Incorporated – B," Harvard Business School Case Services No. 9-384-151 (Boston, 1984).

PRICING

Designing and implementing effective price policies is an especially thorny problem for multinational enterprises. Because of differences in taxes, variations in distribution systems, and other factors, prices are to some extent uncontrollable by management. As one consumer product marketing executive put it:

> Price is probably the marketing mix element which is most difficult to standardize because of country-to-country differences. . . . Unfortunately, in many instances we have almost no discretion over what we charge in a particular market."[7]

For many multinationals, an important motivation for attempting to charge uniform prices is to avoid, or at least minimize, the transshipment of products from one country to another. Transshipments, also called "gray market" sales, occur when differences in prices between countries are sufficiently large to cover the costs involved in moving products from one to the other. For example, during the early 1980s the U.S. dollar was very highly valued relative to other currencies, and gray market imports of higher-priced European cars increased sharply. (The European models did not meet U.S. safety and emission standards, so importers had to incur conversion costs in addition to transportation and import duties. Even so, it was possible to save substantial sums.)

Gray market sales are troublesome for multinationals for several reasons. One is that such product flows often disrupt relationships with dealers or distributors. Mercedes, for instance, must have received strong complaints from U.S. dealers located near ports of entry during the peak period of gray market imports. If cross-border flows are large enough relative to total sales, they can virtually negate a company's efforts to maintain any control over dealer/distributor sales and service programs. Another undesirable result of substantial gray market sales is that they make it hard to hold management in the "importing" country responsible for results.

If price differentials among national markets cause so many disruptions, why are such differentials so common? There are several possible explanations:

- Countries differ in terms of the structure and costs of their distribution systems. The result may be big differences in the total "spread" between factory and end user selling prices, creating an opportunity to buy in the low-cost market and resell in the high-cost one.

---

[7]Sorenson and Wiechmann, *op. cit.*, p. 44.

- Legal restrictions or government policies may constrain latitude more in some countries than others.[8] Multinational pharmaceutical producers, for example, make most of their sales in some countries to governmental health care agencies. Some of these agencies exert strong pressures for lower prices, while others are more lenient. (See Case 1.4 on "The World Pharmaceutical Industry.")

- Managers may believe that the price elasticity of demand differs significantly from one country to another. If there were no cross-border flows, profits would be maximized by setting prices for each market independently. Even if some transshipments do take place, profits may be higher with varying prices than with a uniform worldwide price.

- Tax rates vary among countries. For companies that export products (or components) from one nation to others, taxes may be reduced by establishing intracompany *transfer prices* in such a way as to reduce the total tax burden. (The extent to which this can be done is limited, however, by tax regulations.) If transfer prices differ among countries, the end result is likely to be that final selling prices differ, too.

There are, then, conflicting pressures on prices in a multinational business — some that favor standardization and others that favor diversity. The challenge for managers is to balance all of the factors that are operative in a particular situation.

DISTRIBUTION

Distribution channels perform important functions for producers and for customers — they maintain local stocks, provide promotional support, and supply services including customer education, repairs, and financing. In most cases, multinational businesses would like to have all of these functions carried out in similar ways in all markets. But often there are real limitations on the extent to which distribution mechanisms, or their activities, can be standardized. The retail and wholesale distribution institutions available to a multinational supplier differ considerably among markets — especially the developed countries and LDC markets. The multinational business seldom has any choice but to

---

[8]An extreme case of legal restrictions on pricing is the type of direct price regulation imposed by some countries during periods of severe inflation. In the 1980s, price controls were adopted in Mexico, Kenya, Pakistan, and Brazil, among others. See Victor H. Frank, Jr., "Living with Price Control Abroad," *Harvard Business Review* (March–April 1984), pp. 137–142.

adapt its approaches to the distribution systems that are in place. There are some exceptions: U.S.-based door-to-door selling companies have succeeded in creating entirely new methods of distribution in other countries, as have some fast-food franchisors such as McDonald's and Dunkin' Donuts.

At one time there were major differences in distribution systems even among highly developed countries. These differences have, however, diminished during the 1970s and 1980s. Thus, suppliers of packaged consumer products can distribute through large, self-service outlets in all developed country markets. As living standards rise in the LDCs, it seems likely that their systems will also evolve in similar ways. Moreover, there are now some retailers who operate multinationally themselves. Examples include Benetton (Case 1.3) and Burberry in apparel and Ikea and Conran in home furnishings. Manufacturers supplying this type of channel are assured of very similar distribution services in all of the markets involved. It should be noted, however, that most of the multinational retailers emphasize their own brands rather than manufacturers' branded products.

As noted in the section above on pricing, international variations in distribution costs give rise to differences in end-user prices and thereby lead to cross-border product flows. To limit this problem, and for other reasons, it is important for multinationals to pay close attention to dealer/distributor relationships in each market. This task is complicated by differences in trade practices, legal restrictions, and historical patterns of evolution in distribution systems. Managers of U.S.-based companies, for example, are accustomed to patterns of trade relationships that are governed by U.S. legal restrictions on "price discrimination." In countries that have no such restrictions, negotiating prices and terms of sale with competing dealers or distributors presents unfamiliar problems.

MARKETING COMMUNICATIONS

The communications element of multinational marketing programs has been the focal point of widespread debate during the 1980s. Theodore Levitt's 1983 article on "The Globalization of Markets" (Reading 2.2) provoked a storm of controversy among advertising people, especially executives of major advertising agencies that handle multinational accounts. According to proponents of the global approach, the increasing similarity of consumers' lifestyles around the world, and the increasing standardization of products (owing to scale economies), imply that advertising and sales promotion methods should likewise be standardized among countries. This argument was put forward with particular vigor by those advertising agencies that had "global" capabilities. Others argued, equally strongly, that differences in language, customs, and other national characteristics are still sufficiently important to require at least some modifications in marketing communications.

The idea of a standardized approach to marketing communications has become increasingly appealing in recent years for two reasons. First, as products have become more standardized, both personal selling and advertising are bound to become more uniform among markets. This is especially true for new types of products and services, such as computers, that are relatively "culture free" — at least in comparison with traditional products like foods and cosmetics. But even marketers of some long-established products have adopted global communications approaches: In 1985, for example, International Playtex adopted a uniform worldwide brand name and advertising campaign for its "Wow" brassieres.[9] (The product's specifications were *not* standardized, however, because of differences in customer sizes and shapes.) Other marketers that have employed standardized multinational programs, or that have experimented with this approach, are Coca-Cola and Pepsico, Philip Morris, and Sunbeam.

A second reason for increasing multinational standardization of marketing communications has to do with changes in communications media. Until recently many countries, even highly developed ones, had no commercial television facilities. But traditional government policies in this area have been changing, and by the mid-1980s commercial TV channels were available in most major markets. This, in itself, has led to a greater similarity in advertising, in terms of both budget allocations among media and the use of centrally produced commercials. Differences in the kinds of media available continue to be important, however, in many countries. In LDC markets, in particular, marketers must rely more heavily on such devices as sponsorship of concerts and sporting events, because TV and print media coverage is inadequate.

An even more dramatic change in communications may come about because of the growth of media vehicles that reach multinational, or even global, audiences. Multinational media are most fully developed in professional and technical fields: Producers of machine tools, computer-related products/services, and health care products can reach their major customers on a multinational scale through journals, trade shows, videotapes, and similar channels. More recently, multinational consumer media have begun to emerge. Direct satellite television broadcasting over the "Sky Channel," initiated in the early 1980s, reaches an audience

---

[9]"Playtex Kicks Off a One-Ad-Fits-All Campaign," *Business Week* (December 16, 1985), pp. 48–49.

of viewers in several West European countries. As satellite broadcasting facilities are further developed in the future, it seems probable that more and more advertising will be designed for multinational audiences. There are, however, still many obstacles to this approach. Boris Wilenkin of Unilever concluded in 1983 that " . . . direct broadcasting via satellite is [still] too blunt an instrument for the majority of Pan-European marketers."[10] One important limitation of the approach, in Wilenkin's view, is that it conflicts with the traditional autonomy of local subsidiary managers in individual country markets. Thus, decisions about communications, like those affecting other elements of multinational marketing programs, depend on organizational factors as well as cost-benefit trade-offs viewed from a global perspective. These organizational factors are explored in Part 3 of this volume.

---

[10]Boris C.G. Wilenkin, "A European Perspective on Media Changes and Their Implications," in Robert D. Buzzell (ed.), *Marketing in an Electronic Age* (Boston: Harvard Business School Press, 1985), pp. 175–185.

2.1 *READING*

Can You Standardize Multinational Marketing?

Robert D. Buzzell

Multinational companies emerged in the late fifties as important competitors in an ever-growing number of industries. As the trade barriers in Western Europe and elsewhere diminished, more and more companies found attractive opportunities for expansion in countries other than their traditional home markets. For some of these companies, operations abroad became so extensive and so complex as to require significant changes in organization and operating meth-

Authors note: I wish to acknowledge the valuable contributions of Richard Aylmer and Jean-Louis LeCocq, who conducted interviews with executives of multinational companies under my direction during 1967. This research was conducted under a joint project of the Harvard Business School and the European Institute of Business Administration (INSEAD), and was supported by research grants of The Ford Foundation.

ods. The problems confronting management in a truly multinational company are clearly different in degree, if not in kind, from those of traditional firms.

WHAT ABOUT MARKETING?

The growing importance of multinational companies has stimulated a flood of comment and advice. Conferences, seminars, and surveys have probed the distinctive financial, legal, accounting, organizational, and personnel problems of this new breed of enterprise. In all of this discussion, however, relatively little has been said about marketing.

To be sure, some advertising men have advocated the adoption of uniform advertising approaches, on the grounds that fundamental consumer motives are essentially the same everywhere. This proposition often has a partisan tone, however, especially when it is put forward by executives of large advertising agencies with international networks of subsidiary and affiliate offices. More importantly, the question of advertising approaches cannot be considered realistically in isolation from other elements of a company's marketing "mix" in each market, including its product line, packaging, pricing, distribution system, salesforce, and other methods of promotion.

Is it practical to consider the development of a marketing strategy, in terms of *all* of its elements, on a multinational scale? The conventional wisdom suggests that a multinational approach is *not* realistic, because of the great differences that still exist — and probably always will exist — among nations. For example, George Weissman, President of Philip Morris, Inc., has concluded that "until we achieve One World there is no such thing as international marketing, only local marketing around the world."[1] Apparently most other marketing executives agreed with this view. Millard H. Pryor, Jr., Director of Corporate Planning for Singer Company, wrote:

> *"Marketing is conspicuous by its absence from the functions which can be planned at the corporate headquarters level. . . . The operating experience of many international firms appears to confirm the desirability of assigning long-range planning of marketing activities to local managers."*[2]

---

[1] "International Expansion," in *Plotting Marketing Strategy, A New Orientation,* edited by Lee Adler (New York: Simon & Schuster, 1967), p. 229.

[2] "Planning in a Worldwide Business," *Harvard Business Review,* January-Feburary 1965, p. 137.

The prevailing view, then, is that marketing strategy is a local problem. The best strategy for a company will differ from country to country, and the design of the strategy should be left to local management in each country.

TWO-SIDED CASE

But is the answer this simple? The experiences of leading U.S.-based companies since suggest that there may indeed be something to be said in favor of a multinational marketing strategy. This article is intended to outline some of the possibilities — the limitations — of an integrated approach to multinational marketing. My thesis is that, although there are many obstacles to the application of common marketing policies in different countries, there are also some very tangible potential benefits. The relative importance of the pros and cons will, of course, vary from industry to industry and from company to company. But the benefits are sufficiently universal and sufficiently important to merit careful analysis by management in virtually any multinational company. Management should not automatically dismiss the idea of standardizing some parts of the marketing strategy, at least within major regions of the world.

BENEFITS OF STANDARDIZATION

As a practical matter, standardization is not a clear-cut issue. In a literal sense, multinational standardization would mean the offering of *identical* product lines at identical prices through identical distribution systems, supported by identical promotional programs in several different countries. At the other extreme, completely "localized" marketing strategies would contain *no* common elements whatsoever. Obviously, neither of these extremes is often feasible or desirable.

The practical question is: which *elements* of the marketing strategy can or should be standardized, and to what degree? Currently, most multinational companies employ strategies that are much closer to the "localized" end of the spectrum than to the opposite pole. If there are potential benefits of increased standardization, then they would be achieved by incorporating *more* common elements in a multinational strategy. Each marketing aspect of policy should be considered, first, in its own right, and second, in relation to the other elements of the "mix."

Let us examine the most important potential benefits of standardization in multinational marketing strategy.

SIGNIFICANT COST SAVINGS

Differences in national income levels, tastes, and other factors have traditionally dictated the need for local products and corresponding local marketing programs. The annals of international business provide countless examples, even for such apparently similar countries as the United States and Canada. Philip Morris, Inc., for example, tried unsuccessfully to convert Canadian smokers to one of its popular American cigarette brands. The Canadians apparently would rather fight; they preserved their traditional preference for so-called "Virginia-type" tobacco blends. Examples of this kind suggest that to attain maximum sales in each country, a company should offer products, as well as packages, advertisements, and other marketing elements, which are tailored to that country's distinctive needs and desires.

However, maximizing sales is not the only goal in designing a marketing strategy. Profitability depends ultimately on both sales *and* costs, and there are significant opportunities for cost reduction via standardization. The most obvious, and usually the most important, area for cost savings is product design. By offering the same basic product in several markets with some possible variations in functional and/or design features, a manufacturer can frequently achieve longer production runs, spread research and development costs over a greater volume, and thus reduce total unit costs.

THE "ITALIAN INVASION."   The lesson of mass production economies through standardization, first demonstrated by Henry Ford I, was dramatically retaught during the 1960s by the Italian household appliance industry.[3]

In the mid-1950s, total combined Italian production of refrigerators and washing machines was less than 300,000 units; there were no strong Italian appliance manufacturers. In 1955, only 3% of Italian households owned refrigerators, and around 1% owned washing machines.

Starting in the late 1950s, several companies began aggressive programs of product development and marketing. Ironically, some of the Italian entrepreneurs were simply applying lessons learned from America. One member of the Fumagalli family, owners of the appliance firm, Candy, had been a prisoner of war in the United States and brought back the idea of a "a washing machine in every home."

---

[3]See, for example, Philip Siekman, "The Battle for the Kitchen," *Fortune,* January 1964.

The Italian appliance firms installed modern, highly automated equipment, reinvested profits, and produced relatively simple, *standardized* products in great numbers. By 1965, refrigerator output was estimated at 2.6 million units, and washing machine output at 1.5 million units. Much of this volume was sold in Italy; home ownership of the two appliances rose to 50% and 23%, respectively. But the Italian companies were aggressive in export marketing, too; by 1965 Italian-made refrigerators accounted for 32% of the total French market and for 40% to 50% of the Benelux market. Even in Germany, the home market of such electrical giants as AEG, Bosch, and Siemens, the Italian products attained a 12% market share. The export pattern of washing machines has followed that of refrigerators; by 1965 Italian exports had accounted for 10% to 15% of market sales in most other Western European countries.[4]

The success of the Italian appliance industry was a painful experience for the traditional leaders — American, British, and German — as well as for the smaller French companies that had previously had tariff protection. Whirlpool Corporation, which acquired a French refrigerator plant in 1962, subsequently leased the facility to a French competitor. Even Frigidaire, decided, in mid-1967, to close down its refrigerator production in France.

In competition with other European appliance makers, the Italian companies have benefited from some natural advantages in terms of lower wage rates and government export incentives. But mass production of simple, standardized products has been at least equally important. And, according to *Fortune*, "refrigerators have begun to look more and more alike as national tastes in product design give way to an international 'sheer-line' style."

TURNABOUT AT HOOVER.   To compete with this "Italian invasion" in appliances, some of the established manufacturers tried new approaches. An interesting example was the introduction of a new line of automatic washing machines by Hoover Ltd., the market leader in the United Kingdom. Hoover's previous automatics, introduced in 1961,

---

[4]The estimates of production, exports and so forth cited here are given by Carlo Castellano, *L'Industria Degli Elettrodomestici in Italia*, Universita Degli Studi di Genova (Torino, 1965), or are drawn from *Marketing in Europe*, October 1966 and September 1967.

were designed primarily for the British market. The company's new "Keymatic" models featured:

- An exclusive "pulsator" washing action.
- A tilted, enameled steel drum.
- Hot water provided by the home's central hot-water heater.

In contrast, most European manufacturers, including the Italian producers, offered front-loading, tumble-action washers with stainless steel drums and self-contained water heaters. Either because these features were better suited to continental needs, or because so many sellers promoted them, or perhaps both, Hoover saw its position in the major continental markets gradually decline.

When the Hoover management set out to design a new product line, beginning in 1965, it decided to look for a *single* basic design that would meet the needs of housewives in France, Germany, and Scandinavia as well as in the United Kingdom. A committee including representatives of the continental subsidiaries and of the parent company, Hoover Worldwide Corporation (New York), spent many weeks finding mutually acceptable specifications for the new line.

The result, which went on sale in the spring of 1967, was a front-loading, tumble-action machine, closer in concept to the "continental" design than Hoover's previous washers, but with provisions for "hot water fill" and enameled steel drums on models to be sold in the United Kingdom. By standardizing most of the key design elements in the new machine, Hoover was able to make substantial savings in development costs, tooling, and unit production costs.

OTHER ECONOMIES. The potential economies of standardization are not confined solely to product design decisions. In some industries, packaging costs represent a significant part of total costs. Here, too, standardization may offer the possibility of savings. Charles R. Williams cites the case of a food processor selling prepared soups throughout Europe in 11 different packages. He observes, "The company believes it could achieve a significant savings in cost and at the same time reduce consumer confusion by standardizing the packaging."[5]

---

[5]"Regional Management Overseas," *Harvard Business Review,* January-February 1967, p. 89.

Still another area for cost savings is that of advertising. For some of the major package goods manufacturers, the production of art work, films, and other advertising materials costs millions of dollars annually. Although differences in language limit the degree of standardization that can be imposed, *some* common elements can often be used. To illustrate, in 1966 Pepsi-Cola was bottled in 465 plants and sold in 110 countries outside the United States. Part of its foreign advertising was done by films. According to one of the company's top marketing executives, "We have found that it is possible . . . to produce commercial films overseas in one market, if planned properly, for use in most (but not all) of our international markets." According to company estimates, the added cost of producing separate films for each market would be $8 million per year.[6]

All of these examples illustrate the same basic point: standardization of product design, packaging, and promotional materials *can* offer important economies to the multinational marketer. Even if these cost savings are attained at the expense of lower sales in some markets, the net effect on profits may be positive.

CONSISTENCY WITH CUSTOMERS

Quite apart from the possibilities of cost reduction, some multinational companies are moving toward standardization in order to achieve consistency in their dealings with customers. Executives of these companies believe that consistency in product style, in sales and customer service, in brand names and packages, and generally in the "image" projected to customers, is a powerful means of increasing sales.

If all customers lived incommunicado behind their respective national frontiers, there would be no point in worrying about this matter; only diplomatic couriers and border-crossing guards would ever notice any inconsistencies in products, services, or promotion. But in reality, of course, this is not the case. The most visible type of cross-border flow is international travel by tourists and businesspeople. Especially in Europe, with its relatively high income levels and short distances, the number of people visiting other countries reached flood proportions in the 1960s, and shows no sign of abating today. If the German tourist in Spain sees his accustomed brands in the store, he is likely to buy them

---

[6]See Norman Heller, "How Pepsi-Cola Does It in 110 Countries," in *New Ideas for Successful Marketing*, edited by John S. Wright and Jac L. Goldstucker (Chicago: American Marketing Association, 1966), p. 700.

during his visit. More important, his re-exposure to the products and their advertising may strengthen his loyalty back home or, at least, protect him from the temptation to change his allegiance to a competitor.

Then there is the flow of communications across boundaries. Magazines, newspapers, radio and television broadcasts — all including advertising — reach international audiences. For example, according to estimates by Young & Rubicam International:

- German television broadcasts are received by 40% of Dutch homes with TV sets.
- *Paris Match* has a circulation of 85,000 in Belgium, 26,000 in Switzerland, and substantial readership in Luxemburg, Germany, Italy, and Holland.
- On an average day, over 4 million French housewives tune to Radio Luxemburg; the same broadcast reaches 620,000 Belgian housewives, 30,000 in Switzerland, and 100,000 in Holland.[7]

The possibility of reaching multimarket audiences with common advertising messages, and the risk of confusion that may result from reaching such audiences with different brand names and promotional appeals, has led some of the major consumer goods producers to explore ways and means of standardizing at least the basic elements of their European campaigns. For instance, The Nestlé Company, Inc. and Unilever Ltd., probably the most experienced multinational consumer goods firms at the time, both moved in the direction of more "unified" European advertising during the 1960s. When Nestlé launched "New Nescafé" in 1961–1962, for example, the same basic theme ("Fresh-ground aroma") and very similar creative treatments were used not only throughout Europe, but also in other markets such as Australia. The value of this approach is, perhaps, reflected in the fact that several years later Nescafé was the leading brand of instant coffee in every European country.

PRESSURES FROM CUSTOMERS. During the 1960s an additional argument for consistency in marketing strategy emerged — the needs of the multinational *customer*. Increasingly, both consumer and industrial goods manufacturers find themselves selling to companies which themselves operate on a multinational scale. Industrial users, retail chains, and wholesalers with operations in several countries may buy centrally; even if they do not, personnel in one country often have experience in

---

[7]*When Is a Frontier Not a Frontier?* (pamphlet) Brussels, May 1966.

other countries, or communicate with their counterparts in these countries. In either case, there is a strong pressure on the seller to offer similar products, prices, and services in each market. Thus, IBM standardized the services provided to customers, the duties and training of sales and service personnel, and even the organization of branch offices, on a worldwide basis. A major reason for this policy was the need to provide the same level of service to major customers, such as international banks, in each of the several countries where they do business with IBM.

In some industries, multinational customers virtually force suppliers to standardize products, prices, and terms of sale. If a better deal is available in one country than another, the customer may find it worthwhile to transship goods and will do so.

In certain industries, trade and professional associations exert a pressure toward standardization similar to that exerted by multinational customers. Engineers, chemists, doctors, computer programmers — these groups and many others hold conferences, publish journals, and exchange ideas on an international basis. One result is that companies selling products to professional and technical groups find it advantageous to standardize their offerings. This factor may even affect consumer goods; the marketing director of a major food-processing company told us that dietetic products must be sold on the same basis everywhere because "science and teaching are international anyway."

IMPROVED PLANNING & CONTROL

Flows of people and information across national boundaries may affect multinational marketing strategy in still another way. Consider the following situation:

Philips Gloeilampenfabrieken, one of the world's largest producers of electrical products, found that prices of some of its appliances in Holland were being undercut by as much as 30% by the company's own German subsidiary! How did this come to pass? The German subsidiary had lower costs than the Dutch plant, and sold at lower prices to meet the more intensive competition of the German appliance market. Wholesalers buying from Philips in Germany had a further incentive to sell to outside customers on account of a 7% export subsidy given by the German government. To complete the circle, a European Economic Community anti-trust ruling prohibited manufacturers from interfering with the rights of independent distributors to export freely within the Common Market. Consequently, there was little that Philips could do except to "equalize" prices in the two countries or live with the new sourcing arrangements.[8]

Philips's experience illustrates the difficulty of orderly planning and control by top management if a subsidiary or distributor in Country A is subject to the risk of unpredictable competition from his counterparts in nearby countries B, C, and D.

The feasibility of transshipments among markets obviously varies from one industry to another, depending on the value/weight ratio of the products. Thus, transshipping is common for such items as scientific instruments, cameras, and precision equipment, but relatively rare for major electrical appliances. Even in the food trade, however, cross-border sales increased in volume considerably during the 1960s.

Effective control of transshipping requires harmonization of pricing policies in the multinational company. This does not necessarily mean *equalizing* prices at either the wholesale or retail levels, for if a company's prices to dealers and/or distributors are the same in all countries, then the incentive for transshipping will be eliminated. Rather, it means some adjustments and compromises for the sake of consistency in pricing at the retail and wholesale levels.

EXPLOITING GOOD IDEAS

A fourth argument for standardization is that good marketing ideas and people are hard to find, and should therefore be used as widely as possible. Moreover, good ideas tend to have a universal appeal. This point of view is held especially strongly with regard to the "creative" aspects of advertising and promotional programs. Arthur C. Fatt, Chairman of the Board and Chief Executive Officer of Grey Advertising, Inc., in 1967 stated:

> *"A growing school of thought holds that even different peoples are* basically *the same, and that an international advertising campaign with a truly universal appeal can be effective in any market. . . . If an advertiser has a significant advertising idea at work in one country, not only may it be wasteful but often 'suicidal' to change this idea just for the sake of change."*[9]

---

[8]Reported in *Business Europe,* August 23, 1967, p. 1.

[9]"The Danger of 'Local' International Advertising," *Journal of Marketing,* January 1967, pp. 61–62.

The key word in this statement is "significant." It is the scarcity of really good or significant ideas that encourages standardization. It may be easy to find creative concepts of average quality in each of many different national markets, but really new or unique approaches are not so easily matched.

During the 1960s there were several widely discussed examples of successful application of common advertising themes:

> Esso's "Put a Tiger in Your Tank" campaign, with very minor changes in art and wording, has been used from Southeast Asia to Switzerland. The tiger is, of course, an internationally recognizable symbol for power.
>
> Avis Rent-A-Car has used minor variations on its "We Try Harder" theme throughout Europe as well as in the United States.
>
> Magazine advertisements for Playtex brassieres in many different countries featured the same "stop-action" photographic demonstration of the product's strength and dependability. Although attitudes toward undergarments vary from country to country, Young & Rubicam, Inc. (the Playtex agency) believed that there is a *segment* in each market for which this appeal is effective.

But even the most ardent proponents of the theory that "good ideas are universal" recognize the need to apply the concept with care. Approaches shown to be effective in one market are *likely* to be effective elsewhere, but they do not necessarily apply across the board.

BALANCED APPRAISAL NEEDED

To summarize, then, many companies have found real benefits in a multinational approach to marketing strategy. The gains have included greater effectiveness in marketing, reduced costs, and improved planning and control. Moreover, especially in Western Europe but also in some other parts of the world, social and economic trends are working in favor of more, rather than less, standardization in marketing policies. Tourism, international communication, increased numbers of multinational customers, and other forces are all tending toward greater unification of multinational markets.

But this is just one side of the story. It would be a mistake to assume, as at least a few companies have done, that marketing programs can be transferred from one market to another without careful consideration of the *differences* which still exist. Let us turn next to that side of the picture.

COMMON BARRIERS

Despite the potential benefits of standardization, the great majority of companies still operate on the premise that each national market is different and must therefore be provided with its own, distinctive marketing program. For instance, after a careful study of the marketing policies of U.S. appliance and photographic manufacturers in Europe, Richard Aylmer concluded: "In over 85% of the cases observed, advertising and promotion decisions were based on *local* product marketing objectives."[10]

Why is diversity still the rule of the day in multinational marketing? In many cases, differences simply reflect *customary* ways of doing business which evolved in an earlier period when national boundaries were more formidable barriers than they are today. But even if tradition did not play a role, it must be recognized that there are and will continue to be some important obstacles to standardization.

A comprehensive list of these obstacles would fill many pages, and would include many factors that affect only one or two industries. The most important and generally applicable factors are summarized in *Exhibit 1*. The rows of this exhibit represent the major *classes* of factors which limit standardization in multinational marketing strategies. The columns correspond to different elements of a marketing program. Where they cross is the way in which each factor affects each program element. In effect, each represents a condition or characteristic which *may* differ sufficiently among countries, and *may* require variations in marketing strategies. As we shall see presently, the experiences of multinational companies afford numerous examples of these barriers to standardization. Let us look briefly at each of the four major factors limiting standardization that are listed in *Exhibit 1*.

MARKET CHARACTERISTICS

Perhaps the most *permanent* differences among national markets are those arising from the physical environment — climate, topography, and resources (see the top left of *Exhibit 1*). Climate has an obvious effect on the sales potential for many products, and may also require differences in packaging. Topography influences the density of population,

---

[10]"Marketing Decision-Making in the Multinational Firm," unpublished doctoral thesis. Harvard Business School, 1968.

EXHIBIT 1. Obstacles to standardization in international marketing strategies

Factors limiting standardization	Elements of marketing program				
	Product design	*Pricing*	*Distribution*	*Sales force*	*Advertising & promotion; branding & packaging*
Market characteristics					
Physical environment	Climate Product use conditions		Customer mobility	Dispersion of customers	Access to media Climate
Stage of economic and industrial development	Income levels Labor costs in relation to capital costs	Income levels	Consumer shopping patterns	Wage levels, availability of manpower	Needs for convenience rather than economy Purchase quantities
Cultural factors	"Custom and tradition" Attitudes toward foreign goods	Attitudes toward bargaining	Consumer shopping patterns	Attitudes toward selling	Language, literacy Symbolism
Industry conditions					
Stage of product life cycle in each market	Extent of product differentiation	Elasticity of demand	Availability of outlets Desirability of private brands	Need for missionary sales effort	Awareness, experience with products
Competition	Quality levels	Local costs Prices of substitutes	Competitors' control of outlets	Competitors' sales forces	Competitive expenditures, messages

Marketing institutions

Distributive system	Availability of outlets	Prevailing margins	Number and variety of outlets available	Number, size, dispersion of outlets	Extent of self-service
Advertising media and agencies			Ability to "force" distribution	Effectiveness of advertising, need for substitutes	Media availability, costs, overlaps

Legal restrictions

Product standards Patent laws Tariffs & taxes	Tariffs & taxes Antitrust laws Resale price maintenance	Restrictions on product lines Resale price maintenance	General employment restrictions Specific restrictions on selling	Specific restrictions on messages, costs Trademark laws

and this in turn may have a strong influence on the distribution system available to a manufacturer.

"Product use conditions" include a wide variety of environmental factors affecting marketing strategies. Differences in the size and configuration of homes, for example, have an important bearing on product design for appliances and home furnishings. European kitchens are typically small by U.S. standards, and there is seldom any basement space available to apartment dwellers for laundry facilities. As a result, there is a great emphasis on compactness of design in automatic washers, for they must somehow be fitted into a small and already crowded area. As noted in the example of Hoover Ltd., given earlier, washing machines must also be equipped with self-contained water heating systems to compensate for the lack of central hot-water heaters in most continental homes.

Industrial goods manufacturers also frequently encounter differences in product use conditions. For example, a U.S. producer of farm equipment found that one of his pieces of machinery could not be moved through the narrow, crooked streets of French and Belgian farm villages. In another instance, a chemical industry marketing researcher concluded that there was more dissimilarity than similarity in industrial markets in Europe: "[A factor] which would severely affect the market for surface coatings is the fact that materials used in building construction are vastly different in various parts of Europe. Brick, mortar, and tile are used predominantly in Southern Europe, whereas this is not the case in Northern Germany and in Benelux."[11]

Many similar examples could be cited of differences in the environment which call for variations in product design and other aspects of marketing policy.

DEVELOPMENT STAGE.   Differences among countries in stages of economic and industrial development (second item under "Market characteristics" in *Exhibit 1*) also have a profound influence on marketing strategies. Because of the wide gaps in per capita income levels, many products or models which are regarded as inexpensive staples in the United States or Western Europe must be marketed as "luxuries" elsewhere. Even among the industrialized countries income differences are substantial: Appliance manufacturers such as Philco-Ford Corporation

---

[11]William Gerunsky, "International Marketing Research," in *Chemical Marketing Research*, edited by N.H. Giragosian (New York, Reinhold Publishing Corp., 1967), p. 258.

and Kelvinator of Canada, Ltd. find themselves with little choice but to position their products as deluxe, relatively high-priced, items. This, in turn, implies a very different marketing strategy from that used in the United States.

For industrial products, differences in economic development are reflected in variations in relative costs of capital and labor. Thus, General Electric Company and other companies have sold numerical controls for machine tools to U.S. factories primarily on the basis of labor cost savings. The same approach may be suitable in Germany, where there is a critical shortage of labor. But in most other countries it would be far more difficult to justify numerical controls on the basis of labor substitution.

Differences in income levels may suggest the desirability of systematic price variations. As explained earlier, many companies do charge different prices in different countries, but these variations are seldom, if ever, based solely on incomes.

Consumer shopping patterns and purchase quantities, too, tend to vary with stages of economic development. In underdeveloped countries, there typically are many small retail stores, and many consumers who buy in smaller quantities than do those in highly developed nations. For instance, cigarettes and razor blades are bought one at a time in some countries. Even in England, according to one international marketing executive, "the smallest size of detergent available in U.S. supermarkets is the largest size available in the United Kingdom."

Finally, variations in wage levels may affect choices between personal selling and other forms of promotional effort. One relatively small Italian food processor has a sales force as large as that of General Foods Corporation in the United States. Presumably the salaries of salespersons are proportionately less!

CULTURAL FACTORS. This category is a convenient catch-all for the many differences in market structure and behavior that cannot readily be explained in terms of more tangible factors. Consider, for example, the figures in *Exhibit 2*, which are taken from a survey made by the European Economic Community's Statistical Office. Why do French households consume more than 50 times as much wine as Dutch households, but only two thirds as much milk? No doubt these differences could be explained historically in terms of variations in water, soil and so on. But for practical purposes, it is usually sufficient and certainly more efficient simply to take differences in consumption patterns and attitudes *as given*, and to adjust to them.

There are many examples of cultural differences that have affected

EXHIBIT 2. Average household consumption of beverages, 1963–1964 (in liters)

Country	Milk	Wine	Beer
France	103	116	28
Germany	100	7	46
Holland	153	2	11
Italy	87	95	2

Source: *Le Monde*, weekly overseas edition, February 15–21, 1968, p. 7.

marketing success or failure. One cultural factor is the attitude of consumers toward "foreign" goods. For example, Princess Housewares, Inc., a large U.S. appliance manufacturer in the sixties, introduced a line of electric housewares in the German market. The company's brand name was well known and highly regarded in the United States, but relatively unknown in Germany; and the brand had a definitely "American" sound. The company discovered that the American association was a real drawback among German consumers. According to a survey, fewer than 40% of German individuals felt "confident" about electrical products made in the United States, compared with 91% who were "confident" of German-made products.

Lack of brand awareness, coupled with suspicion of the quality of "American" products, required the company to adopt a very different marketing strategy in Germany than that employed in the United States, where both awareness and a quality image were taken for granted.

INDUSTRY CONDITIONS

A convenient framework for comparing industry and competitive conditions in different national markets is that of the "product life cycle." The histories of many different products in the United States suggest that most of them pass through several distinct *stages* over a period of years, and that marketing strategies typically change from stage to stage.

Some products are in different stages of their life cycles in different national markets. For example, in the sixties, vacuum cleaners were owned by over 75% of the households in Great Britain, Germany, and Switzerland, but by only 10% of the households in Italy and 45% in France. Even more marked contrasts exist today for some newer types of products, such as electric toothbrushes and electric carving knives, which are widely owned in the United States but virtually unknown in most other countries. Such differences in life cycle stages usually call for adaptations of "home country" marketing approaches, if not for completely separate strategies. For example, in late 1965 the Polaroid Corporation introduced the "Swinger" Polaroid Land camera in the United States. The Swinger, with a retail list price of $19.95, was Polaroid's first camera selling for less than $50. The introductory promotion for the new model in the United States placed very heavy emphasis on price; there was no need to explain the basic concept of "instant photography," since millions of Polaroid Land cameras had already been sold over a 17-year period. Surveys indicated that over 80% of U.S. consumers were aware of the name "Polaroid" and of the company's basic product features.

The Swinger was introduced in Europe during 1966. Prior to that time, Polaroid cameras had been extremely high-priced, owing in part to high tariffs, and the company's sales had been at a very low level. Distribution of Polaroid cameras and film was spotty. Most important, fewer than 10% of consumers were aware of the Polaroid instant photography concept.

Under these circumstances, a very different marketing strategy was needed for the Swinger in Europe. Polaroid advertising had to be designed to do a more basic educational job, since awareness of the instant picture principle could not be taken for granted. The promotional program also had to be aimed at building retail distribution, which was also taken for granted in the United States.

If products are in different stages of their life cycles in different countries, then it is tempting to conclude that marketing strategies used in the past in the more "advanced" countries should be used in other "follower" nations. There is some evidence to support this conclusion. For instance, as described earlier, the Italian appliance manufacturers have successfully employed strategies similar to those of Henry Ford in the early 1900s; similarly, Polaroid in the 1960s in Europe profitably used many of the same approaches that it employed in America in the early 1950s. However, history does not repeat itself exactly, and past marketing strategies cannot be reapplied without some modifications.

COMPETITIVE PRACTICES. Another important industry condition, partly but not entirely related to the product life cycle, is the extent of competition in each national market. Differences in products, costs, prices, and promotional levels may permit or even require differences in the strategies used by a multinational company in various markets. Even within the European Common Market, there are still substantial variations in prices of many products, reflecting in part traditional differences in the degree of competition. A survey made in 1967 by the European Economic Community's Statistical Office showed that price variations were still substantial even within the Common Market. Typical prices were compared for some 125 different consumer products by country; on the average, the difference between prices in the countries with the highest and lowest prices was 58%. Even the price of a staple item such as aspirin varied from a high of 38¢ in Germany to a low of 22¢ in Holland.

The growth of multinational companies in itself has tended to reduce traditional differences in competitive practices. For example, advertising expenditures have traditionally been lower in France than in the United States and other European countries; on a per capita basis, total French advertising outlays are around one-eighth those of the United States and one third those of Germany. However, according to M. Andre Bouhebent, a top French advertising agency executive, the entry of foreign competitors is changing the situation: "When German advertisers sell in France, they have the habit of spending at the same rate (as at home), which is three times that of their French competitors. . . ."[12] As an example, *Advertising Age* noted that the German Triumph bra and girdle company spends three to four times as much as a French undergarment company to promote its products.

MARKETING INSTITUTIONS

The multinational company's opportunities in each market depend critically on the marketing institutions available in each country — including retail and wholesale outlets and advertising media and agencies. Some of the most drastic revisions in strategy made by U.S.-based companies overseas have been imposed by the lack of adequate supermarkets, retail chains, and commercial television. Differences in the number, size, and dispersion of distributive outlets call for differences in promotional methods; and differences in prevailing wholesale and/or retail margins may require vastly different price and discount structures. Some of these variations in institutional systems are related to legal regulations, especially in the area of resale price maintenance.

As in the case of competitive practices, traditional disparities in marketing institutions have narrowed considerably since 1945. For instance, one element of the "Americanization" of Europe is the spread of chains,

---

[12]Quoted in *Advertising Age,* August 29, 1966, p. 218.

supermarkets, and other U.S.-style institutions of distribution. In "borrowing" these methods from the United States, the Europeans add their own modifications; their supermarkets are not as large, they rely on walk-in neighborhood trade rather than on vast parking lots, their average transactions are smaller, and there are other adaptations. But there is a clear trend toward similarity in distributive systems.

The combination of continued differences in marketing institutions *now* with the prospect of greater similarities in the *future* creates some difficult problems for multinational marketers. One such problem may be timing. The experience of Princess Housewares in Germany, previously mentioned, is a case in point.

When Princess Housewares went into the German market, the company had a basic choice to make regarding channels of distribution. In the early 1960s, the predominant system of appliance distribution was independent wholesalers selling to retail stores. Small specialty retailers still dominated the market. However, department stores, mail-order firms, and discounters were growing in importance. Most of these large retailers were able to obtain *gross-handler* (wholesaler) discounts from manufacturers, and many of them sold at substantial discounts from "suggested" retail prices. The suggested prices, in turn, were often set at artificially high levels (so-called "moon" prices) to permit the appearance of large price cuts at retail. At the same time, because of public confusion and discontent over artificial list prices and equally artificial discounts, the resale price maintenance law was increasingly under attack.

Princess Housewares, as a relatively unknown brand, felt that its first task was to obtain distribution. To do this, the company decided to establish maintained prices and enforce them, so that small retailers' margins would be protected. But this put the company at a disadvantage in selling to the large discounters. It also meant that the company had to sell direct to retailers, since wholesalers could not be relied on to enforce resale prices.

In some ways, the Princess Housewares case boils down to a choice between a traditional distributive system, similar to that used in the United States in the early 1950s, and an emerging but still undeveloped system. U.S. experience suggests that the emerging system will become the dominant one. But can a manufacturer afford to be ahead of the trend?

LEGAL RESTRICTIONS

Different countries require or permit very different practices in the areas of product design, competitive practices, pricing, employment, and advertising. They also impose different taxes and tariffs, and multinational companies often follow devious paths in the attempt to minimize the total cost effects of these levies. Obviously, such practices can be stumbling blocks for the would-be standardizer.

Some product standards, though ostensibly designed for purposes of safety, are used by governments as a device for protecting home industries. A notable case in point was the imposition of new regulations for electrical appliances by France in 1967, along with delays in issuing approvals. This was generally regarded as a deliberate move to slow down the onslaught of competition by the Italian companies and thus give the domestic industry a breathing space.

But other legal restrictions are established for more legitimate purposes. The use of a 220-volt electrical system in Europe, for example, has led to a stringent set of safety standards for such products as irons — more stringent than U.S. standards. Cord connections must be stronger, and shielding against radio interference is necessary. These requirements, in turn, dictate modifications in product design.

Resale price maintenance and other laws designed to protect small retailers still have a strong influence on distribution policies in many countries. The trend has been away from restrictions of this kind, however, and some nations, such as the United Kingdom, have virtually abolished price maintenance.

Custom and legislative regulation combine to discourage some types of advertising and promotion. Goodyear Tire & Rubber Company, for instance, demonstrated the strength of its "3T" tire cord in the United States by showing a steel chain breaking. In Germany, this visualization was not permitted because it was regarded as disparaging to the steel chain manufacturers.[13] Such exaggerated sensitivity may be amusing, but it cannot be ignored in planning advertising campaigns.

CONCLUSION

Traditionally, marketing strategy has been regarded as a strictly local problem in each national market. Differences in customer needs and preferences, in competition, in institutional systems, and in legal regulations have seemed to require basically different marketing programs. Any similarity between countries has been seen as purely coincidental.

---

[13]*Advertising Age*, May 9, 1966, p. 75.

There is no doubt that differences among nations are still great, and that these differences should be recognized in marketing planning. But the experiences of a growing number of multinational companies suggest that there are also some real potential gains in an integrated approach to marketing strategy. Standardization of products, packages, and promotional approaches may permit substantial cost savings, as well as greater consistency in dealings with customers. The harmonization of price policies often facilitates better internal planning and control. Finally, if good ideas are scarce, and if some of them have universal appeal, they should be used as widely as possible.

All of this adds up to the conclusion that both the pros *and* the cons of standardization in multinational marketing programs should be considered, and that a company's decisions should be based on estimated overall revenues and costs. Obviously, each case must be considered on its own merits — slogans and formulas are not very helpful guides to intelligent planning.

If marketing strategy is to be designed with a multinational perspective, then the firm's organization must make provisions for line and staff marketing positions at appropriate levels. Space does not permit a full discussion of the organizational issues here, but it may be noted that there is a clear trend among leading companies toward establishment of marketing coordinators, international committees, and other mechanisms for at least partial centralization of marketing management. Hoover, Singer, General Electric, Eastman Kodak, and many other companies have made changes in this direction.

Finding the right balance between local autonomy and central coordination is not an easy task, any more than is balancing the gains of standardized marketing strategy against the needs of heterogeneous national markets. But it is an important task, with high potential profit rewards for management. Finding the best solutions to these problems should be high on the priority list for every multinational company.

"He gave man speech, and speech created thought,
Which is the measure of the universe."[14]

---

[14]Percy Bysshe Shelley, 1792–1822.

2.2 *READING*

The Globalization of Markets

Theodore Levitt

A powerful force drives the world toward a converging commonality, and that force is technology. It has proletarianized communication, transport, and travel. It has made isolated places and impoverished peoples eager for modernity's allurements. Almost everyone everywhere wants all the things they have heard about, seen, or experienced via the new technologies.

The result is a new commercial reality — the emergence of global markets for standardized consumer products on a previously unimagined scale of magnitude. Corporations geared to this new reality benefit from enormous economies of scale in production, distribution, marketing, and management. By translating these benefits into reduced world prices, they can decimate competitors that still live in the disabling grip of old assumptions about how the world works.

Gone are accustomed differences in national or regional preference. Gone are the days when a company could sell last year's models — or lesser versions of advanced products — in the less-developed world. And gone are the days when prices, margins, and profits abroad were generally higher than at home.

The globalization of markets is at hand. With that, the multinational commercial world nears its end, and so does the multinational corporation.

The multinational and the global corporation are not the same thing. The multinational corporation operates in a number of countries, and adjusts its products and practices in each — at high relative costs. The global corporation operates with resolute constancy — at low relative cost — as if the entire world (or major regions of it) were a single entity; it sells the same things in the same way everywhere.

Which strategy is better is not a matter of opinion but of necessity. Worldwide communications carry everywhere the constant drumbeat of modern possibilities to lighten and enhance work, raise living standards, divert, and entertain. The same countries that ask the world to recognize and respect the individuality of their cultures insist on the wholesale transfer to them of modern goods, services, and technologies. Modernity is not just a wish but also a widespread practice among those who cling, with unyielding passion or religious fervor, to ancient attitudes and heritages.

Who can forget the televised scenes during the 1979 Iranian uprisings of young men in fashionable French-cut trousers and silky body shirts thirsting with raised modern weapons for blood in the name of Islamic fundamentalism?

In Brazil, thousands swarm daily from pre-industrial Bahian darkness into exploding coastal cities, there quickly to install television sets in crowded corrugated huts and, next to battered Volkswagens, make sacrificial offerings of fruit and fresh-killed chickens to Macumban spirits by candlelight.

During Biafra's fratricidal war against the Ibos, daily televised reports showed soldiers carrying bloodstained swords and listening to transistor radios while drinking Coca-Cola.

In the isolated Siberian city of Krasnoyarsk, with no paved streets and censored news, occasional Western travelers are stealthily propositioned for cigarettes, digital watches, and even the clothes off their backs.

The organized smuggling of electronic equipment, used automobiles, Western clothing, cosmetics, and pirated movies into primitive places exceeds even the thriving underground trade in modern weapons and their military mercenaries.

A thousand suggestive ways attest to the ubiquity of the desire for the most advanced things that the world makes and sells — goods of the best quality and reliability at the lowest price. The world's needs and desires have been irrevocably homogenized. This makes the multinational corporation obsolete and the global corporation absolute.

LIVING IN THE REPUBLIC OF TECHNOLOGY

Daniel J. Boorstin, author of the monumental trilogy *The Americans,* characterized our age as driven by "the Republic of Technology [whose] supreme law . . . is convergence, the tendency for everything to become more like everything else."

In business, this trend has pushed markets toward global commonality. Corporations sell standardized products in the same way everywhere — autos, steel, chemicals, petroleum, cement, agricultural commodities and equipment, industrial and commercial construction, banking and insurance services, computers, semiconductors, transport, electronic instruments, pharmaceuticals, and telecommunications, to mention some of the obvious.

Nor is the sweeping gale of globalization confined to these raw material or high-tech products, where the universal language of customers and users facilitates standardization. The transforming winds whipped up by the proleterianization of communication and travel enter every crevice of life.

Commercially, nothing confirms this as much as the success of McDonald's from the Champs Elysées to the Ginza, of Coca-Cola in Bahrain and Pepsi-Cola in Moscow, and of rock music, Greek salad, Hollywood movies, Revlon cosmetics, Sony televisions, and Levi jeans everywhere. "High-touch" products are as ubiquitous as high-tech.

Starting from opposing sides, the high-tech and the high-touch ends of the commercial spectrum gradually consume the undistributed middle in their cosmopolitan orbit. No one is exempt and nothing can stop the process. Everywhere everything gets more and more like everything else as the world's preference structure is relentlessly homogenized.

Consider the cases of Coca-Cola and Pepsi-Cola, which are globally standardized products sold everywhere and welcomed by everyone. Both successfully cross multitudes of national, regional, and ethnic taste buds trained to a variety of deeply ingrained local preferences of taste, flavor, consistency, effervescence, and aftertaste. Everywhere both sell well. Cigarettes, too, especially American-made, make year-to-year global inroads on territories previously held in the firm grip of other, mostly local, blends.

These are not exceptional examples. (Indeed their global reach would be even greater were it not for artificial trade barriers.) They exemplify a general drift toward the homogenization of the world and how companies distribute, finance, and price products.[1] Nothing is exempt. The products and methods of the industrialized world play a single tune for all the world, and all the world eagerly dances to it.

Ancient differences in national tastes or modes of doing business disappear. The commonality of preference leads inescapably to the standardization of products, manufacturing, and the institutions of trade and commerce. Small nation-based markets transmogrify and expand. Success in world competition turns on efficiency in production, distribution, marketing, and management, and inevitably becomes focused on price.

The most effective world competitors incorporate superior quality and reliability into their cost structures. They sell in all national markets the same kind of products sold at home or in their largest export market. They compete on the basis of appropriate value — the best combinations of price, quality, reliability, and delivery for products that are globally identical with respect to design, function, and even fashion.

That, and little else, explains the surging success of Japanese companies dealing worldwide in a vast variety of products — both tangible products like steel, cars, motorcycles, hi-fi equipment, farm machinery, robots, microprocessors, carbon fibers, and now even textiles, and intangibles like banking, shipping, general contracting, and soon computer software. Nor are high-quality and low-cost operations incompatible, as a host of consulting organizations and data engineers argue with vigorous vacuity. The reported data are incomplete, wrongly analyzed, and contradictory. The truth is that low-cost operations are the hallmark of corporate cultures that require and produce quality in all that they do. High quality and low costs are not opposing postures. They are compatible, twin identities of superior practice.[2]

---

[1] In a landmark article, Robert D. Buzzell pointed out the rapidity with which barriers to standardization were falling. In all cases they succumbed to more and cheaper advanced ways of doing things. See "Can You Standardize Multinational Marketing?" (Reading 2.1).

[2] There is powerful new evidence for this, even though the opposite has been urged by analysts of PIMS data for nearly a decade. See "Product Quality: Cost Production and Business Performance — A Test of Some Key Hypotheses" by Lynn W. Phillips, Dae Chang, and Robert D. Buzzell, Harvard Business School Working Paper No. 83–13.

To say that Japan's companies are not global because they export cars with left-side drives to the United States and the European continent, while those in Japan have right-side drives, or because they sell office machines through distributors in the United States but directly at home, or speak Portuguese in Brazil is to mistake a difference for a distinction. The same is true of Safeway and Southland retail chains operating effectively in the Middle East, and to not only native but also imported populations from Korea, the Philippines, Pakistan, India, Thailand, Britain, and the United States. National rules of the road differ, and so do distribution channels and languages. Japan's distinction is its unrelenting push for economy and value enhancement. That translates into a drive for standardization at high quality levels.

VINDICATION OF THE MODEL T

If a company forces costs and prices down and pushes quality and reliability up — while maintaining reasonable concern for suitability — customers will prefer its world-standardized products. The theory holds, at this stage in the evolution of globalization, no matter what conventional market research and even common sense may suggest about different national and regional tastes, preferences, needs, and institutions. The Japanese have repeatedly vindicated this theory, as did Henry Ford with the Model T. Most important, so have their imitators, including companies from South Korea (television sets and heavy construction), Malaysia (personal calculators and microcomputers), Brazil (auto parts and tools), Colombia (apparel), Singapore (optical equipment), and, yes, even from the United States (office copiers, computers, bicycles, castings), Western Europe (automatic washing machines), Rumania (housewares), Hungary (apparel), Yugoslavia (furniture), and Israel (pagination equipment).

Of course, large companies operating in a single nation or even a single city don't standardize everything they make, sell, or do. They have product lines instead of a single product version, and multiple distribution channels. There are neighborhood, local, regional, ethnic, and institutional differences, even within metropolitan areas. But although companies customize products for particular market segments, they know that success in a world with homogenized demand requires a search for sales opportunities in similar segments across the globe in order to achieve the economies of scale necessary to compete.

Such a search works because a market segment in one country is seldom unique; it has close cousins everywhere precisely because technology has homogenized the globe. Even small local segments have

---

ECONOMIES OF SCOPE

One argument that opposes globalization says that flexible factory automation will enable plants of massive size to change products and product features quickly, without stopping the manufacturing process. These factories of the future could thus produce broad lines of customized products without sacrificing the scale economies that come from long production runs of standardized items. Computer-aided design and manufacturing (CAD/CAM), combined with robotics, will create a new equipment and process technology (EPT) that will make small plants located close to their markets as efficient as large ones located distantly. Economies of scale will not dominate, but rather economies of scope — the ability of either large or small plants to produce great varieties of relatively customized products at remarkably low costs. If that happens, customers will have no need to abandon special preferences.

I will not deny the power of these possibilities. But possibilities do not make probabilities. There is no conceivable way in which flexible factory automation can achieve the scale economies of a modernized plant dedicated to mass production of standardized lines. The new digitized equipment and process technologies are available to all. Manufacturers with minimal customization and narrow product-line breadth will have costs far below those with more customization and wider lines.

---

their global equivalents everywhere and become subject to global competition, especially on price.

The global competitor will seek constantly to standardize his offering everywhere. He will digress from this standardization only after exhausting all possibilities to retain it, and he will push for reinstatement of standardization whenever digression and divergence have occurred. He will never assume that the customer is a king who knows his own wishes.

Trouble increasingly stalks companies that lack clarified focus and remain inattentive to the economics of simplicity and standardization. The most endangered companies in the rapidly evolving world tend to be those that dominate rather small domestic markets with high value-added products for which there are smaller markets elsewhere. With transportation costs proportionately low, distant competitors will enter the now-sheltered markets of those companies with goods produced more cheaply under scale-efficient conditions. Global competition spells the end of domestic territoriality, no matter how diminutive the territory may be.

When the global producer offers his lower costs internationally, his patronage expands exponentially. He not only reaches into distant markets, but also attracts customers who previously held to local preferences and now capitulate to the attractions of lesser prices. The strategy of standardization not only responds to worldwide homogenized markets but also expands those markets with aggressive low pricing. The new technological juggernaut taps an ancient motivation — to make one's money go as far as possible. This is universal — not simply a motivation but actually a need.

THE HEDGEHOG KNOWS

The difference between the hedgehog and the fox, wrote Sir Isaiah Berlin in distinguishing between Dostoevski and Tolstoy, is that the fox knows a lot about a great many things, but the hedgehog knows everything about one great thing. The multinational corporation knows a lot about a great many countries and congenially adapts to supposed differences. It willingly accepts vestigial national differences, not questioning the possibility of their transformation, not recognizing how the world is ready and eager for the benefit of modernity, especially when the price is right. The multinational corporation's accommodating mode to visible national differences is medieval.

By contrast, the global corporation knows everything about one great thing. It knows about the absolute need to be competitive on a worldwide basis as well as nationally and seeks constantly to drive down prices by standardizing what it sells and how it operates. It treats the world as composed of few standardized markets rather than many customized markets. It actively seeks and vigorously works toward global convergence. Its mission is modernity and its mode, price competition, even when it sells top-of-the-line, high-end products. It knows about the one great thing all nations and people have in common: scarcity.

Nobody takes scarcity lying down; everyone wants more. This in part explains division of labor and specialization of production. They enable people and nations to optimize their conditions through trade. The median is usually money.

Experience teaches that money has three special qualities: scarcity, difficulty of acquisition, and transience. People understandably treat it with respect. Everyone in the increasingly homogenized world market wants products and features that everybody else wants. If the price is low enough, they will take highly standardized world products, even if these aren't exactly what mother said was suitable, what immemorial custom decreed was right, or what market-research fabulists asserted was preferred.

The implacable truth of all modern production — whether of tangible or intangible goods — is that large-scale production of standardized items is generally cheaper within a wide range of volume than small-scale production. Some argue that CAD/CAM will allow companies to manufacture customized products on a small scale — but cheaply. But the argument misses the point. (For a more detailed discussion, see the box insert, "Economies of scope.") If a company treats the world as one or two distinctive product markets, it can serve the world more economically than if it treats it as three, four, or five product markets.

WHY REMAINING DIFFERENCES?

Different cultural preferences, national tastes and standards, and business institutions are vestiges of the past. Some inheritances die gradually; others prosper and expand into mainstream global preferences. So-called ethnic markets are a good example. Chinese food, pita bread, country and western music, pizza, and jazz are everywhere. They are market segments that exist in worldwide proportions. They don't deny or contradict global homogenization but confirm it.

Many of today's differences among nations as to products and their features actually reflect the respectful accommodation of multinational corporations to what they believe are fixed local preferences. They *believe* preferences are fixed, not because they are but because of rigid habits of thinking about what actually is. Most executives in multinational corporations are thoughtlessly accommodating. They falsely presume that marketing means giving the customer what he says he wants rather than trying to understand exactly what he'd like. So they persist with high-cost, customized multinational products and practices instead of pressing hard and pressing properly for global standardization.

I do not advocate the systematic disregard of local or national differences. But a company's sensitivity to such differences does not require that it ignore the possibilities of doing things differently or better.

There are, for example, enormous differences among Middle Eastern countries. Some are socialist, some monarchies, some republics.

Some take their legal heritage from the Napoleonic Code, some from the Ottoman Empire, and some from the British common law; except for Israel, all are influenced by Islam. Doing business means personalizing the business relationship in an obsessively intimate fashion. During the month of Ramadan, business discussions can start only after 10 o'clock at night, when people are tired and full of food after a day of fasting. A company must almost certainly have a local partner; a local lawyer is required (as, say, in New York), and irrevocable letters of credit are essential. Yet, as Coca-Cola's Senior Vice President Sam Ayoub noted, "Arabs are much more capable of making distinctions between cultural and religious purposes on the one hand and economic realities on the other than is generally assumed. Islam is compatible with science and modern times."

Barriers to globalization are not confined to the Middle East. The free transfer of technology and data across the boundaries of the European Common Market countries are hampered by legal and financial impediments. And there is resistance to radio and television interference ("pollution") among neighboring European countries.

But the past is a good guide to the future. With persistence and appropriate means, barriers against superior technologies and economics have always fallen. There is no recorded exception where reasonable effort has been made to overcome them. It is very much a matter of time and effort.

A FAILURE IN GLOBAL IMAGINATION

Many companies have tried to standardize world practice by exporting domestic products and processes without accommodation or change — and have failed miserably. Their deficiencies have been seized on as evidence of bovine stupidity in the face of abject impossibility. Advocates of global standardization see them as examples of failure in execution.

In fact, poor execution is often an important cause. More important, however, is failure of nerve — failure of imagination.

Consider the case for the introduction of fully automatic home laundry equipment in Western Europe at a time when few homes had even semiautomatic machines. Hoover, Ltd., whose parent company was headquartered in North Canton, Ohio, had a prominent presence in Britain as a producer of vacuum cleaners and washing machines. Due to insufficient demand in the home market and low exports to the European continent, the large washing machine plant in England operated far below capacity. The company needed to sell more of its semiautomatic or automatic machines.

Because it had a "proper" marketing orientation, Hoover conducted consumer preference studies in Britain and each major continental country. The results showed feature preferences clearly enough among several countries (see *Exhibit 1*).

The incremental unit variable costs (in pounds sterling) of customizing to meet just a few of the national preferences are tabulated below. Considerable plant investment was needed to meet other preferences.

	£	s.	d.
Stainless steel vs. enamel drum	1	0	0
Porthole window		10	0
Spin speed of 800 rpm vs. 700 rpm		15	0
Water heater	2	15	0
6 vs. 5 kilos capacity	1	10	0
	£6	10s	0d

$18.20 at the exchange rate of that time.

The lowest retail prices (in pounds sterling) of leading locally produced brands in the various countries are listed below. The figures are approximate.

U.K.	£110
France	114
West Germany	113
Sweden	134
Italy	57

Product customization in each country would have put Hoover in a poor competitive position on the basis of price, mostly due to the higher manufacturing costs incurred by short production runs for separate features. Because Common Market tariff reduction programs were then incomplete, Hoover also paid tariff duties in each continental country.

EXHIBIT 1. Consumer preferences as to automatic washing machine features in the 1960s

Features	Great Britain	Italy	West Germany	France	Sweden
Shell dimensions[a]	34" and narrow	Low and narrow	34" and wide	34" and narrow	34" and wide
Drum material	Enamel	Enamel	Stainless steel	Enamel	Stainless steel
Loading	Top	Front	Front	Front	Front
Front porthole	Yes/no	Yes	Yes	Yes	Yes
Capacity	5 kilos	4 kilos	6 kilos	5 kilos	6 kilos
Spin speed	700 rpm	400 rpm	850 rpm	60 rpm	800 rpm
Water-heating system	No[b]	Yes	Yes[c]	Yes	No[b]
Washing action	Agitator	Tumble	Tumble	Agitator	Tumble
Styling features	Inconspicuous appearance	Brightly colored	Indestructible appearance	Elegant appearance	Strong appearance

[a]34" height was (in the process of being adopted as) a standard work-surface height in Europe.

[b]Most British and Swedish homes had centrally heated hot water.

[c]West Germans preferred to launder at temperatures higher than generally provided centrally.

HOW TO MAKE A CREATIVE ANALYSIS

In the Hoover case, an imaginative analysis of automatic washing machine sales in each country would have revealed that

1. Italian automatics, small in capacity and size, low-powered, without built-in heaters, with porcelain enamel tubs, were priced aggressively low and were gaining large market shares in all countries, including West Germany.
2. The best-selling automatics in West Germany were heavily advertised (three times more than the next most promoted brand), were ideally suited to national tastes, and were also by far the highest priced machines available in that country.
3. Italy, with the lowest penetration of washing machines of any kind (manual, semiautomatic, or automatic) was rapidly going directly to automatics, skipping the pattern of first buying handwringer, manually assisted machines and then semiautomatics.
4. Detergent manufacturers were just beginning to promote the technique of cold-water and tepid-water laundering then used in the United States.

The growing success of small, low-powered, low-speed, low-capacity, low-priced Italian machines, even against the preferred but highly priced and highly promoted brand in West Germany, was significant. It contained a powerful message that was lost on managers confidently wedded to a distorted version of the marketing concept according to which you give the customers what they say they want. In fact the customers *said* they wanted certain features, but their behavior demonstrated they'd take other features provided the price and the promotion were right.

In this case it was obvious that, under prevailing conditions, people preferred a low-priced automatic over any kind of manual or semiautomatic machine and certainly over higher priced automatics, even though the low-priced automatics failed to fulfill all their expressed preferences. The supposedly meticulous and demanding German consumers violated all expectations by buying the simple, low-priced Italian machines.

It was equally clear that people were profoundly influenced by promotions of automatic washers; in West Germany, the most heavily promoted ideal machine also had the largest market share despite its high price. Two things clearly influenced customers to buy: low price regardless of feature preferences and heavy promotion regardless of price. Both factors helped homemakers get what they most wanted — the superior benefits bestowed by fully automatic machines.

Hoover should have aggressively sold a simple, standardized high-quality machine at a low price (afforded by the 17% variable cost reduction that the elimination of £6-10-0 worth of extra features made possible). The suggested retail prices could have been somewhat less than £100. The extra funds "saved" by avoiding unnecessary plant modifications would have supported an extended service network and aggressive media promotions.

Hoover's media message should have been: *this* is the machine that you, the homemaker, *deserve* to have to reduce the repetitive heavy daily household burdens, so that *you* may have more constructive time to spend with your children and your husband. The promotion should also have targeted the husband to give him, preferably in the presence of his wife, a sense of obligation to provide an automatic washer for her even before he bought an automobile for himself. An aggressively low price, combined with heavy promotion of this kind, would have overcome previously expressed preferences for particular features.

The Hoover case illustrates how the perverse practice of the marketing concept and the absence of any kind of marketing imagination let multinational attitudes survive when customers actually want the benefits of global standardization. The whole project got off on the wrong foot. It asked people what features they wanted in a washing machine rather than what they wanted out of life. Selling a line of products individually tailored to each nation is thoughtless. Managers who took pride in practicing the marketing concept to the fullest did not, in fact, practice it at all. Hoover asked the wrong questions, then applied neither thought nor imagination to the answers. Such companies are like the ethnocentricists in the Middle Ages who saw with everyday clarity the sun revolving around the earth and offered it as Truth. With no additional data but a more searching mind, Copernicus, like the hedgehog, interpreted a more compelling and accurate reality. Data do not yield information except with the intervention of the mind. Information does not yield meaning except with the intervention of imagination.

ACCEPTING THE INEVITABLE

The global corporation accepts for better or for worse that technology drives consumers relentlessly toward the same common goals — alleviation of life's burdens and the expansion of discretionary time and spending power. Its role is profoundly different from what it has been for the ordinary corporation during its brief, turbulent, and remarkably protean history. It orchestrates the twin vectors of technology and globalization for the world's benefit. Neither fate, nor nature, nor God but rather the necessity of commerce created this role.

In the United States two industries became global long before they were consciously aware of it. After over a generation of persistent and acrimonious labor shutdowns, the United Steelworkers of America have not called an industrywide strike since 1959; the United Auto Workers have not shut down General Motors since 1970. Both unions realize that they have become global — shutting down all or most of U.S. manufacturing would not shut out U.S. customers. Overseas suppliers are there to supply the market.

CRACKING THE CODE OF WESTERN MARKETS

Since the theory of the marketing concept emerged a quarter of a century ago, the more managerially advanced corporations have been eager to offer what customers clearly wanted rather than what was merely convenient. They have created marketing departments supported by professional market researchers of awesome and often costly proportions. And they have proliferated extraordinary numbers of operations and product lines — highly tailored products and delivery systems for many different markets, market segments, and nations.

Significantly, Japanese companies operate almost entirely without marketing departments or market research of the kind so prevalent in the West. Yet, in the colorful words of General Electric's chairman John F. Welch, Jr., the Japanese, coming from a small cluster of resource-poor islands, with an entirely alien culture and an almost impenetrably complex language, have cracked the code of Western markets. They have done it not by looking with mechanistic thoroughness at the way markets are different but rather by searching for meaning with a deeper wisdom. They have discovered the one great thing all markets have in common — an overwhelming desire for dependable, world-standard modernity in all things, at aggressively low prices. In response, they deliver irresistible value everywhere, attracting people with products that market-research technocrats described with superficial certainty as being unsuitable and uncompetitive.

The wider a company's global reach, the greater the number of regional and national preferences it will encounter for certain product features, distribution systems, or promotional media. There will always need to be some accommodation to differences. But the widely prevailing and often unthinking belief in the immutability of these differences is generally mistaken. Evidence of business failure because of lack of accommodation is often evidence of other shortcomings.

Take the case of Revlon in Japan. The company unnecessarily alienated retailers and confused customers by selling world-standardized cosmetics only in elite outlets; then it tried to recover with low-priced world-standardized products in broader distribution, followed by a change in the company president and cutbacks in distribution as costs rose faster than sales. The problem was not the Revlon didn't understand the Japanese market; it didn't do the job right, wavered in its programs, and was impatient to boot.

By contrast, the Outboard Marine Corporation, with imagination, push, and persistence, collapsed long-established three-tiered distribution channels in Europe into a more focused and controllable two-step system — and did so despite the vociferous warnings of local trade groups. It also reduced the number and types of retail outlets. The result was greater improvement in credit and product-installation service to customers, major cost reductions, and sales advances.

In its highly successful introduction of Contac 600 (the timed-release decongestant) into Japan, SmithKline Corporation used 35 wholesalers instead of the 1,000-plus that established practice required. Daily contacts with the wholesalers and key retailers, also in violation of established practice, supplemented the plan, and it worked.

Denied access to established distribution institutions in the United States, Komatsu, the Japanese manufacturer of lightweight farm machinery, entered the market through over-the-road construction equipment dealers in rural areas of the Sunbelt, where farms are smaller, the soil sandier and easier to work. Here inexperienced distributors were able to attract customers on the basis of Komatsu's product and price appropriateness.

In cases of successful challenge to prevailing institutions and practices, a combination of product reliability and quality, strong and sustained support systems, aggressively low prices, and sales-compensation packages, as well as audacity and implacability, circumvented, shattered, and transformed very different distribution systems. Instead of resentment, there was admiration.

Still, some differences between nations are unyielding, even in a world of microprocessors. In the United States almost all manufacturers of microprocessors check them for reliability through a so-called parallel system of testing. Japan prefers the totally different sequential testing system. So Teradyne Corporation, the world's largest producer of microprocessor test equipment, makes one line for the United States and one for Japan. That's easy.

What's not so easy for Teradyne is to know how best to organize and manage, in this instance, its marketing effort. Companies can organize by product, region, function, or by using some combination of these. A company can have separate marketing organizations for Japan and for the United States, or it can have separate product groups, one working largely in Japan and the other in the United States. A single manufacturing facility or marketing operation might service both markets, or a company might use separate marketing operations for each.

Questions arise if the company organizes by product. In the case of Teradyne, should the group handling the parallel system, whose major market is the United States, sell in Japan and compete with the group focused on the Japanese market? If the company organizes regionally, how do regional groups divide their efforts between promoting the parallel vs. the sequential system? If the company organizes in terms of function, how does it get commitment in marketing, for example, for one line instead of the other?

There is no one reliably right answer — no one formula by which to get it. There isn't even a satisfactory contingent answer.[3] What works well for one company or one place may fail for another in precisely the same place, depending on the capabilities, histories, reputations, resources, and even the cultures of both.

THE EARTH IS FLAT

The differences that persist throughout the world despite its globalization affirm an ancient dictum of economics — that things are driven by what happens at the margin, not at the core. Thus, in ordinary competitive analysis, what's important is not the average price but the marginal price; what happens not in the usual case but at the interface of newly erupting conditions. What counts in commercial affairs is what happens at the cutting edge. What is most striking today is the underlying similarities of what is happening now to national preferences at the margin. These similarities at the cutting edge cumulatively form an overwhelming, predominant commonality everywhere.

To refer to the persistence of economic nationalism (protective and subsidized trade practices, special tax aids, or restrictions for home market producers) as a barrier to the globalization of markets is to make a valid point. Economic nationalism does have a powerful persistence. But, as with the present almost totally smooth internationalization of

---

[3]For a discussion of multinational reorganization, see Christopher A. Bartlett, "MNCs: Get Off the Reorganization Merry-Go-Round." (Reading 3.2).

THE SHORTENING OF JAPANESE HORIZONS

One of the most powerful yet least celebrated forces driving commerce toward global standardization is the monetary system, along with the international investment process.

Today money is simply electronic impulses. With the speed of light it moves effortlessly between distant centers (and even lesser places). A change of ten basis points in the price of a bond causes an instant and massive shift of money from London to Tokyo. The system has profound impact on the way companies operate throughout the world.

Take Japan, where high debt-to-equity balance sheets are "guaranteed" by various societal presumptions about the virtue of "a long view," or by government policy in other ways. Even here, upward shifts in interest rates in other parts of the world attract capital out of the country in powerful proportions. In recent years more and more Japanese global corporations have gone to the world's equity markets for funds. Debt is too remunerative in high-yielding countries to keep capital at home to feed the Japanese need. As interest rates rise, equity becomes a more attractive option for the issuer.

The long-term impact on Japanese enterprise will be transforming. As the equity proportion of Japanese corporate capitalization rises, companies will respond to the shorter-term investment horizons of the equity markets. Thus the much-vaunted Japanese corporate practice to taking the long view will gradually disappear.

investment capital, the past alone does not shape or predict the future. (For reflections on the internationalization of capital, see the box insert, "The shortening of Japanese horizons.")

Reality is not a fixed paradigm, dominated by immemorial customs and derived attitudes, heedless of powerful and abundant new forces. The world is becoming increasingly informed about the liberating and enhancing possibilities of modernity. The persistence of the inherited varieties of national preferences rests uneasily on increasing evidence of, and restlessness regarding, their inefficiency, costliness, and confinement. The historic past, and the national differences respecting commerce and industry it spawned and fostered everywhere, is now subject to relatively easy transformation.

Cosmopolitanism is no longer the monopoly of the intellectual and leisure classes; it is becoming the established property and defining characteristic of all sectors everywhere in the world. Gradually and irresistibly it breaks down the walls of economic insularity, nationalism, and chauvinism. What we see today as escalating commercial nationalism is simply the last violent death rattle of an obsolete institution.

Companies that adapt to and capitalize on economic convergence can still make distinctions and adjustments in different markets. Persistent differences in the world are consistent with fundamental underlying commonalities; they often complement rather than oppose each other — in business as they do in physics. There is, in physics, simultaneously matter and anti-matter working in symbiotic harmony.

The earth is round, but for most purposes it's sensible to treat it as flat. Space is curved, but not much for everyday life here on earth.

Divergence from established practice happens all the time. But the multinational mind, warped into circumspection and timidity by years of stumbles and transnational troubles, now rarely challenges existing overseas practices. More often it considers any departure from inherited domestic routines as mindless, disrespectful, or impossible. It is the mind of a bygone day.

The successful global corporation does not abjure customization or differentiation for the requirements of markets that differ in product preferences, spending patterns, shopping preferences, and institutional or legal arrangements. But the global corporation accepts and adjusts to these differences only reluctantly, only after relentlessly testing their immutability, after trying in various ways to circumvent and reshape them as we saw in the cases of Outboard Marine in Europe, SmithKline in Japan, and Komatsu in the United States.

There is only one significant respect in which a company's activities around the world are important, and this is in what it produces and how it sells. Everything else derives from, and is subsidiary to, these activities.

The purpose of business is to get and keep a customer. Or, to use Peter Drucker's more refined construction, to *create* and keep a customer. A company must be wedded to the ideal of innovation — offering better or more preferred products in such combinations of ways, means, places, and at such prices that prospects *prefer* doing business with the company rather than with others.

Preferences are constantly shaped and reshaped. Within our global commonality enormous variety constantly asserts itself and thrives, as can be seen within the world's single largest domestic market, the United States. But in the process of world homogenization, modern markets expand to reach cost-reducing global proportions. With better and cheaper communication and transport, even small local market segments hitherto protected from distant competitors now feel the pressure of their presence. Nobody is safe from global reach and the irresistible economies of scale.

Two vectors shape the world — technology and globalization. The first helps determine human preferences; the second, economic realities. Regardless of how much preferences evolve and diverge, they also gradually converge and form markets where economies of scale lead to reduction of costs and prices.

The modern global corporation contrasts powerfully with the aging multinational corporation. Instead of adapting to superficial and even entrenched differences within and between nations, it will seek sensibly to force suitably standardized products and practices on the entire globe. They are exactly what the world will take, if they come also with low prices, high quality, and blessed reliability. The global company will operate, in this regard, precisely as Henry Kissinger wrote in *Years of Upheaval* about the continuing Japanese economic success — "voracious

---

TURTLES ALL THE WAY DOWN

There is an Indian story — at least I heard it as an Indian story — about an Englishman who, having been told that the world rested on a platform which rested on the back of an elephant which rested in turn on the back of a turtle, asked (perhaps he was an ethnographer; it is the way they behave), what did the turtle rest on? Another turtle. And that turtle? "Ah, Sahib, after that it is turtles all the way down." . . .

The danger that cultural analysis, in search of all-too-deep-lying turtles, will lose touch with the hard surfaces of life — with the political, economic, stratificatory realities within which men are everywhere contained — and with the biological and physical necessities on which those surfaces rest, is an ever-present one. The only defense against it, and against, thus, turning cultural analysis into a kind of sociological aestheticism, is to train such analysis on such realities and such necessities in the first place.

From Clifford Geertz, *The Interpretation of Cultures* (New York: Basic Books 1973), With permission of the publisher

in its collection of information, impervious to pressure, and implacable in execution."

Given what is everywhere the purpose of commerce, the global company will shape the vectors of technology and globalization into its great strategic fecundity. It will systematically push these vectors toward their own convergence, offering everyone simultaneously high-quality, more or less standardized products at optimally low prices, thereby achieving for itself vastly expanded markets and profits. Companies that do not adapt to the new global realities will become victims of those that do.

2.3 _CASE_

Hoover: Multinational Product Planning

Robert D. Buzzell and
Jean-Louis LeCocq

In May 1965, the New Products Committee of Hoover Limited met to discuss "Project 7," a major program for developing a new line of automatic washing machines. Mr. G.L. Lloyd, managing director of Hoover Limited and chair of the committee, stated that the purpose of the meeting was to arrive at final recommendations on product design features, range of models, pricing, and sales goals. He emphasized that Project 7 was "the most important single undertaking for Hoover Limited during the next two years" and that it "must be given absolutely top priority."

Note: This case was prepared through the cooperation of the Hoover Worldwide Corporation and Hoover Limited. This version was prepared by Professors Benson P. Shapiro and Robert D. Buzzell as a basis for class discussion.

COMPANY BACKGROUND

Hoover was one of the world's largest and best-known manufacturers of household electrical appliances, with factories in 10 countries and sales outlets in more than 100. It began in 1908 with the Hoover Company of North Canton, Ohio. Hoover began exporting vacuum cleaners to the United Kingdom in 1919; in 1932 it built a factory near London and established Hoover Limited as a wholly owned subsidiary. In 1937 shares in Hoover Limited were offered to the British public. In 1965 the Hoover Company owned 55% of Hoover Limited.

For many years, Hoover[1] concentrated almost entirely on vacuum cleaners. After World War II, however, the product line was diversified to include other household electrical appliances. The company's first washer was an inexpensive, nonautomatic machine, well suited to meet the pent-up postwar demand in the United Kingdom. By 1965 more than 6 million Hoover washers had been shipped.

Hoover's efforts to diversify intensified during the 1960s, and by 1965 the company's household appliance product line included many small appliances, such as hair dryers and electric frying pans. These products were manufactured at 21 factories. A new factory, opened at Dijon, France, to serve the European Common Market, commenced production of twin-tub, semiautomatic washing machines in October 1964.

In some countries products purchased from the manufacturers were marketed under the Hoover brand. In 1965, for example, Hoover sold automatic washing machines purchased from an Italian supplier in most continental European countries, in addition to the machines it produced. New products were often purchased initially from outside suppliers and produced by the company itself after sales justified investment.

Most subsidiaries were essentially marketing companies, responsible for sales, advertising, dealer relations, and product service in their respective countries.

Consolidated sales in 1964 were $248.8 million. The Hoover Company (U.S.A.) accounted for $66.7 million and Hoover Limited (U.K.) for $154.6 million. Consolidated net earnings after taxes in 1964 were $19.7 million, to which the Hoover Company (U.S.A.) contributed $10.4 million.

---

[1]From this point on, "Hoover" refers to Hoover Limited (United Kingdom), not Hoover Company (U.S.A.).

WASHING MACHINES

Two basic types of household washing machines were available to consumers in the 1960s: nonautomatics and automatics.

NONAUTOMATICS. A "nonautomatic" washing machine was controlled by the user, who reset it at each stage in its operation cycle. Thus, the user filled the machine with water, loaded the clothing, and added soap or detergent. After the wash cycle was completed, the user turned the machine off, drained the soapy water, added clean rinse water, and started it again. Finally, when the clothing was rinsed, the user extracted water from the wet clothes either with a wringer, or, in the case of the twin-tub system, by transferring the clothes to a separate drum for spin drying.

AUTOMATICS AND SEMIAUTOMATICS. An "automatic" washing machine was controlled by electric timers operating on preset "programs" which governed the start and finish of each stage in the cycle. A "semiautomatic" machine was automatically controlled through the wash and rinse cycles, but had to be reset by the user for spin drying.

There were many methods of programming fully and semiautomatic machines. Some had a simple one-knob control; on others, temperature, duration of wash, methods, and soaking time could be set separately for different fabrics. Some manufacturers gave only a few programs, others offered up to 15.

The two main types of washing actions in automatic machines were the top-loading, agitator type used in the United States and the front-loading, tumble-action type used in most European machines. In the tumble-action type, a perforated cylinder, of either porcelain-enameled steel or stainless steel, held the load to be washed as it revolved in a tub of water. Projections or baffles in the cylinder caused the clothes to drop back into the water (tumbling action) as it turned. In most machines sold in the 1960s the drum reversed at intervals. Tumble-action machines were generally less costly to manufacture than agitator machines.

HOOVER WASHING MACHINE PRODUCT LINE

Hoover Limited had introduced the nonautomatic pulsator washing machine in the United Kingdom in 1948. The "Mark I," with a retail price of around £25,[2] was quickly accepted by British consumers, and Hoo-

---

[2]One pound sterling (£) = U.S. $2.80 = 14 French francs = 11.45 Deutsche marks in 1964.

EXHIBIT 1. Hoover's washing machine line, 1965

The Mark III washing
machine—compactness
with powered wringing.
Also available—the Mark II.

The Twosome—the
"twin tub" for small
kitchens. Also available
separately—the Spinarinse—
efficiency combined with
value for money.

The Hoovermatic De Luxe.
The Hoovermatic is also
available in standard versions,
with and without heater.

The automated Keymatic.

ver's market share reached 50% by the early 1950s. Later versions featured twin tubs and semiautomatic operation. Hoover's 1965 line is shown in *Exhibit 1*.

Hoover introduced its first fully automatic machine in the United Kingdom, the "Keymatic," in 1961. The Keymatic differed from most other automatic washing machines in its basic configuration. Whereas most American and many English automatics were top-loading, agitator-type machines, and most continental European washers were front-loading, tumble-action machines, the Keymatic had a *tilted* drum and a pulsator action.[3] This had been adopted because, according to Hoover executives, it provided a dual washing action: vigorous cleaning with the pulsator in operation, and a gentler action with the drum motion only. A continental-style front-loading design could not be used because the pulsator had to be under water at all times. Thus, the Keymatic was, in part, a compromise between a front-loading design and the company's desire to retain the pulsator. It also featured a "Keyplate" control system, with which the user selected a program for a given type of wash (such as "heavily soiled whites," or "delicate fabrics") by inserting a small plastic plate.

UNITED KINGDOM MARKET

During the 1950s and 1960s the U.K. market for washing machines had increased considerably, but with wide fluctuations from year to year. Total consumer purchases were estimated by Hoover market research as follows:

1953 — 340,000	1959 — 1,100,000
1954 — 600,000	1960 — 780,000
1955 — 700,000	1961 — 858,000
1956 — 400,000	1962 — 879,000
1957 — 480,000	1963 — 982,000
1958 — 690,000	1964 — 863,000

The liberalization of government restrictions on credit terms and a dramatic decrease in purchase tax rates (60% in 1957 to 25% in 1959) were the main reasons, in the view of most observers, for the dramatic

---

[3]The *pulsator* system was based on a small device like a turbine, which moved the water by both turning and creating currents. It was used only by Hoover, AEG, a German manufacturer, and Electrolux, a Swedish producer, under license from Hoover.

expansion of demand for washing machines (and other appliances) in 1959. The 1959 boom encouraged investments in production facilities, which led to excess capacity. A number of new entrants were attracted. John Bloom's Washing Machine Limited reached a sales level of some 45,000 units by 1960 through aggressive door-to-door selling of inexpensive nonautomatic washing machines imported from Holland.

In April 1960 the government reimposed credit restrictions and in July 1961 the purchase tax was increased from 25.0% to 27.5%. (This rate was still in effect in 1965.) It was the seventh purchase tax change since 1951. Appliance sales declined sharply and remained low for many months.

In 1965 the British economy was still somewhat depressed, and the electrical appliance industry was operating well below capacity. Financial difficulties, created in part by those economic conditions, led to John Bloom's withdrawal from the market.

TYPES OF MACHINES

Hoover had introduced its twin-tub, nonautomatic washing machine in 1957, and in 1964 the twin tub was still dominant in the United Kingdom. Trends in and projections for sales are shown in *Exhibit 2*. Twin tubs accounted for an estimated 20% of the market in 1957, nearly 50% in 1960, and 70% in 1963. Between 1960 and 1963 their growth was aided by aggressive promotion by the John Bloom organization.

Fully automatic washers accounted for a growing share of total U.K. sales in the 1960s. Before 1960 only Bendix (a subsidiary of an American company) offered an automatic in the United Kingdom. English Electric introduced one in 1960. Hoover introduced its Keymatic in 1961, followed by Servis and Imperial in 1963 and Duomatic and Hotpoint in 1964.

The growth of automatic washer sales in the United Kingdom had not fully lived up to the expectations of Hoover and other major manufacturers. Hoover had spent an estimated £500,000 on introductory promotion for the Keymatic during 1961. According to a Hoover staff report,

> *The introduction of the fully automatic coincided with the growing demand for twin tubs. Even if the difference between fully automatics and twin tubs were apparent to homemakers, it is unlikely that the majority of them have seen sufficient advantage in fully automatics to justify the additional expenditure.*

Fully automatic washers typically sold at retail for between £100 and £120; twin tubs could be bought for £50 to £80 (plus purchase taxes). Current Hoover retail list prices were £110 for the Keymatic automatic

EXHIBIT 2. Trends in distribution of washing machine sales by type, 1956–1964, and projections for 1965–1974: United Kingdom

Percent of industry sales

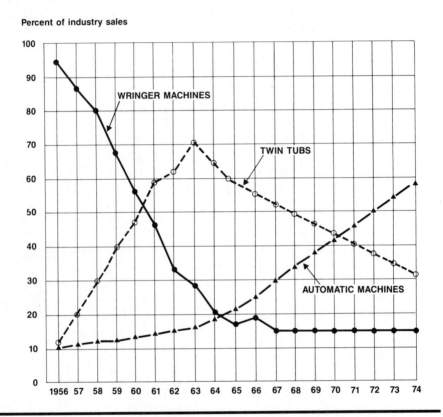

Source: Hoover Limited Market Research Department estimates.

and £83 for the twin tub semiautomatic. See *Exhibit 3* for typical trade margins.

COMPETITION

Approximately 95% of the washing machines sold in the United Kingdom in 1964 were domestically produced (see *Exhibit 4*). Hoover's principal competitors in he domestic market were Wilkins and Mitchell (Servis brand), English Electric, and Hotpoint. Some Italian automatic machines were marketed in the United Kingdom under the Imperial brand.

EXHIBIT 3. Trade margins for primary European countries

	France	Germany	Italy	U.K.
Retailer margin if product sold at manufacturers' suggested list price	25%–40%	30%–45%	35%–45%	25%–35%
Average actual retailer margins (after granting discounts to end consumers)	25	17	20	25
Average wholesaler margin	11	11	11	12

EXHIBIT 4. Washing machine markets in selected European countries, 1964 (000 units)

	France	Germany	Italy	U.K.	Sweden
Local production	770	1,332	1,264*	1,094	66
Imports	114	75	35	41	48
Exports	75	257	167	267	4
Apparent consumption	809	1,146	900	863	110
Hoover sales	70	35	25	285	5

*Italian producers had reportedly experienced some buildup in inventories in 1964 in anticipation of sharp increases in export sales. In 1965, Italian exports of washing machines were expected to more than double to over 350,000 units.

Share of Market (in 1964)

Brand	Wringer washers	Twin tubs	Fully automatics	Total market
Hoover	28%	34%	44%	33%
Hotpoint	33	15	9	16
Servis	24	13	5	13
Bendix	—	—	16	2
English Electric	—	5	15	6
Imperial	—	—	8	1
Others	15	33	3	29
Totals	100%	100%	100%	100%

Imports of washing machines amounted to 41,000 units in 1964, compared with 36,000 in 1961. Exports were substantially more important — 267,000 units in 1964.

FUTURE TRENDS

Early in 1965 Hoover undertook a study of long-term trends in the U.K. market. It indicated that total demand depended on three primary factors (apart from the temporary effects of government restrictions and taxes):

1. The total number of *potential* washing machine owners — the number of homes with electricity.
2. Increases in *market penetration* — the percentage of wired homes owning washing machines.
3. *Replacement* of existing machines.

The study estimated that replacement purchases of washing machines had increased from 10% of the market in 1959 to 25% in 1962 and 35% in 1964. Total market penetration, it concluded, was "approaching saturation" at 55% of households in 1964, and as a result, "a temporary lull in sales is in progress with the minimum in 1967. The depression is caused by a slowing down of market penetration . . . until rising replacement sales catch up."

The report also forecast future industry sales, based on (1) the projected growth in the number of electricity consumers; (2) a slowly increasing market penetration, reaching 70% by 1974; and (3) an "actuarial" model of machine replacements, based on an estimated average machine life of 12 years.[4] The forecasts were:

1967 — 810,000	1971 — 875,000
1968 — 820,000	1972 — 910,000
1969 — 830,000	1973 — 940,000
1970 — 850,000	1974 — 950,000
	1975 — 975,000

---

[4]The actuarial model provided a basis for estimating the number of machines of a given age to be replaced each year. The estimates were derived from a Poisson probability distribution for the uncertain variable "machine life," with a mean of 12 years from the original purchase date.

EXHIBIT 5. Tariffs applicable to washing machines for selected European countries, 1964 (tariffs stated as percentages of invoiced value, ad valorem)

Importing country	Exporting country				
	U.K.	*Germany*	*France*	*Italy*	*Sweden*
U.K.	—	12%	12%	22%	6%
Germany	13%	—	4	4	13
France	16	7	—	7	16
Italy	21	11	11	—	21
Sweden	4	10	10	10	—

As shown in *Exhibit 2*, Hoover studies also indicated that automatics would account for a steadily increasing proportion of the market, rising from 18% in 1964 to 28% in 1967 and 57% in 1974.

CONTINENTAL MARKETS

Export business had long been important for Hoover Limited. In the 1950s, sales in continental Europe had accounted for around a third of total Hoover washing machine output in the United Kingdom, but by 1964, this had declined to 15%. According to Hoover executives, the company had lost ground in Germany and France primarily because "we did not have the right product." Hoover had continued to place major emphasis on twin-tub nonautomatics, which were rapidly displaced by tumble-action automatics. The decline of European export sales, along with the unfavorable economic conditions in the home market, led to underutilization of the factory, Hoover's largest. Hoover management placed a very high priority on increasing this factory's output from its current level of about 60% of capacity.

Two of the major factors contributing to the increasing difficulty of exporting washing machines and other electrical appliances from the United Kingdom to continental Europe were the formation of the Common Market (EEC) and the emergence of an efficient, aggressive appliance manufacturing industry in Italy. The Common Market was designed to reduce, and eventually eliminate, tariffs on goods originating *within* the EEC member countries while imposing standard tariffs on goods imported from other nations. By 1965 tariff rates in the EEC had already been reduced substantially, as shown in *Exhibit 5*. The transition to common external tariffs and tariff-free internal trade was expected to be completed by mid-1967.

The "Italian invasion" of continental European appliance markets began in the mid-1950s when several companies, including Ignis, Zanussi, Zoppas, and Candy, began investing in modern, highly automated facilities. They initially concentrated on refrigerators. Total Italian refrigerator production increased rapidly from an estimated 65,000 units in 1953 to 977,000 units in 1960 and 2,176,000 units in 1964.[5] Refrigerator exports increased even faster, from a value of 619 million lire in 1953 to 17.0 billion lire in 1960 and 36.3 billion lire in 1964.[6] (Official export data were not published in units, but refrigerator exports in 1964 were estimated at nearly 1 million units.) Washing machine production grew less rapidly up to 1961 (262,000 units) but then climbed sharply to 511,000 units in 1962; 916,000 in 1963; and 1,264,000 in 1964. It was estimated that over 167,000 washing machines, virtually all fully automatics, were exported by Italian producers in 1964. Of the total export volume, approximately one-fourth went to Germany and 10% to 15% to France.

Italian appliance manufacturers enjoyed several advantages in competing with other European companies. Wage rates were lower than in other EEC countries or in the United Kingdom. Moreover, the Italian government offered an 8% subsidy on exports. An American executive was quoted in *Fortune* as saying,

> The real reason for Italy's success is high productivity and extensive automation. To this must be added two other factors. First, the Italian industry was fortunate in that just as it began to get up steam, tariffs and quotas within the Common Market were beginning to fall. And second, unlike many of their competitors in other countries, the Italian entrepreneurs were willing to gamble big investments on large-scale, low-unit-cost plants, with the aim of capturing markets all over Europe.[7]

Some commentators also suggested that the Italian success was aided by the fact that they did not "overbuild. . . . They used smaller gauge steel, for example. They deliberately avoided the German zeal for building something to last forever."[8]

---

[5]Estimates by Carlo Castellano, *L'industria degli elettrodomestici in Italia* (Turin: Istituto di Tecnica Economics, Università degli Studi di Genova, 1965).

[6]One pound = 1,736 lire = US$2.80 in 1964.

[7]Philip Siekman, "The Battle for the Kitchen: Europe's Industries, V," *Fortune*, January 1964, 108 ff.

[8]"Italy Finds a Bonanza in Europe's Kitchens," *Business Week*, October 8, 1966, 108.

EXHIBIT 6. Estimated washing machine sales in continental European countries, 1962–1964 (000 units)

Country	1962	1963	1964
Germany	988	853	1,146
Italy	500	600	900
France	593	726	809
Belgium	140	124	150
Holland	199	240	268
Sweden	73	85	110
Norway	49	52	60
Finland	61	52	60
Austria	76	85	90
Totals	2,679	2,817	3,593

Source: Estimated by Market Research Department, Hoover Limited, based primarily on government and trade association reports of production, imports, and exports.

Sales of washing machines in Europe amounted to more than 3.5 million units in 1964, as shown in *Exhibit 6*. Germany, Italy, and France accounted for nearly 80% of total consumption and an even greater proportion of production.

Automatic tumble-action machines constituted an increasing percentage of the market in most continental countries. According to Hoover estimates, 50% of all machines sold in 1964 were automatics, compared with around 30% in 1960. The proportion of automatics was expected to rise further to 67% in 1967 and 80% in 1970.

Consumer preferences, competitive conditions, and other factors differed among the continental countries. These differences are illustrated by the washing machine markets in France, Germany, Italy, and Sweden.

THE FRENCH MARKET

During the 1960s, there were important modifications in the appliance industry in France. The largest domestic company, Thomson-Houston had increased its share of the washing machine business from around 10% to over 20%. The 5 largest manufacturers accounted for over 50% of the French market and the 10 largest for around 80%. Industry observers predicted that further concentration could be expected soon.

The leading brands of washing machines and their estimated shares of the French market in 1965 were as follows:

Brand	Market share
Brandt-Vedette Thomson	23%
Hoover	10
Arthur Martin	7
Lincoln	6
Laden	5
Atlantic	4

All but Hoover originated solely in France. The Hoover machines were built in France, Italy, and the United Kingdom.

Hoover's share of the French market had been as high as 15% in the 1950s. Hoover executives attributed the decline to the lack of a tumble-action automatic until 1965, when it introduced a machine purchased from an Italian supplier.

Foreign competition in washing machines was still limited in France, because domestic manufacturers were indirectly protected by the continued use of gas for water heating.[9] Nevertheless, imports had grown from 61,000 units in 1961 to 114,000 in 1964. The government's electrification policy was expected to permit further expansion of imports, because foreign competition was principally in electrical machines. The share of electrically heated washing machines had increased regularly in France from 15% in 1959 to 20% in 1964.

The growth in sales of fully automatic machines was relatively slow:

French sales of washing machines (by type)

	1961	1962	1963	1964
Nonautomatic	29%	22%	18%	16%
Semiautomatic }	71	71	73	71
Fully automatic }		7	9	13

Horizontally mounted machines accounted for an estimated 83% of French sales in 1964, up from 68% in 1961, while pulsator machines had declined from 19% to 15%.

---

[9]Water heating is described below under the section on product design alternatives.

Washing machines in France tended to be narrower than those in other markets. In 1964 about 60% of those sold in France were "slim-line," less than 50 cm wide. Several manufacturers were emphasizing the corresponding "gain in space" in their advertising. There was, however, a clear-cut increase in the average capacity of French washers. Around half of all machines sold in 1964 had a wash capacity of 3.7 to 4.6 kg and 39% had a capacity of more than 4.7 kg.

Manufacturers' recommended retail prices in 1965 for representative models of washing machines were:

	Retail price	
Brand and type	*Francs*	*Pounds*
Nonautomatic:		
Hoover	860	61.4
Twin-tub:		
Hoover	1,148	82.0
Flandria	1,428	102.0

	Regular		**Slimline**	
	Francs	*Pounds*	*Francs*	*Pounds*
Fully automatic:				
Hoover	2,588	184.9	1,688	120.6
Brandt	1,900	135.7	1,599	114.2
Arthur Martin	1,600	114.3	1,695	121.1
Lincoln	1,991	142.2	—	—
Atlantic	1,980	141.4	1,600	114.3
Frigidaire	2,050	146.4	1,699	121.4
Indesit (Italian)	2,790	127.9	—	—
Average	1,986	141.8	1,656	118.3

Retailers in France generally gave "discounts" from the prices shown, ranging up to 15% in Paris and averaging perhaps 10% on a national basis. (14 francs = £1 = US$2.80 in 1964.)

THE GERMAN MARKET

In Germany the appliance industry was less concentrated than in the United Kingdom. Seven washing machine manufacturers accounted for over 70% of the market.

AEG	25%
Constructa	10
Siemens	8
Zanker	8
Bosch	5
Bauknecht	5

No foreign manufacturer had so far gained a significant share, perhaps because German products had a reputation for good engineering and quality. Imports amounted to only 53,000 units in 1961 and 75,000 units in 1964, compared with exports of 188,000 and 259,000, respectively. Twin-tub machines had enjoyed considerable success in Germany beginning in 1956, but Hoover's market share had decreased to less than 4% in 1964. All the Hoover washers sold in 1964 were imported from the United Kingdom, but in 1965 the company began selling automatics purchased from an Italian supplier in addition to twin tubs and Keymatics.

In Germany, single-tub nonautomatics dominated the market until 1958, when automatics started to gain substantial acceptance. Sales of automatics increased rapidly. In 1960, fully automatics represented 22% of the market; by 1964, 41%. Hoover market research suggested this growth was primarily the result of aggressive promotion and relatively low price spreads between automatics and twin tubs. In addition, German testing authorities recommended tumble-action machines as the most efficient and least damaging.

Constructa and Westinghouse had introduced fully automatic washers before 1954, and by 1959 some 18 different brands were available. The earliest model in the Constructa line, with a capacity of 3 kg, had been sold at a retail price of slightly over £100, only a little more than the least expensive twin-tub machines. Moreover, Constructa had made substantial advertising expenditures, which reached an annual level of nearly £800,000 by 1959. As a result, it was the largest selling automatic brand in Germany, with around 37% share in 1963.

In general, German machines were bulkier than French and similar in size to British machines. The average dimensions of German washing machines were height 85 to 90 cm, width 60 to 68 cm, and depth 57 to 52 cm.

"Going" retail prices (after discounts) for some major brands in Germany in 1965 were:

Brand and type	Retail price*	
	Deutsche marks	*Pounds*
Nonautomatic, single-tub:		
Hoover	398	34.8
Twin tubs, semiautomatic:		
Hoover	598	52.2
AEG	890	77.7
Miele	980	85.6
Siemens	880	76.9
Average	837	73.1

	Regular		Compact	
	Deutsche marks	*Pounds*	*Deutsche marks*	*Pounds*
Fully automatic:				
Hoover (Keymatic)	1,348	117.7	—	—
(Italian source)	765/895/1,225	66.8/78.2/107.0	—	—
AEG	1,150/1,290/1,420	100.4/112.7/124.0	740	64.6
Constructa	1,248/1,475	109.0/128.8	—	—
Miele	1,330	116.2	790	69.0
Siemens	—	—	590/640/845	51.5/55.9/73.8
Zanker	1,148	100.3	670	58.5
Candy (Italian)	690	61.0	—	—
Average (using mid-range models)	1,152	100.7	710	62.0

*£1 = 11.45 DM = US$2.80 in 1964.

THE ITALIAN MARKET

Italy was the most rapidly growing market for washing machines in Europe, as shown in *Exhibit 6*. Before 1960 Hoover had been the leading brand in Italy. With the rapid growth of the domestic industry, however, Hoover's share declined sharply until, by 1964, it was less than 4%. In early 1965, the company began selling automatic machines purchased from an Italian supplier under the Hoover name.

Published statistics on the Italian appliance industry were scarce and of doubtful reliability. The best available estimates indicated that the leading brands of washing machines in 1962 were Candy, with 35%; Indesit, with 15%; and Castor and Zanussi, with 10% to 22% each.

Fully automatic washers, which had accounted for only 14% of the Italian market in 1960, represented over 90% of sales in 1964. Prices of some Italian automatics were lower than in any other European country.

Brand/model	Estimated "going" retail price
Candy-Auto. 3	£57
Indesit	57
Zanussi-Rex 260	80
Zoppas	99
Castor-Drymatic Luxe	100
Hoover Keymatic (U.K.)	186
Constructa (Germany)	234

Virtually all automatic washers sold in Italy were front-loading, tumble-action machines. Consistent with the mass production, low-price policies of the major Italian manufacturers, most domestically produced machines were of relatively simple design.

Estimated ownership of washing machines rose from about 1% of Italian households in 1955 to 4% in 1960 and 16% at the end of 1964.[10]

THE SWEDISH MARKET

A distinctive feature of the Swedish market was the widespread use of communal washing facilities. Thus, although only 30% of households owned their own washers, a roughly equal number had access to machines shared within an apartment building. The three leading brands of washing machines in the Swedish market in rank order were a Swedish firm, Elektroskandia; a German firm, Siemens; and Hoover. Hoover's share of the market had fallen over 20% in the late 1950s to 12% in 1962, and less than 5% in 1964.

---

[10]Estimates by Castellano, *L'industria degli elettrodomestici in Italia*, 24.

The Swedish market showed an increasing preference for the front-loading, tumble-action automatic machine. Consequently, demand for the pulsator type had decreased.

	1961	1962	1963	1964
Nonautomatics:				
Pulsator	31%	16%	6%	3%
Agitator	3	2	—	—
Semiautomatics and twin tubs	47	58	68	71
Fully automatics	18	24	25	26

In 1964, 48,000 machines were imported; 66,000 were produced domestically. Most imports came from Germany. Moreover, Husqvarna, one of the leading Swedish firms, produced machines under license from the German company AEG.

Hoover's market position in Sweden had been adversely affected by the Swedish Consumer Institute's criticisms of its product design. This institute rated various products and its opinions were widely disseminated through published reports. As did the German testing agencies, it criticized the pulsator action as being harsher than tumble action. It also endorsed stainless steel as superior to enameled steel in the drum.

Retail prices of some of the leading brands of automatic washers in Sweden in 1963 were estimated as follows: Husqvarna, £214; Elux-Miele (German), £203; and Hoover Keymatic, £134.

PRODUCT DESIGN ALTERNATIVES FOR PROJECT 7

The Keymatic was the leading automatic washer in the United Kingdom in 1964, but its sales in continental markets were not satisfactory to Hoover management. Hoover dealers were urging the company to provide a front-loading, tumble-action machine.

The New Products Committee's basic problem was to decide whether it would be possible to produce a single "European" machine, one to suit both British and continental consumers. Otherwise, it would be necessary to produce (and/or purchase from other manufacturers) two or more different machines. Mr. Lloyd felt that because of the importance of the domestic market to Hoover's overall operations, it was "essential to develop the type of machine which will find maximum acceptance in the United Kingdom. We realize that this machine may not find equal acceptance in continental markets; some modification would, therefore, be necessary, and this could affect home demand."

The Committee hoped to agree on a common *basic* design for the new line of automatics. Within this concept two or more model variations could be offered with different degrees of automatic operation and different prices. The basic features of exterior dimensions, load capacity, and spinning speed would have to be the same, however, to permit economies of common tooling and common components, such as motors.

Among the important design features to be resolved for Project 7 were load capacity, shell dimensions, spinning speed, drum materials, water heating system, and styling. As a basis for considering alternatives, the Committee studied competing products in each market and a survey of the expressed preferences of automatic washing machine owners in the United Kingdom (see *Exhibit 7*).

LOAD CAPACITY. It was customary to express "stated" capacity in terms of the approximate *weight* of the wash load which could be placed in the machine. Thus, machines were described as "4 kg," "5 kg," and so on.[11]

The problem of design for machine capacity was complicated by continental competitors overclaiming. In consumer advertising it was common to claim capacities from 14% to 25% greater than actual.

To be competitive, Mr. Cutinella, vice-president of marketing of Hoover, felt it was essential to be able to claim a 5 kg capacity in advertising on the continent. Apparently a somewhat smaller machine would be adequate for the United Kingdom. The survey of U.K. automatic owners indicated capacity was the most important single feature. Most users interviewed preferred an 8 to 10 lb (3.7 to 4.6 kg) capacity.

The report submitted to the committee by the Hoover Engineering Department recommended an actual capacity of 4 kg.

SHELL DIMENSIONS. Shell dimensions were basically governed by the capacity of the machine. With a capacity of 4 kg, it was virtually impossible to reduce the height below 85 cm (35.5 in.). Depth and width were interdependent with height and capacity, and it was recommended that the depth be limited to 53.5 cm (21 in.), the minimum that could be achieved. The width of the machine could not be smaller than 68.5

---

[11]In the United Kingdom, load capacities were stated in *pounds* (1 kg = 2.2 lbs).

EXHIBIT 7. Feature comparison of selected brands of automatic washing machines, United Kingdom, 1965

Features	Hotpoint	Servis de Luxe	Bendix	English Elec. (Liberator)	Imperial Super
			Brands/models		
Height (in.)	41.50	36.00	43.00	37.00	35.35
(cm)	105.4	91.4	109.2	94.0	89.5
Width (in.)	22.00	22.63	27.00	25.00	24.75
(cm)	55.9	57.5	68.6	63.5	62.9
Depth (in.)	22.00	24.50	24.00	25.00	21.00
(cm)	55.9	62.2	61.0	63.5	53.3
Drum material	Enamel	Enamel	Enamel	Enamel	Stainless
Loading	Top	Top	Front	Front	Front
Porthole	No	No	Yes	Yes	Yes
Capacity (lbs)	10	6	9	7	9
(kgs)	4.5	2.7	4.1	3.2	4.1
Spinning speed (rpm)	508	650	650	525	400
Controls	Knobs	Knobs	Push button	Knobs	Knobs
"Going" price	£115.1	£113.8	£115.1	£109.4	£83.0

Source: Hoover Limited Market Research Department.

cm (29 in.). The Hoover marketing director felt width should be minimized in view of the space problem in British kitchens.

SPINNING SPEED.   Fully automatic machines in both U.K. and continental markets were showing a definite trend toward higher spinning speeds. Before the introduction of the Keymatic, the generally accepted spinning speed was around 400 rpm, but more recent automatics had speeds of 700 rpm or above. Among the models displayed at a recent trade fair, three Italian machines and one German brand offered speeds around 400 rpm; the Bauknecht provided 600 rpm; Constructa, Bosch, the Juno de luxe, and Scharff had 700 rpm speeds; and Constructa's "V series," 850 rpm.

Mr. Cutinella expressed a strong desire for a speed of 850 rpm. He cited Constructa, as leader in Germany, which had produced an automatic with that spinning speed and had thereby forced other manufacturers to do so. He maintained that the additional speed was important to sell dealers on the superiority of an automatic. He stressed that this also represented a major feature for sales promotion, and because Project 7 would not be available for another 18 months, it was essential to keep pace with the trend toward increased spinning speeds. The cost for 850 rpm was estimated at approximately £0.75 per unit above that for 700 rpm.

From the consumer's viewpoint, spinning speed was important because it affected clothing dryness on completion of the water-extraction phase. Consumers interviewed in the U.K. survey rated "dryness" as the second most important element of performance. Twin-tub machines or separate spin dryers were more efficient in extraction than most automatics; to match spin dryers, a spinning speed of 1,000 rpm would be necessary. The Engineering Department studies indicated, however, that a 1,000 rpm speed would be "too expensive to be justified by the difference in results."

One speed had to be chosen for all machines in the new line, because speed affected the motor and drive design as well as the dimensions and strength of the support structure.

DRUM MATERIALS. The inner drums of Hoover's nonautomatic and Keymatic machines were enameled steel. Most continental manufacturers used stainless steel for their automatics, and Mr. Cutinella stated that it would be preferable in the new Hoover line. The U.K. survey expressed a slight preference for stainless steel too, but this feature was not rated as very important. The market research staff concluded that Hoover could use enameled steel without "prejudicing its sales image" in the United Kingdom. The Engineering Department reported that an enameled steel drum offered a cost saving over stainless steel of approximately £1 per unit.

WATER HEATING SYSTEMS. Previous models of Hoover washing machines featured "hot water fill" — the machine's hot water was provided by the household's central water heater. The U.K. survey indicated 85% of those interviewed preferred this system. Hot water fill offered two basic advantages: speed and economy. In houses equipped with central water heaters, a separate heater in the washing machine ("cold water fill") represented an unnecessary additional cost. Moreover, a heating phase in the wash cycle added to its total time. Over 80% of the users in the U.K. survey wished to maintain the total wash time at approximately two hours, which was based on hot water fill.

Hoover's past promotional efforts in the United Kingdom had emphasized the merits of a hot water fill, and some executives believed that a major new promotional effort would be required to alter the existing attitudes.

On the continent, virtually all automatics featured cold water fill, in part because fewer households owned central water heaters, and in part because many users — especially in Germany — believed that boiling water (100°C) was required for proper cleaning. Tests by the magazine *DM* indicated that 100°C provided no significant benefits over 90°C, either in washing efficiency or in sterilization. Nevertheless, a major German manufacturer emphasized boiling in its advertising.

According to the Hoover Engineering Department, the washing action envisaged for the Project 7 machine would work most efficiently if it commenced with cold water. This was thought to suggest the desirability of a cold water fill.

The variable cost of including a water heater was estimated at £2.8 per unit.

STYLING. Because most major brands of washers would provide satisfactory washing performance, styling was regarded as an important differential design feature. Style preferences varied somewhat among European countries. According to Hoover executives, Italian consumers were apparently attracted to bright colors; German buyers preferred products with an "indestructible" appearance, and U.K. customers were most interested in an inconspicuous design.

Hoover had retained a styling consultant for the Project 7 line, and his tentative concept was a conservative design featuring white with chrome and charcoal gray trim.

Hoover management had also tentatively decided to provide a glass "porthole" window in the door of the machine. Windows were offered by most competing machines on the continent. In the United Kingdom, automatic owners were about equally divided between a desire for the window and a "don't care" attitude. According to Hoover executives, there was no "good reason" for a window. Apparently those who preferred it had been conditioned by the prevalence of window-front machines (primarily Bendix) in coin-operated, self-service laundries.

A window would entail a significant extra cost (approximately £0.5). For this reason, Hoover's Engineering Department recommended a plain metal door design.

RANGE OF MODELS

The New Products Committee recognized that it might be desirable to offer two or more model variations on the same basic product design. From a technical standpoint, the basic design could be modified to include or exclude the window and/or the separate water heater; it was also possible to interchange stainless steel and enameled steel tubs.

PRICES AND COSTS

The investment and development costs for Project 7 before introduction were estimated as follows:

Research, development, and engineering	£238,000
Plant	608,000
Tooling	592,000

These costs would remain in the same order of magnitude, whether one or two models of the same machine were produced. On the other hand, if two basically different machines were produced, incremental costs were estimated at £600,000 for plant and tooling and £100,000 for research.

Introductory promotional expenditures were estimated to be at least £350,000 in the United Kingdom and £200,000 in continental markets.

According to Hoover's Engineering Department, the variable costs of production for an automatic washer with *all* the features proposed — stainless steel drum, window, 850 rpm, and cold water fill — would be approximately £35 per unit. Fixed and semivariable costs for any level of output in the range considered reasonable would be around £1 million per year.[12]

Hoover sold to distributors (wholesalers) in the United Kingdom and to its subsidiaries in other countries, which in turn sold to distributors. General, sales, and administrative expenses were estimated at 15% for sales in the United Kingdom and 5% in continental countries. The GS&A expenses for subsidiaries were added after calculating ad valorem tariffs (see *Exhibit 5*).

The New Products Committee considered pricing requirements for effective competition in continental markets. They anticipated that the new Project 7 models would be available by mid-1967. By this time cus-

---

[12]A major portion of these costs would be eliminated if Hoover discontinued its automatic washing machine business altogether, but they were essentially fixed with respect to output levels.

toms duties would be abolished within the EEC, and all member countries would impose a duty of 10% to 15% on major appliance imports from the United Kingdom. This tariff barrier made it more difficult, of course, for Hoover to match the costs of manufacturers in the EEC. Average unit transportation costs to continental markets, assuming bulk shipments, were expected to be about £1.0.

In 1965 the f.o.b. costs of machines purchased from Italian producers ranged from £36 to £40 for deluxe models, from £31 to £34 for standard models, and from £28 to £30 for simplified models.

Mr. Lloyd had requested a study in the United Kingdom by the Merchandising Department of expected price-volume relationships. It indicated that the maximum total contribution to fixed costs and profit of the deluxe model would be achieved at a suggested retail price of £103.7, excluding purchase tax. The Hoover factory price to wholesalers would average £63.9. If the standard model were to have a suggested retail price of, say, £90.0, the Hoover factory price would be £55.4. Domestic sales at this price level were estimated at 60,000 units per year.

SALES GOALS

The final item on the New Products Committee meeting agenda was to establish sales goals for the new line. Mr. Lloyd asked the committee if they felt that an estimate of 175,000 units annually (for the entire product line) was reasonable. It was based on sales goals of 100,000 units in the home market (60,000 deluxe and 40,000 standard); 50,000 units in continental European markets; and 25,000 units in other export markets.

2.4 CASE

Computervision Japan

Rowland T. Moriarty

In early May 1983, Patrick Alias was returning to the United States from his third trip to Japan in as many months. Ever since his promotion in February to Vice-President, Americas-Far East (AFE), of Computervision Corporation (CV), he had been shuttling back and forth between Boston and Tokyo. With each trip to Japan, his concern about CV's competitive position had increased. Although CV's exclusive Japanese distributor believed it was doing a good job of marketing the CV product line, there were clear signs that the competition — especially IBM and Fujitsu — were gaining market share at CV's expense. Costs for CV's marketing support organization in Japan had also risen dramatically from $200,000 per quarter in 1979 to $1,400,000 for the first quarter in 1983.

When Jim Berrett, President of Computervision, promoted Alias to his new position, he made the following comment:

Japan is by far the largest market in the AFE organization. It certainly is the fastest growing market in the AFE and possibly the world, yet our market penetration there is substantially below the United States and Europe. If we don't take immediate steps to improve our position, we could wind up as a minor player in the Japanese market.

Just before Alias's recent visit to Japan, Berrett had asked him to prepare a detailed plan for improving CV's penetration of the Japanese market. The Japanese market was becoming so important to CV's overall strategy that Jim Berrett wanted Alias to be ready to present his recommendations to CV's board of directors at their May 26 meeting.

COMPUTERVISION CORPORATION (CV)

With 1982 revenues of $325 million, CV was the worldwide leader in CAD/CAM turnkey systems. Headquartered in Bedford, Massachusetts, the company was engaged in designing, manufacturing, marketing, and servicing computer-aided design and computer-aided manufacturing (CAD/CAM) products and systems. These systems were used for increasing productivity and product quality. They shortened the cycle for developing and manufacturing new products by automating many complex or repetitive tasks previously performed manually. CAD/CAM was one of the core building blocks in the newly emerging concept of computer-integrated manufacturing (CIM). The objective of CIM was to automate and computerize all aspects of product design, engineering, and production. CAD/CAM equipment was the fastest growing segment of the industrial automation business. The worldwide market for CAD/CAM equipment was forecast to be a $4–6 billion business by 1987 with an estimated growth rate of 30–50% per year.

COMPANY HISTORY

CV was one of the first entrants into the CAD/CAM industry in 1969, when its cofounders developed an automatic integrated circuit network generator. During the 1970s, CV developed and marketed several leading-edge CAD/CAM products and grew at an annual compound rate of more than 50%. However, in 1981 CV's sales had begun to slow. By 1982, CV's sales grew only 20% over 1981. (See *Exhibit 1* for selected financial data on the company.)

CV claimed to have a 35% share of the turnkey system's market in

EXHIBIT 1. Computervision Corporation
Five-year summary of selected financial data (in thousands except per share data)

	1982	1981	1980	1979	1978
Revenues	$325,185	$270,706	$191,086	$103,004	$48,432
Operating income	$ 48,181	$ 55,339	$ 40,761	$ 24,184	$ 9,722
Income from continuing operations	$ 32,381	$ 35,748	$ 23,464	$ 12,874	$ 4,811
Income per share from continuing operations	$ 1.18	$ 1.30	$ .91	$ .52	$ .24
Research and development expenses as % of revenues	11.2%	10.0%	9.9%	8.6%	7.9%
Operating income as % of revenues	14.8%	20.4%	21.3%	23.5%	20.1%
Income from continuing operations as % of revenues	10.0%	13.2%	12.3%	12.5%	9.9%
Return on average stockholders' equity	19.9%	25.3%	33.8%	39.3%	37.5%
Revenues by geographic areas:					
United States	54.5%	54.3%	59.6%	64.6%	63.3%
Europe	34.7%	36.5%	33.7%	29.7%	30.4%
Other	10.8%	9.2%	6.7%	5.7%	6.3%
Total assets	$274,140	$228,838	$167,479	$ 86,876	$49,112
Long-term debt and capitalized leases	$ 30,689	$ 29,645	$ 19,521	$ 15,934	$ 6,382
Stockholders' equity	$179,780	$144,993	$108,480	$ 40,659	$26,447
Current ratio	2.5	2.5	2.8	1.9	2.2
Debt to total capital	15%	17%	15%	28%	19%

Income statement data for all periods reflect the results of continuing operations only. Balance sheet data and return on average stockholders' equity reflect the financial position and net income of the total company.
No cash dividends have been declared. Applicable data have been restated to reflect two-for-one stock splits in 1981, 1980, and 1979.

232

the United States, where it had focused most of its efforts on the large (Fortune 500) manufacturing companies. CV also had a strong position in Europe with more than 60% of the market in some countries.

PRODUCTS

CV's products were known for their quality and reliability. Its newest high-performance product line was the Designer V system shown in *Exhibit 2*. The price of the system in the U.S. ranged from $200,000 to $600,000, depending on the system's application and its particular hardware/software configuration. The company also marketed a medium-

EXHIBIT 2. Designer V system

scale system called the Designer M series that sold for approximately $120,000.

CAD/CAM systems, like most computer-based systems, had three primary components — the computer hardware, the operating system software, and the application software. The quality, performance, and reliability of a CAD/CAM system depended heavily upon how well the system's hardware and software components were integrated. Most of CV's competitors were systems integrators. They created turnkey systems by adding their software to another company's hardware.

Unlike its competitors, CV designed and produced a substantial portion of the minicomputer-based hardware for the Designer product line. Because much of this hardware was custom-designed for CAD/CAM systems, the software was often easier and less expensive to develop. CV believed their resulting systems were better integrated and provided more features than comparable competitive products.

The operating system software in the Designer product line was specifically developed by CV to enable users to create, design, manipulate, edit, and store data for both two- and three-dimensional diagrams. CV had also developed a variety of specialized software packages for the following applications:

1. Mechanical design
2. Manufacturing and process control
3. Electronic design of printed circuits, integrated circuits, and wiring diagrams
4. Architecture, engineering, and construction (including piping)
5. Mapping

In addition to being vertically integrated, CV distinguished itself from the competition by offering a complete spectrum of support services to its customers, including:

- Preinstallation consulting
- Educational services
- Audiovisual training materials
- Equipment delivery and installation
- Acceptance testing
- On-site consultation and guidance
- Documentation
- Productivity services
- Contract maintenance

- International parts centers
- Remote diagnostics

INTERNATIONAL OPERATIONS

Computervision's international expansion followed the typical pattern for fast-growth, high-technology companies. In 1972, CV hired agents to sell its products in the U.K., France, and Holland. Since they generated little sales volume, CV appointed a European sales manager in 1973. Shortly after his arrival in Europe, the sales manager fired the French agent and hired Patrick Alias as CV's first direct sales representative in Europe. Alias was a 28-year-old Frenchman with master's degrees in electronics and mathematics and three years of experience working for a small American computer company in France. In his first year he booked three times the orders of all the European agents combined.

Alias's success led to CV's decision to phase out the European agents over the next two years and build a European sales, service, and marketing support organization. By 1977 CV-Europe was generating a third of the company's sales revenues and had 150 employees. By 1982, CV-Europe had 450 employees and was generating 35% ($113 million) of the company's yearly revenue.

Alias's career growth paralleled the rapid development of the European market. During the 1970s he held a variety of sales and marketing positions within CV-Europe and was appointed VP marketing for Europe in 1981. CV's senior management felt that Alias's leadership, management, drive, and ambition played an important role in the rapid development of the European sales organization.

In February 1983, when Jim Berrett promoted Alias to the position of VP-AFE, he had high expectations that he would have a significant impact on CV's competitive position in Japan. Unlike Europe, CV had always marketed products in Japan through an exclusive distributor, Tokyo Electron Limited.

TOKYO ELECTRON LIMITED (TEL)

Founded in 1963, TEL had grown rapidly by aggressively marketing imported high-technology systems in Japan. When CV entered the market in 1973, TEL had become its exclusive distributor.

Headquartered in Tokyo, TEL had 1982 sales of $256 million (U.S. dollars) and net profit in $28.1 million. It had been growing at a sus-

EXHIBIT 3. Tokyo Electron Limited nonconsolidated statements of income (years ended September 30, 1982 and 1983)

	U.S. dollars (thousands)	
	1982	*1981*
Net sales	$256,008	$204,277
Operating expenses:		
Cost of sales	192,780	149,152
Selling, G&A expenses	35,055	30,759
Net profit from operations	$ 28,173	$ 24,366

EXHIBIT 4. TEL's sales by sales division

	Sales			
	1982	*1981*		% of total 1982
Sales division	*(millions)*		% change	company sales
Semiconductor production equipment	$105.8	$ 93.4	13.3%	41.3%
Measurement analysis systems	41.3	27.6	49.6	16.1
Computer-controlled systems (CCS)*	40.3	31.4	28.3	15.7
Electronic parts and components	68.6	51.8	32.4	26.8
Totals	$256.0	$204.2	25.4%	100.0%

*1979 sales = $12.6 million.
 1980 sales = $18.5 million.

tained rate of 25% per year for the last 10 years. *Exhibits 3* and *4* contain selected financial data on TEL. TEL's operations were divided between production and marketing. Production was carried out by its subsidiary, Telmec Inc., and four affiliates based on joint venture production agreements with U.S. high-technology companies. The marketing operation had four separate sales divisions whose 1981 and 1982 results are shown in *Exhibit 4*. CV's products were sold through the Computer Controlled Systems (CCS) division of TEL, whose revenues were up 28% in 1982 to $40.3 million. CV's CAD/CAM systems represented about 80% of the CCS division sales.

The director of CCS was Jim Nomura, who joined TEL in 1967 after working for Sumitomo Electric for seven years. He had headed TEL's CAD/CAM sales operation since its beginning in 1973. Having worked in the United States for three years, Nomura spoke excellent English and was familiar with the American style of management. Over the years, CV had assigned responsibility for the Japanese market to a number of different managers, many of whom now held senior management positions. Because Nomura had always handled TEL's relationship with CV personally, he knew many of CV's current executives.

The 10-year relationship between CV and TEL had been uneven. Up until 1977, CV sales in Japan grew slowly and the TEL/CV relationship was amiable. Senior management at CV had been focused primarily on the fast-growth markets in the United States and Europe. However, in 1977 a newly appointed CV manager for Japan undertook a complete review of the CV/TEL arrangement. He was dissatisfied with many aspects of TEL's handling of the CV product line including: market penetration, market coverage, customer support, customer service, new product introduction, new product adaptation, and pricing policies. After a complete review of the options available to CV in the Japanese market, including the establishment of a direct CV sales organization and an analysis of alternative distributors, CV decided not to sever its relationship with TEL. CV felt the overall size of the market at that time did not warrant the risks, the management time, and the expense of switching distributors or establishing its own sales operation. Since that time, the situation in Japan had been under constant review by CV's senior management. A continuing concern that the Japanese CAD/CAM market was about to explode, and that CVJ was not well positioned to be the market leader, developed a constant tension in the CV/TEL relationship.

Along with growth and expansion over the past ten years, TEL's strategic orientation had migrated away from just being an exclusive distributor for American high-technology companies. It now had a strong preference for manufacturing or assembling as well as selling American high-tech products in Japan. In September 1981, TEL established a 50/50 joint venture with GenRad (TEL-GenRad Limited) to begin domestic production of GenRad's electronic testing systems. Similar joint ventures had been established with other U.S. high-tech companies operating under the names TEL-Varian Limited, TEL-Thermco Limited, and TEL-Tre Limited. TEL's complete line of products were sold through its four separate sales divisions.

TEL's joint ventures put additional pressure on the TEL/CV relationship in several ways. First, TEL was assured a long-term relationship with its joint venture partners, whereas its exclusive distribution contract with CV had lapsed two years earlier and had never been replaced. TEL and CV had only a temporary agreement requiring a written 30-day notice by either company to cancel their arrangement. Second, becoming a manufacturing company had significantly increased TEL's prestige and profile within the Japanese business community. This had helped TEL greatly in competing with Japan's largest employers for the best university graduates each year, but now the limited availability of university recruits was constraining TEL's growth. TEL's uncertain relationship with CV was making it increasingly difficult for Jim Nomura to compete internally with the other TEL sales divisions for new people to expand sales coverage. Third, TEL management believed that joint ventures helped its long-term stability by transferring American technologies into the company. This in-house technical knowledge would also increase its options whenever a joint venture agreement expired. Finally, TEL believed that joint ventures gave it a competitive edge in the marketplace. The company's better understanding of the technology improved its ability to adapt American products for their Japanese customers and also helped it provide better applications and service support.

Ever since the mid-1970s, Nomura had been proposing a joint venture with CV. Several factors caused CV senior management to be unreceptive to this idea: (1) CV had no other joint ventures, (2) Japan represented a small proportion of its overall revenues, and (3) the company was extremely concerned about safeguarding its proprietary technology. As a result, Jim Berrett told Alias that a joint venture with TEL would not be possible in the foreseeable future.

CAD/CAM equipment was clearly an important source of revenues and profits for TEL. In spite of the various ups and downs in the TEL/CV relationship, Nomura felt TEL was doing an excellent job for CV in the Japanese CAD/CAM market. Sales results for the CCS division over the past few years were impressive — 47% increase in 1980, 70% increase in 1981, and 28% increase in 1982. Nomura also pointed to the large increase and projected increase in staffing for his division as evidence of TEL's ongoing commitment to CV. (See *Exhibit 5* for staffing projections and *Exhibit 8* for CCS organization.)

CV sold its systems to TEL at about 35% below the U.S. list price. TEL typically sold the system in Japan at U.S. list price plus 15% for shipping, tariffs, and insurance. A typical system that sold in Japan for $500,000 and in the U.S. for $425,000 was purchased by TEL for $275,000 F.O.B., Bedford, Massachusetts. CV management believed that the high Japanese prices for this equipment hurt their market penetration in Japan. TEL discounted the CV systems anywhere from 0% to 30%, depending on the customer, the size of the order, and the date the order was placed in the quarter. Aware of pressure on CV from security ana-

EXHIBIT 5. TEL staffing chart for CCS sales division

	1973	1974	1975	1976	1977	1978	1979	1980	1981	1982	1983	1984	1985	1986	1987
Sales & sales AE[a]	1	2	2	3	5	7	7	14	21	25	37	46	64	88	125
Service CE[b] & AE subcontract	—	3	3	3	6	10	13	16	22	25	31	37	44	53	64
	—	1	2	2	4	5	5	8	10	15	26	35	48	66	90
										(4)	(13)	(21)	(32)	(47)	(68)
Programmer subcontract			1	1	1	1	1	2	3	11	11	14	16	18	20
								(2)	(15)	(21)	(34)	(36)	(40)	(45)	(50)
General management	0	2	3	1	1	1	2	2	2	4	4	5	6	7	8
Administration						1	1	2	2	3	4	5	6	6	6
secretaries	1	1	1	1	3	3	4	5	7	12	18	23	26	33	39
Totals	2	9	12	11	20	28	33	51	82	120	178	222	282	363	470
Averages	(1.17)	(7.17)	(10.9)	(10.83)	(14.00)	(24.83)	(28.58)	(42)	(70)	(107)					
Growth rates	—	350%	33%	(8%)	82%	40%	18%	55%	61%	46%	48%	25%	27%	29%	29%

← PLAN →

[a] AE indicates account executive.
[b] CE indicates customer engineer.

lysts for steady and dramatic increases in quarterly revenue, TEL tended to hold back orders until just before the end of CV's quarter in order to obtain additional discounts and concessions. After all discounting and negotiation, CV averaged 53% gross margin on TEL shipments. This did not include any of the expenses for the CVJ operation.

CV-JAPAN (CVJ)

CV-Japan, headquartered in Tokyo, was by far the largest operation within CV's Americas-Far East organization.

CV's total installed base of systems in the AFE was 282, with 198 in Japan (70%), 21 in Australia, 18 in Singapore, 15 in Taiwan, and 30 in the other 14 countries covered by the AFE. In 1982, the AFE produced about 10% of CV's revenue — $34.8 million — of which $17 million (49%) came from Japan (TEL). Jim Berrett's strategic plan projected CV's revenues from Japan to grow 47% in 1983 to $25 million, 36% in 1984 to $34 million, and 62% in 1985 to $55 million. In the first quarter of 1983, CV's sales to Japan (TEL) were $6.7 million with CVJ expenses of $1.4 million and a cost of goods of $3.2 million. See *Exhibit 6* for TEL's CAD/CAM sales performance 1978–1982.

The CVJ organization, shown in *Exhibit 7*, had grown from 25 people in 1980 to 75 people in 1983. In order to support TEL's efforts in Japan, CVJ had added 20 people to marketing, 14 to software development, 5 to software support, 3 to hardware support, and 8 others to various staff functions. The marketing function was divided into sales and sales support. The salespeople were assigned to specific geographic areas and were responsible for achieving monthly, quarterly, and yearly sales plans by supporting TEL's sales representatives. The sales support account executives were also assigned geographically to support TEL's

EXHIBIT 6. TEL's CAD/CAM sales performance

	1982 ($M)	1981 ($M)	1980 ($M)	1979 ($M)	1978 ($M)
TEL system sales	31.54	19.13	11.47	6.96	5.76
TEL service revenues	1.23	.83	.43	.25	.09
Total TEL sales from CV systems	32.77	19.96	11.90	7.21	5.85
% increase	+64%	+68%	+65%	+23%	
# systems sold	63	39	23	14	11
CV's revenue from TEL	17.1	13.5	8.2	4.9	4.0

EXHIBIT 7. CV-Japan organization

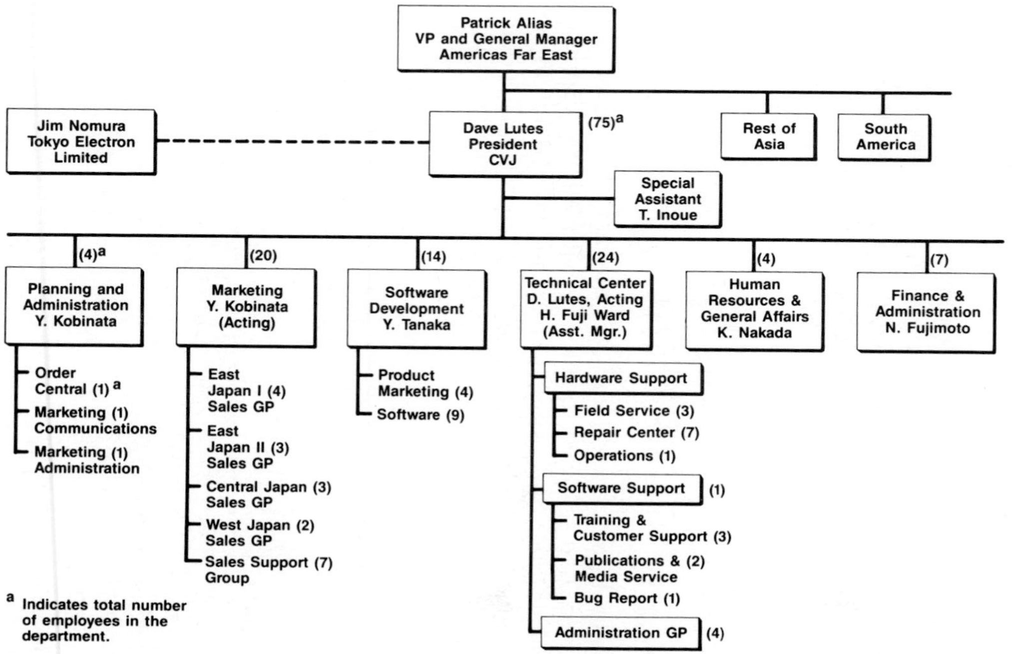

Jim Nomura
Tokyo Electron
Limited

Patrick Alias
VP and General Manager
Americas Far East

South America

Rest of Asia

Dave Lutes
President
CVJ

(75)[a]

Special Assistant
T. Inoue

(4)[a]

Planning and Administration
Y. Kobinata

- Order Central (1)[a]
- Marketing Communications (1)
- Marketing Administration (1)

(20)

Marketing
Y. Kobinata
(Acting)

- East Japan I (4) Sales GP
- East Japan II (3) Sales GP
- Central Japan (3) Sales GP
- West Japan (2) Sales GP
- Sales Support (7) Group

(14)

Software Development
Y. Tanaka

- Product Marketing (4)
- Software (9)

(24)

Technical Center
D. Lutes, Acting
H. Fuji Ward
(Asst. Mgr.)

- Hardware Support
  - Field Service (3)
  - Repair Center (7)
  - Operations (1)
- Software Support (1)
  - Training & Customer Support (3)
  - Publications & (2) Media Service
  - Bug Report (1)
- Administration GP (4)

(4)

Human Resources & General Affairs
K. Nakada

(7)

Finance & Administration
N. Fujimoto

[a] Indicates total number of employees in the department.

241

sales representatives through demonstrations, presales customer consultation, system proposals, and other functions required in promoting sales and closing an order. The software development function was responsible for helping TEL develop special software programs for the Japanese market. Product marketing was a new department within the software development function. Its objectives were stated as follows:

- Survey and analyze customer problems and the competitive situation in all applications areas.
- Help develop the marketing strategy for each application category and promote sales in cooperation with sales management.
- Introduce new CV products to Japanese users and prospects.
- Feed back information to CV's product development group at headquarters.
- Offer consulting services to customers and the sales force.

COMPETITION IN JAPAN

American companies dominated the market in Japan — although many of them had affiliated themselves with various Japanese companies to facilitate their own entry into the market. About 25 companies were competing in the Japanese CAD/CAM market. An independent market research firm estimated the Japanese installed base of CAD/CAM systems to be distributed as follows:

Company	Research firm's estimated 1982 installed base	
	Units	*%*
Computervision, Japan	130	20
Calma/C. Itoh	120	19
Applicon/Marubeni Hytech	100	15
IBM, Japan	80	12
Fujitsu (Facom)	80	12
Daini Seikosha (Seiko)	70	11
Other	70	11
Totals	650	100%

EXHIBIT 8. TEL-Computer Controlled Systems Division functional organization chart (May 1, 1983)

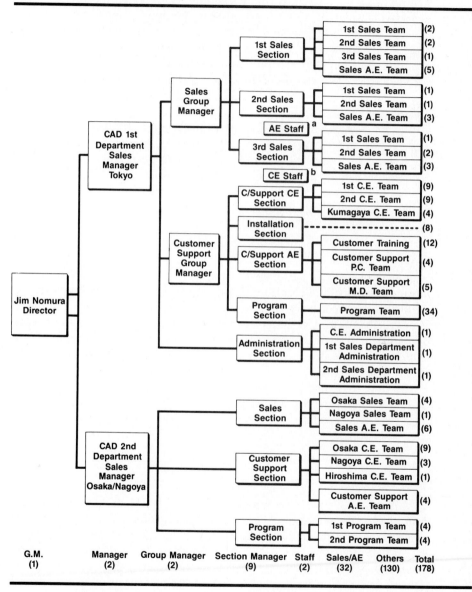

	G.M.	Manager	Group Manager	Section Manager	Staff	Sales/AE	Others	Total
	(1)	(2)	(2)	(9)	(2)	(32)	(130)	(178)

CALMA

Calma was a U.S.-based turnkey systems company with estimated 1982 worldwide sales of about $100 million. Recently acquired by General Electric, it was now part of GE's Industrial Automation Systems group. Calma's products focused heavily on the electronics industry, although it also had systems for mapping and architecture, engineering, and construction (AEC) applications. In Japan, Calma was the leading supplier for the integrated circuit (IC) application which represented 60% of its installed base of systems. Shortly after GE acquired Calma, it entered into a joint venture agreement with the Japanese trading company C. Itoh — the third largest independent trading company in Japan. The agreement included subassembly, service support, sales and distribution of its systems as well as some new product development. A large number of Calma/C. Itoh's sales and sales management people had recently left to join Digital Equipment Corporation in Japan.

APPLICON

Applicon was also a U.S.-based turnkey systems supplier. In 1982 it was acquired by Schlumberger, a leading supplier of data services to the oil industry. Applicon's worldwide sales were estimated to be $75 million. Applicon produced systems for most of the major CAD/CAM applications, but had been most successful in the electronics industry. In Japan, 80% of its installations were used for integrated circuit (IC) or printed circuit (PC) board design. Marubeni Hytech was Applicon's exclusive distributor responsible for sales, service, and support in Japan. Marubeni was the fourth largest independent trading company in Japan. During 1982–83, most of Applicon's orders had come from its existing customer base.

IBM-JAPAN

IBM-Japan was a wholly owned subsidiary of IBM. Its CAD/CAM systems were sold through a large, direct sales force as part of its broad offering of data processing products. During the past two years, IBM-Japan had increased its CAD/CAM sales effort dramatically. In addition to its large staff of CAD/CAM specialists in Tokyo, it also had CAD/CAM sales teams and support groups in Osaka and Nagoya (Japan's second and third largest cities). Industry sources estimated that Japan's CAD/CAM potential was located 50% in the Tokyo area, 20% in the Osaka area, and 20% in the Nagoya area.

Dataquest, a market research company, estimated that, in 1982, IBM-Japan had the largest CAD/CAM revenues in the Japanese market, with Fujitsu being number two. While both companies had a smaller installed base of CAD/CAM systems than the traditional turnkey vendors such as CV, Calma, and Applicon, they had a large installed base of mainframe computers and well-established reputations. Unlike the turnkey vendors, IBM and Fujitsu systems were not based exclusively on minicomputers. Their systems also ran on large IBM and IBM plug-compatible mainframes. Both companies used the CADAM software system that Lockheed had developed for its internal use. The CADAM system provided a two-dimensional drafting ability primarily used for mechanical design applications. IBM and Fujitsu marketed CADAM under a licensing agreement with Lockheed. Fujitsu also sold a three-dimensional software system called ICAD that had originally been developed for Fujitsu's internal use. It was estimated that 90% of IBM's and Fujitsu's installations were used for the mechanical design/drafting application.

FUJITSU

In 1982, the Facom division of Fujitsu surpassed IBM as the largest seller of computers in Japan. All of Fujitsu's mainframe computers were considered IBM plug-compatible. Like IBM-Japan, its CAD/CAM systems were sold through a large direct sales force. Facom invested heavily in the training and support of its customers. Although Facom had been selling CAD/CAM systems only since late 1981, it already had a large group of support people located in the four major cities of Japan — Tokyo, Osaka, Nagoya, and Kyushu. All of Facom's training, training literature, and training exercises were provided in Japanese — unlike most of the American CAD/CAM suppliers that provided Japanese-language training, but English-language text. While Facom was behind IBM in CAD/CAM revenues and units for 1982, it had made major inroads into the Japanese market. Although not known exactly, its 1982 CAD/CAM revenues in the Japanese market were estimated at approximately $50 million.

SEIKO

Daini Seikosha (Seiko) was a worldwide leader in the watch industry as well as a major supplier in Japan of graphics plotters, graphics terminals, and other graphics peripherals. In 1981, it entered the CAD/CAM market by using a variety of approaches. First, it became the exclusive distributor for the Create 2000 printed circuit board design systems that had been developed by another Japanese company — Zuken. Second, Seiko decided to market its own internally developed system for designing integrated circuits, called the SX8000 system. Finally, it agreed to be a nonexclusive distributor for the McAuto Unigraphics product used for mechanical design. This product had been developed for internal use by McDonnell Douglas and was now being marketed by its McAuto division. In Japan, McAuto was also selling the product through a small, direct sales force and other distributors. Seiko had shown a strong commitment to diversifying into the CAD/CAM area from its base in the manufacture of watches and other fine machinery. Many executives believed that Seiko would grow more rapidly than many U.S.-based companies in Japan because of its large investment, the local content of its hardware, and the company's support philosophy. Like Fujitsu, Seiko was providing heavy support for all three of its products. This was a considerable challenge because the Create 2000 was based on Hewlett-Packard equipment, while the SX8000 and the McAuto systems used DEC or Data General equipment. The declining cost of central processors combined with Seiko's locally manufactured peripherals allowed the company to price its systems much lower than CV, Applicon, or Calma. It was estimated that 60% of Seiko's installations were used for mechanical design and 40% for printed circuit board design.

COMPETITIVE OVERVIEW

The recent success of IBM and Fujitsu in the Japanese CAD/CAM market reflected the increased worldwide competition for this fast-growing market. Most of the large computer hardware companies were forward integrating into the CAD/CAM market by licensing third-party software. In addition to the large computer companies, the traditional turnkey systems suppliers (CV, Calma, Applicon, etc.) were encountering new competition from many other directions, including:

- Third-party software houses that packaged their software on hardware stipulated by the customer.
- Component integrators working on a specialized niche. For example, many of the recent start-ups in the field focused on the automated drafting function in order to gain a foothold in the overall CAD/CAM market.
- Some large companies like GM, GE, and Lockheed had developed a leading edge CAD/CAM technology internally in order to gain a

competitive advantage in their industry. Similar to Fujitsu, these companies were starting to sell and/or license their proprietary CAD/CAM knowledge.

In the past two years the Japanese market had attracted the attention of most of the new CAD/CAM suppliers.

THE JAPANESE CAD/CAM MARKET

Japan had a population of 116 million people and a gross national product of roughly one-half that of the United States. Robots were much more heavily used in the manufacturing process in Japan than CAD/CAM was in the design and engineering process. This reflected the strong Japanese emphasis on manufacturing quality and cost control, as well as the easier cost justification for robotics. Because it was hard to put a cash value on fast design turnaround and multiple design iterations, costs of CAD/CAM systems were more difficult to justify. The market situation was just the reverse in the U.S., where total revenues generated by CAD/CAM sales were much larger than total revenues generated by robotics sales.

A Dataquest research report estimated the total installed base of CAD/CAM systems in Japan at the end of 1982 to be distributed by application as follows:

Application[a]	Installed systems base	Percent of installed base
Mechanical design	426	64%
IC design	130	20
PC design	65	10
AEC	32	5
Mapping/other	7	1
Totals	650	100%

[a]In Japan, 60% of CV's systems were used for mechanical design, 20% for PC design, and 20% for all other applications.

The total installed base in the United States was estimated to be 5,800 units. Adjusting for the difference in GNPs, the current Japanese installed base was equivalent to that of the United States in 1977. From

1977 to 1982 the U.S. market grew at a compound annual rate of 47% for systems sold, 53% for workstations sold, and 71% for total annual revenue. During this same period, the compound annual growth rate by application was as follows: mechanical design — 87%; PC board design — 67%; IC design — 62%; mapping — 60%; and AEC —57%. Similar to the United States, the mechanical design applications area was forecast to be the fastest growing application in Japan, followed by printed circuits (PC), integrated circuits (IC), mapping, and architecture, engineering, construction (AEC).

PRICING

Historically, CAD/CAM systems cost much more in Japan than in the United States. For example, a typical CV system with four terminals in Japan cost approximately $500,000 versus $425,000 in the United States. The Japanese prices of the other American turnkey vendors were slightly less but in the same general range. However, Japanese systems did not have to pay import duties and shipping, which could add 15% to the price of a system. In the long run both TEL and CV expected prices to decline in Japan between 5% and 15% per year.

Another factor was the type of central processor used. The first four to eight workstations driven off a large mainframe computer cost about the same as a turnkey system driven off its own minicomputer. However, for an installation involving more than eight workstations, the incremental cost could be as low as $100,000 per workstation if the mainframe computer had unused processing capacity.

UNIQUE MARKET CHARACTERISTICS

The structure of Japanese industry gave the Japanese market several unique characteristics:

1. Japanese industry was centered around 16 industrial groups which employed 16% of all workers and accounted for approximately 29% of goods sold by Japanese companies. *Exhibit 9* shows revenue and employment figures for the 16 groups. Many of these powerful industrial groups had developed out of the pre-World War II "Zaibatsu" companies such as Mitsui, Mitsubishi, and Sumitomo. During the postwar occupation of Japan, Allied forces had broken up the Zaibatsu in an effort to diffuse political power in Japan. However, in the 1950s and 1960s the

EXHIBIT 9. Japan's 16 largest industrial groups

Group	Number of companies	Turnover (yen-billions)		Number of employees (1,000 persons)	
Mitsubishi	136	22,336	(4.8)	387	(2.4)
Mitsui	102	16,058	(3.4)	200	(1.2)
Sumitomo	108	16,407	(3.5)	325	(2.0)
Fuyo	103	14,962	(3.2)	256	(1.6)
DKB	64	16,654	(3.6)	317	(1.9)
Sanwa	80	13,552	(2.9)	217	(1.3)
Tokai	25	3,440	(.7)	38	(.2)
IBJ	19	1,699	(.4)	34	(.2)
Nippon Steel	40	5,310	(1.1)	144	(.9)
Hitachi	37	3,514	(.8)	143	(.9)
Nissan	27	4,370	(.9)	119	(.7)
Toyota	36	8,960	(1.9)	162	(1.0)
Matsushita	24	3,692	(.8)	97	(.6)
Toshiba-IHI	38	3,119	(.7)	131	(.8)
Tokyu	19	1,167	(.2)	41	(.3)
Seibu	21	1,542	(.3)	60	(.4)
Subtotals	879	136,782	(29.3)	2,671	(16.4)
Japan totals	209,195	467,145	(100%)	16,330	(100%)

Source: Dodwell Industrial Groupings in Japan 1980/81.

old Zaibatsu companies and some of the larger post-World War II companies began to form industrial groups centered around banks (for financing) and trading companies (for import/export). The newly formed groups, in compliance with the antimonopoly laws imposed by the Allied occupation, did not recombine into single companies. Instead, they formed company groups through loans, trade agreements, distribution arrangements, and interlocking directorates. Each company acted independently and was targeted at some specific industry or service. The overall group strategy was coordinated by monthly or quarterly meetings of the president's councils, called "Sacho-Kai." In some cases, the industrial groups were associated with each other through common trading companies or banks. For example, the Matsushita group was loosely connected with the Sumitomo group through its use of Sumitomo Bank. Hitachi, Ltd. was a member of the presidential council for the DKB, Fuyo, and Sanwa groups, and it borrowed equally from each group's bank.

The largest industrial group in Japan was Mitsubishi with 139 companies and 388,000 employees. The smallest of the 16 major groups was Seibu with 22 companies and 58,000 employees. It was difficult to directly compare the Japanese groups with large American companies. Unlike divisions in U.S. companies, each group member in Japan was usually targeted at one industry and its stock was individually traded. Consequently, a great deal of information was available for doing industry analysis and targeting industry-specific marketing activities. The Japanese industrial groups were a considerable economic force because, in addition to controlling all of their own companies, each group also had considerable influence over an additional 200 to 500 nongroup companies that were sole source suppliers or subcontractors. It was not unusual for the primary industrial group companies to decide what type of equipment the supplier companies would use.

2. Most Japanese industries were fairly concentrated. In some cases, the top ten companies controlled 90% of the industry.

3. The revenue/employee ratio for most industries was much higher than in the United States, because (1) the extensive use of subcontractors reduced the number of employees involved in producing the goods sold by each company, and (2) many firms did not market their products to the end user but relied on closely aligned trading companies to handle the labor-intensive task of sales and services. The trading companies associated with the 16 industrial groups often played a very significant role in selling their group's products both within their group (to other group companies, suppliers, and subcontractors) and to "outside" markets (domestic and foreign). In addition, the trading companies often acted as distributors' agents or brokers for nongroup products.

4. Cost of capital, return on investment, and rates of profitability were substantially below those in the United States.

JAPANESE MARKET POTENTIAL

Lack of reliable information on the size and potential of the Japanese CAD/CAM market had been a constant source of conflict between CVJ and TEL over the years. Patrick Alias wanted CVJ to achieve a market share of 30% by 1986, rising to 40% by 1990 of the total CAD/CAM market. The recent Dataquest study claimed there were 650 CAD/CAM systems installed in Japan at the end of 1982, of which 130 were CV systems. This would give CV a market share of 20%.

The dramatic strides made by IBM-Japan, Fujitsu, and Seiko in 1981–1982, however, would indicate that CV's recent market share had slipped substantially below 20%. Since CV actually had 198 systems installed in Japan at the end of 1982, Alias felt strongly that the study greatly understated both the current size and growth of the Japanese CAD/CAM market. Jim Nomura also believed the Dataquest figures were inaccurate and unreliable because they did not define what they considered to be a "system," nor did they explain how they developed their data. In his March 1983 meeting with Alias, Nomura had argued that CV/TEL actually had closer to a 50% market share in the Japanese "turnkey" systems market. Based on his own informal appraisal, Nomura felt that the turnkey market was worth about $60 million in 1982.

Patrick Alias's intuition and European experience caused him to question sharply Jim Nomura's estimate of CV's penetration of the Japanese market. He reasoned that "Japan has a population of 116 million and the United States has a population of 230 million. The CAD/CAM market in the U.S. is a $500 million/year market of which CV has about a 35% share. If we assume that Japan's economy is at least as advanced as the U.S. economy, then the market for CAD/CAM equipment should be about $250 million, not $60 million. Since TEL's 1982 sales of CV systems — not including service revenue — were only about $30 million, TEL/CV has a 12% share of the Japanese market."

In addition, Alias had found in Europe that CV's market penetration was highly correlated to the amount of revenue produced per salesperson. The top European sales reps produced $3 million in revenue per year with the average sales rep producing $2 million and the weaker ones about $1 million. These figures were similar to the United States, where an average sales rep produced about $2 million in revenue. Across Europe, where there was reasonably good market information, he found that the top sales reps had about a 60% share. Because TEL claimed to have 30 sales reps devoted to CV, the average revenue per sales rep was about $1 million. Alias felt this was further evidence that CVJ's market share was low.

Through some European contacts, Alias had recently obtained a list of IBM's CAD/CAM customers in Japan. Of these customers, 60% had never appeared on TEL's call reports or loss reports. As a result, he was convinced that additional coverage was necessary in Japan. Alias also felt that low market share made each sale more difficult. In those European countries where CV had 60% of the market, there was a very positive market momentum. In fact, many potential customers called CV first to inquire about buying a system.

CURRENT SITUATION

Alias summarized his views of the current situation as follows:

> *Over the past ten years CV has enjoyed relatively free access to the Japanese market. Our competition has been primarily the other U.S. CAD/CAM companies.*

> *Today, however, the situation is changing; the market is becoming unstable because of the rapidly developing competition from Japanese CAD/CAM suppliers. In other words, the window of opportunity is open, and has been for some time, but it is rapidly going to slam shut unless our strategy is capable of developing significant market share rapidly. Any strategy we recommend to headquarters must therefore be capable of rapid implementation.*

> *A corollary to the goal of establishing local market share is to create a strong defensive posture in the context of our global market share. Already Japanese competition is beginning to move into the U.S. and European markets, the traditional source of CV's strength. By rapidly developing market share in the Japanese market we will limit the ability of our Japanese competitors to encroach on our areas of strength in the U.S. and Europe.*

> *In addition to the need for rapid implementation, another criterion for any strategy we recommend is that it must take into account our current organization and relationships in Japan. We do not begin with a blank piece of paper.*

Before recommending any specific actions for the Japanese market, Alias felt it was essential to (1) develop a reasonable forecast for the CAD/CAM market in Japan, and (2) understand all of the available strategic options.

MARKET FORECAST

In March of 1983, Alias had requested the marketing department of CVJ to forecast the growth of the CAD/CAM market in Japan. He had also requested TEL to develop a separate forecast. CVJ used a local marketing study as a base and modified it using company data and its own market intelligence. TEL had access to the same local marketing study. The results along with TEL's four-year sales forecast had been presented to him this past week in Japan. They were as follows:

	1983		1984		1985		1986	
	Volume[a]	*Market share*	*Volume*	*Market share*	*Volume*	*Market share*	*Volume*	*Market share*
TEL's CV sales forecast (retail)	$42		$55		$75		$100	
TEL's market forecast								
Turnkey only	187	22%	251	22%	341	22%	461	22%
CVJ's market forecast								
Total market	470	9[b]	680	8	930	8	1,200	8
Turnkey only	280	15	410	13	580	13	760	13

[a]All volume figures are millions of U.S. dollars.

[b]To be read as: TEL's sales forecast implies a 1983 CVJ market share of 9% of the total CAD/CAM market as forecast by CVJ.

Regardless of whether CVJ's estimates or TEL's estimates were used, the present strategy would clearly leave CV with results far below its goal of 30% of the total market by 1986. Even with TEL making its 1986 forecast there would be a $260 million shortfall. Based on this analysis, Alias set the following goals for CV in the Japanese market:

CV sales goals, Japanese market

	Sales volume[a]	Market share
1983	$ 42 million	9%
1984	109	16
1985	214	23
1986	360	30

[a]These numbers are for retail, end-user revenues in Japan.

OPTIONS

On the 20-hour flight back from Tokyo, Alias reviewed his options. He wished now that Japan had gone direct back in the mid-1970s when he was converting CV's European operation. In the long run, he felt that having a direct sales force would be the most effective and cost-efficient way of combating the newly emerging Japanese competition. Fujitsu and IBM-Japan both had large direct sales forces of approximately 1500–1800 sales representatives, some of whom were being redeployed against the CAD/CAM market. C. Itoh had 30–40 sales representatives dedicated to CAD/CAM, and Marubeni Hytech had already hired, trained, and deployed 10–15 sales reps in the last two years.

In 1983, the task of building a direct sales and service organization to replace TEL would be enormous. One applications engineer and one service engineer were required to support five installed systems, and it took 6–12 months to hire and train these support people. It took a full year to hire and train a sales representative. Based on CV's experience in the U.S. and Europe, an average sales representative should produce $2 million per year in revenue. However, Jim Nomura felt that $1.5 million was more realistic for Japan. A direct organization would also require supervision, administration, and managers — about one for every six or seven people. In Europe, selling and administrative expenses ran about 20% of sales, but costs in Japan could be expected to run higher. It was extremely difficult for U.S. companies to hire Japanese nationals. The best university graduates generally wanted to work for a company in one of the large industrial groups. Their second choice would be a smaller Japanese company that was growing rapidly. In general, the lack of job security and differences in management style made U.S.-based companies less attractive to work for.

Most U.S. companies relied on higher salaries to recruit people from their competitors. Because of employee loyalty and the consistently tight labor market, this process did not always produce the best results. This was one of many reasons why U.S. companies often entered into joint venture agreements in Japan.

In addition to sales, field service, and applications support, CV would also have to assume responsibility for the other functions and services currently performed by TEL, including:

1. Customer credit — normally 120 days. TEL's cost of credit was approximately 6%. CV's cost would be approximately 10%.
2. Shipping, tariffs, insurance (approximately 15%), and foreign exchange fluctuations — currently all prices to TEL were F.O.B. Bedford, Massachusetts, and payable in U.S. dollars.
3. Extended warranty — TEL provided the customary 1-year warranty in Japan, whereas CV only provided a 90-day warranty. CV estimated the cost of the extended warranty at 1%/month of the end-user price.

4. Preinstallation product/system testing which cost approximately 1% of the end-user price.
5. Product modification — the hardware in all U.S. CAD/CAM systems had to be modified to conform to Japanese Industrial Standards (JIS). In addition, all software had to be converted to Japanese, including the incorporation of special Japanese Kanji figures into the system. For a completely new CAD/CAM system, this could require 30–40 person years of effort. This was currently being done 50% by TEL and 50% by CVJ at a total estimated cost of $1.4 million per new system.

Patrick Alias knew that going direct was very beneficial in Europe, but he was not sure how transferable that experience was to the Japanese market. While CV's agreement with TEL could be canceled with 30 days' notice, TEL had long-established relationships with many of its CAD/CAM customers. TEL was a fast-growing company that had earned the respect of its competitors and the confidence of its customers.

It was apparent from TEL's sales forecast that, on its current course it would not reach CV's goal of 30% of the total CAD/CAM market in Japan by 1986. This would require a dramatic expansion of TEL's marketing efforts. For years CVJ had been asking TEL to accelerate its sales coverage. As recently as February, Patrick Alias, on his first trip to Japan, had asked Jim Nomura to double the size of the sales force this year. Nomura's response had been that TEL was people-constrained and had been for the last five years. The company's policy, as in many other Japanese companies, was to develop its people internally by hiring the best university graduates it could and training them. TEL's management felt that this produced better results than a policy of hiring people away from other companies. The company wanted to grow as fast as possible with internally developed people. All of TEL's sales divisions were growing rapidly and Jim Nomura had to compete with other TEL divisions for available manpower. He was at a considerable disadvantage because most of the other sales divisions' products were made by TEL under joint venture agreements with U.S. companies. These companies had made long-term commitments to TEL not only as a distributor but as a manufacturing partner. Jim Nomura responded to Alias's request for more coverage as follows:

> *First, I think that the CCS division has been very successful at obtaining its fair share of our company's available manpower for CV over the past few years. I would like very much to expand our sales coverage more rapidly — even double it. To do that, I need the support of CV. Our first step should be to*

establish the joint venture which TEL has been proposing for the last five years. TEL and CV are still "dating" after all these years, while TEL and its other U.S. suppliers are married. We have joint ventures with them and both parties have long-term commitments to each other. With a joint venture arrangement I would be in a stronger position to compete for manpower and could more rapidly expand the sales coverage. The joint venture would also help our quest for market share by strengthening our local engineering support. It would also handle final system assembly and check-out, as well as local program development and product adaptation. As needed, it could also develop any custom hardware that was requested for the Japanese market. TEL would provide the joint venture with trained people, local hiring capability, bank credit, and Japanese management know-how. CV would provide the technology and general engineering support in exchange for a 5% licensing fee and half of the joint venture's profits. Sales would continue to be handled entirely by the CCS division of TEL.

If a joint venture is not possible, then CV can help me expand faster by (1) taking over the full responsibility for servicing and supporting our installed base of systems, and (2) assuming full responsibility for all product adaptation and all pre- and post-installation support on new customers. This would allow me to redeploy my available manpower for better sales coverage. I am very anxious to increase the size of our sales force, but TEL needs more support and/ or more commitment from CV in order to achieve increased market share in Japan. In the past few years TEL's performance in the Japanese CAD/CAM market has been outstanding — with some support and commitment we could do even better.

See *Exhibit 5* for TEL's manpower chart for CCS and *Exhibit 6* for TEL's 5-year sales performance on CV systems.

Alias had explored the purchase of TEL's service and support operation by CVJ. However, TEL felt a strong commitment to support its existing customers, and because of its policy of lifetime employment, TEL would not transfer its people to CVJ.

Regarding a joint venture with TEL, Jim Berrett and CV's other senior managers were strongly opposed, for the following reasons:

1. Japanese management in a joint venture tended to have stronger allegiance to the Japanese half owner.
2. There were numerous examples of Japanese companies not needing their American partner a few years after a joint venture or licensing agreement had been signed.
3. CV might lose control of its product in Japan if local sourcing was aggressively pursued.

Another option for Alias was to supplement TEL's marketing efforts with additional distributors, sales agents, or CVJ's own direct sales force. It was not clear whether TEL would tolerate this type of arrangement. TEL's other businesses were growing rapidly — recruiting capable people was its major constraint.

CV had not actively pursued additional distributors, but several capable distributors had approached CV over the past few years. All were anxious to enter the CAD/CAM market. Most suggested an exclusive agreement either replacing TEL or giving them exclusive rights to locations other than the Tokyo area, where TEL had 70% of its sales and service coverage. Other suggestions included dividing the market by industry, application, named accounts, or some combination of these. Most of these distributors preferred that CVJ handle all new product adaptation, field service, and application support.

Another alternative for expanding distribution channels in Japan was for CVJ to enter into multiple distribution arrangements with trading companies associated with the 16 major industrial groups. As a stand-alone trading company, TEL was limited in how it could approach many of the companies associated with industrial groups. In the past three months, Alias had had several discussions with two large trading companies — Toyota and Sony. Toyota Trading Company had about 150 general salespeople and was willing to dedicate at least six salespeople to CV the first year. The trading company did not have the expertise to properly handle the CAD/CAM systems, however, and CV would be responsible for all technical training, service, and support. Sony Trading Company was interested in a similar arrangement of dedicating six sales and sales support people. Both companies were willing to adhere to CVJ's suggested pricing schedule and would expect a 7% commission on all sales.

Alias was confident that CVJ could work out an agreement with Toyota Trading, Sony Trading, and/or other large trading companies not currently selling CAD/CAM equipment. Members of large industry groups bought the best products available. They were not obligated to buy from other companies within their group, even if a member of the group produced a similar, but inferior, product. They were also not obligated to buy products from their own trading company, although the trading company usually had good access to the key decision makers. Trading companies sold to everyone and were motivated primarily by volume and profit considerations. They were expert at identifying prospects, but they were not particularly interested in doing a lot of hand-holding, complex demonstrations, or presales support and analysis. As with most Japanese companies, the trading companies were only interested in entering into long-term agreements, but they did not require exclusive distribution rights.

Alias was also intrigued by the possibilities of using the current CVJ organization to expand market coverage. The CVJ organization had grown rapidly in the past two years with quarterly expenses climbing to a current rate of $1.4 million. After three months on the job, Alias was still uncomfortable about the amount and quality of support being provided by the CVJ organization. It seemed to be a growing bureaucracy with little or no responsibility for achieving sales goals. This concern was shared by Jim Nomura, who thought TEL's efforts were not well supported by CVJ in spite of its growing organization.

Over the past two years CVJ had hired six salespeople away from other CAD/CAM suppliers. These people were currently "supporting" TEL's sales effort and could be converted to sales if CV discontinued the exclusive distribution agreement with TEL.

Patrick Alias knew that achieving a 30% share of market in Japan by 1986 was essential to CV's global strategy. He also realized that any plan he developed for building market share in Japan must fully consider TEL's long-standing relationship with CV and its potential reaction.

2.5 *CASE*

Fisher-Price Benelux

Robert D. Buzzell, Carlos Del Nero, and Stephen Muirhead

In late 1977, executives of Fisher-Price toys met to consider a proposed change in the company's method of distribution in the Benelux market. Stephen Muirhead, Fisher-Price's marketing manager-Europe presented three options to the group: to continue with independent distributors, one in Belgium and one in Holland; to set up a company-owned sales company by early 1979; or to phase out the distributors gradually over a three-year period. Participants in the meeting included, besides Muirhead, Jock Flournoy, vice-president-International; Bob Hoffman, International controller; Manfred T. Wellenbeck, managing director-Europe; Raf Decaluwe, European controller; and Louis Mentor, assistant European controller. Muirhead had raised the question of changing distribution methods in the Benelux countries because he was dissatisfied with the level of sales and promotional support that the two distributors were providing. Changing the distribution system would, however, entail some risks including, possibly, the payment of a substantial indemnity to the Belgian importer/ distributor.

COMPANY BACKGROUND

Fisher-Price Toys, Inc. was founded in East Aurora, New York in 1930 with the concept that solid wood blocks with lithographs applied would sell as toys for preschool children. Herman G. Fisher, president and one of the three founders of the firm, believed that "kids not only want toys to play with, but toys to play with them." Accordingly, he saw in wood lithographing the opportunity to make action toys which would walk, crawl, whine, and generally "respond" to children.

In order to survive the difficult Depression years, Mr. Fisher established as a corporate creed that each Fisher-Price toy must have (1) intrinsic play value; (2) ingenuity; (3) strong construction; (4) good value for the money; and (5) action. These guidelines for toy-making, which were still observed in 1977, led to success in the company's early years. By 1969, Fisher-Price had become a major factor in the toy industry. Sales increased to $32 million in that year and three-fourths of all toy purchasers in the U.S. recognized Fisher-Price as a leading producer of preschool toys (0–4 years). Nonetheless, under the guidance of Mr. Fisher, the firm continued in its conservative ways in terms of both financial and marketing policies. Accordingly, it was not surprising that the Quaker Oats Company of Chicago saw great potential in Fisher-Price and purchased the firm from Mr. Fisher for $50 million in cash.

While Quaker was a far more aggressive company than Fisher-Price had been under Mr. Fisher's direction, Quaker's management was hesitant to meddle in the concerns of the toy manufacturer. They recognized Fisher-Price to be a well-run organization, and sought to ensure continuity of management. At the same time, however, Quaker encouraged Fisher-Price executives to adopt a less conservative posture, specifically in their marketing and advertising programs. Advertising especially took on a dimension of importance with the growth of self-service in toy retailing, creating the need to shift from a push to a pull strategy. To accomplish this desired change in outlook, Quaker made it clear that it stood ready to provide whatever resources would be necessary to ensure a more substantial growth rate.[1] By 1977, Fisher-Price was recognized as one of the world's leading producers of preschool toys. Total worldwide sales reached $270 million. International sales accounted for about one-third of this total.

Examples of Fisher-Price toys are shown in *Exhibit 1*. The company's 1977 International catalog included about 200 different items, classified into categories according to the ages of the children for whom they were designed. The categories were Crib & Playpen (1 day to 18 months); Preschool (18 months to 4 years), and Grade School (4 years to 9 years). Traditionally, Fisher-Price's greatest strength was in the design and marketing of toys for the younger groups (under 4 years).

INTERNATIONAL EXPANSION

In the mid-1970s, the United States was the largest toy market in the world representing approximately one-third of the world market. However, Fisher-Price management recognized that attractive opportunities were also to be found in international markets, primarily in Europe, which (in total) also represented approximately one-third of the world toy market.

Fisher-Price sales in Europe had begun in the 1950s. A general export agent, based in New York, handled all export sales for Fisher-Price. When Fisher-Price became a division of Quaker Oats in 1969, more emphasis was put on international business. Europe, due to its toy market size, high purchasing power, and political stability, was the first region chosen in which to concentrate the company's marketing and production efforts in order to further overseas market development.

By 1977, the general export agent was no longer selling to any market in Europe. All markets were serviced either by local distributors or Fisher-Price-owned sales companies. The original product concepts of Fisher-Price found ready acceptance in the markets of Northern Europe. Price remained a problem until the early seventies when a subcontract manufacturing arrangement was set up with a U.K. toy company. In 1975 the company opened its first European manufacturing facility in Kaulille, Belgium. Fisher-Price's European headquarters office was located nearby, in Brussels.

---

[1]The section on company background is taken from *Fisher-Price Toys,Inc.*, Harvard Business School Case Services #9-572-029, Rev. 12/80, pp. 4–5.

EXHIBIT 1. Excerpt from Fisher-Price 1977 International Catalog

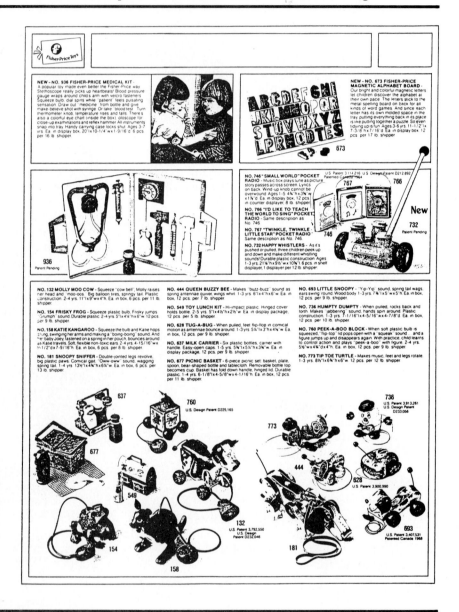

INTERNATIONAL MARKET DEVELOPMENT STRATEGY

In 1977, Fisher-Price products were marketed throughout Western Europe and also in Yugoslavia, Greece, and Turkey. Fisher-Price had its own sales companies in Germany (since the early 1970s) and France (established 1976). In the United Kingdom, Fisher-Price used another company's sales force, but had its own facilities and management staff. In all other countries, exclusive independent distributors were used.

The company's long-term strategy for developing international markets was based on the idea that, over time, national markets evolved through four "stages of development":

1. **Latent stage.** At this stage, sales were inconsequential, either because of small population or low buying power. In such markets, Fisher-Price made only occasional export sales to customers that contacted the company.

2. **Early growth stage.** As sales volume in a country increased, Fisher-Price would shift from direct exporting to selling through a distributor who handled key retail accounts. Ideally, distributors were selected who (a) had established sales organizations, (b) carried few or no competitive lines, and (c) could transact business on the basis of accepted 90-day drafts.

3. **Maturing stage.** In markets that were successfully developed, with Fisher-Price's share of the toy market reaching 1.5% or more, the distributor would call on all significant retail outlets. Fisher-Price gradually took charge of more marketing tasks during this stage, including advertising and point-of-sale display and merchandising. Very small countries such as Iceland would probably never progress beyond this stage, but in other countries it was anticipated that a change to Stage 4 would be made as soon as possible.

4. **Direct sale stage.** Eventually, Fisher-Price would establish its own organization and take over complete responsibility for sales, other marketing activities, warehousing, credit, and general administrative functions. It was expected that Stage 4 markets would have the long-term potential for at least a 5% share of market.

Exhibit 2 shows the stage of development of each European market as of 1977 and the anticipated date for achieving the next stage. The exhibit also shows the "priority level" assigned to each market. A priority ranking of "1" indicates countries to which management would devote substantial attention and resources, while those ranked "3" were

EXHIBIT 2. Actual and expected stages of development for European
countries – 1977

COUNTRY	STAGE 1	STAGE 2	STAGE 3	STAGE 4	PRIORITY LEVEL
GERMANY				→	1
GREAT BRITAIN				→	1
ITALY		→ - - - - - - - → (1980)			1
FRANCE				→	1
TURKEY	→ - - - - - → (1978)				3
SPAIN	→				2
YUGOSLAVIA	→ - - - → (1978)				3
BENELUX			→ - - - - → (1980)		1
IRELAND			→ - - - → (1980)		3
PORTUGAL	→ - - - - - → (1978)				3
GREECE	→ - → (1978)				3
SWEDEN			→		2
AUSTRIA		→ - - - - →			2
SWITZERLAND		→ - - - - →			2
DENMARK		→ - - - - →			2
FINLAND		→ - - - - →			3
NORWAY		→ - - - - →			3
ICELAND			→		3

———— achieved
- - - - planned
(19..) year of
        planned

Source: Company planning documents.

seen as relatively unimportant. As the rankings suggest, most of the
distributor markets were assigned relatively low priorities. Consistent
with this, the company's five-year Development Plan, adopted earlier in
1977, assumed that no "investment spending" would be done in distributor markets. The plan further called for maintaining profitability in all
distributor markets. Even in these markets, however, it was Fisher-
Price's objective to "establish itself as a major brand."

The objectives of the five-year Development Plan for major European markets called for growth in sales from $36.8 million in 1977 to $100.7 million in 1982 — an average annual growth rate of nearly 30%. Projected sales for each country are shown in *Exhibit 3*. (These figures are stated at selling prices to retailers. In countries with sales companies, the projections are for Fisher-Price's sales to retailers; in distributor markets, the figures represent sales *by distributors* to retailers.) Projections for the Benelux countries, assuming they continued as distributor markets, called for an average annual sales increase of 13%, with a slackening of growth in 1981 and 1982. This conservative forecast for Benelux reflected Muirhead's concern about the distributors' lack of aggressiveness in marketing Fisher-Price products.

According to Muirhead, all of the forecasts in *Exhibit 3*, which had been prepared in early 1977, appeared to be on the low side in light of actual sales results for the first nine months of the year. He explained that the management of Fisher-Price Europe had consistently underestimated the growth potential for the company's products.

THE BENELUX MARKET

The term "Benelux" was widely used in international business to designate the adjacent states of Belgium, the Netherlands (Holland), and the Grand Duchy of Luxembourg. While such a grouping was convenient for some purposes, Belgium and Holland were in fact separate and distinct markets.[2] Holland, the larger of the two with a population of some 14 million, was relatively homogeneous in ethnic and linguistic terms. Belgium, with a population of 9.9 million, had two distinct regions: Flanders (Flemish speaking) and Walloon (French speaking).

For the most part, the business and social institutions of the two countries were separate. Each had its own banks, newspapers, department stores, and retail chains. Selected population, economic, and toy market information for the two countries is given in *Exhibit 4*. During the 1970s both countries had enjoyed steady, if unspectacular, economic growth rates. Both had relatively strong currencies, with exchange rates in relation to the U.S. dollar having appreciated by around 10% since 1974.

Sales of toys in Holland were growing at a rate of around 10% annually during the 1970s. Since the number of children had grown only

---

[2]In the discussion that follows, Luxembourg is ignored on account of its small size (1977 population, 340,000).

EXHIBIT 3. Forecasts of market size, sales and market share
Major European countries, 1978–1982 (amounts in millions of dollars)

	1978	1979	1980	1981	1982	Avg. % inc.
United Kingdom						
Mkt. size	$ 456	$ 465	$ 473	$ 482	$ 490	2.0%
Sales	16.3	23.1	28.9	34.0	39.1	
% market	3.6	5.0	6.1	7.1	8.0	
Germany						
Mkt. size	503	507	512	517	521	1.0
Sales	7.6	10.5	13.1	15.7	18.8	
% market	1.5	2.1	2.6	3.0	3.6	
France						
Mkt. size	614	644	677	710	746	5.0
Sales	6.6	10.1	14.6	20.4	26.5	
% market	1.1	1.6	2.2	2.9	3.6	
Italy						
Mkt. size	362	362	362	362	362	—
Dist. sales*	.4	.7	1.5	2.8	4.2	
% market	—	—	—	1.0	1.2	
Benelux						
Mkt. size	244	257	268	279	291	4.0
Dist. sales	4.14	5.04	5.8	6.3	6.7	
% market	1.7	2.0	2.2	2.3	2.3	

Austria						
Mkt. size	47	48	49	50	51	1.0
Dist. sales	.1	.2	.3	.3	.3	
% market	—	—	—	—	—	
Switzerland						
Mkt. size	86	88	90	92	94	2.0
Dist. sales	.5	.6	.9	1.3	1.8	
% market	—	—	1.0	1.4	1.9	
Spain						
Mkt. size	223	243	265	289	315	7.0
Dist. sales	.01	.1	.2	.5	1.1	
% market	—	—	—	—	1.1	
Scandinavia						
Mkt. size	131	135	139	143	147	2.0
Dist. sales	1.1	1.2	1.3	1.5	2.2	
% market	1.0	1.0	1.0	1.0	1.5	
Totals						
Mkt. size	$2,666	$2,749	$2,835	$2,924	$3,017	
Sales	36.8	51.5	66.6	82.8	100.7	
% market	1.4	1.9	2.3	2.8	3.3	

*In distributor markets, sales are stated in terms of amounts expected to be sold by distributors to retailers. Fisher-Price sales to distributors were about two-thirds of the amounts shown above. All of the amounts are forecasts stated at constant local selling prices and constant (1977) exchange rates.

EXHIBIT 4. Selected demographic, economic, and toy market data, 1977

	Holland	Belgium	Total
Population (millions):			
1977	13.8	9.9	23.7
Forecast 1982	14.6	10.0	24.6
Average annual growth rate	1.4%	0.2%	0.7%
Number of children 0–9 (millions):			
1977	2.30	2.27	4.57
Forecast 1982	2.40	2.28	4.68
Average annual growth rate	0.8%	0.1%	0.5%
Consumer income—per capita ($)	$5,321	$5,853	—
Average annual growth rate, 1970–76	10.9%	12.3%	—
Inflation rate:			
1976–77	8.0%	8.0%	
Forecast 1977–82	8–10%	6–7%	
Toy market—at wholesale prices (millions of dollars)	$144	$100	$244
Toy expenditures per child (0–9 yrs.)	$ 65	$ 46	—
Percent of toy volume imported	70%	90%	—
Retail toy outlets—number	1,500	1,100	2,600
Percent of toys sold in			
Toy shops	30%	40%	—
Department stores	40%	50%	—
Discount outlets	20%	10%	—

Source: Company records and estimates.

slightly, the growth in volume reflected rising expenditures per child typically associated with rising consumer incomes.[3]

About 30% of Dutch toy sales were supplied by the country's domestic producers. Imports came from many sources, with Germany ac-

---

[3]Fisher-Price executives emphasized that their estimates of market sizes were subject to considerable uncertainty. Published statistics, they believed, were almost useless. In countries where Fisher-Price operated its own sales companies, purchase diary panels were used to obtain more reliable information. Such a panel cost around $50,000 per year in each country.

counting for over 40% of the total. Very little television advertising was used for toys, because TV commercial time was extremely scarce and expensive. In addition to catalogs, women's magazines and newspapers were used to promote toys. Retailers' margins for toys ranged from 38% to 48% of selling prices.

In Belgium, toy expenditures per child were not growing. Over 90% of toy volume was imported, with Germany and France the leading sources. Retail prices in Belgium were typically 15–20% higher than in Holland, with higher retail margins (45–55%) accounting for about half of the differential. It was believed that Belgian consumers were not very price conscious. Advertising in northern (Dutch-speaking) Belgium was similar to that of Holland, but in the southern part of the country television time (on RTL/Luxembourg) was relatively inexpensive and plentiful.

FISHER-PRICE IN THE BENELUX COUNTRIES

Fisher-Price had marketed its products in the Benelux countries since 1952. In Belgium and Luxembourg the exclusive importer/distributor was Comptoir Boismanu, located in Brussels. Originally, Boismanu had acted as distributor for France and Germany, and for a short time in the late 1950s had manufactured Fisher-Price toys under license. Boismanu was a well-regarded firm, but was thought to be very conservative.

Jean Lagneau, the director of Boismanu, was about 60 years old. His organization was small, consisting of a warehouse, office, and five sales representatives. Lagneau handled major accounts himself, and he had close personal relationships with the buyers in the large Brussels retailers. In total, Boismanu serviced 950 retail accounts and handled 120 Fisher-Price products. Total sales in 1977 were estimated at $2.4 million (85.6 million BFr.), with Fisher-Price products accounting for about three-fourths of this amount. In Stephen Muirhead's opinion, Lagneau did not really have a viable successor at Boismanu.

In Holland, the exclusive distributor (since 1972) was Tiamo, based in the suburbs of Amsterdam. Tiamo's sales of Fisher-Price products had increased fivefold between 1974 and 1977, to about $1.5 million (3.68 million Dfl.). The company also carried other lines directly competitive with Fisher-Price, and they would not give Fisher-Price executives any information on their total sales volume. Tiamo carried 80 Fisher-Price items and serviced 450 retail accounts with a sales force of six.

Historical trends in Fisher-Price product sales by the two distributors are summarized in *Exhibit 5*. (These figures are stated at Fisher-

EXHIBIT 5. **Trends in Fisher-Price sales to distributors**
Selected European countries, 1974–77 (index numbers, 1974 = 100)

Sales stated in local currencies	1974	1975	1976	1977
Belgium	100	142	223	276
Holland	100	141	295	457
United Kingdom	100	74	178	271
Germany	100	206	373	681
France	100	104	431	1,007
Italy	100	67	128	182
Sales stated in dollars*				
Belgium	100	150	225	300
Holland	100	150	300	500
United Kingdom	100	70	138	202
Germany	100	217	383	758
France	100	117	433	983
Italy	100	67	100	133

*Sales in local currencies are converted to dollar amounts for purposes of consolidation in Fisher-Price's accounting system. In each year the average exchange rate is used. For example, in 1977, sales in Belgium were 44.4 million BFr.; at 37 BFr. per dollar, this is equivalent to $1.2 million.
Source: Company records.

Price's selling prices.) The exhibit also shows, for comparison purposes, trends in Fisher-Price sales in selected other European countries.

Both distributors operated on gross margins of around 33% of sales. They were free to set their own selling prices, but as a practical matter had little latitude. Retail selling prices for Fisher-Price products were well established, and discounting from these prices was rare.

Services provided by the distributors included making sales calls on retailers; warehousing and delivering the products; handling orders, complaints, and returns; and extending credit to customers. Neither distributor had spent anything on advertising for Fisher-Price products, nor had Fisher-Price itself advertised in the Benelux countries.

Fisher-Price's major competitors all utilized independent distributors in the Benelux countries and in most other European markets. One competitor had established wholly owned sales subsidiaries in the early 1970s but later switched back to distributors. It was believed that this company had incurred substantial losses because of inadequate internal controls.

EXHIBIT 6. Projected sales, expenses, profits, and investment, 1978–82 (based on continued use of distributors)

Fisher-Price operating results	1978	1979	1980	1981	1982
		(millions of Belgian francs)[a]			
Sales	103.5	126.2	144.8	158.6	166.5
Standard cost of sales	76.0	87.2	100.3	109.5	115.1
Standard gross profit	27.5	39.0	44.5	49.1	51.4
% net sales	27%	31%	31%	31%	31%
Distribution expense	1.6	1.9	2.2	2.5	2.7
Gross margin	25.9	37.1	42.3	46.6	48.7
% net sales	25%	29%	29%	29%	29%
Marketing expenses[b]	6.7	8.2	9.3	10.3	10.8
General and administrative[c]	3.7	4.1	4.5	5.0	5.6
Operating income	15.5	24.8	28.5	31.3	32.3
% net sales	15%	19.7%	19.7%	19.7%	19.7%
Invested capital[d]	39.7	46.8	55.9	60.0	69.1

[a]37BFr. = 1 U.S. dollar.
[b]Marketing expense includes catalogs, samples, participation in toy fairs and exhibits.
[c]Primarily allocated G&A expenses of European HQ office.
[d]Primarily accounts receivable from distributors.
Source: Company estimates.

ALTERNATIVE DISTRIBUTION STRATEGIES

Stephen Muirhead outlined three possible approaches to distribution in the Benelux countries. The first was to continue with the present arrangement, utilizing Comptoir Boismanu and Tiamo as exclusive distributors. Forecasts of sales, expenses, profits, and investment requirements for this option are shown in *Exhibit 6*. According to Muirhead, the advantages of this approach included: low investment requirements, limited credit risks, and the ability to utilize the distributors' market knowledge and experience. On the other hand, he argued, utilizing distributors limited Fisher-Price's growth because

- the distributors provided poor customer service;[4]

---

[4]Both distributors shipped to customers via rail because this was the cheapest means of transport. As a result, deliveries usually took two weeks, while truck delivery could be accomplished in two to three days.

- they were frequently out of stock because of unwillingness to carry adequate inventories;
- they were unwilling to invest in promotion; and
- differences in pricing were likely to lead to cross-border competition.

As Muirhead saw it, the basic problem in using independent distributors was a conflict in objectives. Almost all distributors, he felt, were primarily interested in maximizing *short-term* profits. Most of them, he thought, believed that emphasizing growth was self-defeating because ". . . as soon as sales reach a certain point, the manufacturer will step in and take over the market."

A second possibility was for Fisher-Price to establish its own sales company for Benelux as soon as possible. As a practical matter, this would require about a year to accomplish and would only take effect in early 1979. Projected sales and profits for this strategy were much higher than for continued distributor sales (see *Exhibit 7*). On the other hand, investment requirements were also substantially greater. Moreover, if Fisher-Price set up its own sales company, a separate organization would have to be established. This is reflected in the estimated General & Administrative Expense of 26.2 million BFr. ($708,000) for 1979. In addition, higher sales objectives would have to be supported by substantially higher marketing budgets. As shown in *Exhibit 7*, the first year of operations, 1979, would require an estimated outlay of 72.5 million BFr. ($1.96 million) for field selling, advertising, and merchandising activities. The marketing budget for 1979 included the costs of eight field sales representatives and two sales managers (one for Belgium and one for Holland). Salary, bonus, and expenses were estimated at 1.1 million BFr. per sales representative and 1.9 million BFr. for each sales manager. These costs were essentially fixed. Moreover, much of the advertising and merchandising expense would be "up front" and could not readily be cut back if the projected sales increase did not materialize. A further risk of this strategy was that it relied on continued support from the distributors during 1978, even though Fisher-Price would have to give notice of its intent to terminate them at the beginning of that year.

Muirhead's suggested third option was a compromise between the two extremes. What he proposed was a "phased takeover," in which the distributors would be asked to switch over to a commission arrangement for services rendered during 1978. The key provisions of such a commission arrangement are summarized in *Exhibit 8*. In 1979, Fisher-Price would take over the top 90 accounts in the two countries and service them directly; in 1980, the company would commence operating its

EXHIBIT 7. Projected sales, expenses, profits, and investment, 1978–82 (based on establishing own sales company on January 1, 1979)

Fisher-Price operating results	1978	1979	1980	1981	1982
		(millions of Belgian francs)[a]			
Sales	103.5	331.0	342.0	376.0	402.0
Standard cost of sales	76.0	179.0	185.0	203.0	217.0
Standard gross profit	27.5	152.0	157.0	173.0	185.0
% net sales	27%	46%	46%	46%	46%
Distribution expense	1.6	10.0	10.0	11.3	12.0
Gross margin	25.9	142.0	147.0	161.7	173.0
% net sales	25%	43%	43%	43%	43%
Marketing expenses[b]	6.7	72.5	59.1	45.3	45
General and administrative[c]	6.8	26.2	29.0	32.0	35.2
Operating income	12.4	43.3	58.9	84.4	92.8
% net sales	12%	13%	17.2%	22.4%	23.1%
Invested capital[d]	40.0	127.0	136.0	141.0	150.0

[a]37BFr. = 1 U.S. dollar.
[b]Marketing expense includes advertising, catalogs, samples, merchandising expenses, and sales force salaries and commissions.
[c]In 1978, primarily allocated G&A expenses of European HQ office. Beginning 1979, primarily payroll, warehouse, and office expenses of Benelux sales company.
[d]Beginning 1979, includes inventory and accounts receivable from retailers.
Source: Company estimates.

own warehouse and office; and finally, in 1981, it would establish its own sales force.

Forecasts of sales, expenses, profits, and investment requirements for the phased takeover strategy are shown in *Exhibit 9*. Muirhead saw several advantages in this approach, including:

- an immediate improvement in gross margin in 1978, by reducing the distributors' 33% gross margin to a 20% commission;
- control of pricing and product line selection by Fisher-Price;
- the gradual transition would give Fisher-Price time to acquire expertise, and would permit more gradual build-up of expenses as volume increases materialized.

Under either of the last two approaches, Muirhead argued that customer service would be improved significantly because Fisher-Price would control the delivery system.

EXHIBIT 8. Possible provisions of a commission service agreement between Fisher-Price and Boismanu

Services to be provided by Boismanu

1. During 1978, maintain a sales force and call on all retail accounts; fulfill and deliver orders, handling billing and collections.
2. During 1979, the same services as in 1978 except that Fisher-Price would handle warehousing, delivery, and billing for accounts with actual or anticipated purchases of Fisher-Price products of 150,000 BFr. or more.
3. During 1980, Boismanu would provide only warehousing services and field selling. All billing and delivery arrangements would be handled by Fisher-Price.

Commission rates

1. During 1978, Boismanu would be paid a commission of 20% on all sales in Belgium and Luxembourg.
2. The commission rate would be reduced in 1979 and 1980 in proportion to the reduction in services provided. (Required commissions were estimated at 16% in 1979 and 8% in 1980.)
3. Boismanu would provide to Fisher-Price itemized statements of amounts collected for each customer, as a basis for determining commissions due.

Termination

1. The contract would terminate no later than December 31, 1981.
2. Fisher-Price would have the right to terminate the agreement at an earlier time if
   a. Sales in 1978 did not increase by at least 30% over 1977; or
   b. Sales in 1979 and 1980 did not increase by at least 20% over the preceding year; or
   c. M. Jean Lagneau left Boismanu or otherwise was "no longer able, for whatever reason, to devote his customary effort" to the business.

Exclusive cooperation

1. Boismanu would agree not to handle any product lines directly competitive with Fisher-Price.
2. Fisher-Price would agree not to use any third party for soliciting orders in Boismanu's territory.

Both the "immediate" and the "phased" takeover strategies involved the establishment of a single sales company, located in Belgium, to serve the Benelux market. Consequently, a possible risk of either approach was that retailers in Holland would regard the company as a "foreign" organization. Even within Belgium, the proposed location of the sales company in the Flemish-speaking region might pose problems with respect to relationships with French-speaking retailers. Muirhead

EXHIBIT 9. Projected sales, expenses, profits, and investment, 1978–82
(based on "phased takeover" with own sales company in 1981)

Fisher-Price operating results	1978	1979	1980	1981	1982
	(millions of Belgian francs)[a]				
Sales	178.3	205	249	287	331
Sales commission	35.7	32.8	20	—	—
Net sales after commission	142.6	172.2	229	287	331
% net sales	80%	84%	92%	100%	100%
Standard cost of sales	94.0	111	134	155	179
% net sales	27%	30%	38%	46%	46%
Distribution expense	5.4	6	7.5	9	10
Gross margin	42.9	55.2	87.5	123	142
% net sales	24%	27%	35%	41%	43%
Marketing expenses[b]	10.6	12	14.5	36.7	41.5
General and administrative[c]	4.1	7	22.8	27.6	29.2
Operating income	28.2	36.2	50.2	58.7	71.3
% net sales	15.8%	17.7%	20.1%	20.5%	21.5%
Invested capital[d]	69.0	79.0	97.0	112.0	130.0

[a]37 BFr. = 1 U.S. dollar.
[b]Marketing expense includes catalogs, samples, trade fairs, etc. Beginning 1981, includes advertising expenses.
[c]For 1978 and 1979, primarily allocated G&A expenses of European HQ office. Beginning in 1980, primarily payroll, warehouse, and office expenses of Benelux sales company.
[d]Includes receivables from distributors and, beginning in 1979, inventories and receivables from retailers.
Source: Company estimates.

thought that relationships with retailers could be improved by establishing showrooms in Brussels and Utrecht; by employing Dutch nationals as sales representatives in Holland; and by using a French-speaking advertising agency in Belgium as well as a local agency in Holland.

Another aspect of the proposed switch to a Fisher-Price sales company was that terms of sale to retailers would be modified. It was proposed that a minimum order quantity of one case (usually 12 pieces) per item be established. The two distributors accepted orders for as little as one piece (for examples, see *Exhibit 1*). The proposal also called for establishment of standard, published quantity discounts and credit terms. The distributors often negotiated varying discounts and terms for individual accounts. Muirhead estimated that the proposed new policy might increase prices to retailers on large orders by 3–5%, and shorten the time for which unpaid balances were outstanding by as much as 30 days in some instances.

The estimates of future sales, operating expenses, and profits in *Exhibits 6, 7,* and *9* had been prepared by Muirhead as a basis for comparing the three approaches to distribution in the Benelux countries. The executives present at the meeting realized, however, that such estimates were purely judgmental and subject to considerable uncertainty. No one could really tell how a change in distribution channels might affect future operating results.

LEGAL CONSIDERATIONS

If Fisher-Price moved immediately to set up its own sales company, or if it proposed to shift to a commission arrangement and was rejected by the distributors, the company risked exposure to substantial legal liabilities. In Holland, the problem was not regarded as important; under Dutch law, all that was required of a manufacturer was to give a distributor one year's notice of intent to terminate. In Belgium, however, the situation was different. Belgian law required that a principal (manufacturer) must give "reasonable notice" of his intent to terminate a distribution agreement. This requirement only applied in situations where the distributor, like Boismanu, was the exclusive importer of the manufacturer's line. According to Fisher-Price's Belgian counsel, what constituted reasonable notice depended on several factors, including:

- the importance of the line to the distributor (longer notice would be required if the line represented a large part of the distributor's total sales);
- the degree of the distributor's involvement in the manufacturer's marketing program, i.e., special commitments to advertise, maintain inventories, train salespeople, etc.;
- the size and importance of the distributor's territory;
- the "renown" of the manufacturer's product line or brand name; and
- the duration of the relationship between the manufacturer and the distributor.

Application of these criteria to a specific case was at the discretion of the court, unless the distributor voluntarily settled with the manufacturer. In recent court cases, the periods established as reasonable notice ranged from one year up to as much as three years.

Under the law, if a distributor were terminated without reasonable notice, then the distributor could sue the manufacturer for "just indemnity" in lieu of notice. The amount of such indemnity would be determined by the court, and was intended to compensate the distributor for "damages caused by the termination." According to Fisher-Price's counsel, the indemnity would, *at minimum*, include the distributor's net profits on the manufacturer's product line. It might also include some portion of the distributor's "general expenses," i.e., operating expenses that could not be eliminated if the distributor continued in business.

In addition to an indemnity in lieu of notice, Boismanu might also be entitled to a "complementary indemnity." This was intended to compensate the distributor for losses caused by termination *beyond* the "reasonable notice" period. Factors considered by the courts in assessing complementary indemnities included the following:

- The ongoing value (to the manufacturer) of increases in clientele "resulting from the distributor's efforts."
- Past expenditures by the distributor which would continue to benefit the manufacturer (such as advertising).
- Indemnities which the distributor would be required to pay to its employees who were dismissed on account of the termination.

In the attorney's opinion, if Boismanu sued for damages and Fisher-Price were held liable, the total indemnity it would be required to pay the distributor would be "in the range of $1.2 million to $1.5 million (44 million to 55 million BFr.)."

THE "PHASED TAKEOVER" PROPOSAL

The possibility of a liability for indemnifying Boismanu would arise only if the distributor sued Fisher-Price. Muirhead felt that the likelihood of such an action would be minimized if Comptoir Boismanu could be persuaded to enter into a "commission service agreement" with Fisher-Price covering the years 1978, 1979, and 1980, along the lines shown in *Exhibit 8*. The basic idea was that Boismanu would cease to operate as an independent, full-service distributor. Instead, the company would be paid a commission for specified services. Both the commission rate and the extent of services provided would diminish over the three-year period, as shown in *Exhibit 8* and in the "sales commission" figures shown in *Exhibit 9*.

Muirhead believed that if Boismanu could be persuaded to sign a commission service agreement, Fisher-Price's exposure to possible damages might be substantially reduced. There was, however, no way to know how Lagneau or the owners of Boismanu would react to the proposition.

The group sat down to consider the three possibilities. Mr. Flournoy, the senior executive present at the meeting, said that he wanted to arrive at a definite decision that day, because he was scheduled to return to Fisher-Price headquarters in East Aurora, New York, on the following morning.

2.6 *CASE*

Minolta Camera Co., Ltd.

Ulrich Wiechmann

"We have got to fix this problem," said Mr. Katsusaburo Nakamura as he read the letter he had just received from one of his company's European retailers (see *Exhibit 1*). It was July 1971. Mr. Nakamura was the manager of the International Division of the Minolta Camera Co., Ltd., a leading manufacturer of cameras and camera accessories, headquartered in Osaka, Japan. The letter he was reading came from Mr. Wilfried Reuter,[1] president of a large camera dealership in Germany with stores in Cologne, Düsseldorf, and Essen. Mr. Reuter, who had recently visited the Minolta headquarters in Osaka, complained about the fact that sizeable quantities of Minolta cameras moved through unofficial channels

---

[1]Certain names, places, and financial data have been disguised.

EXHIBIT 1. Letter from a camera retailer in Germany

Dear Mr. Nakamura,

After having safely returned to Cologne, I would like to thank you again for the kind welcome extended to me at the occasion of my visit to Japan. It was certainly a pleasure to see you and have the opportunity to exchange thoughts and discuss various matters with you.

On my way home I spent one day in Hong Kong, where I had to notice the very low prices at which the Minolta cameras and particularly the lenses were offered. For a German photo dealer it is still very much worthwhile to purchase the products in Hong Kong direct. This situation should really urgently be changed. We would like to point out again that this price difference makes business very difficult and has repeatedly been the subject for unpleasant discussions with some of our customers.

We are convinced that you as International Manager can appreciate our difficulties and we suggest that you exchange your position with the Manager of your Domestic Department for a while, which would most certainly make him understand our problems much better afterwards!

We sincerely hope that the "problem Hong Kong" can soon be solved. Meanwhile, we remain, with best regards.

Yours very truly,

REUTER PHOTO AG

Wilfried Reuter
President

from Hong Kong to Germany, where they were sold at prices substantially below Minolta's official suggested retail prices.

Mr. Reuter's letter was not the first of its kind that Mr. Nakamura had received. A number of other authorized dealers in Europe and in the United States had voiced similar complaints about unfair price competition because of an inflow of Minolta cameras through irregular channels. In virtually all of these cases the source of the problem seemed to be that merchants in Hong Kong bypassed Minolta's regular distribution system by exporting directly to camera retailers abroad. The basis of these export transactions was the significant price difference for Minolta cameras that existed between Hong Kong and Japan on the one hand and Europe and the United States on the other.

Mr. Nakamura estimated that these "grey exports," as he called the movement of Minolta cameras through irregular channels, accounted for less than 10% of

EXHIBIT 2. Direct mail promotion of an export firm sent to European camera outlets

Dear Sirs,

Understanding that you are important photographic dealers, we address this letter with the hope of establishing business relations with your esteemed firm.

By way of introduction, we are a Japanese firm with head-office in Tokyo. We specialize in the photo line trade.

From the free port of Hongkong, we are in position to supply you with all Japanese brands of cameras and accessories at low Hongkong prices. We are in position to supply ASAHI PENTAX, CANON, FUJICA, KONICA, KOWA, MAMIYA, MINOLTA, MIRANDA, YASHICA, OLYMPUS, NIKON and also all brands of accessories.

Please specify the brand-name you are particularly interested in. Offers will be promptly submitted for your perusal and consideration.

We are also in position to supply Hongkong-made Transistor Radios.

Very truly yours,

Inter Export Enterprises
Hong Kong B.C.C.

Minolta's total camera sales. A disturbing fact, however, was that the magnitude of these transactions, while hard to measure, seemed to be increasing rather than decreasing. Just a few days ago Mr. Nakamura had received a letter from one of Minolta's exclusive distributors in Europe. The distributor was very concerned that in trying to sell Minolta cameras to the retail accounts in his country he frequently found himself competing against unauthorized exporters in Hong Kong. Attached to the letter was a piece of direct mail promotion that one of these exporters, Inter Export Enterprises, had sent to major camera retailers in the distributor's country (see *Exhibit 2*). The distributor commented:

> *I wish to emphasize that similar direct mail is regularly coming into our market from firms in Hong Kong offering photographic equipment at exceptionally low prices. We are obviously concerned at these overseas firms selling in our market as the recent increase in such selling by overseas outlets causes great discounting to take place in our market and also reduces our market possibilities. There is nothing illegal whatsoever in companies, such as Inter Export, exporting to our country but, like other official photographic equipment distributors, we are being heavily affected because of this unreasonable practice.*

EXHIBIT 3. Consolidated sales 1965–1971

Year	Total sales (billion ¥)	Sales of cameras, lenses, and accessories as percentage of total
1965	8.4	95%
1966	9.0	92
1967	12.1	84
1968	14.7	82
1969	18.5	79
1970	22.8	82
1971[a]	24.5	86

[a]Estimate.
Source: Company records.

COMPANY BACKGROUND

Minolta Camera Co., Ltd. was one of the leading Japanese manufacturers of still and movie cameras, lenses and camera accessories. Founded in 1928, the company reached a 1970 sales volume of ¥22.8 billion.[2] Sales of cameras, lenses and accessories accounted for 82% of this volume. The remaining 18% were predominantly sales of electrostatic office copiers; a small fraction of total company sales was contributed by a diverse line of products, such as light sensing devices, planetaria, hand calculators, and specialized optical instruments. Minolta's sales had shown a rapid growth over the past five years (see *Exhibit 3*). For 1971, management expected to reach a sales volume of ¥24.5 billion.

Minolta's line of cameras covered almost the whole spectrum from modestly priced simple cameras for the beginner or occasional photographer to premium priced sophisticated equipment for the serious amateur or the professional photographer. Throughout its history the company had been a pioneer in the development of advanced Japanese camera equipment. The Auto-Minolta, introduced in 1935, was the first range-finder press camera in Japan when it was marketed in 1937. The Minolta SR-7, introduced in 1962, was the world's first single-lens-reflex camera with a built-in CdS exposure meter. While manufacturing and marketing a full line of still and movie cameras, Minolta's sales volume and marketing efforts concentrated on sophisticated 35 mm single-lens-

---

[2]1 U.S. $ = ¥360 in 1970.

reflex still cameras and a range of interchangeable lenses for these cameras. With these products Minolta competed against other well-known Japanese brands, such as Nikon, Canon, and Asahi Pentax, as well as foreign brands such as Leica. All manufacturers offered essentially similar camera features and equipment. Furthermore, with the exception of the premium-priced Leica, all brands sold at more or less comparable prices.

All of Minolta's products were manufactured in Japan. The company operated four plants for the manufacturing of cameras and lenses, and two plants for the business machines and other products. In spite of the rapid sales growth over the past years, Minolta, like other Japanese camera manufacturers in 1970, was finding it difficult to fill the production capacity in its camera and lens factories. "The whole industry is characterized by a discrepancy between supply and demand and, consequently, intense competition," Mr. Nakamura observed.

INTERNATIONAL ACTIVITIES

Like most Japanese camera manufacturers, Minolta depended heavily on sales outside of Japan. In 1970, Minolta's camera products were sold in about 100 countries. Exports contributed roughly 60% to the company's total sales of cameras and equipment; for 1971, management expected this figure to rise to 65%. Moreover, export sales were considerably more profitable than domestic sales in Japan (see *Exhibit 4*).

Of the various export markets, the United States and Europe were the most important geographical areas for Minolta. The United States accounted for 45% and Europe for 35% of Minolta's export sales of photographic products.

In the United States and in Germany Minolta had established wholly owned sales subsidiaries. In all other foreign countries the company worked through exclusive distributors for the sale and servicing of its products. It was company policy to appoint only one distributor per country. "We want foreign operations to run as orderly as possible," Mr. Nakamura explained. Usually, these exclusive distributors carried only Minolta cameras and equipment. Exceptions were made in some of the smaller countries where the distributors had to carry competing camera brands in order to reach a viable sales volume.

Like most marketers of expensive photographic equipment, Minolta and its distributor attempted to be selective in choosing retail outlets for Minolta cameras. Worldwide, Minolta cameras were sold through ap-

EXHIBIT 4. Profit and loss statement for sales of camera products,
October 1970–March 1971 and April 1971–September 1971,* (million ¥)

	October '70–March '71 (million ¥)		April '71–September '71* (million ¥)	
	Domestic	*Export*	*Domestic*	*Export*
Sales	3,684	5,869	3,510	7,036
Cost of goods sold	2,382	4,105	2,304	5,011
Gross profit	1,302	1,764	1,206	2,025
Selling and administrative expense	1,092	902	1,133	1,045
Operating profit	210	862	73	980

*Estimate.
Source: Company records.

proximately 25,000 retail stores, most of which could be classified as camera specialty stores or camera specialty departments of large department stores.

In most countries the retailer played a very important role in the consumer purchasing process. Consumer studies Minolta had obtained from several major European countries had shown that most consumers relied heavily on the advice and information of the retailer in deciding what type and brand of camera to buy. Moreover, these studies indicated that less than one-fourth of all prospective buyers entered a retail store with a clear idea about the brand of camera they wanted to buy. Even then consumers often would not insist on that particular brand if the dealer argued strongly in favor of another brand.

The marketing of Minolta cameras was fairly standardized from country to country, due to the fact that many of the important dimensions of the marketing activities in each country were determined in Osaka.

The products, model names, and packaging were identical in all markets. Occasionally in the past, a distributor had suggested changes in either the packaging or the model design for his country. So far, such suggestions had never been followed; headquarters management in Japan feared that even slight deviations from a uniform product policy would create serious problems in production scheduling and incur additional costs. It was already not easy to provide the brochures, instruction booklets for the cameras, and dealer manuals in many different languages. Accurate forecasting of demand in each country was a major problem.

Aside from the uniform product policy, the advertising for Minolta cameras was also highly standardized on a worldwide basis. Print media campaigns and posters were mostly prepared in Japan and then sent to the foreign distributors and subsidiaries for placement in local media.

Minolta also granted a uniform worldwide warranty for its products. Within the warranty period of one year, a customer could get free service in case of defective workmanship or materials from any of the authorized Minolta service representatives in the world. Management had always considered free worldwide warranty service, coupled with a uniform worldwide advertising approach, as a mark of quality and prestige in the field of high-priced consumer products. It was the accepted practice not only of most major camera manufacturers but also, for example, of famous watchmakers.

While Minolta's marketing approach showed great similarity from country to country in terms of product, advertising, service, and distribution policy, it varied considerably in terms of price. In 1970, all export prices for Minolta products were quoted in U.S. dollars. Wide differences in retail prices existed between one export market and another and also between certain export markets and the Japanese domestic market. The reason for these price differences was primarily fierce competitive conditions in some markets which forced prices down to a very low level. Hong Kong, Singapore, and also Japan were these low-price markets.

Exhibit 5 gives an example for the price differences that existed between Japan, Hong Kong, the United States, and Germany for a popular Minolta single-lens-reflex camera. For many items in the Minolta product line the price differences were even more drastic. In several instances the price net to dealers in Japan was similar to the landed cost of distributors in Europe and in the U.S. "Generally, the retail prices in Europe and in the U.S. are between 50% and 200% higher than in Hong Kong or Japan; 200% is more typical," said Mr. Nakamura. "Prices in Hong Kong and Japan are very close, usually Hong Kong is only about 5% above retail prices in Japan. Our low prices in Hong Kong and in Japan are dictated by the tough competitive situation and the overhang of supply and demand. Our distributors in Hong Kong and Japan buy from us at prices which are close to our FOB prices for Europe and the U.S. The margins for the distributors and the retailers in Japan and Hong Kong are relatively low; in Hong Kong, in particular, a retailer often takes only a 2–3% markup. Distributors and dealers in Europe and in the U.S. insist on much higher margins. These high margins have

EXHIBIT 5. Price schedule for a Minolta single-lens-reflex camera with case in Japan, Hong Kong, Germany, and the United States, first quarter 1971[a] (in U.S. dollars)[b]

	Japan	Hong Kong	Germany	U.S.A.[c]
Production cost	62	62	62	58
Price net to wholesalers	108	—	—	—
Export price FOB Japan	—	98	94	99
Landed cost to distributors	—	121	130	123
Price net to dealers	136	148	189	205
Retail list price	170	174	270	342
Approximate actual retail price	160	165	248–271	260–280

[a]Disguised data.
[b]*Exchange Rates:* Early 1971: 1 US$ = ¥360 = HK$6.06 = DM 3.66. In mid-1971 there were strong signs that significant changes in the exchange rates would take place. The position of the U.S. dollar had weakened. The German mark had begun to float. Market observers predicted a devaluation of the U.S. dollar by 5 to 10 percent before the end of 1971.
[c]Case not included.
Source: Company records.

largely historical reasons. When Japanese camera manufacturers first started to enter the Western markets after the war, high margins were absolutely necessary to gain distribution. We have thought of reducing these margins in Europe and in the U.S., but we can't do a thing as long as our competitors keep their margins high."

HONG KONG AND THE "GREY EXPORT" PROBLEM

In Hong Kong, Minolta had been represented for more than 10 years by Goddard & Co., Ltd., as their exclusive distributor. Goddard was one of the many medium-size specialist camera distributors that operated in Hong Kong. The company carried only Minolta camera products.

Goddard & Co., Ltd. was founded by Mr. George Ho, a Chinese businessman, well-connected to business and government circles in Hong Kong. Aside from being a camera distributor, Mr. Ho was associated with other businesses in Hong Kong, the most prominent of which was in the field of TV and radio broadcasting. Through his association with Minolta, Mr. Ho had become a personal friend of Mr. Kazuo Tashima, the founder and president of Minolta.

"Through his connections, Mr. Ho is very valuable to us," Mr. Nakamura observed. "Mr. Ho comes from an old family with excellent connections to Chinese merchants, banks, and the Hong Kong government. He has a lot of information that we couldn't get alone."

Goddard & Co., Ltd. sold to roughly 80 regular retail accounts. Many of these retailers carried very little inventory. "When a customer comes into his store and the retailer doesn't have a particular item, he orders it from Goddard for same-day delivery," explained Mr. Nakamura. "Goddard has messenger boys making daily deliveries to retail stores."

Goddard employed two salesmen for sales to retailers. The salesmen were paid a commission and a small fixed salary. The salary amounted to roughly 30–35% of the salesmen's total compensation.

While Goddard served about 80 regular Minolta accounts, there was no effective control of who the salesmen visited and to whom they sold. Mr. Nakamura suspected that they occasionally sold to dealers who re-exported Minolta cameras to other parts of the world. "It is hard for Goddard and their salesmen to turn down an order," Mr. Nakamura commented. "Goddard has done a good selling job for us over the past 10 years and we have a very nice relationship with them. But they don't control distribution. They don't care about 'grey exports,' who they sell to and where the merchandise goes after they have sold it. Of course, distribution control is very hard to do. The people who re-export to Europe and to the U.S. are not easily identified; the frequency and quantity of their purchases may be an indication."

Minolta's export sales to Hong Kong had increased rapidly in the past and in 1970 had accounted for almost 4% of the company's total export sales. This figure was, however, only a fraction of the total volume of Minolta cameras moving from Japan to Hong Kong. Mr. Nakamura explained:

> *Most of the grey exports to Europe and to the United States are organized by traders in Hong Kong. But the Hong Kong market has to be seen together with the Japanese market. The grey exporters in Hong Kong, we call them "smugglers" although there is nothing illegal about their operations, they actually get most of their merchandise from regular camera retailers in Japan. It works like this: Every day a lot of Hong Kong ships and a lot of Chinese sailors come into Japanese ports. Many of these sailors "work" for the "smuggler" in Hong Kong. On his order they each buy one camera tax free[3] in a regular camera store, take it back to Hong Kong, deliver it to the "smuggler," get reimbursed*

---

[3]Under Japanese law, foreign visitors were allowed tax exemption on cameras and several other products — a saving of from 10 to 20 percent.

for whatever they paid, and receive a commission. Since they buy only one camera and some lenses at a time as personal property, there is no export or import documentation necessary.

I don't know how many cameras move this way to Hong Kong. The retail price level and the supply and demand situation in Japan are decisive factors. If the market in Japan is weak, and it frequently is with so many camera makers around, a lot of merchandise flows into Hong Kong.

What I do know is that this is a regular, organized business. Sometimes the "smugglers" also "employ" airline stewardesses and pilots. The annoying thing is that all this happens strictly within the boundaries of the law; so from that angle there is nothing we can do to stop it.

The individual deliveries that reach Hong Kong from Japan in this manner are then pooled and perhaps combined with purchases the "smuggler" makes in the Hong Kong market to form large shipments to Europe and the United States. Again, this whole export operation is perfectly legal. At the moment, most of the cameras go to Europe, Germany in particular. The buyers at the other end are typically large department stores, discount-type operations, specialty camera retailers, and sometimes even our authorized Minolta dealers.

The Hong Kong exporter can offer very low prices to those outlets. First of all, he buys the merchandise cheaply in Hong Kong or in Japan. He takes only a small markup, usually less than 5%. The price difference between the Far East markets and the markets in Europe and the U.S. is large enough to pay for shipping expenses and still offer an attractive price to the Western dealers. For example, for a shipment from Hong Kong to West Germany we figure that an exporter would have to pay roughly 20.5% of the FOB Hong Kong value for freight, insurance, and import duty.

Sometimes the shipments from Hong Kong don't go directly to retailers but to somebody who specializes on "grey imports" from Hong Kong. We have identified a number of these firms in Germany, France, Belgium, and Switzerland. The "grey importer" usually takes another 7% of the FOB Hong Kong price.

This is pretty much all we know about the situation and probably all we are ever going to know. We certainly also know that these "grey exports" are a danger to our idea of orderly marketing. Just recently 3,000 SR-Ts[4] emerged through the Hong Kong system in the U.S. Our regular dealers screamed like hell.[5] In Germany, a department store just offered 600 SR-Ts at "drastically reduced prices." The problem is that these "grey exports" create a lot of attention; the retailers who buy them in Europe or in the United States, of course, heavily advertise that they have a special deal "as long as supply lasts."

---

[4]Model designation for one of Minolta's single-lens-reflex cameras.

[5]Minolta's total export sales of the SR-T model to the U.S. in 1970 had amounted to about 51,000 units.

TACKLING THE PROBLEM

"We have got to fix this problem," said Mr. Nakamura. He had called a meeting with key executives of the International Division. The meeting was attended by Mr. Isao Izuhara, Manager of the Export Department, Mr. Akio Miyabayashi, General Manager of Minolta Camera Handels-gessellschaft m.b.H. in Hamburg, Germany, Mr. Sadahei Kusumoto, President of Minolta Corporation in New York, and Mr. Koji Kusumoto, who had previously been the general manager of Minolta's Hamburg subsidiary and was now working in the Export Department.

"I agree," said Mr. Koji Kusumoto. "I got into some very uncomfortable situations with our regular dealers when I was over in Germany. At the last Photokina[6] a number of our dealers cornered my sales manager and myself; they wanted to know what Minolta is going to do about it. But I am not sure whether there is anything we can do unless we eliminate the current differences in price that exist between the Far East and the Western markets. Water will flow from high points to low points, and cameras will flow from low-price markets to high-price markets."

"Well, our dealers don't see it quite that way," replied Mr. Miyabayashi. "They think that what we should do, first of all, is better control of our distribution. They keep arguing that other companies, prestigious watchmakers like Omega, in particular, which have similar price differences, don't seem to have our problem. Of course, what the dealers don't say is that wristwatch distribution is much more selective, almost exclusive, than ours; I don't think that would be feasible for our products."

"Still, distribution control and stock control is something we can do and we should do better," said Mr. Izuhara. "Goddard in Hong Kong just isn't doing a good job in this respect. We have discussed the matter with them several times. They don't care where our products go. I think we should control the Hong Kong operation ourselves. I have had some very preliminary discussions with George Ho about this. I think there may be a chance of talking him into changing Goddard into a 50:50 joint venture with us. We have made some rough calculations; for a 50:50 joint venture we might need a capital expenditure of roughly HK$600,000."

"But certainly, we would want more than an equity participation," said Mr. Nakamura. "If we do it, we would have to insist on Japanese

---

[6]Important trade exhibition of photographic products in Cologne, Germany.

management of the joint venture. I wonder whether George Ho would go along with that."

"If he doesn't, I believe that we should terminate our agreement with Goddard and establish a wholly owned subsidiary in Hong Kong," Mr. Izuhara replied.

"These are all very drastic steps," commented Mr. Sadahei Kusumoto from New York. "I think there are a number of tactical changes we can make to improve the situation. I believe that if we sold our cameras under different model names in the Far East and in the West we would reduce the inflow of 'grey exports' from Hong Kong significantly. Consumers in the United States would be reluctant to buy the Hong Kong imports if the imports carried a model designation that is different from the models we show in our advertising. They would feel that they would get an inferior model if they bought the lower-priced Hong Kong imports."

"Furthermore, we could change our current warranty policy under which we service any camera free of charge during the warranty period, irrespective of where the camera was bought. Why not impose a handling charge, say $25.00, for any camera we receive for service that was not imported through the Minolta Corporation in New York? We could make similar arrangements in Europe. Since each of our cameras and lenses carries a number, it's easy to determine whether we imported a specific camera or whether it reached the U.S. in some other way."

"These are all very interesting ideas," said Mr. Nakamura. "I wish we had more information about the 'grey export' problem. But I am sure we won't get much more. We have got to make some decisions on the basis of what we know now. The fluctuation in currency exchange rates we are experiencing at the moment certainly doesn't make this job easier."

2.7 CASE

British Airways

John A. Quelch

On Sunday, April 10, 1983, a six-minute commercial for British Airways (BA) was aired in the middle of a weekend talk show. The commercial included a statement by Lord King, BA's chairman, and highlighted BA's achievements during the previous two years. The commercial also included the inaugural showing of a ninety-second advertisement known as Manhattan Landing. This advertisement and three others formed the basis of an unprecedented £31 million advertising campaign designed to promote BA's brand name and corporate image worldwide.[1]

---

[1]BA's fiscal year ran from April 1 to March 30. At the time of the case, £1 was equivalent to about $1.50.

BRITISH AIRWAYS

By many criteria, BA was the largest international airline in the world. In 1982–83, BA carried 11.7 million passengers on 130,728 international departures, well ahead of Air France, which carried 9.6 million international passengers. In terms of international passenger miles, BA's 37 billion a year comfortably surpassed Pan Am. BA flew to 89 cities in 62 countries outside the U.K. during 1982–83. Forty-two percent of BA sales were made in the U.K., 25% in the rest of Europe, and 33% in the rest of the world.

BA was a state-owned enterprise, formed as a result of the 1972 merger of British European Airways and British Overseas Airways Corporation. The economies of scale in the work force which many expected from the merger were slow to materialize. Partly as a result, BA continued to record annual losses throughout the 1970s. BA's financial performance was aggravated by increases in the price of fuel oil stemming from the 1973–74 energy crisis. In addition, greater price competition, especially on transatlantic routes, resulted from the deregulation of international air fares. An example of this trend was the advent of the low-price, no-frills Laker Airways Skytrain service on the lucrative transatlantic route in 1979.

The election of a Conservative government in the U.K. in 1979 prompted a change in approach toward the management of BA. The new administration was determined to reduce the losses which almost all state enterprises showed each year and, in many cases, to restore these enterprises to private ownership. A new chairman, Sir John (later Lord) King, was appointed to head BA in 1980. He initiated programs to improve BA's products and services along with a hiring freeze and an early retirement program to reduce the size of the work force. By March 1983, BA's work force had been reduced to 37,500 people from 59,000 just three years earlier. In addition, BA showed a profit in 1982–83 for the first time in 10 years, compared to a £500 million loss in 1981–82 (see *Exhibit 1*).

Industry observers believed that BA would have to sustain this improved performance if stock was to be offered to private investors by the end of 1984. So the programs of product and service improvement continued, together with further labor cutbacks. Recently introduced Boeing 757s were added to the fleet in 1983, a quality control division was established, and the U.K. Super Shuttle was introduced.[2]

---

[2]Four shuttles operated between London and Manchester, Glasgow, Edinburgh, and Belfast. Tickets could be purchased in advance or on board, and flights typically left every hour during the day.

EXHIBIT 1. British Airways: income statement, April 1, 1982–March 31, 1983

	Million £
Sales revenues	
Passengers on scheduled services	1,771
Passengers on charter services	86
Freight	151
Mail	36
Ground arrangements for package tours	100
	2,144
Expenses	
Staff	593
Aircraft	101
Engineering	107
Operations	863
Marketing	205
Accommodation, ground transport, and administration	159
Recoveries	(158)
Ground arrangements for package tours	102
	1,972
Operating surplus	172
Plus operating surplus from nonairline activities[a]	18
Plus other income[b]	20
	210
Less cost of capital borrowings and tax	149
Profit before extraordinary items	51
Plus profit on sale of subsidiaries	26
Profit	77

[a]Including BA helicopters, BAAC, and IAC.
[b]Investments in other companies, interest earned on cash deposits, surplus from disposal of assets.

The turnaround in performance was recognized when BA received the 1983 Airline of the Year award, based on a survey of business travelers. However, although costs were reduced and the quality of service improved, BA's public image remained weak. Along with other nationalized industries, BA continued to share a reputation for inefficiency and incompetence. Accordingly, Lord King stated that one of his main objectives was "to make the airline proud again."

ADVERTISING DURING THE 1970s

During the 1970s, BA country managers had revenue responsibility for BA's marketing and operations in their individual markets. The advertising agencies with which they dealt were appointed by BA headquarters. Foote, Cone & Belding (FCB) had held the BA account in the U.K. since 1947, and as a result many country managers outside the U.K. also used FCB subsidiaries or affiliates.

In 1978, British Airways appointed FCB as its worldwide agency, meaning that all country managers *had to* deal with the FCB subsidiaries or affiliates in their countries. The purpose was to achieve a more favorable commission rate from FCB rather than to increase centralized control of advertising content around the world. Indeed, in the United States, where the BA account moved from Campbell Ewald to FCB, the BA advertising theme built around Robert Morley and the slogan, "We'll take good care of you" was retained intact since it had only recently been launched (see *Exhibit 2*). Although the Morley campaign was considered a success, building as it did on Britain's favorable reputation in the United States for old-fashioned hospitality, the campaign nevertheless caused problems for BA executives in the United States. In the words of one, "It overpromised on customer service; every time something went wrong, my phone would ring off the hook."

Prior to the appointment of FCB as the worldwide agency, BA country managers were not required to submit their proposed advertising copy to headquarters for approval. There were certain loosely defined guidelines governing the presentation of the BA logo, but beyond that, local country managers and their agencies were free to determine their own advertising copy. Major advertising campaign concepts did, however, require headquarters approval. Following the appointment of FCB as the worldwide agency, this procedure changed. Each December, BA country managers would submit to headquarters requests for advertising funds for the following fiscal year as part of the annual planning process. Once the commercial director at headquarters had allocated these funds, each country manager would then brief the local FCB agency or affiliate, and develop the advertising copy for the coming year. Country managers in the larger markets would submit their advertising copy to the commercial director in London more as a courtesy, while the smaller countries were required to submit their proposed copy for approval. Headquarters required changes in about 5% of cases, typically on the grounds that the advertising overstated claims or was inconsistent with the image BA wished to project.

Whatever the intent, the result of this process was inconsistent ad-

EXHIBIT 2. Robert Morley campaign magazine advertisement

We can beat the experience

British Airways beats Pan Am's experience five times a day. After all, we have more business seats to London than Pan Am and TWA combined.

You'd like a 10 a.m. flight? Of course we have it…we've had it for years. And British Airways offers something really special on it. First Class and Super Club® passengers receive a voucher worth £20 (about $33) for dinner in any one of four exclusive restaurants. Tourist passengers receive a voucher for a choice of one of five evenings of cabaret entertainment with dinner.*

British Airways has the very first flight out daily (9:30 a.m. Concorde). So we're up in the air before most airlines even wake up. We also have the last daily flight out (10:00 p.m.) and three

flights in between. And British Airways Super Club seats are by far the world's widest business class seats.

Need we go on? We could mention our free helicopter service,** or our preferred hotel and car rental rates for business travelers, or our longstanding commitment to our 10 a.m. flight. And you'll be pleased to note that your flight miles between the U.S. and London will count as credit toward the A Advantage® travel award plan.

So you see, British Airways has no trouble beating the experience. It's experience like ours that makes us the world's favourite airline. That's why British Airways flies more people to more countries than anyone else. See your travel agent or corporate travel department.

*Offer valid April 15-October 31, 1983 and subject to government approval. For full fare USA originating passengers only. See vouchers for details.
**Helicopter service free for Concorde, First Class and Super Club passengers.

DEPARTURE	AIRCRAFT	FREQUENCY
9:30AM	Concorde	Daily
10:00AM	TriStar/747	Daily
1:45PM	Concorde	Daily
7:00PM	747	Daily
10:00PM	747	Daily

British airways
The World's Favourite Airline™

vertising from one country to another. First, campaigns varied across markets. The Robert Morley campaign was only considered suitable for the U.S.A. And a recently developed U.K. campaign in which a flight attendant emphasized the patriotism of flying the national flag carrier could likewise not be extended to other countries. Second, commercials and advertising copy promoting the same service or concept were developed in different markets. There were limited procedures within BA and the agency for ensuring that the best ideas developed in one market were transferred to other markets. Finally, the quality of FCB's subsidiaries and affiliates varied significantly from one country to another, aggravating the problem of inconsistency.

BA advertising during this period, like the advertising for most other major airlines, tried to persuade consumers to choose BA on the basis of product feature advantages. Rather than attempting to build the corporate image, BA advertising emphasized superiority and differentiation in scheduling, punctuality, equipment, pricing, seating, catering, and/or in-flight entertainment. Advertising typically focused on particular products such as the air shuttle, BA tour packages, route schedules and classes of service (such as Club[3]). The impact on sales of many of these product-specific and tactical advertising efforts could be directly measured. In addition, the commercial director responsible for BA advertising worldwide insisted that a price appear in all advertisements in all media. Frequently, BA advertisements compared the prices of BA services to those of competitors. The commercial director's insistence on including price information in each advertisement frequently caused problems. For example, in the United States, the APEX fare[4] to London from New York differed from that from Boston or Chicago, so different commercials had to be aired in each city.

The 1982–83 advertising budget of £19 million was allocated almost entirely to advertising of a tactical or promotional nature. Only the patriotic "Looking Up" campaign in the U.K. made any effort to develop BA's corporate image. About 65% of the 1982–83 budget was allocated by the commercial director to the International Services Division (ISD); about 30% to the European Services Division (ESD), and about 5% to the Gatwick Division, which handled BA air tours, package holidays, and cargo business in the U.K.[5] BA advertising expenditures during

---

[3]The BA equivalent of Business Class.

[4]Advance purchase excursion fare.

[5]The geographical coverage of the ISD and ESD mirrored that of the old BOAC and BEA.

1982–83 for 14 representative countries are listed in *Exhibit 3,* together with other comparative market information.

SAATCHI & SAATCHI APPOINTED

In October 1982, the Saatchi & Saatchi (S&S) advertising agency was asked by Lord King to explore the possibility of developing an advertising campaign which would bolster BA's image and which could be used on a worldwide basis. S&S was one of the first agencies to espouse the concept of global brands. In newspaper advertisements such as that shown in *Exhibit 4,* S&S argued that demographic and cultural trends, and therefore the basic factors underlying consumer tastes and preferences, were converging. In addition, S&S noted a growing spillover of media across national borders, fueled by the development of satellite television. Given these trends and the increasing level of international travel, S&S viewed the concept of global brands employing the same advertising themes worldwide as increasingly plausible.

Following its appointment, S&S set up a Central Policy Unit (CPU) to plan and coordinate work on the worldwide BA account. This unit included a director aided by specialists in research, planning, and budgeting. Over a two-month period, the CPU developed into a complete account team, one section of which handled advertising in the U.K. and Europe, while the second handled advertising in the rest of the world. The account team included a creative group and a senior media director with international experience.

After winning the BA account, S&S had to resign its business with British Caledonian, Britain's principal private airline. This business amounted to £3.5 million in media billings in 1982. Three S&S offices in other countries had to resign competitive airline accounts. Of the 62 countries in which BA had country managers, S&S had wholly owned agencies in 20 and partly owned agencies in 17. In the remaining countries, S&S retained a local agency, in some cases an FCB affiliate, to continue to handle the BA account. S&S did not permit its overseas affiliates to collect commissions on locally placed media billings as compensation for working on the local BA account. Rather, each affiliate received a fee or share of the commission for the services it performed from S&S headquarters in London. S&S billed BA headquarters for all of its services worldwide, except in the case of markets such as India where legal restrictions inhibited currency transactions of this nature.

EXHIBIT 3. Comparative BA data for fourteen markets, 1982–1983

	% worldwide passenger revenues	Advertising expenditures (£ 000)	Principal competitors	Market share vs. principal competitor	% Business/ % pleasure passengers
U.K.	42%	6,223	British Caledonian* Pan American	Similar	42%/58%
U.S.A.	14	5,773	Pan American TWA	Lower	26/74
Germany	5	228	Lufthansa British Caledonian	Lower	50/50
Australia	3	967	Qantas Singapore Airlines	Similar	6/94
France	3	325	Air France British Caledonian	Lower	52/48
Japan	3	393	Japan Airlines Cathay Pacific Airways	Lower	30/70
Gulf States	2	134	Gulf Air Kuwait Airlines	Lower	12/88
Canada	2	991	Air Canada Wardair	Lower	11/89
South Africa	2	331	South African Airways TAP (Air Portugal)	Lower	15/85
Italy	2	145	Alitalia Dan Air	Lower	50/50

New Zealand	1	125	Air New Zealand Singapore Airlines	Similar	3/97
Egypt	0.5	53	Egyptair Air France	Similar	26/74
Zimbabwe	0.4	41	Air Zimbabwe KLM	Higher	8/92
Trinidad	0.3	77	BWIA	Higher	7/93

*These are BA's principal competitors on international routes. BA's main competitors on domestic U.K. routes were British Midland Airways and Dan Air.

EXHIBIT 4. Saatchi & Saatchi newspaper advertisement

THE OPPORTUNITY FOR WORLD BRANDS.

Nowadays, life for branded goods manufacturers is not as straightforward as it once was.

Many years ago manufacturers first recognised that advertising could provide a key foundation for their business growth.

They realised that while their customer was the retailer, the actual 'consumer' was the public: that advertising could enable them to build a solid position in their market by building the goodwill of their real customer – the consumer.

They also saw that if they, the manufacturers, did something to move their goods from retailers' shelves as quickly as they arrived on them, trade would be brisk and everyone would be satisfied.

Thus the manufacturer became the advertiser of branded products, the retailer became the purveyor of brands and advertising became a conspicuous feature of the age.

This happy cycle produced 'brands' of startling endurance and longevity, as the table below shows.

US BRAND LEADER

	1923	CURRENT POSITION
SWIFT PREMIUM BACON		NO 1
EASTMAN KODAK, CAMERAS		NO 1
WRIGLEY CHEWING GUM		NO 1
NABISCO BISCUITS		NO 1
EVEREADY BATTERY		NO 1
GOLD MEDAL FLOUR		NO 1
LIFE SAVERS, MINT CANDIES		NO 1
SHERWIN-WILLIAMS, PAINT		NO 1
GILLETTE, RAZORS		NO 1
SINGER SEWING MACHINES		NO 1
COCA COLA SOFT DRINKS		NO 1
CAMPBELL'S SOUP		NO 1
IVORY SOAP		NO 1

Brand Character

Nowadays, when probed deeply, consumers describe the products they call brands in terms that we would normally expect to be used to describe people. They tell us that brands can be warm or friendly, cold or modern, old-fashioned, romantic, practical, sophisticated, stylish and so on.

They talk about a brand's persona, its image and its reputation – and this 'aura' or 'ethos' is what characterizes a brand.

It follows that all brands, like all people, have a 'personality' of one kind or another. But like the strongest individuals, the strongest brands have more than mere personality – they have 'character' – more depth, more integrity, they stand out from the crowd.

Note the importance that one major marketer attaches to this concept.

> 'My acid test on the issue is whether a housewife intending to buy Heinz Tomato Ketchup in a store, finding it has run out, would switch to the store to buy it elsewhere or switch to an alternative product.'

This explains why the best marketers try to develop powerful brand characters. They make them less vulnerable in the market-place. They help a higher quality product to be perceived as such by consumers.

The establishment of such strong and enduring brands is rather more difficult.

☐ Static populations mean static markets which means increased competition for market-share.

☐ Product quality is converging, with increasing technological parity among major marketers.

☐ The influence of the retailer and retailers' own store brands is growing in many parts of the world.

☐ Marketing expenses are growing, as manufacturers respond to the ever-higher cost of reaching the consumer.

All in all, the pressures on manufacturers' brands are immense.

Superior Product Quality

Serious marketers know that in the face of these pressures the success of their brands can only rest on superior product quality.

They know that as the consumer views more products as commodities, it becomes harder to establish a meaningful point of difference for their products. They know that clever marketing and promotion of cosmetic differences cannot paper over this.

They know that the longevity of their brands is helped by good marketing but is founded on superior product performance and this in turn is founded on their ability to produce *a higher quality product at a lower cost.*

Which is why market leaders' priorities are now focusing on a common objective which was not among their priorities in previous decades – to work diligently to be *the low cost producer* in their market.

Low costs provide the means to achieve that happiest of all situations – higher product quality ... lower price increases... and more advertising.

Low costs are the priority as a sound base for all the other steps needed to build growth.

Thus, the competitive intensity of maturing packaged goods markets around the world has brought to the fore the economic logic of world brands – *the opportunity for cost/rational economies at scale as the basis of long term strategic security.*

Today, the most thoughtful companies are adopting a new approach to international marketing.

These companies are moving through the five basic stages in the life of a multinational corporation as seen in the chart below.

And as they pass through stages 4 and 5 the need for pan-regional and world marketing is emerging at the heart of their business strategy.

> *The globalization of markets at hand. With that the multinational commercial world nears its end and so does the multinational corporation.*
>
> *The global corporation operates as if the entire world were one single entity it sells the same things in the same way everywhere.*
>
> *Corporations geared to this new reality can derive enormous benefits of scale in production, distribution, marketing and management. By translating these benefits into reduced world prices they can decimate competitors that still cling to the old assumptions about how the world works.*

A New Approach

After the vicissitudes of the 1950s and 1960s, more companies are now reaching the status of having acquired 'critical mass in various regions of the world. They are now starting to turn from primary concern about 'return on acquisition investment' and 'overhead recovery' towards getting to grips with long term franchise building across each world region.

At the same time the progressive harmonization of headquarters' and 'local' management culture and style, evolving from more frequent two-way movement of personnel, is enhancing the likelihood of successful adoption and execution of pan-regional business strategies.

And meanwhile in Europe, management's strategic thinking is beginning to broaden to match the dimensions of the Common Market as legislative harmonization focuses attention on pan-European issues.

International Growth Priority

Companies have passed through the bygone age when many of them treated 'Overseas Division' as the poor cousin of the organisation, struggling to compete in foreign markets with strongly established indigenous competitors.

The international divisions of many companies are now beginning to 'come of age' and receive their rightful allocation of corporate resource, if only for the practical reason that corporate earnings growth in many multinationals is today often provided by non-domestic markets.

Business System Economics

The strategic value of pan-regional branding lies in the scale economies it affords across the company's business system – to help make the company the low-cost producer.

Where the economies arise will vary by product category, and may include research and development, materials purchasing, manufacturing, distribution and advertising.

The optimum business system for a European beer, for example, is markedly different to that for chewing gum, but the principle is the same. Secure franchise-protected volumes at the regional scale can allow a company to build *a low cost value structure which will eventually put control on each of competition.*

All these factors set the conceptual framework within which a truly pan-regional brand can exist in the years ahead. The international need is the starting point. Research will be conducted to look for market similarities between countries, not to seek out differences. Similarities will be the new fuel for growth.

The creative process will still be as vital as ever, marketers in each location will still be dependent on the intuitive creative judgement of locally based creative management, but this effort will be marshalled to a single-minded overall advertising strategy.

Marketing Learning Curve

There is then a real marketing learning curve that allows the progressive refinement of a success formula, as the pan-regional brands broaden their experience country by country.

The best creative brains are given an opportunity to develop advertising for an entire region of the world, and not simply for one market – to find a real advertising idea *a deep is its appeal* that it can transcend national sales orders previously thought insolate.

Consumer Convergence

In the past, the successes in world branding have been few, and have been achieved by virtue of the sheer will and far-sighted commitment of managements who stayed consistently with a long-term vision for the business. Procter & Gamble is a company in this category that comes to mind.

In the future, the only winners in cross-country branding will be companies who have seen that social developments are making redundant the old idea that differences between nations are decisive in framing marketing strategy.

The most advanced manufacturers are recognising that there are probably more social differences between Midtown Manhattan and the Bronx, two sectors of the same city, than between Midtown Manhattan and the 7th Arrondissement of Paris. This means that when a manufacturer contemplates expansion of his business, consumer similarities in demography and habits rather than geographic proximity will increasingly affect his decisions.

Demographic Convergence

Trends of vast significance to consumer marketing, such as ageing populations, falling birth rates, and increased female employment are common to large segments of the modern industrial world.

Consumer convergence in demography, habits and culture is increasingly leading manufacturers to a consumer-driven rather than a geography-driven view of their marketing territory.

Decline of the Nuclear Family

Some of the most telling developments spring from the same source – the decline of the nuclear family. Observers have attributed this to various causes – the rapid pace of technological development, higher labour productivity which reduces hours of work, and other more metaphysical notions such as the emergence of a 'liberal' philosophy, which increasingly recognizes that a woman's role can exist outside the home.

DECLINE OF THE FAMILY UNIT

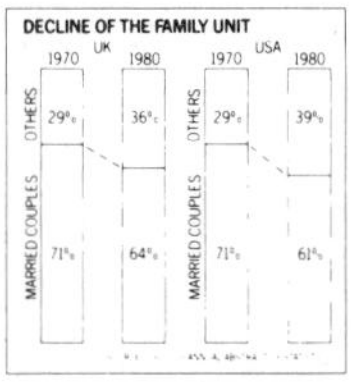

	1970	1980	USA 1970	1980
OTHERS	29%	36%	29%	39%
MARRIED COUPLES	71%	64%	71%	61%

Whatever the causes, the effects in terms of household composition have been dramatic. There are now less children per household, and a declining proportion of households which conform to the two-adult-two-children pattern.

The result is the erosion of the traditional family unit and its clarity of role and relationship. The effects have been illustrated by the decline of formal meal-taking and the corresponding increase in the sales of 'instant' and 'convenience' foods. The multinational expansion of fast-food franchises like McDonalds is another manifestation of the same trend.

Changing Role of Women

The table below shows the change in the role of women in the working population over the past decade. The fact that the majority of women in most modern societies now have a job requires a major adjustment to current ideas on communicating with a consumer group that no longer conforms to the home-centred stereotype of yesteryear.

MORE WORKING WOMEN

	CHANGE 1970-1979 WORKING POPULATION	WORKING WOMEN
USA	+24.6	+37.6
BELGIUM	+8.3	+24.7
NETHERLANDS	+10.1	+24.6
ITALY	+8.1	+22.8
FRANCE	+7.7	+17.3
UK	+4.5	+15.1
GERMANY	-1.6	+3.5

Associated with this change there has been a well documented trend to lower marriage rates and higher divorce rates. This trend has led one group of social scientists to invent the phrase "serial monogamy" to describe what they forecast to be the nature of relationships in the 1980s and beyond. They suggest that there will be an increasing tendency for couples to live together for a number of years, then to change their partners and set up home afresh, changing again after a few years, and so on. This discontinuity in formal relationships, especially where children are involved and re-marriages occur, will have profound effects on family relationships.

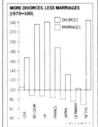

MORE DIVORCES, LESS MARRIAGES (1970=100)

Legend: DIVORCES, MARRIAGES

Static Populations

Population growth is now almost zero in the western world. All modern industrial countries are forecast to produce population growth of much less than 1% per annum over the next 20 years. It is hardly surprising that within this static population, the age structure is undergoing a transformation. The over 65s are a growing group relative to the 25–65s, and that group is growing relative to the fourteen and unders.

STATIC POPULATIONS

	GROWTH PER ANNUM 1960-70	1980-2000 (EST)
AUSTRALIA	2.0	0.8
CANADA	1.8	0.9
USA	1.3	0.7
SPAIN	1.1	0.7
JAPAN	1.0	0.4
FRANCE	1.0	0.4
ITALY	0.6	0.3
UK	0.5	0.2
GERMANY	0.9	0.1

ORGANISATIONAL PROGRESS TO WORLD BRANDS

1	2	3	4	5
COMPANY STARTS TO OPERATE IN ITS OWN COUNTRY	STARTS TO EXPORT	OPENS MARKETING COMPANIES OVERSEAS WITH THEIR OWN MANUFACTURING PLANT	CO-ORDINATES MARKETING AND PRODUCTION ACROSS DIFFERENT COUNTRIES	CENTRALIZES PRODUCTION DISTRIBUTION MARKETING BY CONTINENT

ECONOMIC PROGRESS TO WORLD BRANDS

1	2	3	4	5
PRESSURE OF COST INFLATION IN STATIC MARKETS	NEED TO BE LOW COST PRODUCER TO WIN MARKET SHARE BATTLE	SEARCH FOR MORE EFFICIENT BUSINESS STRUCTURE	ECONOMIES OF SCALE	WORLD BRANDS

EXHIBIT 4 (continued). Saatchi & Saatchi newspaper advertisement

Higher Living Standards

In most western countries, improvements in the material standard of life have resulted in a growing demand for consumer durables and for more leisure. This is reinforced by shorter working weeks that accompany technological progress and productivity growth.

The entry of women into the labour market itself creates a demand for consumer durables to ease the strain of 'keeping house'.

HIGHER LIVING STANDARDS

	GROWTH IN REAL PERSONAL CONSUMPTION 1970–82
USA	+ 42%
UK	+ 26%
FRANCE	+ 60%
GERMANY	+ 34%
JAPAN	+ 65%

SOURCE: HENLEY CENTRE

Cultural Convergence

At the same time as demography is converging, television and motion pictures are creating elements of shared culture. And this cultural convergence is facilitating the establishment of multinational brand characters. The worldwide proliferation of the Marlboro brand would not have been possible without TV and motion picture education about the virile rugged character of the American West and the American cowboy – helped by increasing colour TV penetration in all countries.

Observers believe that cultural convergence will proceed at an accelerated rate through the next decade – particularly with the deployment of L-SAT high-power TV satellites throughout Europe.

EUROPE'S NEW SUPER STATIONS

These developments will reduce cultural barriers as countries exchange their media output through satellite networks – for the first time allowing viewers freer access to international television without the barrier of language.

Marketing Timetables

Analysis of all these demographic, cultural, and media trends is allowing manufacturers to define market expansion timetables. Essentially, marketers will be tracking trends which indicate when a region is ready for attack via programmes they have tested elsewhere.

For example, current changes in European laundry practices were foreshadowed by similar trends in the US during the late '60s and early '70s. Thus a US manufacturer of low-suds detergent would examine the growth in the penetration of front-loading washing machines in the UK to assess the ripening potential for its own product.

MARKET EXPANSION TIMETABLES
% OF HOUSEHOLDS OWNING FRONT LOADING WASHING MACHINES

SOURCE: COMPANY RESEARCH

Consider also Europe's soap powder manufacturers. Driven by improved washing machine technology and the increased popularity of relatively fragile synthetic and coloured fabrics, European laundry habits have converged. Every major nation now washes a majority of its wash loads in under 60°C water. This has created a common need for a product which performs well under these circumstances.

The result has been the marketing of single brands with a common brand name, product formulation, and positioning across the whole of Europe.

In the future, the only winners in cross-country branding will be companies who do a lot of things right and subject their efforts effectively around three golden rules:

1. To market clearly differentiated products that either thrive, or capitalize on, real convergences in consumer habits and tastes.

2. To create a dedicated management value system that mirrors the vision of a pan-regional branded business.

3. To monitor their brands' character on a consistent, continuous, comparable basis across geography and over time.

The opportunity for world brands is there to be seized but only for those companies with the long-term determination to meet these stringent requirements.

Here are two other examples of the global approach in action – for British Airways and Procter & Gamble's Pampers. The Pampers brand was introduced in the US in the late 1960s. Pampers created the disposable diaper market by providing a product that was more convenient and more absorbent than cloth diapers at a price consumers were willing to pay. Pampers is now Procter & Gamble's largest brand and is sold on a similar strategy almost all over the world. If the Pampers business was a separate company, it would rank in the top one-third of the 'Fortune 500' list.

Does a global advertising campaign have to be bland? Not according to the South China Morning Post which described B.A.'s new worldwide campaign as *"unique and imaginative"*; or the Sydney Morning Herald – *"a radical departure from the usual formula"*, or Newsweek – *"a tour de force"*; or the Wall Street Journal – *the most ambitious attempt so far... to use a one world campaign"* or the London Sunday Times – *"a flash of inspiration."*

The Agency is now working on a similar exercise on Silk Cut for American Brands/Gallaher – a Company whose marketing was recently described by the Financial Times as *"an object lesson for its competitors on the mechanics of brand discipline."*

65 OFFICES IN 38 COUNTRIES.

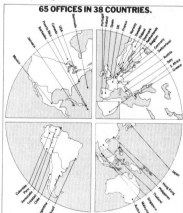

THE UK AGENCY WORKS WITH 6 OF BRITAIN'S TOP 10 ADVERTISERS.

THE US AGENCY HANDLES MORE No. 1 BRANDS THAN ANY OTHER AGENCY IN AMERICA.

THE INTERNATIONAL NETWORK WORKS WITH 44 OF THE WORLD'S TOP 200 ADVERTISERS.

Impact on Agency Structure

What are the implications of these trends for the advertising industry?

Business service companies, such as agencies, benefit from the increasing complexity of problems in their areas of expertise. Knowledge has value, and there is a greater 'value-added' during periods of turmoil and change in the business environment.

Most observers believe that the trend to pan-regional or global marketing will have a marked impact on the structure of advertising agencies... because world brands require world agencies.

A HANDFUL OF WORLDWIDE AGENCY NETWORKS WILL HANDLE THE BULK OF $125 bn WORLD ADVERTISING EXPENDITURE FOR MAJOR MULTINATIONALS.

Many expect to see the advertising industry moving in the same direction as accounting, banking, financial services, etc. – a polarization between worldwide networks servicing global corporations, and strong local firms handling domestic clients in their own country.

SOME OF THE AGENCY'S CLIENTS IN 3 OR MORE COUNTRIES

ALLIED LYONS	IBM
AMERICAN BRANDS	JOHNSON & JOHNSON
AMERICAN MOTORS	NABISCO BRANDS
AVIS	NESTLE
BLACK & DECKER	PEPSICO
BRITISH AIRWAYS	PROCTER & GAMBLE
BSN GERVAIS DANONE	PLAYTEX
CADBURY SCHWEPPES	ROWNTREE MACKINTOSH
CHESEBROUGH-POND'S	TIMEX
DU PONT	UNITED BISCUITS

This is pleasant for the business prospects of those agencies who can serve this global requirement, but leaves open one important question – whether this trend will result in *better* advertising.' On this question opinions differ.

Some agency managers are fond of saying that they would rather operate a solid, disciplined international network than run the best creative agency in the world.

Meantime, others declare that they would rather have high creative standards than succumb to the arthritis of international management structures.

Both these viewpoints ignore the possibility of combining discipline and creativity in one international organisation. This is because it is hard to do.

IN 1982, OUR UK AGENCY WON MORE TOP UK ADVERTISING AWARDS THAN ALL THE OTHER MAJOR MULTINATIONAL AGENCIES PUT TOGETHER.

SOURCE: GOLD AND SILVER AWARDS IN THE CAMPAIGN PRESS AWARDS, D&AD, AND BRITISH TELEVISION ADVERTISING AWARDS.

The Company has always aimed to create *the one type of agency which has somehow eluded the grasp of those few men and women who have tried to achieve it* – a large agency, certainly, with all the stability that gives to employees, and all the back-up that provides for clients – but one which at the same time also succeeds in being progressive, youthful and innovative in approach.

The fact that this combination has so rarely been achieved in our industry increases the sense of purpose with which we continue to pursue it as our goal.

This has been the fundamental spur to our growth over the years.

HIGH CREATIVITY ACROSS A DISCIPLINED WORLD NETWORK. THE COMPANY'S CONSISTENT STRATEGIC GOAL.

Last month Saatchi & Saatchi Company PLC, the parent company of the worldwide agency network, announced its results for the year ended September 30th 1983. It was the Company's 13th successive year of profit growth. In the year pre-tax profits rose by 103%, earnings per share by 40%, dividends per share by 45%.

Over the last five years the Company has shown a compound average growth of 43% in pre-tax profits, 33% for earnings per share, and 37% for dividends per share.

If you would like a copy of the Chairman's Statement on these results please write to the Company Secretary, Saatchi & Saatchi Company PLC, at 80 Charlotte Street, London W1A 1AQ, or 625 Madison Avenue, New York, New York 10022.

SAATCHI & SAATCHI COMPTON WORLDWIDE.

The relationship between S&S affiliates and headquarters was closer than it had been when FCB handled the BA account. A BA country manager would work with the local S&S agency to develop an advertising copy proposal which would be submitted to BA headquarters in London on a standard briefing form. The BA headquarters advertising manager would then decide whether to approach the S&S account team in London to develop a finished advertisement to be sent back to the BA country manager. Under this system, neither BA country managers nor their local agencies were involved in the design of advertising copy except in terms of working requests, stating objectives, and suggesting content. According to S&S executives, the frequency with which certain types of advertisement were requested meant that it might, in the future, be possible to develop standard "ad mats." BA country managers and their local agencies would simply fill in the relevant destination and fare information on these ad mats, and would not have to submit them to London for approval.

The system described above varied somewhat from one country to another. BA country managers and their local agencies in the five most important long haul markets (U.S., Canada, Australia, South Africa, and Japan) had slightly more autonomy than their counterparts in less important markets. Although all advertising had to be approved in London prior to use, finished copy could be developed in the local market by the local agency in conjunction with the BA country manager.

An early example of how commercials might be developed for use in more than one country under the S&S approach occurred at the end of 1982. The U.S. country manager developed an advertising proposal for the "Inbound" line of package tours from the U.S. to the U.K. Members of the U.S. agency creative team and BA executives from New York came to London to develop proposed scripts for the commercials. These were then approved by the U.S. country manager, but the commercials were shot in the U.K. so that British scenery could be included. These same commercials were subsequently used in South Africa and the Caribbean with different voiceovers; these countries' budgets could not be stretched to fund their independent production of television commercials of this quality.

Meanwhile, organization changes occurred at BA. Following the appointment of Mr. Colin Marshall as managing director in February 1983, the three divisions were replaced by eight geographic market centers which handled BA's basic passenger business and three additional business units handling cargo, air charter services, and package tours. These 11 profit centers reported to Mr. Marshall through Mr. Jim Harris, marketing director.[6] Mr. Harris also supervised a central marketing services staff involved with strategic planning, advertising, market analysis, and market research. An advertising manager who reported to the general manager for marketing services was responsible for agency relations and for the review and implementation of advertising by BA country managers. One of his assistants handled relations with the U.K. and European country managers; a second handled relations with the remaining country managers.

Under this new organization, BA country managers submitted their annual marketing plans, including proposed advertising and promotion budgets, to the appropriate market center manager in London. The country managers were informed in 1983 that their future budget proposals would have to provide detailed objectives and research support. In particular, country managers would have to forecast how their overall sales and profits would be impacted by particular advertising and promotion programs. The total advertising budget would be allocated among the country managers according to the quality of the proposals and according to which markets were designated for maintenance or development spending levels.

If a country manager required additional advertising funds during the fiscal year or wished to offer special consumer price deals and travel agency commissions above the norm applicable to the countries in his/her market center, s/he could apply to the market center manager in London. The marketing director held a reserve fund to deal with such contingencies. He also reserved the right to reallocate funds designated for one market to another during the fiscal year if, for example, foreign currency fluctuations altered the attractiveness of one market versus another as a holiday destination.

DEVELOPMENT OF THE CONCEPT CAMPAIGN

The S&S creative team was charged with developing an advertising campaign which would restore BA's image and prestige, and not necessarily by focusing on specific BA products, services, and price promotions. The agency described the qualities of the ideal advertising concept for the campaign: "It had to be simple and single-minded, dramatic and

---

[6]The marketing director performed the tasks previously undertaken by the commercial director. The latter title was no longer used.

break new ground, instantly understood throughout the world, visual rather than verbal, long-lasting, likable, and confident." S&S executives believed that the type of product-feature-based advertising used by BA and traditional in the airline industry could not satisfy these objectives. First, an airline competitor could easily match any product-based claim BA might make. Second, such advertising only impacted that portion of the target market who viewed the benefit on which superiority was claimed (e.g., seat width) to be particularly important. The agency believed that only a brand concept campaign could focus consumers on the permanent and essential characteristics of BA which transcended changes in product, competitive activity, and other market variables.

The agency established five objectives for the worldwide BA concept campaign:

- To project BA as the worldwide leader in air travel.
- To establish BA as the world's most successful airline.
- To demonstrate the superiority of BA products.
- To add value in the eyes of passengers across the whole range of BA products.
- To develop a distinctive, contemporary, and fashionable style for the airline.

The account team had the benefit of consumer research, which S&S had conducted in July 1982 with business and pleasure travelers in the U.K., U.S.A., France, Germany, and Hong Kong to understand better attitudes toward, and preferences for, particular airlines. Based on these data, S&S executives concluded that consumers perceived most major airlines as similar on a wide array of dimensions. To the extent differences existed, BA was viewed as a large, experienced airline using modern equipment. However, BA was rated poorly on friendliness, in-flight service, value for money, and punctuality. In addition, BA's image varied widely among markets; it was good in the U.S.A., neutral in Germany, but weak in France and Hong Kong. The name of the airline and the lack of a strong image meant that consumer perceptions of its characteristics were often a reflection of their perceptions of Britain as a country.[7] BA was often the carrier of second choice after a consumer's national flag airline, particularly among consumers taking a vacation trip to the U.K.

---

[7]In addition, some BA executives believed that BA was perceived more favorably in countries that had previously been served by BOAC than those previously served by BEA.

By November 1982, BA had developed in rough form a series of 11 television commercials around the theme "The world's favorite airline." The lead commercial of the concept campaign, known as "Manhattan Landing,"[8] was to be 90 seconds long with no voiceover during the first 40 seconds and with a total of only 35 words of announcer copy. It would show the island of Manhattan rotating slowly through the sky across the Atlantic to London accompanied after 70 seconds by the statement that "every year, we fly more people across the Atlantic than the entire population of Manhattan."[9] Ten other commercials known as the "preference" series showed individuals (from an Ingrid Bergman look-alike in Casablanca to members of a U.S. football team) receiving airline tickets and being disappointed to find that they were not booked on BA. International celebrities such as Peter O'Toole, Omar Sharif, and Joan Collins were shown at the end of each commercial checking in for a BA flight. The announcer copy for all the preference commercials was identical. Storyboards for Manhattan Landing and one of the preference commercials are presented as *Exhibits 5* and *6*. The intention was to air these commercials in all BA markets worldwide, with changes only in the voiceovers.

In November, the BA board of directors approved production of Manhattan Landing and three of the preference commercials. Production costs for these four commercials were estimated at £1 million.[10] S&S executives were asked to have the finished commercials ready for launch by April 1983, a very tight schedule given the complexity of the executions.

While the commercials were being produced, members of the S&S account team and BA headquarters advertising executives traveled to each BA market. Their purpose was to introduce and explain the worldwide concept campaign at meetings attended by each BA country manager and his/her staff along with representatives of the local BA advertising agency. These visits occurred during January and February 1983 and involved the presentation of storyboards rather than finished commercials.

---

[8]The Manhattan Landing commercial was originally conceived as a corporate advertisement to be shown exclusively in the U.K. to support BA's privatization effort. When it became clear that the offering of BA stock to the public would be delayed until at least the end of 1984, it was decided to include it in the worldwide concept campaign.

[9]BA flew 1.5 million passengers across the Atlantic to the U.K. in 1982–83, more than Pan Am and TWA combined. The population of Manhattan was 1.4 million.

[10]Recent BA television commercials had cost about £75,000 to produce.

EXHIBIT 5. Manhattan Landing storyboard

EXHIBIT 6. Casablanca preference campaign storyboard

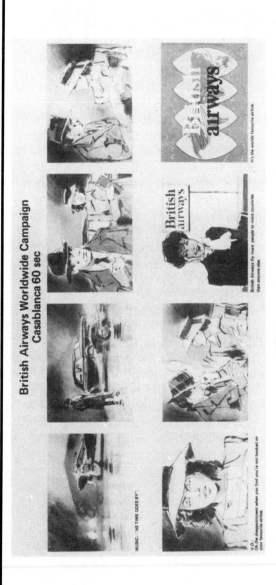

British Airways Worldwide Campaign
Casablanca 60 sec

MUSIC: "AS TIME GOES BY".

V.O.
Oh the disappointment when you find you're not booked on
your favourite airline.

British airways

British Airways fly more people to more countries
than anyone else.

British airways

It's the world's favourite airline.

REACTIONS TO THE CONCEPT CAMPAIGN

Reactions varied. The concept campaign was well received in the U.S.A., although the BA country manager was concerned about its dissimilarity from the existing Robert Morley campaign, which emphasized traditional British values. In India, there was some question as to whether Manhattan would hold any significance for the local audience. In other countries, including former British colonies, the claim "the world's favorite airline" was met with reactions such as "you must be joking!" The claim seemed to lack credibility, particularly in those markets where BA was in a relatively weak share position versus the national flag carrier. In other markets, such as France and Kuwait, only the state-owned airline was allowed to advertise on television, so the BA concept commercials could only be used in cinema advertising.

Questions about the proposed campaign were also raised by S&S affiliates. Since the parent agency had built its reputation on the importance of developing clear-cut positioning concepts, the proposed commercials seemed inconsistent with the philosophy of the agency. Even though the preference commercials were each planned to be 60 seconds long, some agency executives argued that they were too cluttered and tried to achieve too many objectives.

In particular, the 90-second Manhattan Landing commercial was greeted by some with amazement. One agency executive commented: "The net impact of three 30-second commercials would surely be greater?" The South African agency requested a 60-second version of the commercial because the South African Broadcasting Company would not sell a 90-second piece of commercial time. S&S management had to decide whether to accommodate this request.

Other BA country managers were concerned that the concept campaign would reduce the funds available for local tactical advertising presenting fare and schedule information specific to their particular markets. One BA manager, after seeing the proposed campaign, commented, "Where are the smiling girls, the free cocktails, and the planes taking off into the sunset?" Another asked, "Will this campaign sell seats?" The BA proposal to spend half of the worldwide 1983–84 advertising budget of £26 million on the concept campaign meant that the amount available for local tactical advertising would fall from £19 million to £12 million. Preliminary BA concept and tactical advertising budgets for 14 representative countries are presented in *Exhibit 7*. Partly in response to the country managers' concerns, the total budget was raised to £31 million in April when BA's 1982–83 operating results were known. Forty percent of the new budget was allocated to the worldwide concept campaign, 60% to tactical local market advertising.

EXHIBIT 7. BA concept and tactical advertising budgets: initial 1983–84 plan (£000)

	Concept campaign			Tactical campaigns	Row total
	Apr.–Sep.	*Oct.–Mar.*	*Total*		
U.K.	4,700	1,200	5,900	3,200	9,100
U.S.A.	2,600	750	3,350	2,450	5,800
Germany	450	450	900	607	1,507
Australia	500	100	600	350	950
France	150	200	350	269	619
Japan/Korea	200	70	270	400	670
Gulf States	0	35	35	190	225
Canada	900	200	1,100	400	1,500
South Africa	300	75	375	250	625
Italy	150	100	250	225	475
New Zealand	100	0	100	100	200
Egypt	50	0	50	30	80
Zimbabwe	32	0	32	25	57
Trinidad	18	0	18	27	45
Others	N/A	N/A	860	3,220*	4,080
Totals	10,150	3,180	14,190	11,740	25,930

*Includes contingency fund.

Some country managers complained that their control over advertising would be reduced and that a corporate advertising expenditure in which they had no say would be charged against their profits. BA headquarters executives responded that while the country managers were required in 1983–84 to spend 40% of their budgets against the concept campaign, they were free to determine the media allocation of concept campaign expenditures in their markets and the weight of exposures given to each of the four executions. They were also free to spend more than 40% of their budgets on the concept campaign if they wished.

Despite such concessions, the Japanese country manager remained adamantly opposed to adopting the concept campaign. On the London-Tokyo route, Japan Air Lines held a 60% market share compared to BA's 40%. Of the traffic on the route, 80% originated in Japan, and 80% of those on board BA flights were tourists on package tours. The Japanese country manager rejected the concept campaign as inappropriate. He presented market research evidence showing that his main challenge was selling Britain as a destination rather than developing consumer preference for BA.

THE APRIL 10 LAUNCH

Some S&S executives had hoped that BA would commit almost all of its 1983–84 advertising budget to the concept campaign. However, local marketing requirements highlighted by the country managers necessitated the continuation of tactical advertising, albeit at a reduced rate. The logo and slogan from the concept campaign were, however, to be incorporated in BA tactical advertising and the requirement that tactical creative copy be developed by S&S in London ensured that this would be the case.

Despite all the reservations they had encountered, BA and S&S executives in London felt that they had sold the campaign effectively to most of the BA country managers. Thus, an invitation was mailed by Lord King to all BA employees in the U.K. to view the introductory television commercial on April 10. Videocassette copies of this six-minute commercial were mailed to BA offices around the world. BA country managers invited representatives of the travel industry to attend preview parties timed to coincide with the launch of the new concept campaign in their respective countries.

The campaign was launched in the U.K. on April 10 as planned and, within two weeks, was being aired in 20 countries. For two reasons, few country managers adopted a "wait and see" attitude. First, the marketing of package tours for the summer season had already started (in the northern hemisphere). Second, many country managers had exhausted their 1982–83 advertising budgets by the end of January, with the result that consumers had not been exposed to any BA advertising for several months.

THE CONCEPT CAMPAIGN IN THE U.S.A.

The U.S.A. was one of the countries in which the concept campaign was launched on April 10. The BA country manager welcomed the campaign since consumer research indicated that BA's size was not recognized by most consumers in a country where, for many, bigger meant better. When asked to name the airline that carried the most passengers to the U.K., more respondents cited Pan Am and TWA than BA. The results of the survey conducted in New York and Los Angeles in March 1983, also showed

- Unaided awareness of BA as a leading international carrier was 41% in New York (Pan Am – 85%; TWA – 74%) and 33% in Los Angeles (Pan Am – 76%; TWA – 74%).
- Unaided recall of BA advertising was 21% in New York and 17% in Los Angeles.
- BA was mentioned as one of the three largest airlines in the world by 15% of New York respondents and 13% in Los Angeles.
- BA was mentioned as one of the three best international carriers by 11% of New York respondents and 9% in Los Angeles.

The BA country manager viewed the concept campaign as a means of addressing some of these deficiencies. Since the claim "the world's favorite airline" was well-documented, the U.S. country manager did not anticipate a legal challenge from Eastern Airlines, which used the slogan "America's favorite way to fly."

The media plan for the concept campaign (*Exhibit 8*) called for a combination of spot television in BA's six key gateway cities, national network television, and commercials on Cable News Network. The Manhattan Landing commercial was scheduled to be shown four times on national network television. Management argued that this would provide BA with exposure in important markets near gateway cities and would also excite the BA sales force and the travel industry. Four exposures were deemed sufficient given the commercial's creative originality. They would reach 45% of the U.S. adult population an average of 1.2 times.

The budget for the concept campaign from April to June was $4 million. Nevertheless, during this period, the BA country manager expected to be outspent by Pan Am and TWA in BA gateway cities. In 1982–83, Pan Am and TWA advertising expenditures for domestic and international routes combined approximated $65 million and $50 million respectively.

In addition to the concept campaign, the BA country manager had also developed a business campaign and a leisure campaign for 1983–84.

BUSINESS CAMPAIGN.   Recent consumer research indicated that Pan Am and TWA were perceived as superior to BA on attributes important to business flyers. BA advertising directed at business people had not significantly improved these perceptions (BA and TWA advertisements

EXHIBIT 8. Media budget and schedule of the British Airways concept/ brand campaign in the U.S. ($000)

	April–June 1983		September–October 1983	
	# spots	*Expenditures*	*# spots*	*Expenditures*
Spot television (in 6 gateway markets)[a]	686	$2,900	175	$572
Network television[b]	4	1,040	—	—
Cable television	40	104	25	58
	730	$4,044	200	$630
Reach/frequency				
Gateway cities		86%/8.7 times	63%/3.3 times	
Remainder of U.S.		45%/1.2 times	—	
Audience composition		*% of those reached*	*Index[c]*	
Adult men		48	102	
Adult women		52	99	
Age 25–54		73	137	
Household income $30,000 +		47	169	

[a]New York, Washington, Boston, Miami, Chicago, and Los Angeles.

[b]Only the Manhattan Landing execution was shown on network television. It was targeted at the 78% of U.S. households not reached by the spot television advertising.

[c]Each index figure represents the percentage degree to which the audience reached included more or fewer people than the U.S. population at large.

targeting the business traveler are presented as *Exhibits 9* and *10*). However, the perceptions of BA among its business passengers were much more positive than those of non-BA passengers, indicating significant customer satisfaction. BA's U.S. marketing director concluded that BA had a substantial opportunity to increase its share of the transatlantic business travel market.

The following three objectives were established for the 1983–84 business advertising campaign:

1. Increase awareness of the name "Super Club" as a service comparable to (or better than) TWA's Ambassador Class and Pan Am's Clipper Class.

2. Increase the business traveler's awareness and knowledge of the features of all three BA business travel services: Concorde, First Class, and Super Club.

EXHIBIT 9. BA business campaign magazine advertisement

CUT HERE for Pan Am's 18½"
Clipper Class seat.

CUT HERE for TWA's 20⅞"
Ambassador Class seat.

WORLD'S WIDEST AIRLINE SEAT CUTS OTHER AIRLINES DOWN TO SIZE.

British Airways Super Club®
When you're travelling on business, we
offer you the widest seats in the air. We
give you 24 inches between armrests —
more room than TWA or Pan
Am!* You'll always be next to
an aisle or a window, and you
have almost a foot of work
space between you and the next
passenger.

**American Airlines
AAdvantage® Program**
Show us your number at check-in
and your flight miles on British
Airways between the U.S. and
London will count towards your
AAdvantage travel award plan.

First Class Comfort
Lean back in luxury in our
sumptuous First Class,
with its sleeperseats and
impeccable British service.

The Ultimate: Concorde
If you want to reach London in half the usual
time, there's only one way — our Supersonic
Concorde.

It's no wonder that British Airways fly
more people to more countries than anyone
else. After all, we're the World's Favourite
Airline. Call your travel agent or corporate
travel department.

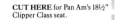

British airways
The World's Favourite Airline™

*Measurements are inside armrest to inside armrest. British
Airways has a few Super Club seats only 22" wide due to
structural requirements. However, all Super Club seats are
wider than our competitors'.

EXHIBIT 10. TWA business segment magazine advertisement

TWA.
Our First is foremost.

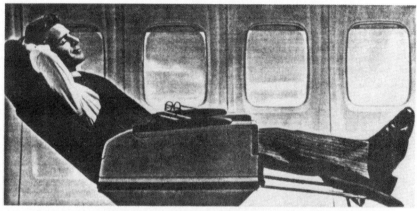

Only TWA has First Class Sleeper-Seats℠ on every widebody.
For First Class comfort.

First and foremost, there are our First Class Sleeper-Seats.

They are available on every 747, every L-1011, and every 767, everywhere we fly in the U.S., Europe and the Middle East. So you can rest easy every time you fly TWA.

Just settle into a Sleeper-Seat, and you'll be impressed with its incredible comfort and legroom. Then settle back—the seat stretches out with you.

Royal Ambassador℠ Service.
First Class service in a class by itself.

TWA's Royal Ambassador Service is available on every transatlantic and transcontinental route we fly, as well as selected shorter domestic flights.

We offer a gourmet menu with a choice of entrees like Chateaubriand. Vintage wines from California and France. A selection of fine liqueurs and cognac. All cordially offered to you in a warm, personal manner.

We even cater to your needs before you take off. In major airports, you'll find a special First Class desk to speed you through check-in. And a special lounge for transatlantic passengers to relax in before flight time.

So call your travel agent, corporate travel department, or TWA.

Because for First Class service that's second to none, there's only one choice. TWA.

You're going to like us /TWA/

3. Maximize the "halo" benefits of BA's Concorde in marketing efforts directed at First Class and Super Club consumers.

The media schedule for the business campaign (*Exhibit 11*) emphasized national magazines and both national and local newspapers. Magazines were selected which had higher-than-average percentages of readers in BA's gateway cities. Newspapers with strong business sections were given preference.

LEISURE CAMPAIGN. BA advertising targeting the leisure traveler had traditionally focused on BA's hotel, car rental, and package tour bargains. Despite high consumer recall of these "bolt-on" features, consumer perception research indicated that BA lagged its competitors on attributes such as "good value for money" and "good deal for leisure travelers." Accordingly, BA's advertising agency suggested that these bolt-on features be subordinated to the objective of creating a general impression of value for money through advertising an airfare bargain along with BA's expertise in things British.

The objectives for the 1983 summer campaign were

1. To capitalize on BA's reputation as a marketer of good vacation buys, reinforcing consumers' willingness to arrange their European vacations with BA.
2. To promote awareness of and demand for BA's summer transatlantic leisure-oriented fare of $549 roundtrip.

A BA summer campaign newspaper advertisement and a Pan Am advertisement targeting the leisure traveler are reproduced as *Exhibits 12* and *13*. BA executives were planning on developing print advertisements targeting the leisure market which would mirror the commercials in the concept campaign if it proved successful.

The media schedule for the leisure campaign (*Exhibit 14*) emphasized spot television and the travel sections of local newspapers. Their late advertising deadlines meant that fare changes could be quickly communicated to consumers.

CONCLUSION

As BA and S&S executives implemented the worldwide concept campaign and the biggest advertising effort in BA history, they contemplated several issues. First, if awareness, recall, and sales data indicated that

EXHIBIT 11. Media budget and schedule of the British Airways business campaign in the U.S. ($000)

	December 1982–March 1983[a]		April–June 1983		September–October 1983	
	# insertions	Expenditures	# insertions	Expenditures	# insertions	Expenditures
22 magazines	8	$121	30	$ 745	22	$674
3 newspapers (WSJ, NYT, LAT)	9	563	13	371	17	276
	17	$684	43	$1116	39	$950

Reach/frequency: men 25–54

	December 1982–March 1983	April–June 1983
Gateway cities	73%/7.4 times[b]	65%/5.4 times
Remainder of U.S.	67%/6.3 times	55%/3.5 times

Audience composition

	% reach to those planning foreign travel for business	Index
Adult men[c]	72	147
Age 25–54	69	126
Attended/graduated college	64	197
Household income $35,000 +	55	284

[a]No insertions prior to February 1983.
[b]Figures for December 1982 through June 1983.
[c]In 1982–83, about 10% of transatlantic business travelers were women.

EXHIBIT 12. BA leisure segment print advertisement

Great Britain Great Price

$549

round trip
(and only $18 a day for a hotel*)

With British Airways' fantastic fares and today's incredible dollar exchange rate, there's never been a better time to visit Britain. Plus, British Airways offers "London Hotel Bargains" including the modern, convenient Kennedy Hotel for only $18 per night (includes private bath and continental breakfast); the Regent Palace for $13 a day (without private bath but a stone's throw from Piccadilly); and "Britain Car Rental" offering a Ford Fiesta with unlimited mileage for only $17 a day. Call British Airways or your travel agent for more information on these and other great deals now!

"Good show"

Britain Salutes
New York 1983

British airways

Airfare valid for travel through September 14. Tickets must be purchased 21 days in advance. Minimum stay 7 days. Maximum stay 6 months. There is a weekend surcharge. Car and hotel rates valid through October 31. Petrol and tax not included with car.
*Hotel rates per person, double occupancy and include VAT and tax.

British Airways, P.O. Box 10010,
Dept. HT, Long Island City, NY 11101
Dear Mr. Morley:
Please send me the following brochures:
☐ DollarSaver™ Holidays in London
☐ Fly-Drive Holidays in Britain

Name _____
Address _____
City _____
State _____ Zip ____

EXHIBIT 13. Pan Am leisure segment print advertisement

the campaign was not having the desired impact in a particular market, would BA headquarters permit the country manager to curtail the concept campaign? Second, if the campaign was successful, how long could it be sustained before becoming "tired?"

A third issue was how competitive airlines would respond to the BA concept campaign. Believing that the major carriers wished to avoid a new worldwide competitive price war, BA executives believed that they would adopt a "wait and see" attitude. However, market share losses would make retaliation inevitable, particularly in markets like the Far East where Singapore Airlines and Cathay Pacific held high market shares and were extremely price-competitive. In such a situation, should BA steadfastly continue to spend 40% of its advertising budget on the concept campaign or should some of these funds be diverted to tactical advertising in particular local markets? The probability of such diversion of funds depended partly on the emerging profit picture dur-

EXHIBIT 14. Media budget and schedule of the British Airways leisure campaign in the U.S. ($000)

	December 1982–March 1983		April–June 1983		September–October 1983	
	# spots, insertions	*Expenditures*	*# spots, insertions*	*Expenditures*	*# spots, insertions*	*Expenditures*
Spot television (10 markets)	—	—	450	$795	—	—
Local newspapers (11 markets)	3–4/market	$641	3–7/market	$620	4–6/market	$550

Reach/frequency: adults 25–54

	December 1982–March 1983	April–June 1983	September–October 1983
Average market	40%/2.0 times	75%/5.0 times	47%/2.9 times

Audience composition

	% reach to those planning a foreign vacation	*Index*
Adult men	45	96
Adult women	55	105
Age 25–54	60	114
Household income $30,000 +	49	175

319

ing the fiscal year and partly on the level of unspent tactical advertising funds. It was, therefore, more likely to become an issue toward the end of the fiscal year.

A further related issue was the appropriate budget split between the concept campaign and tactical advertising in 1984–85. Some BA executives argued that if the concept campaign were successful, it would be possible to reduce expenditures on the campaign to a maintenance level and proportionately restore tactical advertising. They maintained that such a move would shift control of the advertising budget from S&S back to BA. But agency executives argued strongly that the concept campaign should be centrally administered from BA headquarters and that expenditures on the campaign in each country should not, unlike tactical advertising, be regarded as a route operating cost. They also argued that the concept campaign was essential to BA's long-term effectiveness and should not be sacrificed to short-term operational requirements.

PART 3

Organizing and Controlling Multinational Operations

Introduction

Readings

3.1. Customizing Global Marketing by John A. Quelch and Edward J. Hoff

3.2. MNCs: Get Off the Reorganization Merry-Go-Round by Christopher A. Bartlett

Cases

3.3. Nestlé S.A.: International Marketing by John A. Quelch and Edward J. Hoff

3.4. Chandler Home Products by Michael Y. Yoshino and Yaakov Keren

3.5. Procter & Gamble Europe: Vizir Launch by Christopher A. Bartlett

3.6. Yoshida Kogyo K.K. by Ulrich Wiechmann

3.7. Citibank: Marketing to Multinational Customers by Robert D. Buzzell

$\mathbf{I}$n the second part of this text we focused on the issue of standardization versus adaptation and the degree to which different elements of the marketing program should be tailored for particular products in particular countries. Two major concerns of this third section are the process issue of centralization versus decentralization and whether the multinational should be organized principally by product or by geography.

CENTRALIZATION VERSUS DECENTRALIZATION

During the 1950s and 1960s, most multinationals followed a path of decentralization, devolving decision making and profit and loss responsibility to local management. Local nationals were hired as managers, local equity partners sought out, and host governments courted. Global competition intensified in many industries during the 1970s and 1980s, as the Japanese exploited scale economies through worldwide product standardization and the pressure for headquarters centralization increased. Centralization, it was thought, could limit needless country-by-country duplication of effort, capitalize on scale economies in all functional areas, and ensure the rapid, worldwide exploitation of good ideas.

Centralization is not an either-or proposition but rather a matter of degree. A judgment on the appropriate degree of centralization of marketing decision making cannot be divorced from the (de)centralization decision in other functional areas such as finance. manufacturing, and research and development. In many companies, marketing is the last function to be centralized, and autonomy in this area is closely guarded by local managers, particularly in consumer goods companies. In addition to being influenced by a multinational's history of local autonomy, the level of centralized decision making may appropriately vary by product, by element of the marketing mix, and according to the competence and importance of each country subsidiary. Centralization is also more appropriate the greater the international scope of a company's customers and competitors.

As the chart suggests, a centralized decision-making process need not always lead to a standardized marketing program. In many traditionally decentralized multinationals that are inching toward greater standardization (referred to by Bartlett as transnationals[1]), headquarters may well decide that some elements of a marketing program should be locally adapted.

	The program	
	Adaptation	Standardization
Decentralization		
Centralization		

The process (label at left, spanning the two process rows)

Too precipitous a move toward greater centralization of decision making can be risky. Local management may be demotivated, the best managers may quit, and the flow of good ideas from the field may slow, leaving country subsidiaries more dependent than ever on headquarters support. Local management's self-confidence and ability to respond quickly and aggressively to local competition may be diminished.

PRODUCT VERSUS GEOGRAPHY

Initially, most companies handle their international operations through an international division. However, decisions are often made at this stage regarding, for example, local operating unit autonomy from which it is later difficult for the multinational to retreat. The difficulties experienced by Corning Glass in trying to centralize traditionally autonomous international operations illustrate this problem.

When the international division's sales exceed those of the largest domestic division, the international division may be disaggregated into several regional divisions. Alternatively, according to the Stopford and Wells stage model of an international corporation's evolution,[2] worldwide product divisions may be established. This second option is more likely in the case of multinationals selling more technical, less culture-bound products to major customers and against major competitors who are also multinational in their scope of operations.

---

[1]Christopher A. Bartlett, "Building and Managing the Transnational: The New Organizational Challenge," in *Competition in Global Industries*, Michael E. Porter (ed.). Boston, MA: Harvard Business School Press, 1986.

[2]John M. Stopford and Louis T. Wells, Jr., *Managing the Multinational Enterprise*. New York: Basic Books, 1972.

Some companies such as Phillips have attempted to establish a matrix organization structure whereby different managers hold profit and loss responsibility on both a geographic (across product) basis and a product (across geography) basis. Generally, matrix organizations are difficult to manage, so most companies let strategy dictate which of the two dimensions should be dominant and appoint staff personnel to ensure that there is a strong voice articulating the other perspective.

FLEXIBILITY IS KEY

As Chandler has pointed out, a corporation's strategy should adjust to the competitive environment and a corporation's structure should be consistent with its strategy.[3] If care is not taken, an entrenched organization structure can begin to constrain strategy. For example, a multinational bank like Sumitomo that is not constrained by a sprawling global branch structure such as Citibank's can respond much more adroitly to new market opportunities. Moreover, while a change in organization structure can shake up a company or symbolize a change in strategic direction, it cannot by itself change the way executives think and behave.

There is no special virtue in a neat, symmetrical organization chart. The obsession with formal organization common in North America and Europe contrasts with the less structured Japanese multinational in which an emphasis on personal relationships, built up over many years of service to the same company, permits greater flexibility and nimbleness. For the following reasons, the neat organization chart is perhaps more constraining to the multinational of the 1980s than ever before.

- The quickening pace of technological and market change is such that changes to the formal organization simply cannot be implemented and absorbed quickly enough.
- Multinationals increasingly have to accommodate intercompany alliances and coalitions such as those between Xerox and Fujitsu or General Motors and Toyota. Many of these alliances are now strategic in nature rather than merely vehicles for market access, so the organizations of the companies involved must be flexible enough to accommodate them.

---

[3]Alfred D. Chandler, *Strategy and Structure: Chapters in the History of the Industrial Enterprise.* Cambridge, MA: MIT Press, 1962.

- Products differ in stage of market development from one country to another, and country subsidiaries differ in sophistication and resources. The country manager in a small, developing market may have less latitude and decision-making power than the country manager in a more developed market.
- Executives should not be force-fitted into slots on the worldwide organization chart; assignments should be structured to develop executives' capabilities and broaden their experience.

The need for flexibility is especially acute when a multinational's customer base includes, as is often the case, some customers that are national, others that are global. International banks and advertising agencies, for example, must deal with such heterogeneous customer mixes (which, incidentally, offer the advantage of motivating local managements since they remain entirely responsible for managing and developing relationships with local businesses). Typically, such service organizations are willing to create account management teams that mesh with the organization structures and decision-making processes of their major international clients. For example, to serve a multinational with strong regional managers, an advertising agency might appoint regional account coordinators. Agency and client must jointly determine whether the focus of decision making should rest at the country, region, or world headquarters level for decisions about each brand's positioning, copy strategy, media mix and scheduling, advertising budget and evaluation.

There are two caveats to our general advocacy of organizational flexibility that deserve mention. First, flexibility, when unconstrained by a shared set of corporate values, can lead to inconsistency and confusion. Worldwide account coordination for the global customer is essential if the right hand is to know what the left is doing; too much flexibility can backfire when local accommodations are subsequently treated as generalizable precedents. Second, the multinational should follow the customer's organization lead and, for example, shy away from the client who seeks to use the agency as a stalking horse for global policy direction that it has not yet persuaded its field managers to accept. The chairman of the J. Walter Thompson Company advertising agency has been quoted as saying: "We get paid to mirror our clients' organizational structures, not to lead."[4]

---

[4]Stewart Alter, "JWT Disbands Global Account Superstructure," *Advertising Age* (December 15, 1986), p. 3.

BEYOND ORGANIZATION

Bonoma (1985) has identified four skills critical to the implementation of marketing programs: organizing, interacting, allocating, and monitoring.[5]

In this section, we discuss applications of the latter three to multinational marketing management.

INTERACTING. Informal relationships among the executives of a multinational are often so critical to the quick implementation of important tastes that the formal organization and established procedures may not be able to deal with either properly or promptly. There are three principal means of developing such relationships:

1. *Meetings.* In many multinationals, marketing directors from country subsidiaries meet regularly at regional or world headquarters to exchange among themselves and with the corporate staff ideas and information about aspects of marketing programming and the progress of new and existing products.

2. *Teams.* Increasingly, multinationals are organizing teams of executives from different countries to address specific tasks, such as developing a common marketing program for a new product to be introduced at the same time in several countries. The benefits of such a team approach are that involvement enhances both commitment and the probability of success, and that a global marketing program can be achieved without headquarters imposing it on the field.

3. *Career path planning.* Increasingly, multinationals move executives from one country to another and between the field and headquarters to broaden their perspectives and build personal relationships. International career pathing can create a cadre of global executives that share common objectives and values and so cultivate a corporate culture of cooperation rather than competition among country subsidiaries. In addition, the demonstrated ability of nationals of any country to reach the upper levels of management aids the recruitment and motivation of top-quality local nationals down the line; this is true at Coca-Cola where three of the four senior executives in 1986 were non-American by birth. Finally, the greater the continuity of personnel within a company, the stronger and more valuable the network of informal relationships becomes; the nimbleness of Japanese multinationals

---

[5]Thomas V. Bonoma, *The Marketing Edge.* New York: The Free Press, 1985.

is largely a result of personnel continuity and their emphasis on informal relationships over the formal organization.

Interacting skills outside the organization are equally important as multinationals establish more and more cooperative alliances with other companies, as they serve increasingly diverse customer bases, and as global competition and dumping allegations fuel protectionist sentiment and add to the challenge of host governmental relations.

ALLOCATING. In the traditional decentralized multinational, each country manager proposes an annual marketing plan and budget to headquarters. Once agreed upon, the country manager is held accountable for executing the plan and assumes profit and loss responsibility. In the complex multinational of the 1980s, allocations of opportunities, tasks, and resources by headquarters among countries are becoming more complicated. For example:

- Headquarters might assign management in a particular country responsibility for leading the development of the marketing program for a new product or for researching a particular new product idea.
- Headquarters might assign each country marketing director in a region lead responsibility for the strategic direction of an individual product line across the entire region as well as responsibility for the sales of all products in his or her particular country.
- Headquarters might allocate special market development funds to country managers who agree to follow a standard marketing program for designated global brands.

MONITORING. Technological advances and cost reductions in communications and information systems enable the headquarters of multinationals to receive more information from around the world more rapidly than ever before. Particularly when information systems can be standardized across the multinational's network of operational units, these trends facilitate tighter central control and decision making.[6] For example, based on retail store sales information collected in its North American retail outlets, Fisher-Camuto Corp. can, on the following day, adjust its production of different styles and sizes of women's shoes in its Brazilian factories.

Operating information may be gathered by product or by market.

---

[6]Martin D.J. Buss, "Managing International Information Systems," *Harvard Business Review* (September-October 1982), pp. 153–162.

Regardless of whether product or geography is the dominant dimension in their organization structures, most multinationals find it useful to collect and analyze operating information data on both. Internal reporting systems and externally commissioned market research studies are increasingly standardized worldwide to permit easier cross-border comparisons, improved market intelligence at headquarters, and more equitable evaluation and compensation standards for line management.

CONCLUSION

Increasingly, the top managements of multinational corporations are asking the question, "Why not go global?" rather than "Why go global?" Implementing this shift in perspective is especially challenging for the traditionally decentralized multinational facing aggressive, new global competitors that are not constrained by entrenched organizational bureaucracies. The ability to nurture the informal organization, to develop organizational flexibility, and to cultivate a shared set of values worldwide is far more essential to the effective implementation of global marketing programs than the design of the perfect organizational chart.

3.1 *READING*

Customizing Global Marketing

John A. Quelch and
Edward J. Hoff

In the best of all possible worlds, marketers would only have to come up with a great product and a convincing marketing program and they would have a worldwide winner. But despite the obvious economies and efficiencies they could gain with a standard product and program, many managers fear that global marketing, as popularly defined, is too extreme to be practical. Because customers and competitive conditions differ across countries or because powerful local managers will not stand for centralized decision making, they argue, global marketing just won't work.

Of course, global marketing has its pitfalls, but it can also yield impressive advantages. Standardizing products can lower operating costs. Even more important, effective coordination can exploit a company's best product and marketing ideas.

Too often, executives view global marketing as an either/or proposition — either full standardization or local control. But when a global approach can fall anywhere on a spectrum from tight worldwide coordination on programming details to loose agreement on a product idea, why the extreme view? In applying the global marketing concept and making it work, flexibility is essential. Managers need to tailor the approach they use to each element of the business system and marketing program. For example, a manufacturer might market the same product under different brand names in different countries or market the same brands using different product formulas.

The big issue today is not whether to go global but how to tailor the global marketing concept to fit each business and how to make it work. In this article, we'll first provide a framework to help managers think about how they should structure the different areas of the marketing function as the business shifts to a global approach. We will then show how companies we have studied are tackling the implementation challenges of global marketing.

HOW FAR TO GO

How far a company can move toward global marketing depends a lot on its evolution and traditions. Consider two examples:

Although the Coca-Cola Company had conducted some international business before 1940, it gained true global recognition during World War II, as Coke bottling plants followed the march of U.S. troops around the world. Management in Atlanta made all strategic decisions then — and still does now, as Coca-Cola applies global marketing principles, for example, to the worldwide introduction of Diet Coke. The brand name, concentrate formula, positioning, and advertising theme are virtually standard worldwide, but the artificial sweetener and packaging differ across countries. Local managers are responsible for sales and distribution programs, which they run in conjunction with local bottlers.

The Nestlé approach also has its roots in history. To avoid distribution disruptions caused by wars in Europe, to ease rapid worldwide expansion, and to respond to local consumer needs, Nestlé granted its local managers considerable autonomy from the outset. While the local managers still retain much of that decision-making power today, Nestlé headquarters at Vevey has grown in importance. Nestlé has transferred to its central marketing staff many former local managers who had succeeded in their local Nestlé businesses and who now influence country executives to accept standard new product and marketing ideas. The trend seems to be toward tighter marketing coordination.

To conclude that Coca-Cola is a global marketer and Nestlé is not would be simplistic. In *Exhibit 1*, we assess program adaptation or standardization levels for each company's business functions, products, marketing mix elements, and countries. Each company has tailored its individual approach. Furthermore, as *Exhibit 1* can't show, the situations aren't static. Readers can themselves evaluate their own *current* and *desired* levels of program adaptation or standardization on these four dimensions. The gap between the two levels is the implementation challenge. The size of the gap — and the urgency with which it must be closed — will depend on a company's strategy and financial performance, competitive pressures, technological change, and converging consumer values.

FOUR DIMENSIONS OF GLOBAL MARKETING

Now let's look at the issues that arise when executives consider the four dimensions shown in *Exhibit 1* in light of the degree of standardization or adaptation that is appropriate.

BUSINESS FUNCTIONS.   A company's approach to global marketing depends, first, on its overall business strategy. In many multinationals, some functional areas have greater program standardization than others. Headquarters often controls manufacturing, finance, and R&D, while the local managers make the marketing decisions. Marketing is usually one of the last functions to be centrally directed. Partly because product quality and accounting data are easier to measure than marketing effectiveness, standardization can be greater in production and finance.

PRODUCTS.   Products that enjoy high scale economies or efficiencies and are not highly culture-bound are easier to market globally than others.

1. *Economies or efficiencies.* Manufacturing and R&D scale economies can result in a price spread between the global and the local product that is too great for even the most culture-bound consumer to resist. In addition, management often has neither the time nor the R&D resources to adapt products to each country. The markets for high-tech products like

EXHIBIT 1. Global marketing planning matrix: how far to go

		Adaptation		Standardization	
		Full	Partial	Partial	Full
Business functions	Research and development			Nestle	Coca-Cola
	Finance and accounting			Nestle	Coca-Cola
	Manufacturing		Nestle	Coca-Cola	
	Procurement	Nestle		Coca-Cola	
	Marketing			Nestle	Coca-Cola
Products	Low cultural grounding / High economies or efficiencies				Coca-Cola
	Low cultural grounding / Low economies or efficiencies				
	High cultural grounding / High economies or efficiencies		Nestle		
	High cultural grounding / Low economies or efficiencies				
Marketing mix elements	Product design			Nestle	Coca-Cola
	Brand name			Nestle	Coca-Cola
	Product positioning		Nestle		Coca-Cola
	Packaging			Coca-Cola	
	Advertising theme		Nestle		Coca-Cola
	Pricing		Nestle	Coca-Cola	
	Advertising copy	Nestle			Coca-Cola
	Distribution	Nestle	Coca-Cola		
	Sales promotion	Nestle	Coca-Cola		
	Customer service	Nestle	Coca-Cola		
Countries Region 1	Country A			Nestle	Coca-Cola
	Country B			Nestle	Coca-Cola
Region 2	Country C		Nestle		Coca-Cola
	Country D		Nestle		Coca-Cola
	Country E	Nestle			Coca-Cola

Nestle   Coca-Cola

computers are not only very competitive but also affected by rapid technological change.

Most packaged consumer goods are less susceptible than durable goods like televisions and cars to manufacturing or even R&D economies. Coca-Cola's global policy and Nestlé's interest in tighter marketing coordination are driven largely by a desire to capitalize on the marketing ideas their managers around the world generate rather than by potential scale economies. Nestlé, for example, manufactures its packaged soups in dozens of locally managed plants around the world, with some transference of engineering know-how through a headquarters staff. Products and marketing programs are also locally managed, but new ideas are aggressively transferred, with local managers encouraged — or even prodded — to adapt and use them in their own markets. For Nestlé, global marketing does not so much yield high manufacturing economies as high efficiency in using scarce new ideas.

2. *Cultural grounding.* Consumer products used in the home — like Nestlé's soups and frozen foods — are often more culture-bound than products used outside the home such as automobiles and credit cards, and industrial products are inherently less culture-bound than consumer products. (Products like personal computers, for example, are often marketed on the basis of performance benefits that share a common technical language worldwide.) Experience also suggests that products will be less culture-bound if they are used by young people whose cultural norms are not ingrained, people who travel in different countries, and ego-driven consumers who can be appealed to through myths and fantasies shared across cultures.

Exhibit 1 lists four combinations of the scale economy and cultural grounding variables in order of their susceptibility to global marketing. Managers shouldn't be bound by any matrix, however; they should find creative ways to prepare a product for global marketing. If a manufacturer develops a new version of a seemingly culture-bound product that is based on new capital-intensive technology and generates superior performance benefits, it may well be possible to introduce it on a standard basis worldwide. Procter & Gamble developed Pampers disposable diapers as a global brand in a product category that intuition would say was culture-bound.

MARKETING MIX ELEMENTS. Few consumer goods companies go so far as to market the same products using the same marketing program worldwide. And those that do, like Lego, the Danish manufacturer of construction toys, often distribute their products through sales companies rather than full-fledged marketing subsidiaries.

For most products, the appropriate degree of standardization varies from one element of the marketing mix to another. Strategic elements like product positioning are more easily standardized than execution-sensitive elements like sales promotion. In addition, when headquarters believes it has identified a superior marketing idea, whether it be a package design, a brand name, or an advertising copy concept, the pressure to standardize increases.

Marketing can usually contribute to scale economies most significantly by creating a standard product design that will sell worldwide, permitting savings through globalized production. In addition, scale economies in marketing programming can be achieved through standard commercial executions and copy concepts. McCann-Erickson claims to have saved $90 million in production costs over 20 years by producing worldwide Coca-Cola commercials. To ensure that they have enough attention-getting power to overcome their foreign origins, however, marketers often have to make worldwide commercials expensive productions.

To compensate local management for having to accept a standard product and to fit the core product to each local market, some companies allow local managers to adapt those marketing mix elements that aren't subject to significant scale economies. On the other hand, local managers are more likely to accept a standard concept for those elements of the marketing mix that are less important and, ironically, often not susceptible to scale economies. Overall, then, the driving factor in moving toward global marketing should be the efficient worldwide use of good marketing ideas, rather than any scale economies from standardization.

In judging how far to go in standardizing elements of the marketing mix, managers must also be mindful of the interactions among them. For example, when a product with the same brand name is sold in different countries, it can be difficult and sometimes impossible to sell them at different prices.

COUNTRIES. How far a decentralized multinational wishes to pursue global marketing will often vary from one country to another. Naturally, headquarters is likely to become more involved in marketing decisions in countries where performance is poor. But performance aside, small markets depend more on headquarters assistance than large markets do. Because a standard marketing program is superior in quality to what local executives could develop themselves even with the benefit of their local market knowledge, they may welcome it.

Large markets with strong local managements are less willing to accept global programs. This is unfortunate because these are the markets that often account for most of the company's investment. To secure their acceptance, headquarters should make standard marketing programs reflect their needs, rather than those of small markets. Small markets, being more tolerant of deviations from what would be locally appropriate, are less likely to resist a standard program.

As we've seen, Coca-Cola takes the same approach in all markets. Nestlé varies its approach in different countries, depending on the strength of its market presence and each country's need for assistance. In completing the *Exhibit 1* planning matrix, management may decide that it can sensibly group countries by region or by stage of market development.

TOO FAR TOO FAST

Once managers have decided how global they want their marketing program to be, they must make the transition. Debates over the size of the gap between present and desired positions and the speed with which it must be closed will often pit the field against headquarters. Such conflict is most likely to arise in companies where the reason for change is not apparent, or the country managers have had a lot of autonomy. Casualties can occur on both sides. Consider two examples.

Because Black & Decker dominated the European consumer power tool market, many of the company's European managers could not see that a more centrally directed global marketing approach was needed as a defense against imminent Japanese competition. To make his point, the CEO had to replace several key European executives.

In 1982, the Parker Pen Company, forced by competition and by a weakening financial position to lower costs, more than halved its number of plants and pen styles worldwide. Parker's overseas subsidiary managers accepted these changes but, when pressed to implement standardized advertising and packaging, they dug in their heels. In 1985, Parker ended its much heralded global marketing campaign. Several senior headquarters managers left the company.

If management is not careful, moving too far too fast toward global marketing can trigger painful consequences. First, subsidiary managers, who joined the company because of its apparent commitment to local autonomy and to adapting its products to the local environment, may become disenchanted. When poorly implemented, global marketing can make the local country manager's job less strategic. Second, disenchantment may reinforce "not-invented-here" attitudes that lead to game playing. For instance, some local managers may try bargaining with headquarters, trading speed of acceptance and implementation for additional budget assistance. In addition, local managers competing for resources and autonomy may devote too much attention to second-guessing which headquarters' "hot buttons" to push. Eventually good managers leave, and less competent ones who lack their initiative may replace them.

A vicious circle can develop. Feeling compelled to review local performance more closely, headquarters may tighten its controls and reduce resources but without adjusting its expectations of local managers. Meanwhile, local managers, trying to gain approval of applications for deviations from standard marketing programs, are frustrated. The expanding headquarters bureaucracy and associated overhead costs are reducing the speed with which the locals can respond to local opportunities and competitive actions. Slow response time is an especially serious problem with products for which barriers to entry for local competitors are low.

In this kind of system, weak, insecure local managers can become dependent on headquarters for operational assistance. They'll want headquarters to assume the financial risks for new product launches and welcome the prepackaged marketing programs. If performance falls short of headquarters' expectations, the local management can always blame the failure on the quality of operational assistance or on the standard marketing program. The local manager who has clear autonomy and profit-and-loss responsibility cannot hide behind such excuses.

If headquarters or regions assume much of the strategic burden, managers in overseas subsidiaries may think only about short-term sales. This focus will diminish their ability to monitor and communicate to headquarters any changes in local competitors' strategic directions. When their responsibilities shift from strategy to execution, their ideas will become less exciting. If the field has traditionally been as important a source of new product ideas as the central R&D laboratory, the company may find itself short on grassroots creative thinking and marketing research information, both of which R&D needs. The fruitful dialogue that characterizes a relationship between equal partners will no longer flourish.

HOW TO GET THERE

When thinking about closing the gap between present and desired positions, most executives of decentralized multinationals want to accommodate their current organizational structures. They rightly view their subsidiaries and the managers who run them as important competitive strengths. They generally do not wish to transform these organizations into mere sales and distribution agencies.

How then, in moving toward global marketing, can headquarters build rather than jeopardize relationships, and stimulate rather than demoralize local managers? The answer is by focusing on the means as much as on the ends, by examining the relationship between the home office and the field, and by asking which level of headquarters' intervention for each dimension — business function, product, marketing mix element, and country — is necessary to close the gap.

As *Exhibit 2* indicates, headquarters can intervene at five points, ranging from informing to directing. The five intervention levels are cumulative; for headquarters to direct, it must also inform, persuade, coordinate, and approve. *Exhibit 2* shows the approaches Atlanta and Vevey have taken. Reading from left to right, it is clear that things are done increasingly by fiat rather than patient persuasion, through discipline rather than education. At the far right, local subsidiaries can't choose whether to opt in or out of a marketing program, and headquarters views its country managers as subordinates rather than customers.

When the local managers tightly control marketing efforts, multinational managers face three critical issues. In the sections that follow, we'll take a look at how decentralized multinationals are working to correct the three problems as they move along the spectrum from informing to directing.

INCONSISTENT BRAND IDENTITIES. If headquarters gives country managers total control of their product lines, it cannot leverage the opportunities that multinational status gives it. The increasing degree to which consumers in one country are exposed to the company's products in another won't enhance the corporate image or brand development in the consumers' home country.

LIMITED PRODUCT FOCUS. In the decentralized multinational, the field line manager's ambition is to become a country manager, which means acquiring multiproduct and multifunction experience. Yet, as the pace of technological innovation increases and the likelihood of global competition grows, multinationals need worldwide product specialists and executives willing to transfer to other countries. Nowhere is the need for headquarters guidance on innovative organizational approaches more evident than in the area of product policy.

SLOW NEW PRODUCT LAUNCHES. As global competition grows, so does the need for rapid worldwide rollouts of new products. The decen-

EXHIBIT 2. Global marketing planning matrix: how to get there

		Informing	Persuading	Coordinating	Approving	Directing
Business functions	Research and development					
	Finance and accounting					
	Manufacturing					
	Procurement					
	Marketing					
Products	Low cultural grounding High economies or efficiencies					
	Low cultural grounding Low economies or efficiencies					
	High cultural grounding High economies or efficiencies					
	High cultural grounding Low economies or efficiencies					
Marketing mix elements	Product design					
	Brand name					
	Product positioning					
	Packaging					
	Advertising theme					
	Pricing					
	Advertising copy					
	Distribution					
	Sales promotion					
	Customer service					
Countries Region 1	Country A					
	Country B					
Region 2	Country C					
	Country D					
	Country E					

Legend: Nestle   Coca-Cola

tralized multinational that permits country managers to proceed at their own pace on new product introductions may be at a competitive disadvantage in this new environment.

WORD OF MOUTH

The least threatening, loosest, and therefore easiest, approach to global marketing is for headquarters to encourage the transfer of information between it and its country managers. Since good ideas are often a company's scarcest resource, headquarters' efforts to encourage and reward their generation, dissemination, and application in the field will build both relationships and profits. Here are two examples.

Nestlé publishes quarterly marketing newsletters that report recent product introductions and programming innovations. In this way, each subsidiary can learn quickly about and assess the ideas of others. (The best newsletters are written as if country organizations were talking to each other rather than as if headquarters were talking down to the field.)

Johnson Wax holds periodic meetings of all marketing directors at corporate headquarters twice a year to build global *esprit de corps* and to encourage the sharing of new ideas.

By making the transfer of information easy, a multinational leverages the ideas of its staff and spreads organizational values. Headquarters has to be careful, however, that the information it's passing on is useful. It may focus on updating local managers about new products, when what they mainly want is information on the most tactical and country-specific elements of the marketing mix. For example, the concentration of the grocery trade is much higher in the United Kingdom and Canada than it is in the United States. In this case, managers in the United States can learn from British and Canadian country managers about how to deal with the pressures for extra merchandising support that result when a few powerful retailers control a large percentage of sales. Likewise, marketers in countries with restrictions on mass media advertising have developed sophisticated point-of-purchase merchandising skills that could be useful to managers in other countries.

By itself, however, information sharing is often insufficient to help local executives meet the competitive challenges of global marketing.

FRIENDLY PERSUASION

Persuasion is a first step managers can take to deal with the three problems we've outlined above. Any systematic headquarters effort to influence local managers to apply standardized approaches, or to introduce new global products while letting local managers retain their decision-making authority, is a persuasion approach.

Unilever and CPC International, for example, employ world-class advertising and marketing research staff at headquarters. Not critics but coaches, these specialists review the subsidiaries' work and try to upgrade the technical skills of local marketing departments. They frequently visit the field to disseminate new concepts, frameworks, and techniques, and to respond to problems that local management raises. (It helps to build trust if headquarters can send out the same staff specialists for several years.)

Often, when the headquarters of a decentralized multinational identifies or develops a new product, it has to persuade the country manager in a so-called prime-mover market to invest in the launch. A successful launch in the prime-mover market will, in turn, persuade other country managers to introduce the product. The prime-mover market is usually selected according to criteria that include the commitment of local management, the probabilities of success, the credibility with which a success would be regarded by managers in other countries, and its perceived transferability.

Persuasion, however, has its limitations. Two problems recur with the prime-mover approach. First, by adopting a wait-and-see attitude, country managers can easily turn down requests to be prime-mover markets on the grounds of insufficient resources. Since the country managers in the prime-mover markets have to risk their resources to launch the new products, they're likely to tailor the product and marketing programs to their own markets rather than to global markets. Second, if there are more new products waiting to be launched than there are prime-mover markets to launch them, headquarters product specialists are likely to give in to a country manager's demands for local tailoring. But because of the need for readaptation in each case, the tailoring may delay rollouts in other markets and allow competitors to preempt the product. In the end, management may sacrifice long-term worldwide profits to maximize short-term profits in a few countries.

MARKETING TO THE SAME DRUMMER

To overcome the limits of persuasion, many multinationals are coordinating their marketing programs, whereby headquarters has a structured role in both decision making and performance evaluation that is far more influential than person-to-person persuasion. Often using a matrix or team approach, headquarters shares with country managers the responsibility and authority for programming and personnel decisions.

Nestlé locates product directors as well as support groups at headquarters. Together they develop long-term strategies for each product category on a worldwide basis, coordinate worldwide market research, spot new product opportunities, spark the field launch of new products, advise the field on how headquarters will evaluate new product proposals, and spread the word on new products' performance so that other countries will be motivated to launch them. Even though the product directors are staff executives with no line authority, because they have all been successful line managers in the field, they have great credibility and influence.

Country managers who cooperate with a product director can quickly become heroes if they successfully implement a new idea. On the other hand, while a country manager can reject a product director's advice, headquarters will closely monitor his or her performance with an alternative program. In addition, within the product category in which they specialize, the directors have influence on line management appointments in the field. Local managers thus have to be concerned about their relationships with headquarters.

Some companies assign promising local managers to other countries and require would-be local managers to take a tour of duty at headquarters. But such personnel transfer programs may run into barriers. First, many capable local nationals may not be interested in working outside their countries of origin. Second, powerful local managers are often unwilling to give up their best people to other country assignments. Third, immigration regulations and foreign service relocation costs are burdensome. Fourth, if transferees from the field have to take a demotion to work at headquarters, the costs in ill will often exceed any gains in cross-fertilization of ideas. If management can resolve these problems, however, it will find that creating an international career path is one of the most effective ways to develop a global perspective in local managers.

To enable their regional general managers to work alongside the worldwide product directors, several companies have moved them from the field to the head office. More and more companies require regional managers to reach sales and profit targets for each product as well as for each country within their regions. In the field, regional managers often focus on representing the views of individual countries to headquarters, but at headquarters they become more concerned with ensuring that the country managers are correctly implementing corporatewide policies.

Recently, Fiat and Philips N.V., among others, consolidated their worldwide advertising into a single agency. Their objectives are to make each product's advertising more consistent around the world and to make it easier to transfer ideas and information among local agency offices, country organizations, and headquarters. Use of a single agency (especially one that bills all advertising expenditures worldwide) also symbolizes a commitment to global marketing and more centralized control. Multinationals shouldn't however, use their agencies as Trojan horses for greater standardization. An undercover operation is likely to jeopardize agency-client relations at the country level.

While working to achieve global coordination, some companies are also trying to tighten coordination in particular regions. Kodak, for example, recently experimented by consolidating 17 worldwide product line managers at corporate headquarters. In addition, the company made marketing directors in some countries responsible for a line of business in a region as well as for sales of all Kodak products in their own countries. Despite these new appointments, country managers still retain profit-and-loss responsibility for their own markets.

Whether a matrix approach such as this broadens perspectives rather than increases tension and confusion depends heavily on the corporation's cohesiveness. Such an organizational change can clearly communicate top management's strategic direction, but headquarters needs to do a persuasive selling job to the field if it is to succeed.

Procter & Gamble is another example. It established so-called Euro Brand teams that analyze opportunities for greater product and marketing program standardization. Chaired by the brand manager from a "lead country," each team includes brand managers from other European subsidiaries that market the brand, managers from P&G's European technical center, and one of P&G's three European division managers, each of whom is responsible for a portfolio of brands as well as for a group of countries. Concerns that the larger subsidiaries would dominate the teams and that decision making would either be paralyzed or produce "lowest common denominator" results have proved groundless.

STAMPED & APPROVED

By coordinating programs with the field, headquarters can balance the company's local and global perspectives. Even a decentralized multinational may decide, however, that to protect or exploit some corporate asset, the center of gravity for certain elements of the marketing program should be at headquarters. In such cases, management has two options: It can send clear directives to its local managers or permit them to develop their own programs within specified parameters and subject to headquarters approval. With a properly managed approval process, a multinational can exert effective control without unduly dampening the country manager's decision-making responsibility and creativity.

Procter & Gamble recently developed a new sanitary napkin, and P&G International designated certain countries in different geographic regions as test markets. The product, brand name, positioning, and package design were standardized globally. P&G International did, however, invite local managers to suggest how the global program could be improved and how the nonglobal elements of the marketing program should be adapted in their markets. It approved changes in several markets. Moreover, local managers developed valuable ideas on such programming specifics as sampling and couponing techniques that were used in all other countries, including the United States.

Nestlé views its brand names as a major corporate asset. As a result, it requires all brands sold in all countries to be registered in the home country of Switzerland. While the ostensible reason for this requirement is legal protection, the effect is that any product development in the field has to be approved by Vevey. The head office had also developed detailed guidelines that suggest rather than mandate how brand names and logos should appear on packaging and in advertising worldwide (with exceptions subject to its approval). Thus the country manager's control over the content of advertising is not compromised, and the company achieves a reasonably consistent presentation of its names and logos worldwide.

DOING IT THE HEADQUARTERS WAY

Multinationals that direct local managers' marketing programs usually do so out of a sense of urgency. The motive may be to ensure either that a new product is introduced rapidly around the world before the competition can respond or that every manager fully and faithfully exploits a valuable marketing idea. Sometimes direction is needed to prove that global marketing can work. Once management makes the point, a more participative approach is feasible.

In 1979, one of Henkel's worldwide marketing directors wanted to extend the successful Sista line of do-it-yourself sealants from Germany to other European countries where the markets were underdeveloped and disorganized as had once been the case in Germany. A European headquarters project team visited the markets and then developed a standard marketing program. The country managers, however, objected. Since the market potential in each country was small, they said, they did not have the time or resources to launch Sista.

The project team countered that, by capitalizing on potential scale economies, its pan-European marketing and manufacturing programs would be superior to any programs the subsidiaries could develop by themselves. Furthermore, it maintained, the already developed pan-European program was available off the shelf. The European sales manager, who was a project team member, discovered that the salespeople as well as tradespeople in the target countries were much more enthusiastic about the proposed program than the field marketing managers. So management devised a special lure for the managers. The project team offered to subsidize the first-year advertising and promotion expenditures of countries launching Sista. Six countries agreed. To ensure their commitment now that their financial risk had been reduced, the sales manager invited each accepting country manager to nominate a member to the project team to develop the final program details.

By 1982, the Sista line was sold in 52 countries using a standard marketing program. The Sista launch was especially challenging because it involved the extension of a product and program already developed for a single market. The success of the Sista launch made Henkel's field managers much more receptive to global marketing programs for subsequent new products.

MOTIVATING THE FIELD

Taking into account the nature of their products and markets, their organizational structures, and their cultures and traditions, multinationals have to decide which approach or combination of approaches, from informing to directing, will best answer their strategic objectives. Multinational managers must realize, however, that local managers are likely to resist any precipitate move toward increased headquarters direction. A quick shift could lower their motivation and performance.

Any erosion in marketing decision making associated with global marketing will probably be less upsetting for country managers who have not risen through the line marketing function. For example, John Deere's European headquarters has developed advertising for its European country managers for more than a decade. The country managers have not objected. Most are not marketing specialists and do not see advertising as key to the success of their operations. But for country managers who view control of marketing decision making as central to their operational success, the transition will often be harder. Headquarters needs to give the field time to adjust to the new decision-making processes that multicountry brand teams and other new organizational structures require. Yet management must recognize that even with a

THE UNIVERSAL DRINK

In the postwar years, as Coca-Cola strove mightily to consolidate its territorial gains, its efforts were received with mixed feelings. When limited production for civilians got under way in the Philippines, armed guards had to be assigned to the trucks carting Coke from bottlers to dealers, to frustrate thirsty outlaws bent on hijacking it. In the Fiji Islands, on the other hand, Coca-Cola itself was outlawed, at the instigation of soft-drink purveyors whose business had been ruined by the Coke imported for the solace of G.I.s during the war. Most of the opposition to the beverage's tidal sweep, however, was centered in Europe, being provoked by the beer and wine interests, or by anti-American political interests, or by a powerful blend of oenology and ideology. Today, brewers in England, Spain, and Sweden are themselves bottling Coke, on the if-you-can't-lick-'em-join-'em principle. . . . In Western Europe, Coca-Cola has had to fight a whole series of battles, varying according to the terrain, not all of which have yet been won, though victory seems to be in sight. Before Coca-Cola got rolling in West Germany, for instance, it had to go to court to halt the nagging operations of something called the Coördination Office for German Beverages, which was churning out defamatory pamphlets with titles like "Coca-Cola, Karl Marx, and the Imbecility of the Masses" and the more succinct "Coca-Cola? No!" In Denmark, lobbyists for the brewers chivied the Parliament into taxing cola-containing beverages so heavily that it would have been economically absurd to try to market Coke there. . . . At last word, the Danes were about to relent, though. But in Belgium the caps on bottles of Coke, including bottles sold at the Brussels Fair, have had to carry, in letters bigger than those used for "Coca-Cola," the forbidding legend *"Contient de la cafeine."*

From THE BIG DRINK (Random House), © 1959 by E.J. Kahn, Jr. Originally in *The New Yorker.*

one-or two-year transition period, some turnover among field personnel is inevitable. As one German headquarters executive commented, "Those managers in the field who can't adapt to a more global approach will have to leave and run local breweries."

Here are five suggestions on how to motivate and retain talented country managers when making the shift to global marketing:

1. Encourage field managers to generate ideas. This is especially important when R&D efforts are centrally directed. Use the best ideas from the field in global marketing programs (and give recognition to the local managers who came up with them). Unilever's South African subsidiary developed Impulse body spray, now a global brand. R.J. Reynolds revitalized Camel as a global brand after the German subsidiary came up with a successful and transferable positioning and copy strategy.

2. Ensure that the field participates in the development of the marketing strategies and programs for global brands. A bottom-up rather than top-down approach will foster greater commitment and produce superior program execution at the country level. As we've seen, when P&G International introduced its sanitary napkin as a global brand, it permitted local managers to make some adjustments in areas that were not seen as core to the program, such as couponing and sales promotion. More important, it encouraged them to suggest changes in features of the core global program.

3. Maintain a product portfolio that includes, where scale economies permit, local as well as regional and global brands. While Philip Morris's and Seagram's country managers and their local advertising agencies are required to implement standard programs for each company's global brands, the managers retain full responsibility for the marketing programs of their locally distributed brands. Seagram motivates its country managers to stay interested in the global brands by allocating development funds to support local marketing efforts on these brands and by circulating monthly reports that summarize market performance data by brand and country.

4. Allow country managers continued control of their marketing budgets so they can respond to local consumer needs and counter local competition. When British Airways headquarters launched its £13 million global advertising campaign (see Case 2.7), it left intact the £18 million worth of tactical advertising budgets that country managers used to promote fares, destinations. and tour packages specific to their markets. Because most of the country managers had exhausted their previous year's tactical budgets and were anxious for further advertising support,

they were receptive to the global campaign even though it was centrally directed.

5. Emphasize the general management responsibilities of country managers that extend beyond the marketing function. Country managers who have risen through the line marketing function often don't spend enough time on local manufacturing operations, industrial relations, and government affairs. Global marketing programs can free them to focus on and develop their skills in these other areas.

3.2 READING

MNCs: Get Off the Reorganization Merry-Go-Round

Christopher A. Bartlett

For many companies, international expansion has been the major strategic thrust of the postwar era. Yet even successful, well-established organizations face difficult problems in managing global operations. Heady years of overseas expansion have been followed by a persistent organizational hangover, unresponsive to traditional remedies.

In the 1960s, the answer to the international challenge seemed clear: Managers simply needed to identify key strategic goals and restructure the corporation around them. But after two decades of experimentation, an "ideal international structure" remains elusive. Many companies still reorganize in the hope of finding it — but with only isolated cases of success.

With so many companies searching for this structural solution, why have results been so poor? Could it be that managers, obsessed with structure, were focusing on the wrong variable? A study I have made of 10 diverse and successful MNCs indicates that companies that persistently reorganize may be misdirecting their efforts. (For the background and overview of the research, please see the boxed insert on page 354.) The companies I studied have *not* continually reorganized their operations. Each has retained for years a simple structure built around an international division — a form of organization that many management theorists regard as embryonic, appropriate only for companies in the earliest stages of worldwide growth.

These companies see the international challenge as one of building and maintaining a complex decision-making process rather than of finding the right formal structure. The critical task is to develop new management perspectives, attitudes, and processes that reflect and respond to the complex demands companies with international strategies face. Such a process might sound too time consuming, too subtle, or too difficult to imitate. But companies that want to better meet the challenge can use as a guide the patterns established by these successful companies.

BROKEN PROMISE

To understand why these companies have succeeded, we first should look at the reasons others have failed. As companies began to feel the strain of controlling fast-growing foreign operations, managements intuitively looked for structural solutions. This generation of top managers was on the front line when the wave of postwar product diversification led to the widespread shift from functional to multidivisional organization structures. They saw, firsthand, the powerful linkage between strategy and structure. The conventional wisdom was that if the divisional organization structure had helped managers implement the corporate strategy of diversification, surely an equivalent structure would facilitate their new international strategic thrust.

Managers had other reasons to reorganize. For one, changing the formal structure was recognized as a powerful tool through which management could redefine responsibilities and relationships. Top managers could make clear choices, have immediate impact, and send strong signals of change to all hierarchical levels. Furthermore, companies were encouraged to pursue such international reorganization because it seemed many others were doing likewise. In fact, the pattern of reorganization became so familiar that management theorists had documented and classified it (see the boxed insert on pages 361–362).

Frustration came when managers discovered that no one structure provided a long-term solution. To many executives, it seemed they had no sooner developed a new set of systems, relationships, and decision-making processes than the international operations again needed to be reorganized. For example, Westinghouse disbanded its separate international division in 1971 when the 125 domestic product division managers were given worldwide responsibilities. By early 1979, however, concern about the lack of coordination among divisions and the insensitivity to certain nations had mounted. A task force recommended a global matrix, and by mid-year the new structure was in place. It was the third reorganization of international operations in one decade.

Like the executives at Westinghouse, many managers turned to a global matrix because they were frustrated by the one-dimensional biases built into a global-product or area-based structure. It was supposed to allow a company to respond to national and regional differences, while simultaneously maintaining coordination and integration of worldwide business. But the record of companies that adopted this structure is disappointing. The promised land of the global matrix quickly turned into an organizational quagmire, forcing a large number of companies to retreat from it. Some of these cases were widely publicized, such as that of Dow Chemical.

Dow, which served as the textbook case study of the global matrix, eventually returned to a more conventional structure in which the emphasis is on geographically based managers. Citibank became the new case illustration in one important book on matrix organization.[1] Yet within a few years, Citibank was reportedly retreating from its global matrix structure.

The same problems with the global matrix kept coming up: Tension and uncertainty built into dual reporting channels sometimes escalated to open conflict, complex issues were forced into a rigid two-dimensional decision framework, and minor issues became the subject of committee debates. More important, the design of matrix organization implied that managers with conflicting views or overlapping responsibilities communicate problems and confront and resolve differences. Yet barriers of distance, language, and culture impeded this vital process.

---

[1] See Stanley M. Davis and Paul R. Lawrence, *Matrix* (Reading, Mass.: Addison-Wesley, 1977). Citibank CEO Walter Wriston acknowledged in his foreword to this book the difficulty of managing in a global matrix.

MANAGING THE PROCESS

The 10 companies that escaped the organizational merry-go-round had a number of things in common, but the most fundamental was their adaptability to complex demands without restructuring. Underlying the approach to global operations of managers of these companies was the way they thought about the strategic demands and the appropriate organizational response.

Two major forces exerted opposite pressures on international strategies during the 1970s. First, as global competitors emerged in many industries, skirmishes for single-country markets gave way to battles for worldwide market position and global-scale efficiencies. Second, host-country governments raised their demands, and competition for market access tilted the bargaining power more in the governments' favor. MNCs had to increase local equity participation, transfer technology, build local manufacturing and research facilities, and meet export quotas.

With one set of pressures suggesting global integration and the other demanding local responsiveness, it is easy to see why executives of many companies thought in either-or terms and argued whether to centralize or decentralize control and whether to let the product or the geographic managers dominate corporate structure.

While managers in the 10 companies remained sensitive to those conflicting demands, they resisted the temptation to view their tasks in such simple either-or terms. The managers understood that such clear-cut answers would not work since *both* forces are present to some degree in all businesses. Moreover, thinking of strategy in "global" or "local" terms ignored the complexity, diversity, and changeability of the demands facing them.

For example, a growing threat of Japanese competitors forced Timken, the leading bearings manufacturer, to become more globally competitive in the 1970s. Unlike the Japanese, Timken chose not to compete solely as the low-cost producer of standard bearings. Rather, the company opted to reinforce its position as the technological leader in the industry. While this strategy required the strengthening and integrating of a worldwide research function, Timken's management thought such global integration was unnecessary in manufacturing. It trimmed and standardized product lines to gain efficiencies, but plants still specialized on a regional — not a worldwide — basis. Moreover, because customer service and response time were at the core of Timken's strategy, sales forces and engineering services retained their strict local focus.

Savvy managers realize that it is often difficult to know how to focus responsibility even within a single function. For example, Corning Glass Works's TV tube marketing strategy required global decision making for pricing and local decision making for service and delivery.

THE CHALLENGE OF SUBTLETY

It is not surprising that with this subtle perception of the nature of strategy, the managers in the 10 corporations set objectives, adopted a focus, and used tools that were different from those in most other MNCs. They realized that if the pressures in the international operating environment were intrinsically complex, diverse, and changeable, they had to create an internal management environment that could respond to those external demands and opportunities.

With this perception, managers viewed the organizational challenge not as one of finding and installing the right structure but as one of building an appropriate management process. As a result, they focused attention on the individual decision and the way it was reached rather than on the overall corporate structure. Questions changed from "Do we need worldwide product divisions or an area structure?" to "How can the company take the regional product group's perspective more into account in capacity expansion decisions?"

Finally, they looked for management tools with a finer edge than the blunt instrument of formal structural reorganization. Managers in other companies seemed so captivated by architectural problems that they forgot that the boxes they sketched on the back of an envelope represented not just positions but also people: The lines they casually erased and redrew stood not only for lines of authority but also for personal relationships. It was not unusual then to announce major reorganization very suddenly and install the structure in a few weeks or months. The result was often traumatic readjustment, followed by a long recovery. At Westinghouse, for example, the decision to reorganize into a global matrix structure was made by a senior management task force after a 90-day study of the problems and was put in place over the following 90 days.

Managers in the companies that were studied used tools that influenced individuals' behavior and attitudes or group norms and values in a more discreet and flexible manner.

A MULTIDIMENSIONAL DECISION PROCESS

The experience of the companies studied suggests that development of the diverse and flexible organizational processes follows three closely related stages. First, because an organization must take into account the richness of the environment it faces rather than view the world through a single, dominant management perspective, the companies developed internal groups that allowed the organization to sense, analyze, and respond to a full range of strategic opportunities and demands.

In most companies, a necessarily formal organizational structure limits interaction between such diverse interests. Therefore, during the second stage, the company builds additional channels of communication and forums for decision making to allow greater flexibility.

Finally, in the third stage the company develops norms and values within the organization to support shared decisions and corporate perspectives. Value is placed on corporate goals and collaborative effort rather than on parochial interests and adversary relationships.

DEVELOPING MULTIPLE MANAGEMENT PERSPECTIVES

In this environment of changeable demands and pressures, managers must sense and analyze complex strategic issues from all perspectives. Top management's job is to eliminate the one-dimensional bias built into most organizations.

The traditional bias in companies with international divisions, for example, allowed country and regional managers to dominate decision making from their line positions, with product and functional staff groups relegated to support and advisory roles. As a result, the companies underestimated or even ignored strategic opportunities that might have been realized by global coordination and integration of operations.

Similarly, organization by product divisions fostered decisions favoring worldwide standardization and integration. The power of headquarters' product managers over their geographic and functional counterparts was usually reinforced within the structure in formal as well as informal ways. For instance, the companies constructed information systems around products that allowed headquarters-based product management to collect and analyze data more easily than their functional or geographic counterparts. Furthermore, the strongest managers were appointed to product management positions, which reinforced their influence over the decision process.

Top management can begin to gradually eliminate these biases in the decision process in the following the ways.

1. **Upgrading personnel.** Assigning capable people to the right positions not only allows skills to be brought to bear in important areas but also sends strong signals that top management is serious about its ob-

THE RESEARCH BACKGROUND AND APPROACH

By the 1970s, some clear patterns of international organization change were beginning to emerge, and it was probably inevitable that the most common reorganization sequence be proposed as a prescriptive theory for stages of international organization. Perhaps the best known of these theories suggested that as a company's autonomous foreign subsidiaries grew, they should be consolidated under the umbrella of an international division structure. As product diversity increased abroad and overseas sales and profit grew in size and strategic importance, the stages theory suggested that a global product or an area division structure be adopted. Finally, as product and geographic diversity continued to increase, a global matrix or grid structure was prescribed.*

While numerous companies followed this structural evolution, many others did not. The research project examined ten U.S.-based MNCs that, according to the theory, should have adopted a global product, area, or matrix structure but instead retained this supposedly embryonic international division form. Through extensive interviews within each of these companies, I was able to observe how these companies adapted to changing strategic demands. In the broad philosophy and assumptions of top management and in the particular tools used, these companies offered an alternative to the one implied by the macro structural stages theories described above.†

*John M. Stopford and Louis T. Wells, Jr., *Managing the Multinational Enterprise* (New York: Basic Books, 1972).

†Detailed reporting of the research is presented in my unpublished doctoral thesis "Multinational Structural Evolution: Changing Decision Environment in International Divisions." Harvard Business School, 1979.

jectives and priorities. For example, top managers of the hospital supply company Baxter Travenol decided to counterbalance the strength of country managers in the international division with a strong global business perspective. First, they replaced existing product managers with MBAs who, while lacking the product expertise of their predecessors (ex-sales representatives), brought a more analytical and strategic perspective to the role. While this interim step upgraded the role, it was only with the appointment of more experienced managers from the domestic product divisions and foreign subsidiaries that the company achieved a strong global business perspective in its international strategy decisions.

2. **Broadening responsibilities.** Aggressive, ambitious, and able managers will naturally resist transfer to positions viewed as less powerful and having fewer responsibilities and lower status. So companies must redefine the role of the positions at the same time they upgrade the personnel. In the example of Baxter Travenol, when top management appointed MBAs to product manager positions, it enlarged the role from primarily a support responsibility to one that focused on monitoring and analyzing global product performance. When experienced product and country managers superseded the MBAs, the company allowed them to get involved in the budgeting and strategic planning processes, making recommendations about the management of their lines of business worldwide.

Such progression of roles is fairly typical when a company is trying to develop groups previously underrepresented in the decision process. The company first broadens advisory and support roles to encompass responsibility for monitoring and control. Exposure to the information necessary to undertake these new tasks then helps develop the ability to make analyses and recommendations of key issues, and finally to implement strategy.

3. **Changing managerial systems.** The biggest impediment to these changes is often the existing line management group; as happened at Baxter Travenol, country subsidiary managers may greatly resent the increased "interference" of product and functional staff. So top management needs to back up the desired changes.

If the newly upgraded managers are to succeed, they need information tailored to their responsibilities. Management systems usually parallel the formal organization structure and give line managers a tremendous information advantage. Top executives must be sure managers representing other perspectives also have the information needed to support their proposals and arguments.

Originally, Corning consolidated data only by geographic entity. When the company decided to upgrade the role of product and functional managers, however, it found that consolidating data along these dimensions was both difficult and expensive. Inconsistent product-line definitions, different expense allocation practices, and numerous tangled cases of double counting were impediments to system restructuring. By the time management sorted out these problems (with the help of a consultant and a couple of high-powered software packages), the new systems had cost well over $1 million.

Through these three steps, the company elevates previously under-represented management groups. The organization recognizes the need to monitor the environment from their perspective, acknowledges their competence to analyze the strategic implications of key issues, and accepts the legitimacy of representing such views in the decision process. Happily, many old distinctions between line and staff blur, and organization clichés about the locus of power become less relevant. As the president of Bristol-Myers's international division told me: "The traditional distinctions between line and staff roles are increasingly unclear here. . . . But by motivating managers and giving them latitude rather than writing restrictive job descriptions, we believe we can achieve much more."

CREATING SUPPLEMENTARY INFORMATION CHANNELS

It is not enough for a company simply to develop an organization that can sense and analyze issues from various perspectives. Managers representing diverse points of view need access to the decision-making processes.

As I mentioned earlier, in most companies formal communication channels parallel formal organization structures. The focus is one-dimensional and the decision-making process, hierarchical and formal. The structure reinforces the power of dominant line managers while limiting the influence of managers representing other perspectives.

Top management must create forums for decision making that take many perspectives into account and are flexible. While the formal reporting lines and management systems provide one way to channel communications, management can use an equally strong set of informal channels.

INFLUENCING INFORMALITY.   Informal relationships among people, of course, naturally develop in any organization, and to date, many corporate executives have regarded them as an uncontrollable by-product of the formal organization. Increasingly, however, they recognize that they can, and indeed should, influence the organization's informal systems if the environment is to allow people representing diverse and frequently conflicting interests to influence decisions. In any MNC, managers are separated by barriers of distance, time, and culture; the extent to which top management works to overcome these barriers, the way in which it builds bridges, and the groups among which it develops contacts and relationships all have an important influence on the organization's informal network and processes.

A variety of tools is available. By bringing certain individuals together to work on common problems, for example, or by assigning a specific manager to a position that requires frequent contact with colleagues, management can influence the development of social relationships. Such personal bonds break down the defensiveness and misunderstanding that often build when line managers feel their power is threatened.

Senior management of Eli Lilly's international division was conscious of this dynamic. As a normal part of career development, it transferred managers from line to staff positions, from one product line to another, and from headquarters to country subsidiaries. Although the original idea was to develop a broad perspective, an equally important benefit has been the development of an informal network of friends and contacts throughout the organization. In the words of one manager, "Those who moved about had far better information sources than computer reports, and more important, they developed the influence that comes with being known, understood, and respected."

Baxter Travenol's top management used frequent, well-planned meetings to help develop informal relationships. The company had long held annual general managers' meetings in which country and regional line managers listened to formal presentations of the year's financial results, of the latest corporate plans, and of one or two new products. Recognizing that staff-line relationships were becoming very strained, the division president changed the traditional meeting into a senior management conference to which product managers and functional managers were also invited. He replaced most formal presentations with discussions, during which senior managers jointly identified and tried to resolve strategic and organizational issues.[2] The team formed bonds that endured far beyond the meetings.

AVOIDING STRATEGIC ANARCHY. Of course a company cannot resolve complex issues by simply allowing different interests to clash in a trading-room-floor atmosphere. The formal hierarchy will still constrain and limit the influence of nonline managers as key issues are actually

---

[2]For a description of the process used, see my article, written with David W. DeLong, "Operating Cases to Help Solve Corporate Problems," *Harvard Business Review*, March-April 1982, p. 68.

decided. There are, however, ways to ensure the representation of appropriate interests and at the same time allow headquarters to retain control.

Most managers are familiar with such things as task forces, interdepartmental teams, and special committees. These devices are often used ad hoc, after the formal decision process has failed, for example, or in response to a crisis. But managers can also use them in a more routine manner to pull certain issues out of the mainstream and to tailor the analysis and decision making.

Bristol-Myers's international organization, for instance, feared that the company was dissipating scarce research resources. Each project typically had the backing of a country subsidiary manager who claimed that the project was absolutely essential to his or her national strategy. By creating a "pharmaceutical council" comprised of senior geographic line managers and division-level business development staff managers, the division president forced these managers to make compromises and to combine these separate proposals into a single cohesive program. By appointing the business development director as the council's chairman he increased this manager's influence and leverage and ensured that the deliberations would have a global perspective.

In Warner Lambert, country managers had for years influenced decisions on manufacturing capacity toward constructing local plants. Believing that such decisions compromised efficiency, the division president set up a task force of geographic and functional managers to conduct an 18-month review of global capacity needs. Recognizing the sensitivity of country managers to any loss of autonomy, he appointed regional managers to represent the line organization. The task force's manufacturing, finance, and marketing managers convinced regional managers of the need for greater coordination of manufacturing operations and rationalization of facilities to gain scale economies. With regional managers behind the idea, country managers were forced to recognize the program's considerable savings.

One note of caution: The purpose of such temporary task groups is to supplement rather than replace the mainstream decision process. The company must consider carefully which decisions cannot be resolved by the regular managerial process. It should clearly define and limit the number of issues taken "off line" and keep them out of the mainstream only as long as necessary.

BUILDING A SUPPORTIVE CULTURE

There is no guarantee that decisions will reflect the mix of interests and views represented in the process. Simply putting people together does not mean they will interact positively and productively. It is necessary to build an organizational culture that supports multidimensional, flexible decision making.

In many companies, a culture that stresses internal competition has proven the major barrier to the development of a flexible decision process. In one of the companies studied, a well-known motto was that "only your final result counts." The company's formal structure and reward systems reinforced the value.

When internal competition is overemphasized, managers with different perspectives easily become entrenched adversaries and the decision-making process deteriorates, as protecting territory and even subversion become the norms. In fact, many companies discovered that upgrading nonline management groups and supplementing the hierarchical decision process triggered such adverse reactions.

To make the organization flexible, top management of the companies studied made certain that managers understood how their particular points of view fit with corporate strategies; it reinforced this understanding with a culture supportive of cooperation and compromise. The organizational norms and values creating such an environment obviously could not be established by management fiat. Rather, they were carefully developed through a variety of small actions and decisions.

ARTICULATE GOALS & VALUES.   Elementary and simplistic as it may seem, one of the most powerful tools for top management is the precise formulation and communication of specific strategic objectives and behavioral norms. In a surprising number of companies, however, middle managers have only the vaguest notion of overall corporate objectives and of the boundaries of acceptable behavior.

Eli Lilly places great importance on mutual trust, openness, and honesty in all interpersonal dealings. In an orientation brochure for new employees, the late Mr. Eli Lilly, grandson of the founder, was quoted as saying: "Values are, quite simply, the core of both men and institutions. . . . By combining our thoughts and by helping one another, we are able to merge the parts [of this organization] into a rational, workable management system." It is clear that adversary relationships and parochial behavior do not fit in the culture he envisioned.

At Baxter Travenol, senior management conferences provided an ideal communication forum for the international division president. In addition to articulating overall objectives and priorities, he acknowledged the conflicts implicit in particular important issues and encouraged managers to discuss how they might subjugate individual interests to the overall strategy. The participation of managers ensured not only their understanding of the issues but also their involvement in, and commitment to, corporate goals.

MODIFY REWARD SYSTEMS.   It is clear that a company cannot ask managers to compromise parochial interests for a broader good if it continues to evaluate and reward them on the basis of indicators tied tightly to a small area of responsibility. Successful international companies in the sample made sure managers understood they did not compromise career opportunities or expose themselves to other organizational risks by adopting a cooperative and flexible attitude. Many companies altered management evaluation criteria and modified formal reward systems.

As the decision-making processes became increasingly complex at Corning Glass Works, top managers changed the criteria for promotion. One top manager said to me: "In addition to the analytic and entrepreneurial capabilities we have always required, managers must now have strong interpersonal skills to succeed in key positions. To contribute to our decision-making process, they must be good communicators, negotiators, and team players. We had to move aside some individuals who simply could not work in the new environment."

Eli Lilly's formal evaluation and reward systems are tied even more directly to the need for cooperation and flexibility. Rather than being evaluated only by a direct superior, each manager's performance is also appraised by others with whom he or she deals. This multiple review process not only encourages cooperative behavior but also serves as a control to identify those who are unwilling or unable to develop positive work relationships.

PROVIDE ROLE MODELS.   Top managers know that their words and actions are models that strongly influence values and behavioral norms in the organization. Yet few top managers routinely use these powerful tools. With a little thought and planning, they can send signals that encourage behavior conducive to achieving the organization's goals.

After one restructuring failed, Corning's president and vice-chairman recognized that the role model they were providing as top management was one of the fundamental problems. They were simply not communicating and cooperating on efforts to integrate the international and domestic operations, and this lessened the willingness of domestic division managers to share information and cooperate with their overseas counterparts. Later, as these top managers made a strong effort to work closely on issues and to let the organization see their joint com-

THE CARAVAN AND THE FLEET

"The good merchant," says quaint old Thomas Fuller, "is one who by his trading claspeth the Islands to the Continent, and one country to another; an excellent gardener, who makes England bear wine, and oil, and spices; yea herein he goes beyond nature in causing that *omnis fert omnia tellus*." The mission of the merchant is indeed, when rightly viewed, one of the most important of the occupations of men, and has in all ages exerted a deep influence on the progress of society and the destiny of nations. Geologists have begun to discover that the steady flow of water is, after all, accountable for greater terrestrial changes than spasmodic bursts of volcanic fire. Thus, too, Commerce, in its earnest, ceaseless, silent, undemonstrative way, has produced more momentous and permanent revolutions among the peoples of the earth than war, dazzling us with the glitter of its arms, deafening us with the blare of its trumpets and the thunder of its guns, and awing us by the visible signs of its victories and desolations.

It was Commerce which quickened the primitive faculties of man, and brought the early races into communion with each other; which opened up the rich and varied treasury of India to peoples further from the rising sun; which made princes of the camel-drivers of Babylon and the fishermen of Tyre; which raised up imperial cities on the hot sands of the African seashore, on the muddy refuse of the Po, and on the quaking marshes of Holland; which made London the capital of an empire extending to the furthermost ends of the earth; which first developed and then checked the rapid growth of the giant Republic of the New World. Agriculture, manufacture, navigation, most of the arts and many of the sciences, owe their origin to the promptings of Commerce, and their progress to its stimulus. Alternately the nations have taught and learned; and along with material products, religion, poetry, and philosophy have been disseminated by means of the caravan and the fleet.

There does not, at first sight, appear to be much heroism and romance in the occupation of a merchant; but it is not difficult, on reflection, to discover that there may be, and often is, both; and it is well that he should not lose sight of the great influences he may be setting at work, and the responsibility he

is incurring, even when engaged in seemingly commonplace
and trivial details of routine work.

From J. Hamilton Fyfe *Merchant Enterprise; or, the History of Commerce from
the Earliest Times* (London: T. Nelson and Sons, 1864).

mitment to decisions, they saw their cooperative behavior reflected
throughout the organization.

THE KEY IS FLEXIBILITY

Clearly, the approach outlined is vastly different from one in which a
company installs a new structure to "force the product managers to interact with geographic specialists."[3] Building a multidimensional and
flexible decision process means the company will sense and respond to
the complex, diverse, and changeable demands most MNCs face.

Several benefits flow from this approach. First, matching decision
processes with the task keeps managers' attention focused on the business issues. By contrast, in an organization going through a major restructuring, management's attention tends to be riveted on changes in
formal roles and responsibilities, as people debate the implications of
the new structure and jockey for position and turf.

Second, by working to achieve a gradual organizational evolution
rather than a more rapid structural change, a company can avoid much
of the trauma associated with reorganization. Changes in roles and relationships are best achieved incrementally.

Finally, by thinking in terms of changing behavior rather than
changing structural design, managers free themselves from the limitations of representing organizations diagrammatically. They are not restricted by the number of dimensions that can be represented on a chart;
they are not tempted to view the organization symmetrically; and they
are not limited by the innately static nature of an organization diagram.

---

[3]This was the objective of the Westinghouse reorganization study, according to the
report in "Westinghouse Takes Aim at the World," *Fortune*, January 14, 1980, p. 52.

3.3 *CASE*

Nestlé S.A.: International Marketing

*John A. Quelch and
Edward J. Hoff*

In July 1983, Mr. Jean Robin, marketing counselor to the general manager of Nestlé's headquarters marketing staff, was reviewing the marketing organization of the company. Nestlé was the world's oldest multinational company and, with 1983 revenues of SFr. 27.9 billion ($14.0 billion), one of the world's largest and best-known food manufacturers. From its founding in 1866,[1] the company had followed a "uniquely Swiss and neutral philosophy," pursuing global expansion through the creation of local operating companies with their own local managements. The Swiss headquarters provided the brand names and most of the product concepts and manufacturing processes, held its local managers to

---

[1]Nestlé official history.

high quality standards, and maintained a large, influential central staff. At the same time, the individual country organizations retained the primary responsibility and authority for managing each local market.

However, several factors prompted an examination of how marketing at Nestlé was managed — and whether any changes were in order. Some observers believed that emerging market forces worldwide called for a more centrally coordinated or common marketing approach. They also contended that, with greater central coordination of the marketing function, Nestlé could reduce costs through economies of scale and could employ proven ideas more effectively throughout the world. Moreover, Nestlé's chief executive had stated that management should be unconstrained by the practices of the past as the company strove to revive profits which had declined as a percent of sales during the late 1970s and in 1980.

Robin pointed to two decisions that illustrated the influence of the central marketing staff and the issues involved in determining whether marketing policies and programs at Nestlé ought to be more centrally coordinated or harmonized. The first case concerned the advantages of developing a centrally coordinated advertising campaign. In 1980, the director of advertising and promotion had had to consider whether an advertising concept that was highly successful in West Germany should be employed in Latin America. The second decision faced the product director for culinary products in 1983.[2] It concerned whether or not to persuade the Nestlé operating companies in France and West Germany to accept a package with a common design for a product that had been launched successfully in both countries in 1981 in distinctly different packages and under different brand names.

NESTLÉ HISTORY AND PERFORMANCE

In 1866, Charles and George Page, American brothers, founded a company in Cham, Switzerland to manufacture condensed milk for export throughout Europe. The Pages chose the name Anglo-Swiss Condensed

---

[2]Culinary products included bouillons, dehydrated soups, liquid soups in tins, seasonings and condiments, cold and hot sauces, and preparations for simple, easy-to-make dishes.

Milk Company to give the company an international image and to help sales in the large British market. In 1867, Henri Nestlé founded Ste Henri Nestlé in Vevey, Switzerland to produce an infant food made of milk, grain, and carbohydrates. Doctors throughout Europe were soon recommending this food for malnourished infants. The Anglo-Swiss Company introduced its own infant food in the 1870s and Nestlé responded by selling its own condensed milk.

The Page brothers began building processing plants in their largest markets since rapid sales growth necessitated supplies of milk beyond those available only in Switzerland. European wars further convinced both the Pages and Nestlé that self-sufficient production was needed in each major market to ensure uninterrupted production and distribution. Anglo-Swiss opened its first non-Swiss plant in England in 1874, and Charles Page returned to the U.S. in 1882 to open the first non-European plant.

In 1905, Nestlé and Anglo-Swiss merged. Subsequently, Nestlé grew rapidly through mergers, geographical expansion, and entry into new product categories. The company opened milk and infant food processing plants in Australia (1910), South America (1921), Africa (1927), and Asia (1932). In 1929, Nestlé merged with a large Swiss chocolate company Peter-Cailler-Kohler, which also had international business. In 1937, Nestlé's R&D laboratories invented the "Nescafe" process to manufacture premium-quality instant coffee. Nescafe was launched in Switzerland and in the large U.S. coffee market in 1938–1939. After World War II, Nestlé merged with Maggi, a large European producer of food enhancers and prepared foods such as packaged soups. Acquisitions continued throughout the 1960s and 1970s, including Crosse & Blackwell (1960), an old and well-known British food company, Locatelli (1961), an Italian cheese producer, Findus (1962), a Swedish frozen food company, Libby McNeill & Libby (1970), an American fruit and vegetable processor, Ursina Franck (1971), an important Swiss firm in the milk and dietetic food businesses, the Stouffer Corporation (1973), an American frozen food manufacturer and hotel chain operator, and Alcon Laboratories (1977), a pharmaceutical manufacturer. The operations of these acquired companies typically reported to the Nestlé country managers in each market.

By 1982, Nestlé was the 25th largest international corporation outside the U.S., with registered operating companies in 75 countries, 282 plants in 56 countries, and 140,000 employees of whom only 3% were Swiss nationals. Nestlé competed in a wide variety of product categories:

	%1982 sales	% 1983 sales
Instant drinks	27.1	27.7
Dairy products	21.4	20.4
Culinary products	14.4	13.9
Frozen foods and ice cream	9.5	10.3
Infant foods and dietetic products	8.9	8.4
Chocolate and confectionery	8.0	8.1
Restaurants and hotels	2.9	3.0
Liquid drinks	2.8	2.9
Refrigerated products	3.0	2.9
Pharmaceuticals, dermatologicals, and cosmetics	2.0	2.4

Net after-tax profit during the early 1970s was consistently above 4% of sales but fell below 4% from 1978 to 1981. Due to mismanagement by its Argentinian subsidiary, 1980 was a particularly difficult year. The loss, "unprecedented in the company's long history genuinely shocked headquarters at Vevey." Helmut Maucher, a new chief executive officer, who had risen primarily through the Nestlé marketing organization in West Germany, announced the pruning of unprofitable product lines in several countries, including the $180 million Libby canned food business in the U.S. An industry analyst described Maucher as "very tough and not very sentimental about company traditions." Maucher described his style as "management by provocation. If everything is settled and solid and well thought of, you sometimes must play the provocateur."[3] Net after-tax profit in 1983 reached 4.5% of sales.

NESTLÉ ORGANIZATION

In 1983, each of the 75 operating companies was run by a country manager who had full responsibility for profit and loss and for management of all marketing, manufacturing, financial, and administrative functions.[4] Most country managers were local nationals who had risen through the marketing function.

---

[3]*International Management*, February 1983, p. 22.

[4]Nineteen operating companies had no manufacturing facilities under their control and imported all the Nestlé products that they marketed.

COUNTRY ORGANIZATION

Two types of country organization were evident at Nestlé in 1983. In smaller markets, the country manager usually oversaw a production manager, a financial manager, and a marketing manager. The marketing manager in turn supervised a single sales force for all Nestlé products, a number of product managers, and a small marketing services staff.

In larger markets, the country managers typically supervised several product division managers, each of whom was responsible for marketing and sales for a particular product line. In some cases, these division managers also shared responsibility for production and finance with the local technical and financial managers. The deciding factor in creating a separate division was whether a product line's sales volume or trade situation in that country called for a separate sales force. Some countries were partially divisionalized, with one or two product divisions coexisting with a basic functional organization which covered all other product lines.

The local product managers were a key element in Nestlé's marketing organization. They had responsibility for the marketing objectives, positioning, and marketing programs of the Nestlé products they managed. At the same time, the country managers were particularly involved in advertising decision making, especially the choice of and relationships with their organizations' advertising agencies.

The career paths of product managers concerned Nestlé management in Vevey. Product managers tended to be switched too frequently from one product category to another and to be promoted to manage a more important product line in the same country rather than to manage the same product line in a larger market. Personnel transfers across national boundaries had become increasingly difficult partly as a result of local labor laws requiring employment of nationals.

REGIONAL MANAGERS

As indicated in *Exhibit 1*, the 75 country organizations reported through five zones, each run by a regional manager. Zone I covered Continental Europe; Zone II, Asia, Australia, and New Zealand; Zone III, South and Central America; Zone IV, U.S., Canada, U.K., and Ireland; and Zone V, Africa and the Middle East.

The regional managers, who all had their offices at headquarters, were described by Robin as "representing the interests of the sharehold-

EXHIBIT 1. Partial Nestlé organization chart, 1983

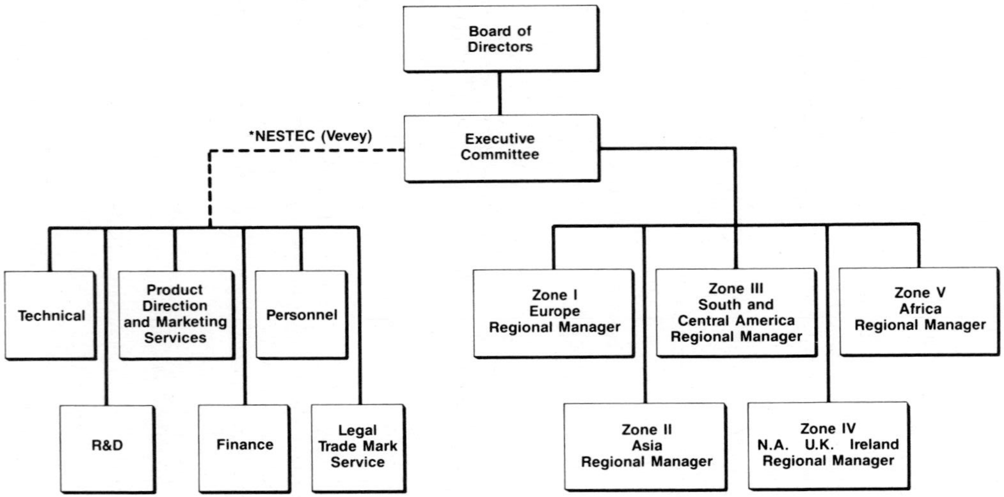

ers" in their regions.[5] They managed their regions country by country, working with each country manager to set revenue and profit goals. They did not set formal goals for their regions by product line.

THE CENTER

Nestlé had long employed a central headquarters staff which grew rapidly after World War II. In 1961, Nestlé management concluded that a more structured central marketing organization was required. A marketing division, run by a general manager, was therefore instituted at the Center in 1961 alongside the already existing finance and technical divisions at the Center. The marketing division initially held a high degree of centralized power. However, several of its functions were decentralized in 1972. In 1983, the level of decentralization was increased and the headquarters marketing function was consolidated in the Product Direction and Marketing Services Department (PDMS).

The Finance Division managed both the controller and treasurer functions. Nestlé's financial control system was designed to give Vevey early warning of problems in a particular country. The system was streamlined and tightened after the losses in Argentina, not in order to increase control but to improve monitoring.

The Technical Division had responsibility for ensuring that Nestlé's commitment to product quality, described by Robin as "Nestlé's quality religion," was followed worldwide. The production directors at the Center worked with the local production managers to monitor and improve production operations around the world.

The Research and Development Department within the Technical Division managed 17 separate research companies (RECOs) located throughout the world. Each concentrated on a single region and a specific range of products. For example, a new RECO in Quito, Ecuador worked on culinary, dairy, and infant food products for the country organizations in South and Central America. These RECOs worked on product improvements for existing businesses, product extensions to

---

[5]Years of disappointing performance for Nestlé Enterprises (U.S.) caused Maucher to create a regional management for Zone IV in Vevey for the first time. Maucher commented: "I think we've found the right way of combining a big decentralized unit run by Americans with all the European and Nestlé experience and know-how. It was a problem of what kind of management we should establish, how much we should adapt ourselves to American mentalities and habits, and how much we should draw on our own experience."

new geographical areas, and the development of new products adapted to local consumption habits and environmental conditions.

Robin noted that the financial, technical, and research functions were "certainly more heavily supervised and controlled from Vevey than marketing. If marketing is to focus on the needs of consumers, nobody is in a better position to identify these needs than our local country organizations." Robin strongly believed that marketing had to be more decentralized than the financial and technical functions.

PRODUCT DIRECTION AND MARKETING SERVICES

Although Nestlé gave country organizations complete responsibility for managing their respective markets, it also sought to infuse certain policies, goals, and standards worldwide. The PDMS was responsible for monitoring and promoting these corporate interests.

Mr. Peter Ferrero was general manager of PDMS in 1983. He supervised eight product directors[6] and six marketing services directors. An organization chart is presented as *Exhibit 2*.

PRODUCT DIRECTORS

The concept of product management at Nestlé headquarters had been introduced in 1958, but the first worldwide "product managers" were essentially coordinators with relatively little influence. In 1974, product directors were appointed at the Center and they assumed an increasingly important role in Nestlé's headquarters organization. Both the product directors and their staff members were former line managers in country organizations. Some of them, especially at the middle management level, returned to the local markets after having been exposed to the management challenges of the Center. Mr. Walther Mueller, product director for culinary products, had most recently been culinary product division manager in West Germany, running a $250 million business. The main functions of the product directors were to establish global and/ or regional product market strategies, to search for new product ideas and initiate their development, to ensure maximum cross-fertilization of

---

[6]The product line boundaries separating the responsibilities of the eight product directors corresponded to those used in most of the large country organizations and by headquarters: drinks, dairy products and cheese, culinary products, frozen foods and ice cream, infant foods and dietetic products, chocolate and confectionery, refrigerated products, and food services products.

EXHIBIT 2. Product direction and marketing services: organization chart, 1983

Product Direction and Marketing Services

Marketing Counsellor
- Graphics and Printing
- Administration
- Commercial Secretariat

Product Directors
- Drinks
- Infant and Dietetic Products
- Culinary Products
- Dairy Products and Vegetable Proteins
- Chocolates and Confectionery
- Frozen Food and Ice Cream
- Refrigerated Products
- Food Service

Marketing Services Manager
- Advertising and Promotion
- Packaging
- Marketing Research
- Sales Force and Trade Services
- Consumer Services
- Marketing Communications

product information among regions and markets, and to provide in exceptional cases operating assistance to those markets lacking particular skills.

PRODUCT POLICY AND STRATEGY.   The product directors established worldwide or regional goals and strategies for their product lines. In addition, they developed branding, positioning, packaging, and advertising guidelines. Once approved by top management, the guidelines were transmitted to the regional managers who would, if justified, adapt the product directors' strategies to local market conditions. Major differences of opinion were resolved by top management.

Sometimes, a product director might attempt to coordinate the marketing efforts of two or more country organizations when their positionings of a particular product line were different and when their marketing communication campaigns spilled over from one country to the other, as was often the case in Europe. However, product positionings were often established before such a situation was identified by the Center, and country organizations were then unwilling to change.

PRODUCT INNOVATION AND NEW PRODUCT DEVELOPMENT.   The product director was the central figure in the product development process. A RECO which made a technological advance resulting in a new product idea was required to inform the appropriate product director so that he or she could assess its marketing potential and help steer its further development. There was constant contact between the product director, the RECO, and the regional manager during all phases of a new product's development. If a local manager conceived a new product idea, the manager was to inform the appropriate product director who would then work with a RECO to develop it. Increasingly, however, product directors and their staffs worked on identifying and developing new product ideas themselves. Mr. Carl Freeman who worked for Mr. Mueller on new product development pointed out that most new culinary product ideas in recent years had originated in the product director's staff at the Center.

The product directors also had to promote investment in new product ideas. To commercialize a new product concept, a product director would usually select one or more "prime-mover markets," large enough to assume the financial risk of an unproven product and in which the product had a good chance of success. The product director, supported by the regional manager, had to convince the country manager to make the necessary investment. Once a product was successful in one market, it became easier to persuade other country organizations to launch the product. As Mr. Freeman said, "Our country managers are our customers. Our competitors are not only other companies, but also the other product groups as we strive to secure the attention and investment of the country organizations."

PRODUCT EXTENSIONS. The product directors also sought opportunities to extend existing products to new countries. Often local raw materials or consumer uses differed, and the product director would work with a RECO to adapt the product concept to a new environment. The director again had to convince the country manager to make the necessary investment. Managers in developing countries often asked for operational assistance in return for taking the investment risk.

BRANDING. Nestlé S.A. retained total ownership and control of all its brand names, treating them as corporate property. Brand names were "licensed" to the operating companies which paid fees for their use. *Exhibit 3* presents excerpts from the introduction to a 1979 policy statement on branding still valid in 1983. Top management set policy on the use of brand names. For example, no sweet product could be introduced under the Maggi (culinary) brand name. Within the framework of the general policy, the product director developed detailed guidelines on logo and packaging design for each brand name for which he was responsible. *Exhibit 4* presents excerpts from the introduction to the Maggi packaging design manual, issued by the culinary product director. As of 1980, the local markets were no longer required to submit to the Center for approval new labels and packages which complied with the guidelines. However, exceptions to the guidelines did require the approval of the appropriate product director. The local markets continued to be responsible for ensuring compliance with local labeling regulations.[7]

KNOWLEDGE AND EXPERIENCE TRANSFER. The product directors worked to transfer knowledge and experience among countries. Together with the marketing services staff, they contributed articles and case histories to an internal monthly publication, *Marketing Communication*. *Exhibit 5* lists the table of contents from the January 1983 issue. Knowledge transfer was also fostered through personal visits by central staff members to the country organizations and through the training of marketing personnel.

---

[7]The European Economic Community issued a Food Labeling Directive in 1982 requiring information on food packages including the list of ingredients and the minimum durability date.

EXHIBIT 3. Excerpts from the introduction to a policy statement on branding, 1983

The purpose of this paper is to facilitate decisions involving branding.
Our first attempt, some twelve years ago, to establish guidelines for an international branding policy has proved its value but is in considerable need of updating because

- the worldwide expansion of our business over the last decade has enlarged the repertoire of brands employed by us, or available for use;
- through a period of rapid economic growth, followed by recession, further experience has been gained on both the consequences of inventing additional brands, and of employing the brands we already possess;
- consumers are now known not to be overly sensitive to the spread of brand names in the food industry even into apparently unrelated food areas, so long as the name is perceived as belonging to a large, successful company whose products are valued by consumers;
- the ever-increasing cost of being clearly heard among the ever-louder barrage of communications aimed at consumers forces us to be even more pragmatic and to proceed in an even more orderly fashion;
- of the now very high cost of registering new brands internationally.

The extreme importance of branding decisions and their international connotations makes this publication a statement of group policy.

Branding is the prerogative of the Center's Product Departments in consultation with Regional Managements and the Trade Mark Service. The final decision rests with a member of the General Management.

The high visibility of branding on packages necessitates that packaging be also the prerogative of the Center's Product Departments in consultation with Regional Managements and the Trade Mark Service, the final decision again resting with a member of General Management.

On the other hand, the markets are responsible for implementing branding policies, as well as for proposing, developing and defining the necessary local branding strategies.

HUMAN RESOURCE DEVELOPMENT.   The product directors were responsible for organizing regional seminars at which local product managers were educated on marketing strategies and new developments in their particular product categories. This time-consuming task was made more burdensome by the frequency with which product managers changed their assignments. The directors also advised regional and country managers on the selection and evaluation of their marketing personnel.

EXHIBIT 4. Introduction to Maggi packaging design manual, 1980

This manual replaces the 1976 edition.

With the growth in competition and expansion of the range, three factors have acquired importance:

1. The clear display of the brand name in an outstanding position on all the packages.
2. The need to have a clear category identification within the Maggi family.
3. The identity of each particular product, but also its quality/price level, must be able to be quickly recognized and memorized where there are several ranges within the same category.

The red and yellow identification colors, if properly used, serve to draw the customer's attention to Maggi, a function that is particularly important in self-service stores.

The presentation of a pack is one of the basic elements of communications. Consequently this must not be gauged independently but within the overall context of the other Maggi products.

In any good presentation, priority should be given to:

1. Maggi identity
2. General clarity
3. Readability of the product name
4. Quick identification of the main elements
5. Appetite appeal

It is essential that all the elements are combined in such a way that in a self-service store the housewife can easily find and identify the particular Maggi products she wants among thousands of other food packages. Fractions of a second can be decisive, which is why instant identification is of paramount importance.

However, you are not being asked to sit down and redesign your packages. Unless there are compelling reasons, a package should only be modified every 5 to 10 years (at the earliest).

Will you be working on further suggestions for improving the packaging presentation?

If the answer is yes and you come up with any new and better solutions, these will be very welcome and, as common property, be included in the manual so that all interested markets can benefit from them.

How compulsory are the guidelines?

These are compulsory as regards the main elements, such as the brand, its dimension in the presentation and the positioning, also the distribution of the red/yellow surfaces, their shape and delimitation. The rules also apply to the typography unless there are national or linguistic obstacles.

In short, the new rules should be interpreted and applied with discrimination but must be strictly observed in principle. Since all modifications require the consent of your advisers, each of your suggested packaging modifications will be examined in detail and a final solution found for your market in agreement with you.

EXHIBIT 5. Marketing communication (CM): table of contents

NESTEC

January 1983

Milk Products and Desserts
USA — Successful launch of *Soft Wispride*

Refrigerated Products
Spain — Launch of *Petit Chamburcy*

Frozen Foods
United Kingdom — Launch of *Bacon and Egg Savoury Toasts*

Switzerland — Two new pizzas: *Panizza Famosa* and *Panizza Rustica*

Culinary Products
Switzerland — Maggi improves and expands its sauce range

Sales Force and Trade
Germany — What is *your* sales force doing in the petrol crisis?

NESTEC
Training model/salesman's career

CM is aimed to be as widely distributed as possible to all the marketing
personnel of the Operating Companies. In particular, these publications are
meant for Product Group specialists in the following sectors: Catering,
Vending, Home Economics, Market Research, Advertising — and for
promotion and sales executives, that is to say, all who can benefit from CM
information. Additional copies can be requested to ensure the widest possible
distribution, but this publication remains an internal communication tool and
is not supposed to be distributed outside of the Nestlé Group.

OPERATIONAL ASSISTANCE.   Product directors and the marketing services staff provided operational assistance to the country organizations
when requested. However, in 1982, it was decided that the Center
should provide such assistance only in exceptional cases, so that, in
Robin's words, the central staff "would have time to think and not be
overloaded with tactical work for the local markets."

MARKETING SERVICES

Six marketing services units reported to Mr. Engel, Marketing Services Manager. The heads of these units were technical experts who, according to Robin, served "as advisers to the product directors, the regional managers and the local organizations within the framework of the overall corporate policy guidelines adopted for their specialized functions."

In the 1960s, the *Advertising and Promotion Manager* worked with the local markets primarily on enhancing the "quality, execution, and tone" of their advertising, rather than on influencing its content. With the help of more than sixty people, the advertising manager used to review all local advertising produced by the operating companies. By 1983, this was no longer the case; the current staff comprised only three specialists. Instead of attempting to review and approve the advertising of each market, the advertising manager sought to influence local practices through regional training seminars for local personnel,[8] through visits to the local markets, and through technical guidelines (see *Exhibit 6* for the introduction to one such guideline on print advertising for culinary products). The manager received frequent requests from the markets for technical advice and estimated that, in 1982, he had visited markets representing 55% of Nestlé's worldwide sales. He cited as his important tasks "maintaining communication with the markets, providing technical expertise, and transferring experience and knowledge." He also helped to coordinate relationships with the 15 principal advertising agencies working with Nestlé. Each local market controlled its own agency relationships, but might sometimes ask the advertising manager at the Center to contact the agency at a higher level on an agency personnel or policy matter.[9] While the advertising manager worked primarily with the local markets, product directors would sometimes ask him to help coordinate a product's positioning or image across several countries by suggesting an appropriate standard visual or graphic concept.

The main objective of the *Packaging Design Manager* was to be competitive on quality and cost with any external supplier of the services his unit provided. Two-thirds of all Nestlé packages and labels were developed or modified by this unit. This represented between 2,000 and 3,000 labeling projects per annum. Members of the packaging unit

---

[8]Advertising agency personnel were often invited to attend these seminars.

[9]Nestlé organizations worked with 137 different agencies worldwide. Culinary products in Europe alone were handled by 14 different agencies.

EXHIBIT 6. Introduction to manual on advertising culinary products in print

The objective of this book is to provide management with a convenient frame of reference for the creation and assessment of print advertising. You will find here the basic fundamentals upon which successful print campaigns have been built over the years, and which will continue to hold good all the while that basic reading habits remain unchanged.

Advertising is our principal "voice to the consumer" and probably the most powerful Brand Franchise Builder at our disposal. Therefore, since budgets are always limited, it behooves us to use it well.

Results have proven that good, intelligent advertising works many times harder than mediocre advertising.

The following guidelines are easily stated, and one must have a sound understanding of the principles upon which they are based in order to apply them effectively. We invite you, therefore, to study the accompanying commentary with some care. Because food advertising is a carefully controlled combination of pictures and words, illustrations and text should always be considered together.

Since our advertising reflects the company as a whole, and the sort of people we are, it must be truthful and defensible. But it must also be interesting, because "you can't bore people into buying your product." Finally, our advertising must be persuasive; it must always provide the consumer with justification and reassurance in her choice of our products.

Although what follow are rules, creative workers should not regard them as any kind of prison. Rather, they are a professional framework within which any amount of imagination and creativity can be generated by those who have the necessary talent.

EXHIBIT 7. Title page from policy and method paper on packaging research: Nestec Marketing Research Guidelines (No. 8)

Why Packaging Research

The product package is a very powerful selling tool. The final promotional item the consumer sees prior to making her buying decision about a retail product is the pack itself, and the decision of whether or not to purchase is frequently influenced or even determined by the packaging. The pack also goes with the product into the home, where it continues to communicate messages to the consumer about the product we are selling.

The need to ensure that our packaging is effective leads to an examination

(continued)

EXHIBIT 7. (continued)

of the role that consumer feedback can play, both as an aid to marketing and the designer in developing new packages and as a management tool for assessing the effectiveness of different pack designs. This is why management in Vevey has asked the Marketing Research Service to prepare the present guidelines on packaging research.

These guidelines, which have been developed in close collaboration with the Marketing Packaging Service at Vevey, set forth a series of general principles on the uses as well as the limitations of research in packaging and present a number of recommended methods for conducting packaging research.

It is the view of management at Vevey that consumer feedback, if applied correctly, can play an important role in the development and evaluation of packaging. Thus, this policy and method paper should be a useful tool for you and your staff in your efforts to maximize the effectiveness of the packaging supports for your brands.

Table of Contents

Page

Part 1: Policy Section
When to consider packaging research and when not 2
Link with advertising research.. 4
Predesign research 6
Communication research 7
Summary of key principles 8
Part 2: Methods Section
Predesign research methods.. 10
Communication research methods... 11
Package handling research methods 15
Shelf impact research methods 16
Package design briefing form...................................... Appendix

This document is one in a series of marketing research related policy guidelines. Earlier publications are:

No. 1 Management Paper on Test Marketing
No. 2 Standardized Questions for Concept and Product Testing
No. 3 Management Paper on Advertising Research
No. 4 Technical Paper on Advertising Research Methods
No. 5 Technical Paper on Marketing Research Report Standards
No. 6 Technical Paper on Marketing Research Supplier Standards
No. 7 Policy and Method Paper on Sales Promotion Research

worked primarily for the product directors and, on occasion, directly for the operating companies. They also contributed to the development of branding policies at the Center.

The *Marketing Research Manager* estimated that 20% of his time was spent providing direct technical assistance to the local markets. In the future he expected to reduce that level of commitment by concentrating his assistance on research methodology and the organization of the marketing research function rather than on what specific research should be done. He spent 30% of his time working with product directors on special projects and an increasing proportion of his time upgrading local technical skills, both through training of local personnel and through development and dissemination of technical guidelines (see *Exhibit 7*).

The *Sales Force and Trade Services Manager* provided advice to the markets on sales force management. He was often consulted on whether a product line in a country warranted a separate product division and was also involved in sales training in smaller markets. In addition, he followed the comparative evolution of distribution channels and the progressive concentration of the trade across markets.

The *Consumer Services Manager* worked to develop and enhance the effectiveness of Nestlé home economists employed by the country organizations.

THE STANDARDIZATION DEBATE

The appropriate role of the Center in influencing and directing marketing policies and programs executed by the country organizations was discussed frequently at Vevey. Most Nestlé executives believed that the country managers had to have decision-making authority commensurate with their profit responsibility. However, many also expressed concern that the autonomy of the country organizations reduced Nestlé's ability to capitalize on the size and collective wisdom of the corporation. In discussing the role of the Center and the implementation of its policies and proposals, Robin, Mueller, and Freeman recalled the following four situations:

1. In the 1950s, the country manager in France decided to introduce an instant potato line under a new premium quality brand name, Mousline, rather than under the Maggi brand. He argued that although Maggi was well established, its image in France was old. The line was successful and introduced later under the Maggi brand in West Germany with the same positive result.

2. In the late 1970s, the Center sought to standardize the packaging of Nescafe in Europe. Nescafe was roasted and blended in individual markets to suit local tastes. However, the product director at the Center thought the brand's franchise in Europe would be strengthened if all European countries used the same package, label design, and visual advertising concept. Most European country managers accepted the proposed changes; a few, including the French and German managers, declined.

3. The Center proposed a standard European bottle for the original and best-selling Maggi liquid food enhancer.[10] Many countries accepted, but Mueller, then culinary division manager in West Germany where Maggi held a dominant market share, refused, arguing that the existing bottle and package design had almost universal consumer recognition in West Germany.

4. The Maggi logo was presented differently on packages in four contiguous Latin American countries. In 1982, the Center worked with the regional manager to direct all four country managers to change to the standard "talking bubble" Maggi logo which had been developed first for West Germany and was later incorporated into the Maggi packaging design manual.

CULTURAL CONVERGENCE AND TECHNOLOGICAL CHANGE

In considering the arguments for and against greater coordination of marketing plans by the Center, Robin noted that demographic and cultural trends, and therefore the basic factors underlying consumer tastes and preferences, were increasingly converging across national boundaries. Some studies indicated that most countries in Western Europe and North America were experiencing in 1983 a decline of the traditional family and an increase in smaller and single-person households; a dramatic rise in the percentage of women working; low population growth; increasing away-from-home food consumption; and steady but slow increases in the standard of living. They also noted a cultural convergence across these countries, resulting from an increase in travel, migration, and cultural interchange. One advertising agency asserted that the Marlboro cigarette brand had become successful internationally because

---

[10]This product was the liquid equivalent of a spiced bouillon cube used as a seasoning.

a cultural understanding of the American West, stemming from American movies and television shows, existed in most countries.

Many advertising agencies perceived growing opportunities for the development of "global" brands and pointed to the many consumer products such as Marlboro that had been marketed internationally under centralized direction. In launching its highly successful Pampers brand of children's diapers worldwide, Procter & Gamble marketed a standardized product and employed a common packaging design and advertising concept in every country. In 1983, Cadbury Schweppes was employing the "Schwepping" theme, Coca-Cola was employing the "Coke Is It" theme, and Pepsi-Cola was employing the "Pepsi Challenge" theme in almost every country in which their beverages were marketed.

Agency executives further pointed to the spillover of commercial television programming across national borders, particularly in Europe. In 1983, the availability of commercial television in Western Europe varied widely because of differences in public policy. A large percentage of households in smaller countries, such as Belgium, where little commercial television programming was available, watched channels originating in neighboring countries. People were especially likely to view foreign programming from neighboring countries that shared their primary language. For example, 65% of the programming watched in the French-speaking part of Switzerland emanated from France. Such spillover across national boundaries contributed to the occasional conflicts in product positioning discussed earlier. Little data existed, however, measuring the effects of such positioning differences on consumer brand preferences and behavior.

Satellite television was expected to present an additional opportunity to the marketer of a global brand. Satellites would permit the delivery of programs to several countries, and advanced satellites would have the capacity to dub the same program simultaneously in several languages. Many European broadcasting companies had indicated plans to launch satellites in the mid-1980s. Some advertising agencies believed that satellite broadcasting would further break down cultural barriers and offer in Europe the same type of advertising cost efficiencies that network television afforded in the U.S. However, product positioning, packaging, promotion, and perhaps even pricing, would have to be harmonized to take advantage of this new medium. *Exhibit 8* provides data on commercial television penetration, programming, and planned satellite launches in Europe as of 1983.

However, some Nestlé executives, including the Advertising and Promotion Manager, were skeptical of the potential of satellite television

EXHIBIT 8. Television penetration and programming in Western Europe

	Population (000)	Households (000)	Own TV (%)	Own color-TV (%)	No. of TV stations	No. stations advertising allowed	Cable TV penetration % of households end of 1981	Planned satellite project	Projected satellite launch	No. of TV channels
Austria	7,500	2,700	93%	64%	2	1	6	—	—	—
Belgium	9,900	3,300	96	71	5	1	75	—	—	—
Denmark	5,100	2,200	90	67	1	0	51	—	—	—
Finland	4,800	1,700	97	56	2	2	4	—	—	—
France	53,800	19,300	93	56	3	3	3	TDF-1	1985	3
Greece	9,700	2,800	93	14	3	2	0	—	—	—
Ireland	3,400	900	92	60	2	2	18	—	—	—
Italy	56,000	18,400	96	43	4	3	0	L-Sat	1986	5
Luxembourg					5	1		Luxsat	1986	5
Netherlands	14,200	4,800	97	82	2	2	60	—	—	—
Norway	4,100	1,450	93	79	1	0	31	—	—	—
Portugal	9,900	3,000	90	14	2	2	0	—	—	—
Spain	37,700	10,500	94	42	2	2	0	—	—	—
Sweden	8,300	3,300	97	60	2	2	0	Tele-X	1986	3
Switzerland	6,300	2,300	85	69	3	3	46	Tel-Sat	1986	3
United Kingdom	54,500	20,750	98	77	4	2	13	Unisat	1986	2
West Germany	61,700	25,100	98	80	3	2	4	TV-Sat	1985	3

in Europe. Broadcasting in every country in Europe was either highly regulated or actually owned by a nationalized PTT (Post, Telephone & Telegraph) company. Governments had the power to regulate or even proscribe the reception of satellite broadcasting. The development of direct broadcasting systems with an individual reception dish mounted on each home might make such regulation more difficult or unpopular, but the widespread availability of such a system was not expected until the late 1980s. In addition, a satellite system was expensive, with initial capital expenses estimated at $200 million per satellite. Such costs were expected to dissuade some governments and broadcasting companies from carrying out their planned launches.

THE STANDARDIZATION DEBATE: TWO EXAMPLES

Mr. Robin detailed two situations involving the Maggi line of culinary products that illustrated the work of the Center's product directors and the issues involved in the debate over the standardization of marketing policies and programs.

THE MAGGI PRODUCT LINE

As a result of acquisitions, Nestlé marketed five brands of culinary products around the world. The Center had developed a branding policy and packaging guidelines for each. The most important brand, Maggi, had been developed by a Swiss company acquired by Nestlé in 1947. Maggi products were not marketed by all Nestlé operating companies and market shares varied substantially, both overall and item by item, in those countries where the line was available.[11] To accommodate local flavor and taste preferences, 775 different Maggi products were marketed worldwide. Six hundred were marketed in Europe, which accounted for almost three-quarters of total Maggi sales. A selection of Maggi soups and a picture of the standard red and yellow "talking bubble" Maggi logo are shown in *Exhibit 9*. Mr. Freeman suggested that the Maggi line could be broadly divided into two groups of products, a group of mature, standardized, ingredient-type products such as bouillon cubes and seasonings, and a group of more recently introduced sauces and quick-fix recipe-based products.

---

[11]For example, in the U.K., the Crosse & Blackwell brand, acquired by Nestlé in 1960, was Nestlé's principal culinary product line.

EXHIBIT 9. Maggi "talking bubble" logo and the Maggi canned soup product line

ADVERTISING IN MEXICO AND SOUTH AMERICA

In 1979, the Nestlé country manager of Mexico was involved in expanding the Maggi culinary product line, introduced in Mexico 10 years earlier. Nestlé marketed only four Maggi products in Mexico which, with combined sales of $10 million, held only 10% of the packaged culinary products market. Nestlé's market share was well behind that of CPC International's Knorr brand, Maggi's principal competitor worldwide.

The Mexico country manager requested assistance from the Center in further developing the Maggi line. In particular, he wanted an advertising concept that could provide an umbrella theme which would not only build consumer brand recognition for the entire line but also permit focus on specific new products that he intended to introduce.

The Advertising and Promotion Manager at the Center took the lead in handling this request for assistance. He thought of the Maggi "Koch (Cooking) Studio" advertising concept that had proved so successful in West Germany and considered whether it could possibly be successfully adapted for use in Mexico.

Maggi held a 70% share of the West German market for culinary products. Backed by $15 million in advertising, 70 Maggi items accounted for $150 million in sales in West Germany in 1979. The quality image and consumer recognition of the Maggi brand in West Germany was so strong by the mid-1970s that the culinary products division had begun to provide special educational and cooking services to consumers. A Maggi cooking encyclopedia was compiled, and more than 120,000 copies were sold by 1979. Maggi provided a telephone recipe service that consumers could call, changing the recipe twice a day.

The Maggi Koch Studio advertising program was also part of this service. Each Tuesday night, Maggi presented a 60-second commercial educating consumers on how to prepare a particular meal using Maggi products. The commercial always featured the voices of a man and a woman in their thirties or forties, engaged in an easy, upbeat conversation about how to prepare the meal of the week. The man and woman were never shown; only the food, the Maggi products, and the woman's hands appeared. Each week, the television advertisements were supported with complementary full-page recipe ads in family and women's magazines (see *Exhibit 10*). These ads generated extremely high consumer recall and their popularity never faded over a 10-year period. Maggi Koch Studio advertising comprised 30% of the total West German culinary product line advertising budget.

The advertising manager in Vevey believed that this advertising concept might provide an answer for the country manager in Mexico. The concept had proven overwhelmingly successful in West Germany, and it had the flexibility to promote the entire brand while focusing each week on one or two individual products. The Mexico country organization conducted a limited "communications check" of the advertising concept with 30 Mexican housewives. This research indicated high recall and interest.

EXHIBIT 10. Maggi Koch Studio magazine advertisement

Im ZDF-Werbefernsehen
Dienstag, 16. Nov., gegen 18.12 Uhr   **Fernseh Rezepte**   Im ZDF-Werbefernsehen
Dienstag, 9. Nov., gegen 18.48 Uhr

Eine Abwechslung im Koch-Alltag: Herzhaftes Bauern-Gulasch.

Weil gutes Essen nicht immer teuer sein muß, machen Sie doch einmal Schweinegulasch mit roten Bohnen. Und mit Maggi Gulasch Fix ist es einfach gemacht und schmeckt noch mal so gut.

Damit gelingt's immer:
Maggi Gulasch Fix. Da ist alles drin, was dran gehört.

Zutaten für 4 Portionen:
1 Beutel Maggi Gulasch Fix, ⅜ l Wasser, 100 g geräucherter, durchwachsener Speck, 500 g Schweinegulasch, ½ Dose rote Bohnen, gehackte Petersilie.

Zubereitung:
Maggi Gulasch Fix in warmes Wasser einrühren, zum Kochen bringen und den gewürfelten Speck mit dem Gulasch hineingeben. Kurz aufkochen, 45 Minuten schmoren. Die abgetropften Bohnen zufügen und alles noch 15 Minuten schmoren lassen. Am Ende das fertige Gericht mit gehackter Petersilie bestreuen.
1 Portion ca. 3040 kJ/723 kcal.

Der Kochstudio-Tip:
Stromersparnis beim Kochen: Topf und Plattendurchmesser stimmen überein: ca. 30 %.
Deckel auf Topf: bis 6 %!

Gemüse im Winter: Deftiges Gemüseallerlei.

Dieses Rezept sorgt dafür, daß Sie gerade im Winter Geschmack finden an Gemüse. Der kleine Kniff bei der Zubereitung: mit Maggi Instant Klare Brühe aus dem Glas wird alles fein gewürzt.

Maggi Instant Klare Brühe aus dem Glas würzt und gibt einen feinen Geschmack.

Zutaten für 4 Portionen:
500 g Möhren, 4 Zwiebeln, 500 g Rosenkohl, 50 g geräucherter, durchwachsener Speck, 1 EL. Gänseschmalz, 3 KL Instant Klare Brühe, ⅛ l Wasser, 1 Apfel (Cox-Orange).

Zubereitung:
Möhren und Zwiebeln putzen bzw. schälen und in Scheiben schneiden. Rosenkohl putzen, waschen, Stiel kreuzweise einschneiden. Speck in Würfel schneiden, in Gänseschmalz auslassen und die Zwiebelscheiben darin anbraten. Möhren und Rosenkohl zufügen und mit Instant Klare Brühe bestreuen und alles bei geringer Wärmezufunr 15 Minuten kochen. Apfel schälen, halbieren, Kerngehäuse entfernen, Apfel in Würfel schneiden und weitere 5 Minuten kochen.
1 Portion ca. 1105 kJ/265 kcal.

Der Kochstudio-Tip:
Frischer Rosenkohl wird gleichmäßiger gar, wenn der Strunk kreuzweise eingeschnitten wird.

After considerable debate, the Mexico organization decided to devote all its 1980 culinary advertising budget to television and magazine advertisements based on the Koch Studio concept, to be known in Mexico as "Momentos Maggi." A magazine advertisement from the campaign is presented as *Exhibit 11.* Having developed several Spanish language commercials, the manager of advertising in Vevey then considered whether to suggest this approach to other Nestlé organizations in South America. He wanted to develop the technical competence of Zone III managers in using videotape rather than film in television commercial production. One way to promote an understanding of both videotape technology and the Momentos Maggi concept would be for a team from Vevey to travel to the major Nestlé operating companies in South America to prepare, in conjunction with country organizations and their advertising agencies, Momentos Maggi commercials on videotape. The commercials would differ in each country depending on the local recipes sold under the Maggi brand.

5 MINUTEN TERRINE, BOLINO, AND QUICK LUNCH

In 1978, Mr. Freeman had identified a new product concept: instant noodles that could be sold with different sauces and recipes, packaged in a cup from which the heated product could be eaten directly. Mr. Freeman had noticed the product in the Orient, where the noodles were fried and then dried, both to suit local tastes and to provide sufficient shelf life. A Nestlé RECO devised a way to dry the noodles for long shelf life without frying, thus better suiting Western tastes. The product was ready for launch in 1981.

The culinary product director selected West Germany as the prime-mover market, and the country manager agreed to invest in its launch. The noodles, topped with different recipes of traditional German and Italian sauces and spices, were packaged in a double-walled bowl, shaped like a formal German terrine. The consumer had to peel back an aluminum lid, pour in boiling water, let the noodles absorb the water for five minutes, and then consume the product. The double-walled package was designed to retain the heat from the boiling water so that the noodles could rehydrate without the lid having to be placed back on and so that the consumer could hold the package comfortably.

The culinary product division in West Germany positioned 5 Minuten Terrine as good nutritious food that was also convenient. Women and men in their thirties and forties offered testimonials in television advertisements, backed by lighthearted jingles. The advertisements emphasized that the product was made by Maggi, building on the strength

EXHIBIT 11. "Momentos Maggi" magazine advertisement

of the brand name. The launch proved successful, and 40 million units were sold in the first year, exceeding break-even.

In 1981, the Nestlé organization in France decided to launch the product. However, the French culinary product division manager decided to use a new brand name, Bolino, designed to be short and easy to remember, to conjure up a bowl in the consumer's mind, and to sound Italian, since French consumers were believed to associate pasta with that country. Although the West German organization was willing and able to supply packages as well as the noodles, the French product manager and packaging manager decided to package the noodles in a single-wall, wide-mouthed bowl, which was cheaper but could not be held by the consumer while the noodles absorbed the water. French market research indicated that consumers saw no special benefit in being able to do this, and were willing to place the lid back on the bowl while the noodles were rehydrating. The product, in four new recipes, was positioned as a convenient instant snack for young, single consumers. The Maggi brand name was downplayed on the package and in the advertising.[12] The product was also successful in France, selling 13 million units in its first year, slightly exceeding break-even.

At the end of 1981, the Swiss organization introduced the product with the brand name Quick Lunch. The Swiss product was manufactured in West Germany and was packaged in the terrine-style bowl. The Swiss advertisements also emphasized the Maggi brand and positioned the product as good, nutritious food endorsed by homemakers and mothers. The Austrian and Norwegian organizations were next to introduce the product, and also used packages made in Germany. Like the Swiss, they expected to sell about 3 million units annually. Pictures of the West German, French, and Swiss packages are presented in *Exhibit 12*. Transcripts of the television commercials used in the three countries are presented in *Exhibit 13*.

In 1982, Knorr introduced in France a similar noodle-based product packed not in a bowl but in a unit-size cellophane packet at a price 20% below Bolino on a per-serving basis. Early in 1983, both France and West Germany sought assistance from the Center for improvements in their packaging. The French package had faulty lamination that attracted dust and detracted from the product's appearance on the store shelves. The French country organization intended to use new lamination, but it would increase the cost of the package which already accounted for 20% of cost of goods sold.[13] France asked for assistance in selecting the spec-

---

[12]Maggi held a 30% share of the culinary product market in France, second to Knorr.

[13]The current package cost was equivalent to about 10 cents in U.S. currency.

EXHIBIT 12. 5 Minuten Terrine, Bolino, and Quick Lunch packages

EXHIBIT 13. 1982 advertisements for 5 Minuten Terrine, Bolino, and Quick Lunch

---

5 Minuten Terrine (translated from German)

Video	Audio	
Man (in his 40s) singing and smiling, holding a cup of 5 Minuten Terrine.	*Man singing:* *(the jingle rhymes)*	5 Minuten Terrine by Maggi — I'll do it myself.
		If I go on a break far from home, then wait and I'm going to get it.
		5 Minuten Terrine, that's a great idea.
Woman (in her 30s) singing while holding a cup.	*Woman singing:* *(same jingle music)*	The 5 Minuten Terrine. You add water and good appetite!
		5 Minuten Terrine from Maggi.

Bolino (translated from French)

Two young women in early 20s moving in unison — having fun.	*Women singing:* *(in rhyme)*	When you don't want to prepare the food . . .
Two young men in early 20s moving in unison — having fun.	*Men singing:* *(in rhyme)*	You can still give yourself a nice little meal.
All four together.	*Together singing:*	Today, Bolino, Bolino.
The women pouring water into the Bolino package.	*Women singing:*	It's new. It's easy to prepare Bolino.
The men holding the package with fork in hand.	*Men singing:*	Five minutes to prepare it. It tastes good.
Close up to the Bolino dish.	*Announcer:* *(music overlay)*	It's already precooked the Napolitaine (from Naples) way.
		A good dish of precooked pasta already completely prepared.
		It's nutritious food, with cheese and fine herbs.
Close-up of the two women singing and smiling.	*Women singing:*	Bolino, Bolino.

(continued)

EXHIBIT 13. (continued)

Close-up of package with Maggi logo.	*Announcer:*	A little dish when you're on the run.

Quick Lunch (translated from French)*

Shot of the Quick Lunch package.	*Announcer:*	Quick Lunch.
Three women eating Quick Lunch.		Suddenly everybody is eating Quick Lunch.
Scene of man eating Quick Lunch with woman (wife) standing behind.		Quick Lunch, a completely new type of food. Quick Lunch from Maggi.
Shot of pouring boiling water into package.		Add a little bit of boiling water. Stir. Wait for five minutes and it is ready.
Shot of hand holding the package, stirring the noodles with a fork.		Quick Lunch is prepared in a bowl and can be eaten in the same bowl.
Shot of the package.		Quick Lunch. The little hot dish. Completely new.
		The best pasta with five different sauces. Quick Lunch from Maggi.

*Identical ads were shown in German in the German-speaking part of Switzerland.

ifications for the lamination and in finding ways to lower the cost of the package, such as through the use of a new lid made of paper and aluminum rather than aluminum alone.

West Germany also asked for assistance to lower the cost of its package which accounted for 30% of variable cost.[14] The retail price of the product was approaching the price point of two Deutschemarks beyond which the local culinary product division manager believed many consumers would not be willing to buy it.

Mr. Freeman was working with technicians at the Center to devise ways to lower the costs of these packages. They had determined that a single-walled bowl similar to the German package with an outer cardboard sleeve that could be changed to carry the appropriate labeling information for each country could be made at a unit cost 20% below

---

[14]Equivalent to about 12 cents in U.S. currency.

EXHIBIT 14. Planning chart for Nestlé Center involvement in international marketing

Elements of marketing function	No HQ initiative	HQ promotes cross-fertilization among countries	HQ persuasion for standardization	HQ decision making	HQ enforced standardization
Marketing strategy					
Product positioning					
Product characteristics					
Branding					
Packaging					
Distribution					
Trade promotion					
Consumer promotion					
Media advertising					

that for the existing German bowl. Although there were no significant economies of scale to producing a single package beyond 10 million cups, Mr. Freeman wondered whether he should use this opportunity to influence the three country organizations to accept a common package design. While watching television at home in Vevey, he had seen advertisements for all three products.

CONCLUSION

Nestlé executives periodically reviewed how much influence the Center should have over the local markets. Some argued that Nestlé could achieve greater efficiency and significant economies of scale if marketing policies were more coordinated, if not directed from the Center, with country organizations being given the opportunity to "opt out" with appropriate justification, rather than "opt in."

Robin wondered whether coordination by the Center was more feasible and productive for some elements of the marketing mix than others, for some product categories more than others, and in some countries more than others. He also noted that the level of headquarters intervention could vary. It could range from cross-fertilization of ideas and experiences, through headquarters efforts to persuade the country organizations to follow standard programs, to headquarters control of local decisions through enforced standardization. Robin wondered under what circumstances each of these approaches was more appropriate. Mulling over this question, he developed the chart shown in *Exhibit 14.*

3.4 _CASE_

Chandler Home Products

*Michael Y. Yoshino and
Yaakov Keren*

As Antonio (Tony) Pesci, General Manager of Chandler Home Products Italia, left the offices of his Torino-based headquarters on a rainy April night in 1976, he pondered how he might best present the delicate issue of sourcing alternatives to the European management of Chandler. Pesci firmly believed that the existing practice of total centralized sourcing from Chandler's Complant[1] located in Nijmegen, The Netherlands, no longer made economic sense in the Italian environment. Then too, he was convinced that the use of the transfer pricing system currently employed with Complant production and other cost-related accounting practices had unfairly represented the performance of the Italian subsidiary, especially following the recent precipitous drop in the value of the Italian lira (see *Exhibit 1*).

---

[1]Common Market Plant.

EXHIBIT 1. Exchange rates (# of local currency = US $1) end of year or month

	1971	1972	1973	1974	1975	J' 76	F' 76	M' 76	A' 76
Netherlands/Guilders	3.254	3.226	2.824	2.507	2.688	2.666	2.676	2.686	2.686
Italy/Lira	594.00	582.50	607.92	649.43	683.55	751.10	766.90	840.28	896.92
Exchange Guilder–Lira	183	181	215	259	254	282	287	313	334

Source: Bulletin Mensuel de Statistique United Nations, Juillet, 1976

Minutes earlier he had completed an intense round of day-long discussions with his Chandler Italia staff. These talks were in preparation for next week's scheduled meeting with Pierre Genet, Executive Vice-President and Director of Chandler Europe (see *Exhibit 2*). Genet, already familiar with the general outline of CI's claims, had temporarily placed both CI and Complant in a direct reporting relationship to him. As budgets for the rapidly approaching new fiscal year were being finalized, it was expected that he would shortly respond to the Italian proposals. Despite the beating of windshield wipers and the reflection of street lights against newly formed puddles, Pesci's mind reviewed the day's discussions in light of the future of CI and his own career.

CHANDLER HOME PRODUCTS

Chandler Home Products was a privately owned, family controlled corporation. Headquartered in Peoria, Illinois, Chandler's lines of household care products were marketed worldwide. Though no company figures were released, industry observers estimated Chandler's 1975/76 sales at nearly $800 million from the approximately 1,500 different items sold in 47 countries. More than half its sales were made outside the USA. Of these, a majority were recorded in Europe.

The bulk of the company's business was concentrated in four product areas: floor care products, furniture polish, air fresheners, and insecticides. Chandler's strategy had always been to secure a dominant position in each category while selling a heavily advertised, premium priced product. The resulting high gross margins (60% was not unusual) were needed to finance the costs of advertising and channel support while still providing adequate returns.

In recent years attempts had been made to diversify into the personal care field with deodorants and shaving gels. Household care products had also been extended into laundry additives. Broadening the company's offerings was largely seen as an effort to become less dependent upon the traditional household care products. The latter markets were mature with dimming prospects for substantial growth. In addition, the large market shares which Chandler commanded in its traditional product lines were thought likely to be the target of increasing competitive assault. Competing in new markets, however, frequently pitted Chandler against such international giants as Procter & Gamble, Unilever, and Gillette.

EXHIBIT 2. Chandler European organization

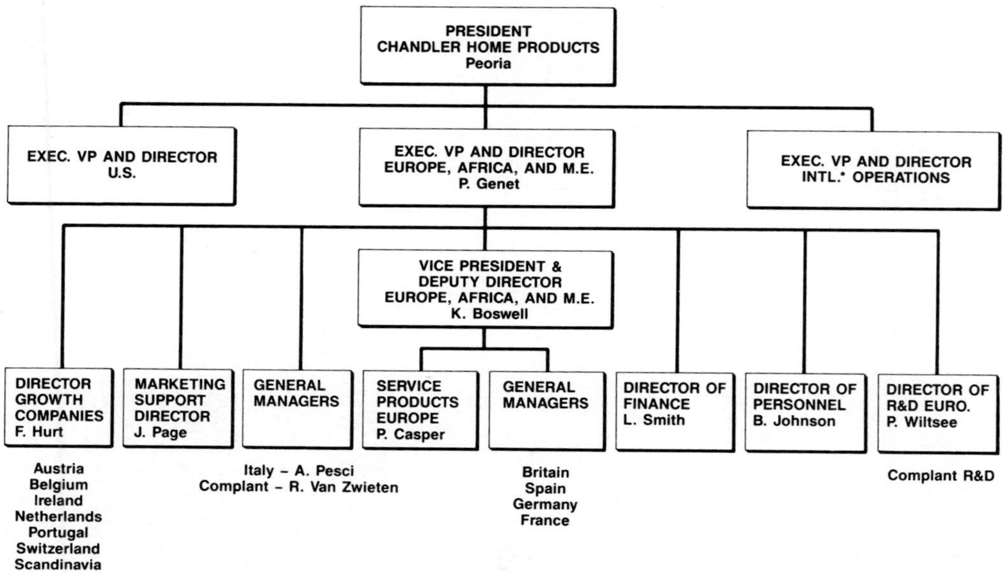

PRESIDENT
CHANDLER HOME PRODUCTS
Peoria

EXEC. VP AND DIRECTOR
U.S.

EXEC. VP AND DIRECTOR
EUROPE, AFRICA, AND M.E.
P. Genet

EXEC. VP AND DIRECTOR
INTL.* OPERATIONS

VICE PRESIDENT &
DEPUTY DIRECTOR
EUROPE, AFRICA, AND M.E.
K. Boswell

DIRECTOR
GROWTH
COMPANIES
F. Hurt

Austria
Belgium
Ireland
Netherlands
Portugal
Switzerland
Scandinavia

MARKETING
SUPPORT
DIRECTOR
J. Page

GENERAL
MANAGERS

Italy – A. Pesci
Complant – R. Van Zwieten

SERVICE
PRODUCTS
EUROPE
P. Casper

GENERAL
MANAGERS

Britain
Spain
Germany
France

DIRECTOR OF
FINANCE
L. Smith

DIRECTOR OF
PERSONNEL
B. Johnson

DIRECTOR OF
R&D EURO.
P. Wiltsee

Complant R&D

399

CHANDLER EUROPE

The decade of the '60s witnessed a significant expansion of the Chandler presence in Europe. While some European subsidiaries actually predated World War II, none had represented a major source of revenues until this growth period. Subsequently older subsidiaries grew in size and new subsidiaries rapidly blossomed throughout Western Europe. At that time Chandler decided to centralize its production for its EEC member subsidiaries under a single roof, much as U.S. production was centralized in Peoria. Until then all production had been done on the country level. Constructed in 1962, the Nijmegen site (Complant) was capable of producing all aerosol and liquid product requirements for the EEC subsidiaries.

It was believed that Complant would provide both better quality control and the economies of scale resulting from concentrated production. The former objective was important due to the rapid proliferation of aerosol products in the Chandler line which typically complicated quality control. Then, too, aerosols demanded capital-intensive production lines[2] which complemented the objective of scale economies by requiring high utilization for economic use. In addition, centralized purchasing promised significant cost advantages in a production process in which nearly three-quarters of the full costs (including overheads) were the cost of raw material and packaging. Complant was also envisioned as a central warehouse facility and as a center for research, development, and other technical services to be provided individual European subsidiaries.

Overseas sales while generally anchored upon products developed at Peoria frequently differed as to the product mix of sales. Even neighboring European subsidiaries often significantly differed as to the relative popularity of Chandler products in the diverse product categories in which they competed. Products were adapted to local consumers by means of local brand names and even ingredients specifically designed for local needs. Thus a country's income level distribution or its home furnishing styles had substantial influence upon the product offerings of the local Chandler subsidiary. Some foreign subsidiaries even sold products which had been developed for their own use and which were unavailable in the U.S. These products, too, were generally manufactured at Complant.

Therefore country managers had considerable autonomy in deter-

---

[2]By 1976 an aerosol line cost upwards of $2 million, while a comparable volume liquid line cost only a fraction of that.

mining their product lines. They could add, drop, position, or emphasize products according to their perception of local market conditions. Complant functioned strictly as a service arm designed to provide subsidiaries with their product requests. Despite this relative freedom, country managers had to justify particular product decisions (e.g., dropping a product, an unusual pricing strategy, etc.) before Mr. Genet. In such cases Genet could seek the advice of such European staff members as the Household Marketing Support Director, the Director of Service Products, or the Director of R&D Europe.

CHANDLER ITALIA

Founded by a licensee in 1960, Chandler Italia was taken over by the parent company while still in the early '60s. After a couple of years of small losses following the takeover, the company successfully launched in 1965 a furniture polish called ANTICA (in the U.S., GLOW). For the next decade this product would account for a substantial share of total company contribution.

In 1967 local manufacturing was discontinued in Italy. Instead, CI began to source exclusively from Chandler's Complant in Holland which had been in operation for several years already. CI's yearly sales figures prior to 1967, while steadily climbing, nonetheless had not yet approached $1 million per annum. With the successful launch of ANTICA and bright prospects for rapid growth horizontally into other traditional Chandler product categories, however, the benefits of centralized sourcing seemed alluring.

Tony Pesci took over the helm at CI in 1971. In the mid-'60s Pesci had left Italy to study in the United States at a well-known Eastern business school. Upon graduation he accepted a position as marketing manager of the Brazilian subsidiary of Chandler Home Products. Within a short time he was promoted to General Manager of that operation. His meteoric rise continued with his transfer back to his native Italy as General Manager of Chandler Home Products Italia.

After Pesci's ascension to the head of CI, turnover skyrocketed, as sales increased threefold within three years (see *Exhibit 3*). From virtually a one-product subsidiary (ANTICA), Pesci succeeded in enlarging its presence in other product categories (see *Exhibit 4*). Insecticides, air fresheners, floor waxes, and deodorants were among major market segments in which new CI products competed vigorously. The costs associated with launching these generally premium-priced lines and surfacing competitive pressures restricted advances in profits.

By 1976/77 CI's sales were expected to reach $33 million, making it

EXHIBIT 3. Operating performance of Chandler Italia

	1970–1	1971–2	1972–3	1973–4	1974–5
Sales (net)	5898	9651	11,870	16,472	17,673
Cost of sales	2061	3601	4147	6907	7580
Advert. & pro.	1366	2492	3434	4036	4572
Freight	206	260	328	559	586
Net profit	692	469	552	783	(464)

All numbers in local currency (000,000 omitted).

the third largest Chandler subsidiary in Europe and the second largest user of aerosols from Complant. CI's product mix was heavily weighted toward aerosols (80%) as opposed to the customary roughly equal split between liquids and aerosols. This preponderance of aerosols was expected to remain as CI believed that Italian acceptance of premium-priced household products was best in an aerosol form.

Parallel to the introduction of new products Pesci had consistently rationalized his existing lines, pruning low-volume products. By 1976 CI's product offerings were among the most rationalized of any Chandler European subsidiary. Chandler service products which were sold to industry and which accounted for about 10% of both CI and total European turnover, indeed, had become increasingly rationalized across European borders having generally a single name and package. Rationalization of consumer products, however, remained on a national basis. Recently CI had participated in some simultaneous launchings of new consumer products across national borders, yet even then the number of Complant product codes[3] quickly multiplied to meet the tastes of the fickle consumer in different countries.

BUSINESS CONDITIONS IN ITALY

Following World War II, Italy's transition to an industrialized society encountered serious problems. While wage rates were considerably lower than most other Western nations, frequent labor strikes and high

---

[3]Every variation in container size, shape, material, or label or ingredient composition required a separate product code. Manufacture of a specific product code required a set-up of a few minutes to several hours. In addition, inventories were maintained by product codes.

EXHIBIT 4. Retail price and market share information of selected products

Product category	Price per oz. compared to competition	Market shares		Change in market share	Market position
		units/kg	Lira		
1) Furniture waxes (ANTICA)	Premium priced (25–60% higher)	49.6%	71.2%	Increase	1
2) Spray starch (AMIDORISSO)	Slightly higher than competition	44.6	48.3	Decrease	1
3) Air freshener (PINETA)	Premium priced (20% higher)	17.1	24.2	Decrease	2
4) Fabric care (CARINA)	About 15% higher	8.4	11.9	Stable	3
5) Insecticides (FLIT)	20% higher	6.1	8.2	Decrease	4
6) Floor wax (BRIO, TORNA)	Slightly higher than competition	7.6	8.8	Stable	3
7) Deodorant (HAWAII)	Competitive	2.1	2.2	Increase	7

Size of market

Less than 5 billion Lira − spray starch, fabric care

5 to 15 billion Lira − furniture waxes, air freshener

15 to 30 billion Lira − insecticides, floor wax

More than 30 billion Lira − deodorant

rates of absenteeism often negated this business advantage. The post-war period witnessed continual political instability while government after government collapsed without executing the long overdue reforms needed to deal with the country's economic problems. The labor unrest and lack of political stability were potent disincentives to investment, thus hampering industrial growth.

The 1973 OPEC price hike ended the era of cheap energy for Italy, which imported over 90% of its energy requirements. During the world-wide recession of 1975 Italy was hit particularly hard. Real GNP declined nearly 4%, industrial production dropped nearly 10% (back to 1971 level), and inflation continued at a high level (see *Exhibit 5*).

The difficulties of operating in Italy were impressed upon the CI management soon after the oil price hike had its impact on Western Europe. Increased manufacturing costs in Nijmegen, coupled with in-

EXHIBIT 5. Index of prices (1970 = 100) (average of year or month)

	1971	1972	1973	1974	1975	J' 76	F' 76	M' 76
Italy								
General wholesale price index	102.7	106.8	125.9	177.2	192.4	202.4	208.7	218.2
Raw material wholesale index	105.7	105.5	123.7	274.0	290.4	303.0	312.3	
Chemical products wholesale index				178.0	185.9	191.8	199.2	204.5
Personal hygiene & health products consumer price index				127.4	144.0	149.4	152.4	154.7
Manufactured products consumer price index				151.3	173.0	180.9	183.4	188.5
Netherlands								
General wholesale price index	100.9	104.5	117.7	134.0	143.2	157.4	161.4	163.6
Raw material wholesale index	105.8	107.4	122.2	155.0	168.8	180.4		
Chemical products wholesale index				140.3	151.8	153.7	154.4	154.7
Personal hygiene & health products consumer price index				175.5	206.7	221.6	222.2	222.2
Manufactured products consumer price index				136.2	150.0	154.6	156.1	157.7

Source: 1. Bulletin Mensuel de Statistiques Générales, Eurostat 1/6, 1976. 2. Bulletin Mensuel de Statistiques, United Nations, Juillet, 1976.

flation and devaluation in Italy, caused price lists to be revised almost monthly in early 1974. Nonetheless strong demand for Chandler products continued, which led by June to a 40% increase in monthly unit sales as compared to the previous year. CI management believed that a recent advertising and promotional campaign to relaunch ANTICA was responsible for the surge in sales. Indeed, a Nielsen survey of Chandler's retailers indicated that their inventory levels were normal (see *Exhibit 6* for typical Nielsen data), thus indicating, they thought, that the "pull" of the campaign had succeeded.

In the summer of 1974 the Bank of Italy began to apply tough credit measures in order to stem inflation and a worsening B-O-P deficit. Among these was an import deposit scheme which required that importers deposit 50% of the value of their imports with the Bank for six months without interest. Soon afterward Chandler Italia's sales began to plummet. At first CI believed that the slowdown in sales could have been just a cyclical downturn in an industry in which deals, advertising, and some seasonal products make such movements common. The drop in sales, however, continued into the winter. It soon became apparent to CI that during the summer its wholesalers had stockpiled literally months of Chandler products in order to accrue inventory gains as prices went up. The Bank of Italy's decree, though, placed these wholesalers, who imported many items directly, in a severe liquidity bind. These wholesalers then proceeded to reduce inventories to an absolute minimum, waiting hopefully for the repeal of the import deposit.

CI'S ORGANIZATION AND CONTROL SYSTEM

As elsewhere in the Chandler family the General Manager of Chandler Italia had considerable latitude in running his subsidiary. Certainly he had to shape his budget within the general guidelines that Chandler Europe suggested, nevertheless CI had substantial discretion in regard to the pricing, advertising level, and promotional expenditure of individual products. Corporate expectations were summarized in a yearly fiscal budget (July 1-June 30) which was then broken into monthly budgets (see *Exhibit 7*). Similarly, a three-year subsidiary plan was drawn to project the annual progression of CI's operations. In addition, projections were made by product or product group, including new product introductions. Cash flow forecasts informed Chandler Europe of future CI cash generation.

Tony Pesci not only occupied the position of General Manager but also acted as Marketing Manager (see *Exhibit 8*). In his role as General

EXHIBIT 6. Sample Nielsen data

Type of floors in Italian homes	
Wood	6.4
Ceramic	13.8
Tiled	58.6
Marble	10.2
Linoleum	1.1
Carpet	2.0
Brick	4.2
Cement	1.7
No indication	2.0

Base: 1053 interviews

Progression of sales in 1,000 kilos — Convenience Floor Wax

Period	Total Italy	BRIO	Other products
N/D '73	629	78	551
J/F '74	745	103	642
M/A	915	133	782
M/J	1024	137	887
Total half year	2684	373	2311
J/A	863	125	738
S/O	896	142	754
N/D	902	128	774
Total half year	2661	395	2266
Total year	5345	768	4577
± preceding year	+21.6%	+9.8%	+23.8%

(continued)

Manager he had financial, marketing, and miscellaneous operations-related staff members reporting directly to him. This staff usually had a dotted-line reporting relationship to their counterparts at Chandler Europe (i.e., Financial Manager and Director of Finance Europe). As Marketing Manager Pesci had several product or product group managers reporting to him. These managers had the responsibility of coordinating their marketing activities with the other staff departments.

While no fixed performance evaluation system was used at CI, it was widely believed that adhering to budget was a key indicator of per-

EXHIBIT 6. (continued)

Progression of sales in million Lira — Regular Floor Wax

Period	Total Italy	TORNA	Other products
J/A '71	1625	147	1478
S/O	1815	175	1640
N/D	1793	149	1644
Total half year	5233	471	4762

Regular Floor Wax + Convenience Floor Wax
(% composition by kilo sales)

% of Italy	Area 1 37.2		Area 2 24.0		Area 3 21.9		Area 4 16.9	
Period	R	C	R	C	R	C	R	C
J/F '75	67.3	32.7	74.2	25.8	69.8	30.2	46.5	53.5
M/A	65.4	34.6	75.6	24.4	57.7	42.3	48.2	51.8
M/J	68.1	31.9	69.8	30.2	58.4	41.6	41.8	58.2
J/A	67.2	32.8	72.7	27.3	53.5	46.5	39.3	60.7

formance. There was no direct monetary compensation system for superior performance except for the sales staff.

MARKETING

Since Chandler Italia was to all interests a marketing subsidiary only, all of its efforts were funneled in that direction. While marketing responsibility was largely decentralized, individual subsidiaries could and did receive comparative marketing information from Chandler Europe.

CI's product line strategy had progressed in three directions:

1. Maintenance of dominant yet mature products — relaunchings, formula changes, etc. (e.g., ANTICA).
2. Introduction of new products in familiar product categories — new formulas, specialty segmentation, etc. (e.g., solid PINETA air freshener, BRIO convenience floor wax).
3. Introduction of new products in new product categories — (e.g., HAWAII deodorant in personal care category).

EXHIBIT 7. Monthly subsidiary (CI) reporting form

No.	Description (in local currency 000 omitted)	Month of March 1976						Year-to-date 75/76					
		Actual		Budget		Last year		Actual		Budget		Last year	
		Amt.	% NS	Amt.	% NS	Amt.	% NS	Amt.	% NS	Amt.	% NS	Amt.	% NS
30-00	*Gross sales*	2,329,822	102.1	2,192,184	105.0	1,498,264	103.9	19,134,851	106.5	17,286,756	105.9	12,821,642	105.1
31-10	Less: returns	47,225	2.1	62,649	3.0	49,207	3.4	740,921	4.2	652,947	4.0	340,202	2.8
31-20	allowances	703	—	41,712	2.0	6,903	0.5	404,587	2.2	310,141	1.9	270,099	2.2
31-30	cash disc.	511	—	—	—	109	—	19,722	0.1	—	—	11.632	0.1
31-40	sales & turn. tax	2	—	—	—	20	—	160	—	—	—	240	—
	Total sales ded.	48,441	2.1	104,361	5.0	56,239	3.9	1,165,440	6.5	963,088	5.9	622,173	5.1
	Net sales	2,281,381	100.0	2,087,769	100.0	1,442,025	100.0	17,969,411	100.0	16,323,668	100.0	12,199,469	100.0
41-00	*Cost of sales*	1,085,960	47.6	855,985	41.0	607,429	42.1	8,323,653	46.3	6,774,322	41.5	5,263,931	43.0
	Gross profit	1,195,421	52.4	1,231,784	59.0	834,596	57.9	9,645,758	53.7	9,549,346	58.5	6,935,508	57.0
	Expenses:												
62-00	Sales force	229,096	10.4	232,146	11.1	190,684	13.2	1,930,340	10.7	2,018,250	12.4	1,695,725	13.9
63-00	Marketing admin.	61,346	2.7	44,662	2.1	32,987	2.3	471,403	2.6	439,219	2.7	315,961	2.6
64-00	Warehousing	27,884	1.2	24,209	1.2	15,798	1.1	228,028	1.3	199,754	1.2	170,236	1.4
65-00	Advertising	390,801	17.1	296,417	14.2	239,717	16.6	2,665,251	14.8	2,210,350	13.5	2,072,120	16.7
66-00	Promotion deals	188,625	8.3	150,151	7.2	112,333	7.8	1,412,210	7.9	1,319,267	8.1	1,235,033	10.1
	Total mkt. exp.	897,752	39.4	747,585	35.8	591,519	41.0	6,707,232	37.3	6,186,840	37.9	5,489,075	45.0
67-00	Sales freight	88,974	3.9	66,212	3.2	45,040	3.1	651,511	3.6	542,169	3.3	420,203	3.4

Merchand. profit	208,695	9.1	417,987	20.0	198,037	13.7	2,287,015	12.7	2,820,337	17.3	1,026,230	8.4
77–00 Research & dev.	2,824	0.1	3,610	0.2	2,253	0.2	32,145	0.2	34,767	0.2	29,821	0.2
82–00 Financial	46,360	2.0	49,265	2.4	40,219	2.8	349,032	1.9	326,219	2.0	358,953	2.9
83–00 Admin. mgement.	30,241	1.3	22,915	1.1	20,095	1.4	273,793	1.5	258,014	1.6	272,454	2.2
88–00 Service fees	68,441	3.0	62,633	3.0	43,261	3.0	539,082	3.0	489,710	3.0	365,984	3.0
Total expenses	1,134,592	49.7	952,220	45.6	742,387	51.5	8,552,795	47.6	7,837,719	48.0	6,936,490	56.9
Operating profit (loss)	60,829	2.7	279,564	13.4	92,209	6.4	1,092,963	6.1	1,711,627	10.5	(982)	0.0
90–00 Profit sharing	4,814	0.2	8,613	0.4	2,115	0.1	57,748	0.3	69,210	0.4	39,448	0.3
91–00 Other income/ deductions (net)	—	—	—	—	—	—	1,228	—	—	—	963	—
93–00 Interest income/ expense (net)	43,932	1.9	50,000	2.4	39,224	2.7	516,299	2.9	450,000	2.8	301,210	2.5
Profit before income tax	12,083	0.5	220,951	10.6	50,870	3.5	517,688	2.9	1,192,417	7.3	(342,603)	(2.8)
94–00 Income taxes	6,042	0.3	110,476	5.3	25,435	1.8	258,844	1.4	596,209	3.7	—	—
Net profit (loss)	6,041	0.3	110,475	5.3	25,435	1.8	258,844	1.8	596,208	3.7	(342,603)	(2.8)

EXHIBIT 8. Chandler Italia organization

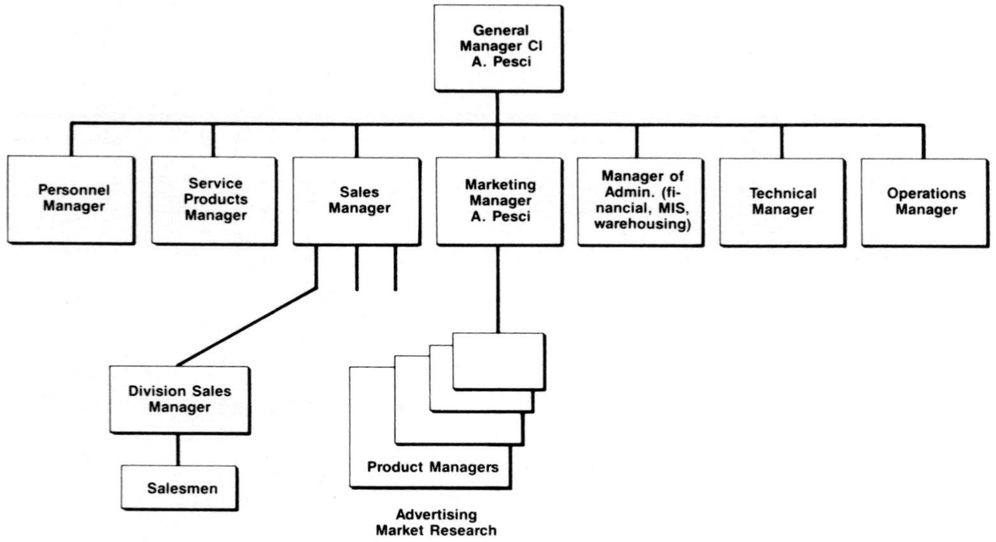

The elements of a marketing strategy in the Italian environment included pricing, promotion and deals, product quality, advertising, and distribution. Since Italy had no government enforced price controls, pricing was subject only to corporate design and competitive pressures. Promotion and deals were aimed mainly at the trade, since it was believed that they didn't actively merchandise household care products nor lower their prices to retailers in response to deals.

In Italy television advertising had to be reserved months in advance. The amount of government-controlled air time was restricted so that requests for increases were usually met only with approval of past allocation levels. Thus marketing staffs had to be extremely flexible to design their campaigns within this constraint and to respond quickly to changes in allocations.

Advertising was believed to be an important tool in CI's product categories. Only 20% of its unit sales were made in large chain stores. Out of the other 80%, which included traditional, small Italian outlets, only 20% was made to stores with self-service operations. Therefore open shelves and price comparisons were not frequent. Customers, consequently, often either requested a specific branded product or left the product choice to the discretion of the owner/operator of the small store.

Until a few years ago, Chandler's competition was very weak. Competitors' products were of substandard quality and their packaging shoddy. This state of the marketplace allowed Chandler to stake out a strong gross margin position on its products. By 1976, though, the locally produced products of competitors had nearly equalled Chandler in quality.

Competition differed as to size and affiliation. One major competitor, Moro Inc., who competed in almost every Chandler category, had begun as the Italian distributor of the products of a large multinational corporation in similar personal and house care products (i.e., dentifrice, deodorants, oven cleaner). Soon Moro began independently to compete in Chandler categories. Another competitor, though small in size, was attached to a corporation partially owned by the government. In insecticides and air fresheners Chandler competed with a local division of a large multinational. The division, though, was quite small. There were other small local companies who competed with one or two Chandler products. The new push into deodorants and other personal care products pitted Chandler against large subsidiaries of multinationals, the only area where Chandler was currently outsized by its competition.

CI's competition relied upon local manufacture either in-house or by local contract fillers. During the past several years price competition had increased in severity. It was not unusual to see some competitive products priced 25–30% lower than similar Chandler products. While inflation in Italy pressed ahead at approximately a 20%/year rate from 1974 onward, wholesale prices in the household care and personal care categories lagged behind significantly. Thus CI felt beleaguered to maintain the current spread.

Apart from those competitors who coupled low price and low advertising expenditures (e.g. Moro), there were others who maintained high advertising budgets and presumably high gross margins. Generally they did not approach, however, the quality of Chandler media presentation.

Chandler product sales were aided by a sales force of nearly 75 salespeople who serviced approximately 25,000 accounts (retail and wholesale). Chandler was thought to have a strong relationship with its retailers and wholesalers. Despite this, Moro, for example, had a larger and seemingly stronger sales force.

SOURCING

Since 1967 CI had sourced all its products from Complant. CI was charged in guilders Complant's fully allocated costs plus a mark-up of 10%.[4]

Complant, which served all of Chandler's EEC subsidiaries except the United Kingdom, had in the early '70s been increased substantially in capacity. Though it produced both liquid and aerosol products, the capacity utilization at Complant between the two types of products differed markedly. Liquid lines were in 1976 nearly at two-shift capacity; aerosol lines had considerable excess capacity. Currently CI took about 35% of the total Complant aerosol output.

Complant's production was recognized as superior in quality and reliability. This was especially important in the aerosol lines, which demanded some technical expertise in their manufacture. Liquid products were generally less complicated, though closures or bottles required some attention in certain solutions (e.g., corrosive).

Due to Complant's large capacity and its strong concentrated buying power with suppliers, unforeseen requirements of individual subsidiaries could usually be met with fairly short notice. On the other hand, CI's relatively long distance from Complant obliged it to hold several

---

[4]The fully allocated costs were based on an assumed 100% capacity utilization. Complant management believed that the Dutch tax authorities would not accept a lower transfer price.

weeks of inventory as a buffer against production or transport difficulties.

THE PROBLEM OF EARLY 1976

In the first four months of 1976 the lira plummeted 30% in relationship to the guilder. Concomitantly the Italian wholesale index, especially in Chandler's segments, lagged far behind (see *Exhibit 1*). The effect upon CI was both severe and immediate. Complant's products, since they were billed in guilders, became rapidly more expensive in translation.

This problem of floating currencies was not new to CI. As early as 1974 CI had expressed its dismay about the cost instability of products from Complant. Some preliminary inspections of sourcing or pricing alternatives had been done. When the lira-guilder rate stabilized in 1975, however, that interest waned. In 1976 this interest was, again, obviously, rekindled.

That evening following the day's meetings Tony Pesci wrote the following memo to Pierre Genet to serve as a basis for their upcoming meeting. Pesci looked forward to seeing Genet again as they had been classmates at the well-known Eastern business school in the United States. Pesci knew, however, that it would take solid justification and not their long-time acquaintance to convince Genet of CI's peculiar difficulties and the needed remedy.

INTERNAL MEMO

From: A. Pesci – Torino   *Date:* April 26, 1976
To: P. Genet – Paris

Re: Strategy for Italy

Dear Pierre:

I am greatly concerned for the future of Chandler Italia. I feel that the important intercompany decisions now under consideration should be made in the best interest of all of Chandler.

Sometimes we say that it is better to make hard Guilder profits than weak Lira profits in Italy. This is a mistake because to buy those hard Guilders in Complant we've had to pay with devaluated Lira, so every conversion gain between Guilder and Dollar is offset simultaneously by an equal conversion loss between Guilder and Lira. In other words, in this exchange nothing is gained by the Corporation.

Apart from this, we have always assumed that inflation differentials between Holland and Italy would balance the effects of the Lira weakening vis-à-vis the Guilder.

The result of this assumption has been that we had thought that the only additional cost Chandler would incur in manufacturing in Nijmegen and shipping the goods to Italy is the extra freight cost. This is a substantial amount, so much so that the nearly 800,000 dollars paid yearly for freight would itself pay for the construction of a liquid filling plant here within a single year. Chandler's belief, however, has always been that the Nijmegen filling lines by virtue of their economies of scale and quality control would more than make up for that freight expenditure.

However, several findings lead me to believe that these arguments are not sound:

1. A cost comparison between Complant and an Italian filler for BRIO and PINETA.
2. An Economic Model Study prepared by Chandler Europe's chief economist.

1. Cost comparison: Complant and Italian filler

	BRIO Liquid Convenience Floor Wax 6143D 850cc x 24 units	
Lira per case	*Complant (March '76)*[a]	*Contract filler*
Raw material	2148	2256
Components and packing	3546	2231
Less allowance (materials)	224	251
Complant — direct labor	826	—
— direct overhead[b]	292	—
Contract filler charge	—	1625
CI overhead	—	80
Direct production cost	7036	6443
Freight to Torino + duty & clear.	1325	75
Direct delivered cost	8361	6518
+ temp. import surcharge/deposit	1235	
	9596	

(continued)

Lira per case	BRIO Liquid Convenience Floor Wax 6143D 850cc x 24 units	
	Complant (March '76)[a]	*Contract filler*
Complant — other overhead[c]	1285	
— admin. + markup[d]	2010	
Total current cost to Italy	12891	
Less: temp. surcharge/deposit	1235	
Total normal cost to Italy	11656	6518

Rate L. 325/DF1.

[a]Estimates provided by engineering staff at Complant in March, 1976.

[b]Direct overhead includes: supervision and indirect labor, repairs and maintenance, depreciation, supplies.

[c]Other overhead includes: distribution, production control, purchasing, quality control, engineering, project installation.

[d]Administration and markup includes: finance and administration, MIS, personnel and general services, Complant debt interest, R&D, and profit markup.

The difference between the current cost to CI of BRIO from Complant versus the cost quoted by a local filler is substantial. It would cost CI literally one-half its current cost from Complant. Even if the import surcharge is lifted,[5] the savings will remain substantial.

That 200–250 Lira savings per unit will permit us to keep our premium-price differential small yet increase our advertising budget substantially. We're counting on increased volume with a stable gross margin to finally turn BRIO into the money-maker we had planned with its introduction three years ago. As you know, the convenience wax segment, while growing, is becoming more and more competitive. To sustain our position as a respected premium quality product will take heavy advertising support.

The figures on PINETA lead to the same conclusion. The cost to CI by local filling will be markedly reduced. Though the difference on aerosols is not as great because of lower freight costs, the savings would nevertheless be substantial.

---

[5]The Italian government had periodically required that all importers of goods deposit with the Bank of Italy a percentage of their value for a specified duration without interest. While these deposits were subsequently returned to the depositers, there was an implicit loss of liquidity and investment income from the monies deposited.

Cost comparison: Complant and Italian filler

Lira per case	PINETA Aerosol Air Freshener 7261A 12 oz. x 24 units	
	Complant (March '76)[a]	Contract filler
Raw material	959	638*
		503*
Components and packing	2856	2801
Less allowance (materials)	135	185
Complant — direct labor	325	—
— direct overhead[b]	104	—
Contract filler charge	—	915
CI overhead	—	80
Direct production cost	4379	5122
Freight to Torino + duty & clear.	485	35
Direct delivered cost	4864	5157
+ temp. import surcharge/deposit	800	
	5664	
Complant — other overhead[c]	789	
— admin. + markup[d]	1017	
Total current cost to Italy	7470	
Less: temp. surcharge/deposit	800	
Total normal cost to Italy	6670	5157

Rate L. 325/DF1.
*Supplied by contract filler.
[a]Estimates provided by engineering staff at Complant, March 1976.
[b]Direct overhead includes: supervision and indirect labor, repairs and maintenance, depreciation, supplies.
[c]Other overhead includes: distribution, production control, purchasing, quality control, engineering, project installation.
[d]Administration and markup includes: finance and administration, MIS, personnel and general services, Complant debt interest, R&D, and profit markup.

As I mentioned, Chandler has always assumed that inflation differentials between Italy and Holland would compensate for the weakening of the Lira versus the Guilder. In fact, you recently sent me a study done at our U.K. subsidiary that attempts to substantiate the claim of linkage between comparative inflation rates and exchange rates (see *Exhibit 9*).

EXHIBIT 9. 5-year comparison of cost per 100 units in Guilders of Complant and U.K.

	1970–71		1971–72		1972–73		1973–74		1974–75	
	Cost of production per 100 units	Index 70/71 = 100	Cost of production per 100 units	Index 70/71 = 100	Cost of production per 100 units	Index 70/71 = 100	Cost of production per 100 units	Index 70/71 = 100	Cost of production per 100 units	Index 70/71 = 100
I. U.K. cost in Sterling:										
Raw material cost	2.27	100	3.02	133	3.22	142	4.38	193	5.97	263
Component cost	4.21	100	5.41	128	5.94	141	6.95	165	7.62	181
Direct labor & overheads	2.20	100	2.76	126	2.53	115	3.41	155	4.16	189
Total cost of product £	8.68	100	11.19	129	11.69	135	14.74	169	17.75	203
II. U.K. cost in Guilders:										
Average exchange rate £1	8.631	100	8.366	97	7.519	87	6.399	74	5.928	69
Raw material cost	19.59	100	25.27	129	24.29	124	28.01	143	35.46	181
Component cost	36.34	100	45.26	125	44.70	123	44.33	122	45.06	124
Direct labor & overheads	18.99	100	23.09	122	18.99	100	21.84	115	24.69	130
Total cost of product DF1.	74.92	100	93.62	125	87.98	118	94.18	126	105.21	140
III. Complant cost in Guilders:										
Raw material cost	22.98	100	22.94	99	22.89	99	30.33	132	34.70	151
Component cost	37.40	100	40.10	107	41.89	112	46.00	123	50.86	136
Direct labor & overheads	16.42	100	16.18	99	16.63	101	18.55	113	25.62	156
Total cost of product DF1.	76.80	100	79.22	103	81.41	106	94.88	124	111.18	145
IV. Comparison of total production cost:										
U.K. DF1.	74.92	100	93.62	125	87.98	118	94.18	126	105.21	140
Complant DF1.	76.80	100	79.22	103	81.41	106	94.88	124	111.18	145

I do not believe that this is so in Italy. The recently produced Economic Model shows that, contrary to that theory, in the future the inflation differential between Holland and Italy does not compensate for the Lira/Guilder weakening. We can sell an Italian-made 16-oz. can at the same price of a Dutch-made 12-oz. can and still make the same gross profit for Chandler. And this assumes that in the base year the landed costs are the same, which the Cost Comparisons show is not the case.

	1975	1976	1977	1978	1979
Dutch inflation index	100	108.6	119.5	130.2	141.5
Lira/Guilder dev. index	100	114.8	123.6	132.1	141.4
Combined effect	100	124.7	147.7	172.0	200.1
Italian inflation index	100	117.4	131.5	149.0	167.2
Cumulative differential	—	+7.3%	+16.2%	+23.0%	+32.9%

I am not an economist so I can't explain the divergences between inflation and exchange rates in Italy. Simply stated, there must be other considerations besides inflation which influence exchange rates. In any event, even for that correlation between the two which exists, there are such irregularly spaced time lags that the stability of the cost input of production evaporates. How can a country manager plan if his gross margin is so erratic?

As you surely recall, we had substantial problems in making ends meet in the 1975/76 budget. Our assumption has been that we could at least "survive" if we were to reduce our aggressiveness in the market by reducing our advertising spending and by cutting our personnel count.

ADVERTISING

In the past three years, we have reduced advertising as follows:

	1973/74 actual	1974/75 actual	1975/76 April estimate
Lira	2650	2895	3616
Dollars	4015	4488	4702
% N.S.	16.1	16.4	14.5

As you can see, our spending has decreased slightly in amount in Lira. But if you take into account the inflation cost in that period, the total has decreased much more as shown in the dollar figures. Obviously today's dollars are worth less than two-year-old dollars, so the decrease is even more substantial. In addition, the Advertising-to-Sales ratio has dropped to such a point where we soon risk losing considerable market share, especially as we are already priced far above our competitors.

PERSONNEL COUNT

During the year we have reduced the Personnel Count substantially:

September 1974	June 1975	June 1976 budget	June 1976 estimate
319	306	286	265

I don't think that it is realistic to expect further savings in this area. Our Personnel Count will be only marginally higher than five years ago when sales were less than one-third of today.

This mad scramble to reduce costs in order to approach our budgeted operating profit cannot be repeated. Already advertising and overheads appropriations are pared to the bone. Any further cuts will directly erode our volumes. Yet Complant's products are increasing in price far more than can be reasonably expected to be recovered through price increases.

Can all this be caused only by the additional freight cost? I think that the Cost Comparisons and Economic Model show definitively not.

A major strategic decision is therefore required that balances the opportunity for profits in Italy, the investments required to make those profits, and the spare capacity in Complant. The issue requires either a major modification of CI's sourcing pattern, namely, use of local contract fillers, and/or a modification of Chandler's intercompany pricing policy in line with the "arms-length" concept.

We have examined three alternatives:

A. MAINTAIN THE PRESENT POLICY OF FULL COST + 10% FROM COMPLANT. As the Economic Model suggests, our costs will rise substantially above Italian inflation levels. If prices for our products are raised in proportion to costs in order to maintain profit margin, volume will be reduced drastically as the price differential with locally producing competition yawns ever larger. Keeping pace with competitive pricing will eliminate any profit margin. The effect will be especially severe on markets in which we have less than 15% market shares (i.e., fabric care, insecticides, floor wax, and personal care). (See *Exhibit 10* for price versus cost history.)

B. CONTRACT FILL LOCALLY.   In this case, volume will go up substantially, as we'll be able to reduce the spread versus our competitors while maintaining a healthy gross margin.

C. MANUFACTURE IN COMPLANT AT A LANDED COST IN LIRA EQUAL TO CONTRACT FILLERS + 5%.   In this case, the only change for us from alternative B is a loss of product contribution equal to the 5% cost increase which we are willing to pay to Complant because of its reliability as a supplier.

Our marketing manager has estimated the impact of the three alternatives on PINETA 12 oz. The results would be as follows:

PINETA AEROSOL (000,000 Lira)	Alternative A	Alternative B	Alternative C
Suggest. retail price	1290	1090	1090
Cases x 24	30,000	64,000	64,000
GROSS SALES	574	1062	1062
Net sales	544	1007	1007
Gross profit	317	586	565
% N.S.	58.3%	58.2%	56.1%
Advertising	120	120	120
Deals	35	65	65
PRODUCT CONTRIBUTION	76	307	286
OPERATING PROFIT	16	129	108
% N.S.	2.9%	12.8%	10.7%

On some of our products that are more price-sensitive, or that have lower initial gross margins, the results would be even much lower for the "full-cost" alternative A.

We think it only in Chandler's interest that the company adopt either B or C. Our marketing programs demand some stability in the cost input. We are very close to dropping several of the less popular household lines since plainly with the spiraling costs of Complant pro-

EXHIBIT 10. Price versus cost history

Product	MSP/MCG	1973/74	1974/75	1975/76
ANTICA 10 oz.	MSP	100	107.2	109.4
	MCG	100	119.4	151.6
BRIO 850 cc.	MSP	100	103.0	110.2
	MCG	100	126.4	152.8
CARINA 16 oz.	MSP	100	102.5	103.7
	MCG	100	117.2	126.9
FLIT 20 oz.	MSP	100	105.2	113.8
	MCG	100	99.7	121.8
PINETA 12 oz.	MSP	100	106.4	112.7
	MCG	100	116.8	134.6

Mean selling price (MSP)
Mean cost of goods (MCG)
and Italian inflation indices (1973 = 100)

duction there is little hope that these lines can provide sufficient contribution to Chandler Italia.

As for local sourcing through contract fillers, we realize that Chandler has a large investment in Complant and the strategic decision to build it more than a decade ago was correct under the existing conditions. Indeed, CI was greatly aided by Complant's reliability and competitive prices. Yet the decision to expand it several years back — to which I admit I gave my approval — was likely a mistake. CI has grown large enough where local sourcing tied to the local economy becomes advantageous, as borne out by the cost comparisons.

Apart from this major strategic decision that faces Chandler, I wish to address two other cost issues that remain to be adjusted if CI continues to source in part or totally from Complant.

1. *Freight.* By virtue of its location, CI currently pays the highest freight bills of all our EEC subsidiaries. In essence, CI is penalized in comparison to Chandler France, Belgium, Holland, and West Germany, due to the proximity of Complant to those markets. We believe that some form of freight equalization scheme would be much more appropriate.

2. *Allocation of overhead.* Overhead of Complant is currently charged on a per-unit basis. We believe that this penalizes large

subsidiaries like us who provide long production runs of a single product in favor of the small subsidiaries who have low-volume products.

I will be willing to assist in any way I can to solve these problems, but I need definite direction on what to do for fiscal 1976/77, which begins in another two and a half months, because I cannot see how to make profits in Italy given the current sourcing arrangement and inter-company costing system.

Tony Pesci
General Manager
Chandler Italia

3.5 *CASE*

Procter & Gamble Europe:
Vizir Launch

Christopher A. Bartlett

There were three critical decisions facing Procter & Gamble's (P&G) senior management in June 1981 as they reviewed the German test market results for Vizir, the new heavy duty liquid (HDL) detergent.

- Should they follow the recommendation of Wolfgang Berndt and his German team and authorize a national launch on the basis of four months of test results? Or should they wait until final test market results were in, or perhaps even rethink their entire HDL product strategy?
- If and when the decision was taken to launch Vizir, to what extent could this be considered a European rather than just a German

product? If a coordinated European rollout was planned, to what degree should the company standardize its product formulation, packaging, advertising, and promotion?

■ Finally, what organizational implications would these decisions have? For example, to what extent should individual country subsidiary managers retain the responsibility to decide when and how this new product would be introduced in their national market?

PROCTER & GAMBLE: COMPANY BACKGROUND

To understand anything in P&G, one had to appreciate the company's strong and long-established culture that was reflected in the corporate values, policies, and practices. The following paragraphs outline how the company saw itself in each of these areas.

CORPORATE VALUES

Established in 1837 by two men of strong religious faith and moral conviction, P&G soon had developed an explicit set of corporate standards and values. From their earliest contact, prospective employees were told of P&G's firm belief that the interests of the company were inseparable from those of its employees. Over the years, this broad philosophy had been translated into a variety of widely shared management norms such as the following:

■ P&G should hire only good people of high character.

■ P&G must treat them as individuals with individual talents and life goals.

■ P&G should provide a work environment that encourages and rewards individual achievement.

The shared beliefs soon became part of the company's formal management systems. General managers would tell you they were evaluated on the achievements in three areas: volume, profit, and people. P&G also tried to attract people willing to spend their entire career with the company. Promotions were made from within, and top management was chosen from career P&G people rather than from outside the company.

MANAGEMENT POLICIES

Over its almost 150-year history, P&G had also accumulated a broad base of industry experience and business knowledge. Within the company, this accumulated knowledge was seen as an important asset and a great deal of it had been formalized and institutionalized as management principles and policies. In the words of Chairman Ed Harness, "Though our greatest asset is our people, it is the consistency of principle and policy which gives us direction."

It was in the marketing area that these operating principles and management policies were the most strategically important for a company with a reputation as a premier consumer marketer. One of the most basic policies was that P&G's products should provide "superior total value" and should meet "basic consumer needs." This resulted in a strong commitment to research to create products that were demonstrably better than the competition in blind tests. (In the words of one manager, "Before you can launch a new brand, you must have a win in a white box.")

Furthermore, P&G believed strongly in the value of market research. In a business where poorly conceived new product launches could be very expensive and sometimes not very successful, continuous and detailed market research was seen as insurance against major mistakes. Chairman Ed Harness had described their market research objectives as being "to spot a new trend early, then lead it."

For similar reasons, P&G also believed in extensive product and market testing before making major brand decisions. Having spotted a trend through market research, the company typically spent two or three years testing the product and the marketing strategy it had developed before committing to a full-scale launch. One paper goods competitor said of them: "P&G tests and tests and tests. They leave no stone unturned, no variable untested. You can see them coming for months and years, but you know when they get there, it is time for you to move."

Finally, P&G believed that through continual product development and close tracking of consumer needs and preferences, brands could be managed so that they remained healthy and profitable in the long term. Their rejection of the conventional product life cycle mentality was demonstrated by the fact that Ivory Soap was over 100 years old, Crisco shortening was more than 70, and Tide detergent more than 35, yet each was still a leader in its field.

ORGANIZATION PRACTICES

In addition to strong corporate values and clear management principles, the P&G culture was also characterized by well-established organization practices and processes. Its internal operations had been described as thorough, creative, and aggressive by some, and as slow, risk-averse, and rigid by others. There was probably an element of truth in both descriptions.

Perhaps the most widely known of P&G's organizational characteristics was its legendary brand manager structure. Created in 1931, the brand management system was designed to provide each brand with management focus, expertise, and drive at a low level in the organization. By legitimizing and even reinforcing the internal competition that had existed since Camay Soap was launched in competition with Ivory in 1923, the brand manager system tended to restrict lateral communication. This resulted in a norm among P&G managers that information was shared on a "need to know" basis only.

While the brand manager system may have impaired lateral communication, vertical communication within P&G was strong and well established. Proposals on most key issues were normally generated at the lower levels of management, with analysis and recommendations working their way up the organization for concurrence and approval. In P&G, top management was intimately involved in most large decisions — (e.g., all new brand launches, capital appropriations in excess of $100,000, and personnel appointment and promotion decisions three levels down). Although the approval system could be slow and at times bureaucratic (one manager claimed that a label change on Head and Shoulders shampoo had required 55 signatures), it was designed to minimize risk in the very risky and expensive consumer marketing business. Once a project was approved, it would have the company's full commitment. As one manager said, "Once they sign off [on the new brand launch], they will bet the farm."

A third characteristic of the P&G management process was that proposals were committed to paper, usually in the form of one- or two-page memos. The purpose was to encourage thoroughness and careful analysis on the part of the proposal originators, and objectivity and rationality on the part of the managers who reviewed the document. Written documents could also flow more easily through the organization, building support or eliciting comments and suggestions.

P&G INTERNATIONAL: EUROPEAN OPERATIONS

EXPANSION PRINCIPLES

Although P&G had acquired a small English soap company in 1926, it was not until the postwar years that the company built a substantial European presence. In 1954 a French detergent company was acquired; two years later, a Belgian plant was opened; and by the end of the decade P&G had established operations in Holland and Italy. A Swiss subsidiary served as a worldwide export center. In the 1960s, subsidiaries were opened in Germany, Austria, Greece, Spain, and the Scandinavian countries. The European Technical Center (ETC) was established in Brussels in 1963, to provide R&D facilities and a small regional management team.

By 1981 Europe represented about 15% of P&G's $11 billion worldwide sales, with almost all of that substantial volume having been built in the previous two and a half decades. The German and U.K. subsidiaries were the largest, each representing about one-fifth of the company's European sales. France and Italy together accounted for another 30%, and Belgium, Holland, Spain, Austria, and Switzerland together made up the balance.

As international operations grew, questions arose as to how the new foreign subsidiaries should be managed. As early as 1955, Walter Lingle, P&G's Overseas V.P., laid down some important principles that guided the company's subsequent development abroad. Recognizing that consumer needs and preferences differed by country, Lingle emphasized the importance of acquiring the same intensive knowledge of local consumers as was required in the U.S. Lingle said: "Washing habits . . . vary widely from country to country. We must tailor products to meet consumer demands in each nation. We cannot simply sell products with U.S. formulas. They won't work — they won't be accepted."

But Lingle insisted that the management policies and practices that had proven so successful for P&G in the U.S. would be equally successful overseas. He said: "The best way to succeed in other countries is to build in each one as exact a replica of the U.S. Procter & Gamble organization as it is possible to create."

EUROPEAN INDUSTRY AND COMPETITIVE STRUCTURE

From their earliest exposure to the European market for laundry detergents, U.S. managers realized how important the first of these principles would be. Washing habits and market structures not only differed from the familiar U.S. situation, but also varied from one country to the next within Europe. Among the more obvious differences in laundry characteristics were the following:

- Typical washing temperatures were much higher in Europe, and the "boil wash" (over 60°C) was the norm in most countries. However, lower washing temperatures were commonplace in some countries where washing machines did not heat water (e.g., U.K.) or where hand washing was still an important segment (e.g., Spain, Italy).

- European washing machines were normally front loading with a horizontal rotating drum — very different from the U.S. norm of an agitator action in a top loaded machine. The European machine also had a smaller water capacity (3–5 gallons versus 12–14 gallons in the U.S.) and used a much longer cycle (90–120 minutes versus 20–30 minutes for U.S.).

- Europeans used more cottons and less synthetics than Americans, and tended to wear clothes longer between washes. Average washing frequency was 2–3 times per week versus 4–5 times in the U.S. Despite the lower penetration of washing machines, much higher detergent dosage per load resulted in the total European laundry detergent consumption being about 30% above the U.S. total.

Market structures and conditions were also quite different from the U.S., and also varied widely within Europe, as illustrated by the following examples:

- In Germany, concentration ratios among grocery retailers were among the highest in the world. The five largest chains (including co-ops and associations) accounted for 65% of the retail volume, compared with about 15% in the U.S. In contrast, in Italy, the independent corner store was still very important, and hypermarkets had not made major inroads.

- Unlimited access to television similar to the U.S. was available only in the U.K. (and even there was much more expensive). In Holland, each brand was allowed only 46 minutes of TV commercial time per annum; in Germany and Italy, companies had to apply for blocks of TV time once a year. Allocated slots were very limited.

- National legislation greatly affected product and market strategies. Legislation in Finland and Holland limited phosphate levels in detergent; German laws made coupons, refunds, and premium offers all but impossible; elsewhere local laws regulated package weight, labeling, and trade discounts.

The competitive environment was also different from P&G's accustomed market leadership position in the U.S. In Europe, P&G shared the first-tier position with two European companies, Unilever and Henkel. By the early 1970s each company claimed between 20% and 25% of the European laundry detergent market. P&G's old domestic market rival, Colgate, had a 10% share and was in a second tier. At a third level were several national competitors. Henkel was present in most European markets but strongest in Germany, its home market; Unilever was also very international, dominating in Holland and U.K.; Colgate's presence in Europe was spottier, but it had built up a very strong position in France. National companies typically were strong at the lower priced end of their local markets.

Each company had its own competitive characteristics. Unilever had long been a sleeping giant, but was becoming much more aggressive by the mid-1970s. Henkel was a strong competitor and could be relied on to defend its home market position tenaciously. Colgate was trying to elbow its way in, and tended to be more impulsive and take bigger risks, often launching new products with only minimal testing. As a result, P&G's market share varied by national market.

Laundry detergent market ($ million)

	Total market	P&G share
Germany	950	200
U.K.	660	220
France	750	160
Italy	650	140
Spain	470	90
Total Europe	3,750	950

By the mid-1970s, the rapid growth of the previous two decades dropped to a standstill. Not only did the oil crisis add dramatically to costs, but almost simultaneously washing machines approached the

85% penetration rate many regarded as saturation point. In the late 1970s, volume was growing at 2% per annum. As market growth slowed, competitive pressures increased.

P&G EUROPE'S STRATEGY AND ORGANIZATION

These differences in consumer habits, market conditions, and competitive environment led to the development of strong national subsidiaries with the responsibility for developing products and marketing programs to match the local environment. Each subsidiary was a miniature Procter & Gamble, with its own brand management structure, its own product development capability, its own advertising agencies, and, typically, its own manufacturing capability. The subsidiary general manager was responsible for the growth of the business and the organization. (See *Exhibit 1.*)

Most subsidiaries faced a major task of establishing P&G in the basic detergent and soap business in their national market. The general manager typically tried to select the best volume and profit opportunity from the more than 200 products in the company's portfolio. The general manager of the Italian subsidiary described the choices he faced when he took over in 1974:

> *Given the limits of P&G Italy's existing brands (a laundry detergent, a bar soap, and a recently acquired coffee business), we had to build our volume and profit, and broaden our base. The choices we had were almost limitless. Pampers had been very successful in Germany and Belgium, but Italy couldn't afford such an expensive launch; Motiv, a new dishwashing liquid, was being launched in France and Germany, but we were unconvinced of its potential here; Mr. Propre (Mr. Clean in U.S.) was successful in three European countries, but competition in Italy was strong; finally we decided to launch Monsavon, the French bar soap. It represented an affordable new product launch in a traditionally good profit line.*

Each of the country general managers reported to Tom Bower, an Englishman who had headed up P&G's European operations since 1961. Bower had a reputation as an entrepreneur and an excellent motivator. He believed that by selecting creative and entrepreneurial country general managers and giving them the freedom to run their business, results would follow. The strategy had been most successful for P&G, and sales and profits had grown rapidly throughout the '60s and into the early '70s. Growth had been aided by P&G's entry into new national markets and new product categories, and by the rapid growth of the core detergent business with the penetration of washing machines into European homes.

Tom Bower made sure that his small headquarters staff understood that they were not to interfere unduly in subsidiary decisions. Primarily, it was the subsidiary general manager's responsibility to call on ETC if there was a problem.

When Tom Bower retired in 1975, his successor, Ed Artzt, was faced with a situation quite different from the one that existed in the 1950s and '60s. As growth slowed, competition intensified, prices weakened, and profits dipped. Artzt felt that if profit and sales growth were to be rekindled, the diverse country operations would have to be better coordinated.

Over the next five years, under his leadership, the role of ETC took on new importance. (*Exhibit 1* shows an abbreviated organization chart). If increased competition was leading to declining margins, more emphasis must be placed on controlling costs, and Artzt moved to strengthen the ETC finance manager's role. The finance manager described the problems:

> *Largely because of duplication of marketing and administrative groups in each subsidiary, our overhead expense per unit was almost 50% higher than in the U.S. parent. We needed to get it under control. Our problem was that we couldn't get meaningful or comparable costs by subsidiary. Our introduction of better cost and reporting systems helped put pressure on subsidiaries to control their costs. It had a very beneficial effect.*

Artzt was also concerned about the slowing of innovation in P&G Europe, and felt that part of the sales and profit problem was due to the fact that too few new products were being developed, and those that were, were not being introduced in a coordinated manner. Under the strong leadership of Wahib Zaki, Artzt's new R&D manager, ETC's role in product development took a dramatic shift.

Previously each subsidiary was responsible for initiating its own local product development. These groups drew on the company's basic technology from the U.S., as modified by ETC. The R&D group in a subsidiary the size of France was around 30, while Germany's technical staff was perhaps twice that size. Responding to its own local market, the subsidiary defined and developed products with the appropriate characteristics, perhaps calling on ETC for specialized technical support or backup. There was no requirement for a subsidiary to use standard formulations or technology. As a result, Ariel detergent had nine different formulas Europe-wide, having been positioned diversely as a low- and a high-suds powder, and for low- and high-temperature usage, depending on the country.

The problem with developing products in this way, concluded Zaki,

EXHIBIT 1. Abbreviated organization chart: P&G Europe

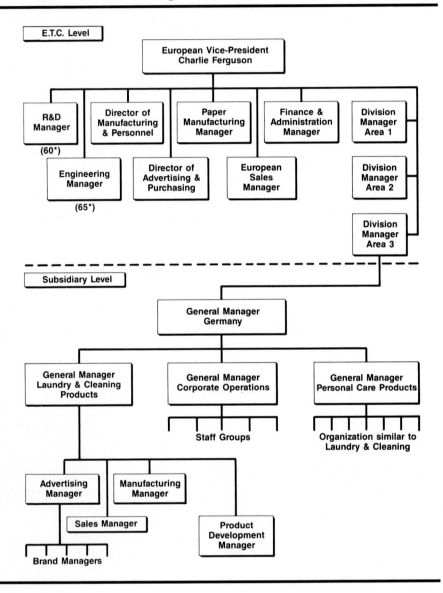

was that there was insufficient focus, prioritization, or strategic direction for the work. As a result, the strong technical capabilities housed in the European Technical Centers as well as in the United States were not being fully or effectively utilized. Furthermore, their efforts were not being appreciated by local country management who tended to view the Technical Center as a high cost, perfectionist group that did not respond rapidly enough to market needs.

Zaki aimed to change this by having ETC take a stronger leadership role in R&D and by assuming responsibility for coordinating the new product development efforts among the subsidiaries. He felt the time had come where this was possible. His analysis indicated that habit differences between countries were narrowing and no longer justified product differences of the type that then existed from one country to another. He felt the need to establish priorities, to coordinate efforts, and, to the extent possible, to standardize products Europe-wide. To achieve these goals he needed the involvement and cooperation of the subsidiaries.

In 1977, Zaki reorganized European R&D, creating European Technical Teams to work on products and technologies that had Europe-wide importance. In his vision, European products would be superior to existing local national products, but without compromising performance or increasing cost. The objective was to focus the resources of the total European R&D community around key brands and to define a long-term European approach to product development.

As roles became clearer, the ETC technical groups were seen as being the developers of new technologies ("putting the molecules together," as one described it), while the subsidiaries took responsibility for testing and refining the products in the field. After a couple of painful years, the new process seemed to be working. "Lead countries" were named for each of the key products, thereby giving more local subsidiary responsibility and ownership for the development process, and also to ensure ongoing coordination among subsidiaries. Transfer of technical staff between ETC and subsidiaries further encouraged the interdependence and cooperation.

An experimental attempt at "Europeanization" in marketing, however, had been less successful. In a break from the philosophy of product adaptation, a group of managers in Cincinnati had concluded that "a baby is a baby" worldwide, and that the laborious market-by-market evaluations necessary for cleaning products would not be needed for disposable diapers. In line with this decision, it was decided to gain experience by managing key elements of Pampers (such as product and copy strategy) on a Europe-wide basis. A senior manager was transferred from the German subsidiary where Pampers had been launched in 1973 to ETC where he was given responsibility for leading key activities on Pampers in all subsidiaries.

The brand promotion manager responsible for Pampers in France at the time recalled the experiment:

> *As soon as it was known I would be principally working with the European Pampers manager in ETC and not the subsidiary GM, my local support dried up. I couldn't get a brand manager or even an assistant to work with me. The French subsidiary manager was preoccupied with the Motiv (dishwashing liquid) launch, and was trying to regain leadership with Ariel (laundry powder). The Pampers situation was a disaster. Eventually Pampers was given back to the subsidiaries — it was the only way to get their support.*

This experience conveyed a very important lesson to P&G's top management. It appeared that while coordination and planning could be effectively centralized and implemented on a European basis, the day-to-day management of the business had to continue to be executed at the local subsidiary level.

In 1980, Ed Artzt was transferred back to Cincinnati as executive vice-president of P&G, and Charlie Ferguson was named Group V.P., Europe. Ferguson had a reputation as an energetic, creative, and intelligent manager who got things done. Impressed by the effectiveness of the European approach to technical development, Ferguson was convinced that a similar approach could succeed in product marketing.

With the encouragement and support of his boss, Ed Artzt, who remained a strong advocate of Europeanization, Charlie Ferguson began to test the feasibility of developing Europe-wide brand and marketing strategies. In pursuing the Eurobrand concept, as it was becoming known, Artzt and Ferguson saw Vizir, the new heavy duty liquid being prepared for launch in Germany, as being a good test case.

THE VIZIR PROJECT
PRODUCT DEVELOPMENT

Following Lever's success in the U.S. with a product called Wisk, in 1974 P&G launched Era as their entrant in the fast-growing heavy duty liquid (HDL) detergent segment. As a late entrant, however, they were unable to match Wisk's dominant share. P&G managers watching developments from Europe realized that if the HDL product concept was transferable to their market, the first company to stake out the territory would have a major advantage. The success of liquids in other product

categories (e.g., household cleansers), the trend toward low-temperature washes, and the availability of liquid product plant capacity, all
provided additional incentives to proceed with the project.

ETC initiated its HDL project in late 1974, and as a first step tested
the U.S. product Era against European powders in a small-scale test
panel. Given the differences in laundry habits on either side of the Atlantic, it was not surprising that Era was evaluated poorly. The problems
reported by the panel related not only to the product's washing performance (e.g., whitening ability, suds level), but also to its form. European washing machines were built with drawers that allowed different
powdered products (pretreatment, main wash detergent, fabric softener) to be activated at different times in the typical 90-minute cycle. To
win acceptance of a laundry liquid would be difficult. First consumers
would have to be convinced that this product would achieve similar
results; then their established usage behaviors would have to be
changed.

Undeterred, a group at ETC began to work on a HDL product that
would be more suited to European laundry practices. It was with high
hopes and considerable corporate visibility that the modified European
HDL product was placed in six full-scale blind tests in Germany, France,
and U.K. The results were disastrous in all tests. Given the high level
of internal expectations that had been created, many P&G insiders felt
that the product was dead, since it would be impossible to rebuild internal support and credibility.

However, the scientists at ETC were convinced that they should be
able to capitalize on the intrinsic ability of a liquid detergent to incorporate three times the level of surfactants compared to a powder. (The
surfactant was the critical ingredient that removes greasy stains.) The
challenge was to compensate for the shortcomings of the HDL that offset this important advantage. Unlike U.S. products, European powdered detergents normally contained enzymes (to break down proteins)
and bleach (to oxidize stains) in addition to builders (to prevent redis-
position of dirt), phosphates (to soften water), and surfactants. Unfor-
tunately, it was not then possible to incorporate enzymes and bleach in
a liquid detergent, and it was this limited capability that was behind the
new product's blind test failure in Europe.

The challenge of overcoming these deficiencies excited P&G's scientists at ETC and in the U.S. Eventually they were able to patent a
method to give enzymes stability in liquid form. Soon afterwards, a
bleach substitute that was effective at lower temperatures was developed. The product modifications showed in improving consumer blind
test results. In late 1976, the new HDL product won a blind test against

the leading French powder, Ariel; the following year it won against Persil, the German market leader.

Although the project was still on shaky ground within P&G, the successes resulted in the establishment of a HDL brand group in Germany. The group reported to Germany's newly appointed Advertising Manager for laundry and cleaning products, Wolfgang Berndt, a 34-year-old Austrian who started his career 10 years earlier in the company's Austrian subsidiary, and after gaining training and experience in brand management in Austria, U.K., and Germany, had spent two years in Cincinnati as a Brand Manager in the parent company's Toilet Goods Division. He returned to Europe in 1973 as Brand Promotion Manager in P&G Italy, before transferring to Germany a year later. He was appointed Advertising Manager in 1977, and having been in this new position only a few months, Berndt was keen to ensure he gave appropriate attention to this important but delicate new HDL responsibility.

In early 1977, Colgate began test marketing Axion, a HDL formula that was similar to its U.S. product, Dynamo. Axion showed excellent initial results, gaining almost 4% share in three months. However, sales declined from this peak and within 18 months Colgate closed down the test market and withdrew Axion.

Meanwhile, P&G's research team had developed three important additional breakthroughs: a fatty acid that provided water softening performance similar to phosphate, a suds suppressant so the product would function in European drum washing machines, and a patented washing machine anticorrosion ingredient. By 1979, European development efforts had shifted to product aesthetics, and the search began for perfumes compatible with the newly formulated *HDL-Formula SB*, as it was known.

Meanwhile, during this period Henkel had been working to reformulate their leading powder and relaunch it as New Persil. Blind tests against New Persil in early 1980 were a breakeven. Finally, in October 1980 with a new fragrance, Procter's Formula SB won a blind test against New Persil by 53 to 47. The product's superiority was confirmed in subsequent tests against the main competitive powders in France (58 to 42 win for Formula SB) and in the U.K. (61 to 39 win).

Now, Berndt and his German brand group were ready to recommend a full-scale test market. During the previous 18 months they had cleared the proposed brand name (Vizir), appointed an advertising agency (Grey), designed packaging (bottles and labels), and collected and analyzed the masses of consumer and market data that were necessary to justify any new product launched in P&G. Management up to the highest level was interested and involved. Although an initial capital approval had been received for $350,000 to buy molds and raw materials, the test market plan for Berlin was expected to involve a further investment of $1.5 million plus $750,000 for original advertising production and research. A national launch would involve an additional $1.5 million in capital investment and $16 million in marketing costs and would pay out in about three years if the product could gain a 4% market share. A Europe-wide launch would be five or six times that amount.

While Berndt and his team had decided to proceed with the test market, a great deal of uncertainty still surrounded Vizir. There were some in the company questioning whether it made sense to launch this product at all in Germany, particularly with the proposed marketing positioning and copy strategy. Others were less concerned about the German launch but were strongly opposed to the suggestion that Vizir be made a Eurobrand and launched in all key European markets.

VIZIR LAUNCH DECISION

One issue that had resulted in some major concern in P&G's senior management related to Vizir's positioning in the detergent market. Its strength was that it gave superior cleaning performance on greasy stains at low temperatures and (following the product improvements) matched powder performance on enzymatic stains and whiteness. The problem was that P&G's Ariel, the leading low temperature laundry powder in Germany, made similar performance claims, and it was feared that Vizir would cannibalize its sales. So close were their selling propositions that two separate agencies operating independently produced almost identical commercials for Vizir and Ariel in early 1981 (*Exhibit 2*).

The German brand group argued that Vizir had to be positioned in this way, since this was the promise that had resulted in high trials during the Axion test. To position it as a pretreatment product would severely limit its sales potential, while to emphasize peripheral benefits like fabric care or softness would not have broad appeal. They argued that it had to be seen as a mainwash product with superior cleaning performance at lower temperatures.

Another concern being expressed by some managers was that P&G was creating a product segment that could result in new competitive entries and price erosion in the stagnant heavy duty detergent market. Liquids were much easier to make than powders and required a much smaller capital investment. ("For powders, you need a detergent tower — liquids can be made in a bath tub" according to one manager.) Al-

EXHIBIT 2. Comparative scripts: Vizir and Ariel commercials

Vizir ("Peter's Pants")	Ariel ("Helen Hedy")
(Woman in laundry examining newly washed pants on her son)	(Woman in laundry holding up daughter's blouse)
Announcer: Hey, Peter's things look pretty nice.	*Announcer:* Looks beautifully clean again, doesn't it?
Woman: Thanks.	*Helen:* Yes, sure.
Announcer: Too bad they're not completely clean.	*Announcer:* Also close up?
Woman: What?	*Helen:* Well, no. When you really look up close — that's gravy. A stain like that never comes out completely.
Announcer: There's still oily dirt from his bicycle.	*Announcer:* Why is that?
Woman: I can't boil modern fabrics. And without boiling they don't get cleaner.	*Helen:* Because you just can't boil these modern things. I can't get Barbel's blouse really clean without boiling.
Announcer: Oh yes! Here is Vizir, the new liquid detergent Vizir, the liquid powder that gets things cleaner. Without boiling!	*Announcer:* Then use Ariel. It can clean without boiling.
Woman: Bicycle oil will come out? Without boiling?	*Helen:* Without boiling? Even these stains? That I want to see.
Announcer: Yes, one cap of Vizir in the main wash and on tough soil pour a little Vizir on directly. Then wash. Let's test Vizir against boilwash powder. These make-up stains were washed in powder at 60° — not clean. On top we put this unwashed dirty towel, then pour on Vizir. Vizir's liquid power penetrates the soil and dissolves it, as well as the stain that boilwash powder left behind.	*Announcer:* THE TEST: With prewash and mainwash at low temperature we are washing stubborn stains like egg and gravy. The towel on the right had Ariel's cleaning power.
Woman: Incredible. The bicycle oil — gone! Without boiling. Through and through cleaner.	*Helen:* Hey, it's really true. The gravy on Barbel's blouse is completely gone. Even against the light — deep down clean. All this without boiling.
Announcer: Vizir — liquid power to get things cleaner.	*Announcer:* Ariel — without boiling, still clean!

though P&G had patented many of its technological breakthroughs, they were a less effective barrier to entry than might be expected. One product development manager explained:

> *Our work on Vizir was very creative, but not a very effective barrier to com-petition. Often it's like trying to patent a recipe for an apple pie. We can specify ingredients and compositions in an ideal range or a preferred range, but com-petitors can copy the broad concepts and work around the patented ranges. And, believe me, they are all monitoring our patents! Even if they don't (or can't) copy our innovations, there are other ways to solve the problems. If enzymes are unstable in liquid form, you could solve that by dumping in lots of enzymes so that enough will still be active by the estimated usage data.*

If capital costs were low, and products could be imitated (at least partially), the concern was that new entrants could open up a market for "white labels" (generic products). Without the product or the market development costs of P&G, they probably could undercut their prices. The German's proposed pricing strategy had been to price at an equiv-alent "cost-per-job" as the leading powders. This pricing strategy re-sulted in a slightly higher gross profit margin for Vizir compared to powders. The pricing decision was justified on two grounds: A premi-um price was required to be consistent with the product's premium im-age, and also to avoid overall profit erosion, assuming that Vizir would cannibalize some sales of the company's low temperature laundry de-tergent brands.

At this time P&G was a strong number 2 in the German detergent market — the largest in Europe. Henkel's leading brand, Persil, was positioned as an all-temperature all-purpose powder, and held a 17% share.[1] P&G's entrant in the all-temperature segment was Dash, and this brand had 5½% share. However, the company's low-temperature brand, Ariel, had a share of 11% and was a leader in this fast-growing segment, far ahead of Lever's Omo (4½%) and Henkel's new entrant, Mustang (2½%).

The final argument of the opponents was that even ignoring these risks there were serious doubts that this represented a real market opportunity. P&G's marketing of its HDL in the U.S. had not been an outstanding success. Furthermore Colgate's experience with their Eu-ropean test market had been very disappointing.

---

[1]These share data related to the total detergent market (including dishwashing liquid). The heavy duty segment (i.e., laundry detergent) represented about ⅔ of this total.

In early 1981, Wolfgang Berndt's attention was drawn to an interesting article that concluded that it would be difficult for a liquid to compete in the European heavy duty detergent field. The paper was presented to an industry association congress in September 1980 by Henkel's director of product development and two other scientists. It concluded that heavy duty liquids would continue to expand their penetration of the U.S. market, due to the less-demanding comparison standard of American powder detergents, and also to the compatibility of HDLs with American washing practices. In Europe, by contrast, the paper claimed that liquids would likely remain specialty products with small market share (1% compared to 20% in the U.S.). This limited HDL market potential was due to the superiority of European powder detergents, and the different European washing habits (higher temperatures, washing machine characteristics, etc.).

While managers in Brussels and Cincinnati were wrestling with these difficult strategic issues, Wolfgang Berndt was becoming increasingly nervous. He and his Vizir brand group were excited by the product and committed to its success. Initial test market readings from Berlin were encouraging (see *Exhibit 3*), but they were certain that Henkel was following Vizir's performance in Berlin as closely as they were. The product had now been in development and testing for seven years, and the German group felt sure that Henkel knew their intentions and would counterattack swiftly and strongly to protect their dominant position in their home market. By the early summer, rumors were beginning to spread in the trade that Henkel was planning a major new product. Henkel salespeople had been recalled from vacation and retailers were being sounded out for support on promotional programs.

On three separate occasions Wolfgang or a member of his group presented their analysis of the test market and their concerns about a preemptive strike; but on each occasion it was decided to delay a national launch. Senior management on both sides of the Atlantic explained it was just too risky to invest in a major launch on the basis of three or four months of test results. Experience had shown that a one-year reading was necessary to give a good basis for such an important decision.

EUROBRAND DECISION

Another critical issue to be decided concerned the scope of the product launch. Within P&G's European organization, the budding Eurobrand concept, whereby there would be much greater coordination of marketing strategies of brands in Europe, was extremely controversial. Some

EXHIBIT 3. Selected test market results — Vizir Berlin test market

A. Total shipments and share

Month	Shipments: MSU (volume index)		Share (%)	
	Actual	*Target*	*Actual*	*Target*
February	4.6	1.8	—	—
March	5.2	2.5	2.2	1.8
April	9.6	4.5	5.2	2.7
May	3.1	3.1	3.4	3.4

B. Consumer research results

Use and awareness (at 3 months; 293 responses)	*Vizir*	*Mustang*[a]	Attitude data (at 3 months: including free sample only users)	*Vizir*	*Mustang*[a]
Ever used (%)[b]	28	22	Unduplicated comments on:		
—past 4 weeks	15	9	—whiteness, brightness, cleaning or stain removal	65/11[c]	58/8[c]
Ever purchased[b]	13	15			
—past 4 weeks	8	6	—cleaning or stain removal	49/8	52/4
—twice or more	4	NA			
Brand on hand	15	11	—cleaning	12/2	17/NA
—large sizes	3	5	—stain removal	37/6	35/NA
Advertising awareness	47	89	—odor	30/4	15/3
Brand awareness	68	95	—effect on clothes	7/—	13/6
			—form (liquid)	23/11	NA

[a]Mustang was a recently launched Henkel low-temperature powder on which comparable consumer data was available. It was judged to have been only moderately successful, capturing 2½% market share compared to Ariel's 11% share as low-temperature segment leader.

[b]Difference between use and purchase data due to introductory free sample program.

[c]Number of unduplicated comments favorable/unfavorable about the product in user interviews (e.g., among Vizir users interviewed, 65 commented favorably about whiteness, brightness, cleaning or stain removal, while 11 commented negatively about one or more of those attributes).

thought it might conflict with the existing philosophy that gave country subsidiary managers the freedom to decide what products were most likely to succeed in their local market, in what form, and when.

The primary argument advanced by Artzt and Ferguson and other managers with similar views was that the time was now ripe for a common European laundry detergent. While widely differing washing practices between countries had justified, up until now, national products tailored to local habits, market data indicated a converging trend in consumer laundry habits (see *Exhibit 4*).

Others were quick to point out that, despite the trends, there were still huge differences in washing habits that were much more important than the similarities at this stage. For example, Spain and Italy still had a large handwash segment; in U.K. and Belgium top loading washers were still important; and in Southern Europe, natural fiber clothing still predominated. Besides, the raw statistical trends could be misleading. Despite the trend to lower temperature washing, even in Germany over 80% of housewives still used the boilwash (over 60°C) for some loads. In general, they regarded the boilwash as the standard by which they judged washing cleanliness.

Some subsidiary managers also emphasized that the differences went well beyond consumer preferences. Their individual market structures would prevent any uniform marketing strategy from succeeding. They cited data on differences in television cost and access, national legislation on product characteristics and promotion tool usage, differences in distribution structure, and competitive behavior. All these structural factors would impede standardization of brands and marketing strategies Europe-wide.

The second point Artzt and Ferguson raised was that greater coordination was needed to protect subsidiaries' profit opportunities. (However, they emphasized that subsidiary managers should retain ultimate profit responsibility and a leadership or concurrence role in all decisions affecting their operations.)

Increasingly, competitors had been able to imitate P&G's new and innovative products and marketing strategies, and preempt them in national markets where the local subsidiary was constrained by budget, organization, or simple poor judgment from developing the new product category or market segment. For example, Pampers had been introduced in Germany in 1973, but was not launched in France until 1978. Meanwhile, in 1976, Colgate had launched a product called Calline (a literal French translation of Pampers) with similar package color, product position, and marketing strategy, and had taken market leadership. Late introduction also cost Pampers' market leadership in Italy. The

EXHIBIT 4. Selected market research data

A. *Selected washing practices*

	Germany		U.K.		France		Italy		Spain	
	1973	1978	1973	1978	1973	1978	1973	1978	1973	1978
Washing machine penetration										
% households with drum machines	76	83	10	26	59	70	70	79	24	50
Washing temperature										
To 60°C (including handwash)	51	67	71	82	48	68	31	49	63	85
Over 60°C	49	33	29	18	52	32	69	51	37	15
Fabric softener use										
% loads with fabric softener	68	69	36	47	52	57	21	35	18	37

B. *Selected consumer attitude data (German survey only)*

*Laundry cleaning problems (% respondents claim)**	Grease based	Bleach sensitive	Enzyme sensitive
Most frequent stains (%)	61	53	34
Desired improvement (%)	65	57	33
—in washes to 60°C	78	53	25
—in washes above 60°C	7	36	65

*Do not add to 100% because multiple responses allowed.

443

product was just being introduced in the U.K. in 1981. An equally striking example was provided by Lenor, a product similar to Downy in the
U.S. This new brand was launched in 1963 in Germany, creating a new
fabric softener product category. It quickly became an outstanding market success. Nineteen years later, Lenor made its debut in France as the
number-three entrant in the fabric softener category, and consequently
faced a much more difficult marketing task.

Artzt and Ferguson were determined to prevent recurrences of such
instances. Particularly for new brands, they wanted to ensure that product development and introduction was coordinated to ensure a consistent Europe-wide approach, and furthermore that marketing strategies
were thought through from a European perspective. This meant thor-
oughly analyzing the possibility of simultaneous or closely sequenced
European product introductions.

At the country level, many were quick to point out that since the
company wanted to keep the subsidiary as a profit center, the concept
was not feasible. To establish a new brand, and particularly to create a
new product category like disposable diapers, was an incredibly expensive and often highly risky proposition. Many country general managers
questioned whether they should gamble their subsidiary's profitability
on costly, risky new launches, especially if they were not at all convinced their local market was mature enough to accept it. In many cases
they had not yet completed the task of building a sound base in heavy-
and light-duty detergents and personal products. They felt that their
organization should not be diverted from this important task.

The third set of arguments put forward by the advocates of the Eurobrand concept related to economics. They cited numerous examples:
the fact that there were nine different Dash formulas in Europe; Mr.
Clean (known as Mr. Propre, Meister Proper, etc.) was sold in nine different sizes Europe-wide. To go to a single formula, standard-size packs
and multilingual labels could save the company millions of dollars in
mold costs, line downtime for changeovers, sourcing flexibility, reduced
inventory levels, and so forth.

Other managers pointed out that the savings could easily be offset
by the problems standardization would lead to. The following represent
some of the comments made at a country general managers' meeting at
which Charlie Ferguson raised the Eurobrand issue for discussion:

> We have to listen to the consumer. In blind tests in my market that perfume
> cannot even achieve breakeven.

> The whole detergent market is in 2-kilo packs in Holland. To go to a European
> standard of 3 kg. and 5 kg. sizes would be a disaster for us.

We have low phosphate laws in Italy that constrain our product formula. And we just don't have hypermarkets like France and Germany where you can drop off pallet loads.

One general manger put it most forcefully in a memo he wrote to ETC management:

There is no such thing as a Eurocustomer so it makes no sense to talk about Eurobrands. We have an English housewife whose needs are different from a German hausfrau. If we move to a system that allows us to blur our thinking we will have big problems.

Product standardization sets up pressures to try to meet everybody's needs (in which case you build a Rolls Royce that nobody can afford) and countervailing pressures to find the lowest common denominator product (in which case you make a product that satisfies nobody and which cannot compete in any market). These pressures probably result in the foul middle compromise that is so often the outcome of committee decision.

ORGANIZATION DECISION

The strategic questions of whether to launch Vizir, and if so on what scale, also raised some difficult questions about the existing organization structure and internal decision-making processes. If product market decisions were to be taken more in relation to Europe-wide strategic assessments and less in response to locally perceived opportunities, what implications did that have for the traditional role and responsibility of the country general manager? And if the Eurobrand concept was accepted, what organizational means were necessary to coordinate activities among the various country subsidiaries?

By the time Charlie Ferguson became vice-president of P&G Europe, the nontechnical staff in ETC had grown substantially from the 20 or so people that used to work with Tom Bower in early 1970s. Ferguson was convinced that his predecessor, Ed Artzt, had been moving in the right direction in trying to inject a Europe-wide perspective to decisions, and in aiming to coordinate more activities among subsidiaries. He wanted to reinforce the organizational shift by changing the responsibilities of the three geographic division managers reporting to him.

In addition to their existing responsibilities for several subsidiaries, Ferguson gave each of these managers Europe-wide responsibility for one or more lines of business. For example, the division manager responsible for the U.K., French, Belgian, and Dutch subsidiaries was also given responsibility for packaged soaps and detergents Europe-wide.

Although these roles were clearly coordinative in nature, the status and experience of these managers meant that their advice and recommendations would carry a good deal of weight, particularly on strategic and product planning issues.

Following this change, for the first time clear Euro-wide objectives and priorities could be sent by line of business, product group, or brand. Not surprisingly, some country subsidiary managers wondered whether their authority and autonomy were being eroded. Partly to deal with this problem, and partly because the division managers had neither the time nor the resources to adequately manage their product responsibilities, Ferguson created a new organizational forum he termed the Euro Brand Team.

Borrowing from the successful technical team concept, each key brand would have a team with a "lead country." Typically the country subsidiary with the most resources, the leading market positions, or the most commitment for a product would be given the lead role so it could spread its knowledge, expertise, and commitment. The charter of the lead country would be to coordinate the analysis of opportunities for the standardization of the product, its promotion and packaging. It would also be asked to facilitate the simplification of the brand's management by coordinating activities and eliminating needless duplication between subsidiaries.

The main forum for achieving this responsibility would be the Euro Brand Team meetings. It was envisioned that various managers from the regional office and the subsidiaries would be invited to these meetings. From ETC, the appropriate European division manager and European functional managers (e.g., technical, manufacturing, purchasing, advertising, etc.) would be invited. Advertising and brand managers from all countries selling the product would also be invited. It was proposed that the meeting be chaired by the brand manager from the lead country. Thus, a typical team might have more than 20 invited participants.

At the subsidiary level, the proposal received mixed reviews. Some saw the teams as a good way to have increased local management participation in Eurobrand decisions. These individuals saw the European technical teams as evidence such an approach could work, and felt it represented a far better solution than having such decisions shaped largely by an enlarged staff group at ETC. Another group saw the Euro Brand Teams as a further risk to the autonomy of the country manager. Some also saw it as a threat to intersubsidiary relations rather than an aid. One general manager from a smaller country subsidiary explained:

> *When a big, resource-rich subsidiary like Germany is anointed with the title of Lead Country, as it probably will be for a large number of brands, I am concerned that they will use their position and expertise to dominate the teams. The rich will become more powerful, and the small subs will wither. I believe this concept will generate further hostility between subsidiaries. Pricing and volume are the only tools we have left. The general manager's role will be compromised if these are dissipated in team discussions.*

Another concern was that team meetings would not be an effective decision-making forum. With individual subsidiaries still responsible for and measured on their local profitability, it was felt that participants would go in with strongly held parochial views that they would not be willing to compromise. Some claimed that because the teams' roles and responsibilities were not clear it would become another time-consuming block to decision making rather than a means to achieve progress on Eurobrands. A subsidiary general manger commented:

> *The agenda for the Euro Brand Teams is huge, but its responsibilities and powers are unclear. For such a huge and emotionally charged task, it is unrealistic to expect the "brand manager of the day" to run things. The teams will bog down and decisions will take forever. How many of these meetings can we attend without tying up our top management? Our system is all checks and no balances. We are reinforcing an organization in which no one can say yes — they can only veto. With all the controls on approvals, we've lost the knack to experiment.*

At least one manager at ETC voiced his frustration directly: "If we were serious (about standardization), we would stop paying lip service, and tell everyone 'Like it or not, we're going to do it.' "

Charlie Ferguson remained convinced that the concept made sense, and felt that *if* Vizir was to be launched and *if* it was to be considered a Eurobrand, it might provide a good early test for Euro Brand Teams.

3.6 *CASE*

Yoshida Kogyo K.K.

Ulrich Wiechmann

"Here we go again," said Mr. Seijiro Nishizaki, Manager of the Overseas Enterprise Department of Yoshida Kogyo Kabushiki Kaisha (Y.K.K.), a leading zipper manufacturer headquartered in Tokyo. It was February 1974. Mr. Nishizaki had just received a letter from the Commission of the European Economic Community (E.E.C.) in Brussels, Belgium. The letter informed him that, acting on a petition filed by an association of European notions manufacturers, the Commission was investigating whether or not Y.K.K. was using dumping practices to promote the sales of its zippers in Europe.

Mr. Nishizaki vividly recalled a similar charge that had been brought against Y.K.K. in the United States in early 1973. The association of U.S. manufacturers had charged that Y.K.K. was using dumping prices for its zipper exports to the United States and had requested the United States International Trade Commission to remedy the situation. As a result, an extensive investigation was started by the International Trade Commission. It lasted for more than six months and involved, for example, lengthy questionnaires to be completed by Y.K.K. headquarters in Japan and its U.S. subsidiary, checking of Y.K.K.'s domestic and overseas selling prices and manufacturing costs by product item, and visits by U.S. and Japanese officials to Y.K.K. to verify the data.

Throughout this investigation in the U.S., Y.K.K. firmly denied ever having resorted to dumping practices. The investigation proved that Y.K.K. was, in fact, not guilty of dumping and the charges were dropped.

Management of Y.K.K. had noted the result of the U.S. investigation with satisfaction. Still, the whole procedure had involved a lot of management time and expense for Y.K.K. Mr. Nishizaki estimated that the out-of-pocket costs amounted to at least $200,000. In addition, 20 members of management and 3 lawyers had devoted almost full time to the case, and several lengthy trips between Japan and the United States had been necessary.

It was against this background that Mr. Nishizaki now studied the letter from the E.E.C. Commission. He wondered what action he should take. He was confident that the charges brought against Y.K.K. in Europe were just as unjustified as they had been in the United States. Still, fighting against these charges in court would again entail a lengthy procedure, and tie up valuable management time. Furthermore, Mr. Nishizaki was not sure what the impact of such a procedure would be on Y.K.K.'s image. He also knew that the E.E.C. Commission, before engaging in a full-fledged investigation and administrative procedure against Y.K.K., might very likely propose an "amicable settlement." There were several such precedents. While Mr. Nishizaki could not be sure what precisely the terms of an "amicable settlement" would finally be, they would undoubtedly include voluntary curtailment of Y.K.K. zipper exports to Europe and some increase in Y.K.K.'s prices in the European community.

PRODUCT AND INDUSTRY INFORMATION[1]

The term "zipper" was originally a trademark of the Goodrich Rubber Co. The trademark fell into the public domain, however, and became the common term for closure devices officially called "slide fasteners."

---

[1]Based on *Slide Fasteners and Parts Thereof.* United States International Trade Commission, Publication 757, Washington, D.C., 1976, pp. A-4–A-10.

The zipper industry started its growth in 1893. Since then the product had been incorporated in a wide variety of articles including wearing apparel, footwear, handbags, luggage, furniture, tents, and sleeping bags. Zippers were also used for such purposes as closing fishnets, bags of grain, and radar domes. Worldwide, the garment industry, however, was by far the largest market for zippers.[2]

As a result of this heavy dependence on the garment industry, zipper sales were heavily influenced by fashion trends and changes. For example, the advent in 1972/73 of the wrap-around look in women's fashion, instead of the fitted look, caused designers to discard zippers in favor of other types of closures, such as buttons, or hooks and eyes. Also, stretch fabrics, such as elastic waistbands for women's slacks, supplanted zippers. When women's fashion boots lost popularity, a marked contraction of zipper sales occurred.

The dependence of zipper sales on fashion trends forced zipper manufacturers to supply and inventory an endless variety of zipper styles, sizes, and colors. One Y.K.K. manager estimated that, at any one point in time, Y.K.K. was turning out zippers in three types (metal, nylon, and plastic), 15 sizes, and about 300 colors.

A zipper consisted of two cloth "tapes" upon which were mounted, in a row along one edge of each tape, either (1) individual interlocking elements of metal, nylon, or plastic, called "scoops," or (2) a "coil" of nylon or plastic. Such scoops or coil mounted on two tapes constituted the zipper "chain." The chain was fitted with a moveable element, called a "slider," which spanned the two rows of scoops or coil. When moved in one direction the slider caused the scoops or coil on one tape to intermesh with the scoops or coil on the other tape. When moved in the opposite direction the slider caused the scoops or coil to disengage.

Only a few large manufacturers in the world manufactured all the parts for a complete zipper themselves. The smaller firms bought tape from the textile trade, sliders and zipper chain from specialized manufacturers, and then assembled the components into complete zippers. In general, U.S.-made sliders and chains were standardized so that one company's slider would fit another company's chain. European-made sliders also fitted American chains. In contrast, the chain manufactured by Y.K.K. could only be fitted with a Y.K.K. slider.

The most important contenders in the world zipper market were Talon (U.S.), Opti (Germany), Lightning (U.K.), and Y.K.K. (Japan). Together these four companies held about 50% of the world market.

---

[2]In the United States, 68 percent of the 1971 zipper consumption went to the apparel industry and home sewing (Source: U.S. International Trade Commission).

The metal zipper had been perfected by German firms in the 1930s. Y.K.K. had popularized the invisible zipper for dresses and the molded, plastic zipper for sportswear in the late 1960s. Talon had introduced the nylon coil zipper into the market in 1960. In general, there had been a high international transfer of technology, as a combination of United States, German, Japanese, French, and Swiss licenses and machinery were employed by each integrated zipper manufacturer.

COMPANY BACKGROUND

Yoshida Kogyo K.K. was the largest manufacturer of zippers in the world. It was estimated that Y.K.K. commanded a share of about 90% of the zipper market in Japan and approximately 25% of worldwide zipper sales.

Total company sales in 1973 amounted to roughly ¥ 130 billion[3] (see *Exhibit 1*). Approximately 55 percent of this volume were sales of zippers; the remaining 45 percent of total sales were sales of aluminum building material. Exports of zippers and zipper sales from foreign production accounted for roughly 30% and 40% of total zipper sales respectively.

Y.K.K. zippers were manufactured in 2 plants in Japan and in 27 overseas factories. It was an important feature of Y.K.K.'s operations that the company had vertically integrated all of the manufacturing steps that were necessary to turn out finished zippers. Y.K.K. had its own metal smelting, extrusion, die-casting, and stamping factories for metal zipper parts, its own textile spinning, weaving and dying plants to produce the zipper tapes, and plastic molding operations to make plastic zipper parts. In addition, the company had a large machinery factory which provided most of the production and assembly machines, tools and die sets needed for the zipper production process. Management believed that vertical integration coupled with high-volume, automated plants gave Y.K.K. a significant cost advantage.

Y.K.K. was a privately held company. Of the total capital stock of ¥ 5.6 billion, roughly 20% were owned by the company founder and president, Mr. Tadao Yoshida, 10% by banks and Y.K.K. distributors, and 70% by company employees. Mr. Yoshida explained:[4]

---

[3]$1.00 = ¥ 300

[4]Quoted in *Y.K.K.*, Keio Business School case, 1974, prepared by Hideo Ishida.

EXHIBIT 1. Development and breakdown of total company sales, 1965–1974

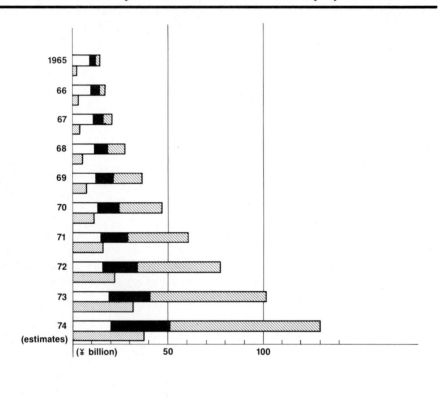

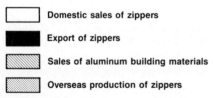

Domestic sales of zippers

Export of zippers

Sales of aluminum building materials

Overseas production of zippers

Source: *Y.K.K.*, Keio Business School case, 1974, prepared by Hideo Ishida.

Y.K.K. does not put its stock on the market; we are trying to give Y.K.K. stocks to Y.K.K. employees as much as possible. As we cannot afford to pay our workers as much as we wish, we make them our stockholders so that they can get dividends and enjoy better life. Because our employees have a sense of responsibility to the company performance as stockholders of Y.K.K. and try to work harder to exercise their assertiveness, Y.K.K. can make products with better quality at smaller costs.

MANAGEMENT PHILOSOPHY

Virtually every aspect of Y.K.K.'s far-flung operations were influenced by the personality and philosophy of Mr. Tadao Yoshida. He had started his own company for the manufacturing and marketing of zippers in 1934, when he was only 25 years old. During World War II Mr. Yoshida's manufacturing facilities were completely destroyed. Shortly after the war ended in 1945, however, Mr. Yoshida made a new start with the establishment of Y.K.K.

In 1976 Mr. Yoshida was still actively involved in the day-to-day management of the company which he had grown into the largest manufacturer of zippers in the world. He ascribed the phenomenal success of Y.K.K. to his personal management philosophy which he called "The Cycle of Goodness." In several speeches and company documents Mr. Yoshida had explained the meaning of "The Cycle of Goodness."

I firmly believe in the spirit of social service.

Wages alone are not sufficient to assure our employees of a stable life and a rising standard of living. For this reason, we return to them a large share of the fruits of their labor, so that they may also participate in capital accumulation and share in the profits of the firm. Each employee, depending upon his means, deposits with the company at least 10 percent of his wages and monthly allowances, and 50 percent of his bonus; the company, in turn, pays interest on these savings. Moreover, as this increases capital, the employees benefit further as stockholders in the firm. It is said that "the accumulation" of savings distinguishes man from animals. Yet, if the receipts of a day are spent within that day, there can be no such cycle of saving.

The savings of all YKK employees are used to improve production facilities, and contribute directly to the prosperity of the firm. Superior production facilities improve the quality of the goods produced. Lower prices increase demand. And both factors contribute to the prosperity of other industries that use our products.

As society prospers, the need for raw materials and machinery of all sorts increases, and the benefits of this cycle spread not just to this firm, but to all

related industries. Thus the savings of our employees, by enhancing the pros-
perity of the firm, are returned to them as dividends that enrich their lives. This
results in increased savings which further advance the firm. Higher income
means higher tax payments, and higher tax payments enrich the lives of every
citizen.

In this manner, business income directly affects the prosperity of society; for
businesses are not mere seekers after profit, but vital instruments for the im-
provement of society.

This cycle enriches our free society and contributes to the happiness of those
who work within it. The perpetual working of this cycle produces perpetual
prosperity for all.

This is the cycle of goodness.[5]

In an interview with a casewriter in 1974, Mr. Yoshida had further
elaborated on his management philosophy:[6]

My business philosophy is based on the concept of the "cycle of goodness." Since
my boyhood, I was very fond of reading biographies of great men and when I
read a biography of Andrew Carnegie, I was deeply inspired by his "Unless you
render profit or goodness to others you cannot prosper." I was deeply impressed
and inspired. At the same time I wondered if and how I could do as he had said.
Gradually I came to believe that it is not good to make money without working
so hard as to sweat, and that to buy things other people made when their prices
go up is nothing but a rake-off. What is important is to make things by yourself.
What is the most precious in man, I believe, is the ability to create something
tangible out of nothing. By means of creativeness, man can make his life richer
and can gain lots of profits. Now suppose that we succeed in reducing the cost
of a certain product to ¥50 while other companies make the same product for
¥100. Then, we will return two-thirds of the balance or the cost saved to con-
sumers and related industries, and we will retain the remaining one-third to
ourselves, which we will use as much as possible for future investments. This
is my idea of profits. Savings make the difference between human beings and
animals. Inventiveness and savings are the two indispensable wheels for human
progress. I would dare say that those people who made money without toiling
but just through rising prices in a concerted way, as you have seen recently,
are committing a sin against society . . .

From last year to this year, costs of our raw materials went up more than 50
percent, and some of them as much as 200 percent. Even if we had boosted

---

[5]*The World of YKK*, Company publication.

[6]Quoted in *Y.K.K.*, Keio Business School case, 1974, prepared by Hideo Ishida.

prices of our products by 50 percent, our competitors could not have competed against us and we could have earned profits amounting to hundreds of million yen. But we did not. We did increase our prices last year, but we made our utmost efforts to make our price-hike as small as possible. As a result, we decided to squeeze this year's production cost on an assumption that we could have purchased raw materials ¥10 billion less than what we actually paid. Even with this, we will not go into red. We can rely on our own excellent production facilities. . . . But our wages have not been on the high side in the country and some of our people wanted larger price increase and bigger bonuses. I admonished them and reminded them making money by buying things at low prices and selling them at high prices is not compatible with the Y.K.K.'s principle because that money is not earned by our own efforts and toils. I told them that now was the time for the Y.K.K. group to exert itself to serve society better by keeping prices as low as possible even if we were to use up the last bit of our stockpile. I also told them, "Situations are very bad, we cannot deny it. We are now, so to speak, in winter. But for Y.K.K. the winter will be crisp and clear. We need not to be miserable because we are sure that at this time next year we will be able to get raw materials more cheaply and abundantly. Let's prepare ourselves, therefore, for a new spring when we can offer society newly developed materials and products." I believe this is the way to contribute to society. Y.K.K. achieved the present position of the world's largest zipper manufacturer because we were and are aiming to serve society . . .

The basis of management philosophy of Y.K.K. should not be changed. But when my son and his colleagues assume responsible positions in the company, it will reflect their own value judgments and will be slightly different from what it is. Similarly, our principal idea must take different forms from country to country. Management philosophy must have flexibility to adapt itself to different times and different countries. Through this process. we can make it closer to the ideal one.

INTERNATIONAL OPERATIONS

Early in Y.K.K.'s development Mr. Yoshida recognized the need for international expansion to maintain Y.K.K.'s growth. Initially, the company's international effort concentrated on *less developed countries*. In the 1950s Y.K.K. established export markets in South East Asia, Latin America, and Oceania. This move was followed, in the 1960s, by the establishment of joint ventures with local partners for the assembly of zipper parts into finished products in a number of Asian and Latin American countries (see *Exhibit 2*). These joint ventures enabled Y.K.K. to further its exports of raw materials, semi-finished goods, and zipper-making machinery.

EXHIBIT 2. Overseas operations in 1973

Company	Country	Location of main office	Established in	Type of ownership	Number of establishments	Type of establishment	Number of employees		
							Local nationals	Y.K.K. expatriates	Total
YKK Zipper (U.S.A.) Inc.	U.S.A.	New Jersey	Aug. 1960	Fully owned	15	Office, plant	190	32	222
Union Yoshida Industries Corp., Ltd.	Thailand	Bangkok	Apr. 1962	Joint venture	1	Office, plant	672	3	675
Malayan Zips Sdn., Bhd.	Malaysia	Johore Bahru	Jun. 1963	Joint venture	2	Office, plant	181	3	184
Slidefast (N.Z.) Ltd.	New Zealand	Auckland	Dec. 1963	Joint venture	1	Office, plant	51	0	51
Yoshida De Costa Rica Ltda.	Costa Rica	San Jose	Dec. 1963	Joint venture	1	Office, plant	181	2	183
Yoshida (Nederland) B.V.	Holland	Sneek	May 1964	Fully owned	3	Office, plant	76	4	80
YKK Zipper (W.I.) Ltd.	Trinidad	Port of Spain	Apr. 1965	Joint venture	1	Office, plant	83	1	84
Taiwan Zipper Co., Ltd.	Taiwan	Chung Li	May 1965	Joint venture	2	Office, plant	925	5	933
YKK Zipper Co. (Hong Kong) Ltd.	Hong Kong	Kowloon	Sep. 1966	Fully owned	2	Office, plant	175	7	182
YKK Fasteners (U.K.) Ltd.	England	London	Mar. 1967	Fully owned	3	Office, plant	180	12	192
Yoshida (France) S.A.R.L.	France	Paris	Dec. 1967	Fully owned	5	Office, plant	77	10	87
Yoshida (Deutschland) G.m.b.H.	West Germany	Monchen-gladbach	Dec. 1967	Fully owned	7	Office, plant	68	12	80
YKK Zipper Co. (Canada) Ltd.	Canada	Montreal	Jun. 1968	Fully owned	4	Office, plant	64	10	74

YKK Australia Pty., Ltd.	Australia	Sydney	Jun. 1968	Joint venture	2	Office, plant	56	3	59
Yoshida De El Salvador	El Salvador	San Salvador	Dec. 1968	Joint venture	1	Office, plant	135	2	137
Yoshida-Fossanese S.p.A.	Italy	Vercelli	Jan. 1969	Joint venture	6	Office, plant	99	8	107
YKK Zipper (S'pore) Private Ltd.	Singapore	Juron	Dec. 1969	Joint venture	1	Office, plant	88	2	90
Yoshida Espanola S.A.	Spain	Barcelona	Feb. 1971	Joint venture	3	Office, plant	18	4	22
N.V. Yoshida (Belgium) S.A.	Belgium	Gent	Apr. 1971	Joint venture	1	Office, plant	9	1	10
YKK Zipper (Middle East) S.A.L.	Lebanon	Beirut	Aug. 1971	Joint venture	1	Office, plant	5	2	7
YKK Indonesia Zipper Co., Ltd.	Indonesia	Djakarta	Jan. 1972	Joint venture	1	Office, plant	155	3	158
YKK-Belding, Inc.	U.S.A.	Atlanta	May 1972	Joint venture	3	Office	6	1	77
YKK Industries (U.S.A.) Inc.	U.S.A.	Macon	Jan. 1973	Fully owned	1	Plant	155	11	166
Hong Kong Ing Kwok Investments	Hong Kong	Hong Kong	Apr. 1973	Fully owned	1	Office	2	1	3
YKK Export, Inc.	U.S.A.	New Jersey	May 1973	Fully owned	1	Office	4	1	5
Hong Kong Ing Kwok Industrial Co., Ltd.	Hong Kong	Hong Kong	Sep. 1973	Fully owned	1	Plant	53	2	55

In addition to the above overseas subsidiaries, Y.K.K. had technical assistance arrangements with the following seven companies in five countries: Korea Zipper Co., Ltd. (Korea, Seoul), Union Fastener Corporation (Pty.) Ltd. (South Africa, Johannesburg), Ecuadorian Agency For Foreign Firms (Ecuador, Guayaquil), Satco, Inc. (Philippines, Quezon), United Fastener Corporation (Philippines, Quezon), Pagasa Industrial Corporation (Philippines, Quezon), Manufacture Bao Ly (Combodge, Phonom-penh).

Source: *Y.K.K.*, Keio Business School case, 1974, prepared by Hideo Ishida.

Y.K.K. had a policy of establishing wholly owned subsidiaries wherever possible. Mr. Yoshida commented on the joint venture route as an expansion strategy with the following words:[7]

> From the viewpoint of the Y.K.K. management principles, local partners tend to be obstacles rather than partakers. Many of them lack the willingness to consider about betterment of employees. More often than not, they are eager to let employees work for wages as low as possible and to put all the profits into their pockets. When establishing joint ventures in Southeast Asian countries, most of the Japanese companies go into business with Chinese residents with whom they have dealings. But in many cases, that choice turns out to be the cause of failure. I always recommend those people who seek joint venture partners to choose nationals of the host country . . . You should not forget that every country has its own nationalism. It is all right to have a Chinese manager in the sales department, but management of factories should be put in the hands of a local national. Unlike commercial business, a manufacturing company must have its roots deep in the soil of the host country. You cannot pull it out easily even if you come to face unforeseeable and unfavorable situations. A factory is like a bridge; once you have built one at a certain place, you cannot move it to another place for many years to come. In many cases, local businessmen are short of money and are not good at doing business. But we must think in long-run terms and help them in financing and transferring technical and management know-how.

While the less-developed areas were the first places for Y.K.K.'s direct foreign investment, Mr. Yoshida realized that the major growth he envisaged for his company would have to come from the industrialized countries. In 1960 Y.K.K. set up a wholly owned importing and assembly operation in *New York*. In the late 1960s and early 1970s additional assembly plants were established all over the United States and a full-scale manufacturing plant was expected to start operation in Macon, Georgia in March 1974.

In penetrating the U.S. market, Y.K.K. initially concentrated its marketing efforts on those customers that purchased a narrow variety of zippers in large volume.[8] Since these customers could accept longer delivery times, Y.K.K. was able to fill their orders from its high-volume factories in Japan. The longer lead-times together with long production

---

[7]Quoted in *Y.K.K.*, Keio Business School case, 1974, prepared by Hideo Ishida.

[8]The information on Y.K.K.'s U.S. market penetration is based on *Slide Fasteners and Parts Thereof.* United States International Trade Commission, Publication 757, Washington, D.C., 1976, p. A-46.

runs frequently allowed Y.K.K. to offer volume discounts in the U.S. below the prices of U.S. competition.

About 1970, Y.K.K. started the next plan of its penetration of the U.S. market. The company offered substantial discounts to volume accounts for purchases of zippers in basic colors. Most U.S. manufacturers followed the practice of average pricing, i.e., they charged the same price for rarely used colors as for basic colors. In general, the basic colors guaranteed a margin that was high enough to cover the relatively higher cost of filling orders for more unusual colors.

The third method of attacking the U.S. market was a special emphasis Y.K.K. put around 1970 on invisible zippers and plastic zippers, replacing metal zippers for sportswear. The invisible zipper gave dresses the "no zipper look" while the molded plastic zipper, in bold colors, transformed the zipper into an eye-catching element of fashion design. The technology for these two innovative products had been widely known; but U.S. manufacturers had not anticipated the popularity these zippers rapidly gained among designers and final consumers. While the U.S. manufacturers began in a hurry to set up manufacturing facilities for the production of similar invisible and molded plastic zippers, Y.K.K. steadily gained sales and market share in the United States.

In *Europe*, Y.K.K. first established a zipper plant in Holland in 1964. Mr. Nishizaki had been responsible for getting the European operations off the ground. He was 32 years old at that time, and had neither sales nor substantial international experience. He recalled Mr. Yoshida's words when he left for his new assignment:

> *Our company is sending a pigeon to the high mountains. If you fail that's not your problem; you will be alone with no team to support you. Don't worry. Only I am responsible to the board for any failure.*

Mr. Doguchi, who went to Holland with Mr. Nishizaki as an engineer, reminisced:[9]

> *We left Japan with a firm resolution. We told ourselves that we would not come back alive to Japan unless we succeed . . .*

The Dutch subsidiary turned out to be a very successful operation, and it became the basis for the establishment of other subsidiaries in France, England, Germany, Italy, Belgium, and Spain (see *Exhibit 2*). While Y.K.K. preferred to set up wholly owned subsidiaries in Europe,

---

[9]Quoted in *Y.K.K.*, Keio Business School case, 1974, prepared by Hideo Ishida.

the subsidiaries in Italy, Belgium, and Spain were joint ventures. Reflecting on the joint venture in Belgium, Mr. Nishizaki explained:

> Our local partner in Belgium is our former import agent. We didn't want him to get into trouble or go out of business. People are very important to us, not just profit.

All of Y.K.K.'s foreign subsidiaries were guided by certain principles that Mr. Yoshida had often expressed to his managers. One of these principles was that, because Y.K.K.'s objective in opening overseas plants was to serve the local community, all the profits of each subsidiary were to be reinvested in the country in which it was operating.

Another principle said that every effort should be made to integrate each Y.K.K. subsidiary and its managers into the local environment. Mr. Yoshida was reported to tell the Japanese managers who were about to move abroad:[10]

> Do not mix with the other Japanese working abroad. Avoid joining Japanese associations over there unless you find difficulties in doing business without being a member of such associations. Try to learn the language of the country where you are going to work. Do not teach local employees Japanese. Try to be a good citizen in your new community. Do not forget to contribute your share to the program of the local economy and welfare. Remember that if you do not render services to your new community, you will neither be accepted by them nor succeed.

Mr. Nishizaki felt that Y.K.K.'s endeavor to be a good citizen in each foreign country often appeared to be in conflict with the economic success of Y.K.K.:

> We are expanding very fast all over Europe. We also import a lot of parts from Japan. We have a big problem. If the local manufacturers receive too much pressure from us our image and our relations with the host country may be hurt. What we are trying to do to reduce such pressure is to stimulate primary demand for zippers in each country. Our introduction of plastic zippers for ski pants and jackets is one example. It made zippers a fashion item.

In managing its overseas operations, Y.K.K. tried to apply essentially the same management philosophy that Mr. Yoshida had established to guide the business in Japan. This worked well in most

---

[10]Ibid.

countries. A senior executive in the Tokyo head office nevertheless cautioned:[11]

> *I think we should take a fresh look at the Japanese way of management. Management philosophy of Y.K.K. is based on a belief that all human beings, in spite of differences in races, customs, and so on, have many things in common. I must admit that I am wondering if our local workers understand what we tell them of our policies as the Japanese workers do. But if they think there is something with which they can have sympathy or something challenging to them, we should be satisfied with them. . . . If not, we had better leave management in the hands of the locals.*

COMPETITIVE SITUATION IN EUROPE

Europe accounted for roughly 45 percent of Y.K.K.'s overseas sales and profits and was consequently an area of particular interest to top management. As previously noted, Y.K.K. operated subsidiaries in seven European countries. In addition, the company exported to virtually every country in Europe, both from its European subsidiaries and from Japan.

The subsidiaries in Germany and in the U.K. each contributed about 20% to Y.K.K.'s European sales; France and Italy each about 15%; the remaining 30% of sales came from the subsidiaries in Holland, Belgium, and Spain. Each subsidiary concentrated its production and marketing activities primarily on its own market and on export sales. So far, Y.K.K. had not made any attempt to move toward plant specialization in Europe. As a result, each subsidiary plant produced the full line of products that its individual market required.

All subsidiaries depended heavily on import of zipper parts and finished zippers from Japan. Metal zippers were mostly produced in Europe. In contrast, virtually all of the molded plastic zippers and some of the nylon zipper volume were imported from Japan.

Industry analysts estimated that of the total Y.K.K. sales volume of finished zippers in Europe roughly 30% was imported from Japan. The percentage varied substantially by country. It was estimated that it was as high as 50% for Italy and as low as 10% for Holland in 1973.

Mr. Nishizaki calculated that the zipper market in Europe was about

---

[11]Quoted in *Y.K.K.*, Keio Business School case, 1974, prepared by Hideo Ishida.

three times the size of the Japanese market and was growing at a rate of
5–10% annually. A total of about 40 zipper manufacturers competed in
this market. Y.K.K.'s principal competition in Europe were Opti (Germany) and Lightning (U.K.), a subsidiary of I.C.I., Ltd. In the 1960s
Opti and Lightning had formed a joint holding company. Opti and
Lightning were operating in virtually every European country. Their
subsidiaries were tightly controlled. Moreover, Opti and Lightning had
accomplished some specialization of their various European plants.

A third major competitor for Y.K.K. in Europe was the U.S. company, Talon. Talon was a division of Textron, Inc. and had about 45%
share of the U.S. market.

Market share data for Europe were not easily obtainable. Several
industry analysts estimated, however, that Opti and Lightning combined held about 55% of the total Western European zipper market,
Y.K.K. about 35%, and that the remaining 10% were spread over more
than 30 other manufacturers, including Talon. The same analyst also
estimated that Y.K.K.'s market share in Italy and in the U.K. might be
as high as 50%.

In comparing the relative strengths of Y.K.K. and its major competition, Mr. Nishizaki made the following observations:

> *Technologically all major companies are strong, but they go different ways. Opti
> seems to buy more technology from outside. Talon seems rather old and not as
> aggressive in developing new products.*

> *Y.K.K. is weakest in finance. We are a relatively small company. Both Opti/
> Lightning and Talon belong to huge diversified concerns.*

> *But that may also be a disadvantage. Because they are just subsidiaries of I.C.I.
> or Textron they don't have the direct access to top management we have, and
> they have to fight for resource allocation. In Y.K.K. we have to sell zippers,
> and we probably have to do it for the next 50 years. So everybody here, includ-
> ing top management, has a vital interest in what happens to zippers.*

> *We certainly differ in our management style. We are fair to competition; we
> don't believe in cut-throat competition.*

> *Y.K.K. men do not have to be afraid of any mistakes.*

The demand for zippers in Europe as elsewhere was derived from
the demand for the end products into which zippers were incorporated.
Analysis of sales trends in various industries as well as cooperation with
apparel manufacturers for new applications of zippers were, therefore,
important marketing tasks.

For the distribution of its products, Y.K.K. used no intermediaries
but sold its products directly to the large number of garment makers,

footwear manufacturers, and other industrial customers. Management of Y.K.K. felt that direct sales were necessary to obtain fast feedback from the market and to give rapid delivery.

Fast delivery was seen as the most important competitive tool. "About 40–50% of our customers want delivery within one day," said Mr. Ueno, General Manager of Y.K.K.'s subsidiary in Holland. Management of Y.K.K. felt that a company's capability to effect fast delivery and to supply a wide selection of products were even more important than low price. Mr. Nishizaki explained:

> *Obviously, the price has to be reasonable. But we are not selling cheap; we are selling at a reasonable margin. What gives us strength in Europe is the fact that our delivery is good, that each of our subsidiaries carries a full line, and that we respond quickly to changing customer needs.*
>
> *A price cut of 1–2¢ is not an important reason for a customer to switch suppliers. Some of our competition learned that when they tried to break into the market with price cuts. Our approach is to emphasize reliable, fast supply and trouble-free zippers. But again, the price has to be reasonable. I would guess if price differences between competing products of more than 10% existed — assuming the same quality — customers would switch.*

DEALING WITH THE DUMPING ACCUSATION

The letter that Mr. Nishizaki had received from the E.E.C. Commission was the result of a dumping complaint against Y.K.K. initiated by zipper producers in Belgium, France, Italy, Holland, The United Kingdom, and Germany. Mr. Nishizaki realized that Y.K.K.'s penetration of the European market had certainly intensified the competitive struggle. He was confident, however, that the dumping charges were absolutely unfounded.[12] Mr. Nishizaki commented:

> *We are certainly not selling below costs, nor are our export prices lower than our domestic prices minus domestic marketing costs. In fact, our prices in Europe are actually not lower than those of our major competition. But, many of our competitors are not making profits at current prices. Our costs are lower than theirs, even lower than those of Opti and Lightning. What competitors are*

---

[12]The General Agreement on Tariffs and Trade (GATT) defined dumping as the practice of setting the price at which a product leaves the exporting country below the normal domestic price in that same country. The legislature of several countries had established both broader and narrower definitions.

really after with this complaint against Y.K.K. is to force us to raise our prices so that they can get their own prices up.

Although Mr. Nishizaki was convinced that the dumping accusations were unjustified, he felt that he had to take some action rather than just sit and wait for the end of a lengthy investigation. He knew that some of Y.K.K.'s competitors were visiting customers, spreading the rumor that Y.K.K. was dumping and suggesting that Y.K.K. would soon be forced to raise prices. "They are fighting with all means," Mr. Nishizaki said.

He was not sure what exactly the legal procedure would be if Y.K.K. took a stern attitude, simply denied all charges, and waited for the investigation to find the company not guilty.

It could take years! The E.E.C. Commission is understaffed. There are only three officers in the whole department dealing with dumping issues. In the U.S. 300–400 officials worked on our case.

Moreover, even after the investigation has shown that we are not guilty of dumping, the thing may still not be over. I believe there is a GATT regulation that says that if imports of a given product have increased and if such increased imports are a substantial cause of serious injury to local industry, then import restrictions may be unilaterally imposed by the respective country government. Any government could take such action, and it will obviously be influenced by the lobbying of the local industry. In reaction to such import restrictions, the Japanese government could impose similar restrictions on goods from the other country.

I really don't know enough about all the legal implications and they are probably difficult to predict. What complicates the legal situation even further is that Y.K.K.'s European subsidiaries, I believe, would actually be treated as part of the local industry.

Mr. Nishizaki felt confident that the E.E.C. Commission, before embarking on a lengthy investigation, would propose an "amicable settlement" to Y.K.K. management. The terms of such a settlement would have to be negotiated, but the Commission would undoubtedly insist on some voluntary import restrictions, in particular for high import countries such as Italy. Also, the Commission would most probably demand a voluntary increase of Y.K.K.'s European selling prices; the requested increase might range from 5% to 25%.

Mr. Nishizaki thought that a price increase would not have to put Y.K.K. at a competitive disadvantage. Cost inflation was pushing prices upward anyway. Moreover, although he could not be sure, Mr. Nishizaki expected that once Y.K.K. raised its prices, competition would raise theirs, too.

A curtailment of exports from Japan to Europe, he felt, would be more difficult to deal with. In the short run, any import quota to which Y.K.K. might agree would endanger customer service in terms of product availability and fast delivery until the manufacturing output of Y.K.K.'s European subsidiaries had been sufficiently increased to meet demand. The longer-term effect of import restrictions would be additional investment in European plant facilities. Mr. Nishizaki made a rough estimate: In Italy, for example, imports as a percentage of Y.K.K's total sales were particularly high, so the E.E.C. and the Italian industry would surely demand some quota for this country. If Y.K.K. agreed to reduce imports by 30% below current levels, the company would have to invest an additional ¥1–¥1.5 billion in local manufacturing facilities to meet demand. Besides, manufacturing costs in Italy were close to 10% higher than in Japan.

ORGANIZATIONAL ISSUES

Mr. Nishizaki realized that there would be no easy solution to the dumping problem. He could think of a number of alternative courses of action, and he tried to assess how each of these alternatives would affect Y.K.K. and the individual subsidiaries and, most importantly, how the European subsidiary managers would react to any of these decisions he could envisage. He began to reflect on Y.K.K.'s organization and management of the international operations.

Y.K.K. had essentially a functional organization structure. The principal departments at headquarters in Japan were seven manufacturing departments,[13] accounting, finance, purchasing, domestic zipper marketing, building materials marketing, export, and Overseas Enterprise. The export department handled all exports from Japan. The Overseas Enterprise Department, managed by Mr. Nishizaki, supervised the activities of Y.K.K.'s foreign subsidiaries.

In most of the subsidiaries Japanese managers occupied the key positions. A common characteristic of these roughly 140 Y.K.K. managers working abroad was that they were very young, usually in their early 30s. One senior executive in the Overseas Enterprise Department commented on the selection criteria for an overseas manager:[14]

---

[13]Metal zipper, plastic zipper, zipper parts, textile, metal, machinery, and aluminum building material.

[14]Quoted in *Y.K.K.*, Keio Business School case, 1974, prepared by Hideo Ishida.

What is most important is whether he is good or not as an individual human being. In other words, whether he can be accepted as a representative of Y.K.K. However fluent in foreign languages and competent as a manager he may be, he cannot be qualified for overseas assignments unless he understands fully the spirit of Y.K.K. And he must not be reserved. Our overseas managers are sent to their new assignments without much orientation and training. But since they are young, they are rich in vitality and flexibility in their thought and action. Because our president always encourages them by telling them, "Do not be afraid of two or three misfires," they can freely exercise their own initiative and potentialities. And in most cases, this resulted in satisfactory achievements.

Once assigned to their overseas jobs, the subsidiary managers had considerable autonomy for decision making in virtually every area of their businesses. "Tokyo exercises very little influence on our operations," said one European subsidiary manager:

Of course we consult with the Overseas department or functional departments on very important issues, such as major product changes, joint ventures, acquisitions, and financing, especially when corporate guarantees are necessary. But the head office never tells me what to do in marketing, product mix, or pricing because each subsidiary knows more about its local market than the head office.

The General Manager of another European subsidiary commented:

Perhaps the only thing where the parent company has decision power over the affairs of our company is treatment of me.

Mr. Nishizaki elaborated on the relationship between headquarters and foreign subsidiaries in Y.K.K.:

The emphasis in our company is not on who is in charge, *but who* knows most. *We don't have a very formal organization, we just stress people. Our basic philosophy is: Always talk to the expert, go to the department that really knows rather than waste time going through a complicated structure.*

Our subsidiary managers are the experts in their local markets. They know best, and giving them a lot of autonomy assures the best customer service in each country. Also, our people abroad are quite normal. If they have a lot of autonomy then they think that the business really belongs to them, and they do their utmost to succeed.

But we emphasize interaction between the parent company and the subsidiaries. The subsidiaries have many visitors from the parent company and there are a lot of occasions when our overseas employees come to Japan.

No one person has almighty wisdom, so it's important that he who knows best makes the decision. Y.K.K. is like a forest and not like just one big tree. Every individual has special competence. The subsidiary managers, and not just the head office, have special competence. When a typhoon hits the forest the stronger trees must support the weaker ones. The system works very well.

The major reports sent from the subsidiaries to headquarters were monthly sales reports, monthly balance sheets, and annual plans and budgets. The annual plans were presented and discussed in February each year at the "Joint Meeting of Directors." About 300 managers of the Y.K.K. subsidiaries and branches in Japan and abroad got together for a 3-day meeting to review the annual production and sales plans. These meetings were also attended by managers of the major functional departments, people reporting to them, recent university graduates that Y.K.K. had hired, and foreign employees. One subsidiary manager commented on this plan presentation and discussion: "The plans are submitted not so much for approval but to inform the head office and to make sure we get the new equipment we need from Japan."

Y.K.K. had no explicit guidelines for evaluating the performance of overseas managers. "When I went to Holland, Mr. Yoshida just told me: 'Do the best you can,' " related Mr. Ueno, General Manager of Yoshida Nederland.

Another executive stated:

There are 5–10 criteria top management looks at, market share, growth rate of sales and profits, sales targets, employee relations, popularity in the local community. But senior management does not get mesmerized by the actual figures as I think U.S. companies do. The potential is just as important as the actual results. We are more concerned with next year's strengths than this year's weaknesses.

Mr. Takahashi of Y.K.K. Fasteners (U.K.) commented:[15]

I am happy to say that the parent company takes a long outlook in evaluating our overall performance. If you have good records for one or two years, they take it calmly. But three or four years later, you will understand that they accurately measure and reward your contribution.

While high subsidiary autonomy was firmly established, not everybody in Y.K.K. agreed that this was the best approach and problems occasionally arose. The General Manager of one of Y.K.K's European subsidiaries made the following observation:

Most of the Y.K.K. subsidiaries over here engage in exports and Y.K.K. also exports from Japan. As a result, at least once or twice a year we find ourselves

---

[15]Quoted in *Y.K.K.*, Keio Business School case, 1974, prepared by Hideo Ishida.

competing against another Y.K.K. subsidiary or against the export department in Japan for the same larger customer. It has actually happened that a large customer has tried to play out one Y.K.K. subsidiary against the other.

Such competition against each other is nonsense. Who loses is the Y.K.K. group as a whole. We also confuse our customers, and we are losing face, especially if different Y.K.K. subsidiaries quote different prices and conditions.

The problem is getting bigger every day as the European markets grow closer and closer together. I am not interested in competing against other Y.K.K. units. To avoid that, I think every subsidiary should be assigned a certain geographic territory.

For the future, Y.K.K. has to be strong, and that means we all have to go into the same direction. In the future there has to be more integration and centralization; otherwise it will be difficult to manage the growing organization. We all don't like a very rigid organization. We all like to be on the same level. But eventually we need a control center in Europe to coordinate the subsidiaries over here. You can't do that easily from Japan.

Headquarter's management, of course, knew about these concerns but did not feel that any major change from the current way of operating was indicated. "We don't want to get involved in the local subsidiaries' operations," said Mr. Nishizaki. "We are very afraid of interference. We believe in fair competition, even among our own subsidiaries. As long as no subsidiary sells under cost we are satisfied. Besides, if conflicts arise our managers can usually work them out by talking to each other. They are all part of the Y.K.K. group. The nature of the product — which means low margin, high volume, quick fashion changes, and fast delivery — does not allow central direction from a European or the Japanese head office."

3.7 *CASE*

Citibank: Marketing to Multinational Customers

Robert D. Buzzell

In April 1984, Larry Lee, task force coordinator for Citibank's Global Account Management System (GAMS), was reviewing the bank's progress in improving the system during 1983. GAMS was designed for coordinating the bank's dealings with some 500 large, multinational corporations (MNCs). Originally, it had been developed for use by a major organizational unit, the World Corporation Group (WCG), that had line responsibility for relationships with the MNCs. As part of an overall reorganization of the bank in early 1980, WCG had been disbanded as a separate unit. Account managers responsible for MNCs were integrated into the newly constituted Institutional Banking Organization which assumed worldwide responsibility for dealings with all corporate customers. Following the reorganization, there was some concern about a loss of momentum in the bank's maintenance and development of business with the MNCs formerly served by WCG. A task force appointed to study the subject in mid-1982 had recommended several actions, and Lee had been appointed to coordinate their implementation. He felt that considerable progress had been made since that time, but was aware that some of the bank's account managers who were responsible for relationships with MNCs were not satisfied with the way the system was working. A consultant had recently submitted to Lee a draft report of an investigation of GAMS. As he reviewed the report, Lee wondered what modifications in the system might be considered next.

CITIBANK: COMPANY BACKGROUND

Citibank, N.A. was the principal operating subsidiary of Citicorp, a holding company formed in 1967. Founded as the City Bank of New York in 1812, Citibank was by any measure one of the leading financial institutions in the world. In 1983, the bank employed over 60,000 people and had about 2,400 locations in the United States and 94 countries. *Exhibit 1* gives selected financial data for Citicorp, the parent company of Citibank.

Citibank's activities were organized into three principal business units: institutional banking, individual banking, and the capital markets group.

Institutional Banking (IB) units provided loans and other financial services to corporations and governmental agencies. IB's principal business was lending: Its worldwide volume of commercial loans in 1983 was $60 billion. Other services included foreign exchange, international payments, electronic banking, and asset-based financing. Within the North American Banking Group, responsible for the U.S. and Canada, IB had in recent years pursued a strategy of decentralization. In order to develop closer contacts with corporate clients, the bank had started opening offices throughout the country; by 1983, there were locations in 40 states and the District of Columbia. International operations were organized around three geographic groups — Asia/Pacific, Caribbean/Central and South America, and Europe/Middle East/Africa. In addition, the International Financial Institutions Group was responsible for coordinating the bank's dealings with banks and other financial institutions around the world.

Individual Banking units in the U.S. and 18 other countries provided a wide range of deposit, loan, and other service to consumers. Until the

EXHIBIT 1. Selected financial statistics — Citicorp and subsidiaries 1978–1983

	1978	1979	1980	1981	1982	1983
Millions of dollars:						
Net interest revenue	$2,256	$2,509	$2,545	$2,479	$3,526	$4,043
Fees, commissions, and other revenue	739	807	1,171	1,617	1,641	1,840
Total revenue	$2,995	$3,316	$3,716	$4,096	$5,167	$5,883
Total expense	2,168	2,445	2,872	3,241	3,871	4,277
Pre-tax income	$ 827	$ 871	$ 844	$ 855	$1,296	$1,606
Net income	470	541	499	531	723	860
Total assets	$88,195	$106,371	$114,920	$119,232	$129,997	$134,655
Return on equity (%)	15.5	16.0	13.3	13.1	15.8	16.5

Source: Citicorp annual reports.

471

1980s, regulatory constraints limited Citibank's domestic individual banking operations to New York State. These regulations were, however, gradually breaking down. In the fall of 1982, the bank acquired its first unit outside New York with "full deposit-taking capability" — Fidelity Savings & Loan, in California.

The *Capital Markets Group* was formed in 1982, combining the bank's securities underwriting, distribution, and trading activities with international private banking, venture capital, and investment advisory services. Although U.S. regulations prohibited it from functioning as such domestically, CMG was one of the world's largest merchant (investment) banks, with a staff of 3,500. Multinational corporations were major users of these services outside the U.S.

In addition to the three core businesses, Citibank also provided information and transaction processing services through its Financial and Information Services Group.

INTERNATIONAL OPERATIONS

For many years, Citibank had emphasized international operations. First among U.S. banks to open a foreign branch (in 1912), the bank in 1983 operated in 94 countries. This was clearly the most extensive branch network of all U.S.-based banks, and included small nations such as Sudan and Peru as well as all of the major industrial countries. Citibank also had by far the largest volume of foreign loans, deposits, foreign exchange revenue, and earnings of any of the U.S.-based banks. An industry comparison for 1982, for example, showed that the bank's foreign branch loans amounted to $43.7 billion, while second-place Chase Manhattan's figure was $31.9 billion.

A rapid expansion of the international network took place between the mid-1950s and the mid-1970s, with the number of branches increasing more than threefold. By 1973, international operations accounted for 59% of worldwide revenue and 60% of net income. According to one senior vice-president who had spent several years in the United Kingdom during the 1970s:[1]

---

[1]Quotations of statements by Citibank personnel in this case study are drawn from one of several sources: interviews by the casewriter, the consultant's draft report, published Citibank reports, and case studies written in 1975 by Stanley M. Davis. ("First National City Bank: Multinational Corporate Banking," A, B, C, and D, HBS Case Services Nos. 9-476-079, -080, -081, and -082.) In the interest of brevity, the sources of the quotations are not cited individually.

At first our overseas expansion was basically a matter of following our U.S. customers as they built their international business. Later, in the mid-seventies, we were in a great position to serve the foreign multinationals when they began to make acquisitions or set up operations in the U.S. This, in turn, led to opportunities that didn't involve North America at all, such as a German corporation financing a facility in South America.

Exhibit 2 summarizes trends in the relative importance of domestic and international operations from 1975 to 1983.

THE CHANGING FINANCIAL SERVICES MARKETPLACE

Both within the United States and elsewhere, the once-tranquil world of commercial banking underwent radical changes between the 1960s and the 1980s.

For many years up to the 1960s, Citibank and other banks defined their business as *lending,* not as the provision of services. Bank relationships with corporate customers were based primarily on personal contacts, and competition was limited to other commercial banks, all of whom played by essentially the same rules. As one Citibank executive put it:

"We all followed the "3-6-3 rule" — pay 3% for deposit money, lend it out at 6%, and be on the golf course by 3:00 p.m.!"

A series of "shock waves" disrupted the banking industry, and financial services in general, beginning in the early 1960s.

1. First in the United States, and then elsewhere, the "commercial paper" market emerged. This provided a mechanism for companies to borrow from each other, and from private investors, without going through banks at all. The effect, according to Citibank Executive Vice-President Lawrence Small, was that "routine borrowing by top-rated corporations, which was the bread and butter of corporate banking, was no longer done."

2. The passage of the Bank Holding Company Act in 1968 led to the formation of regional chains of banks within the U.S. These banks began to compete more aggressively with Citibank and other "money center" banks for large corporations' business.

3. Insurance companies, traditionally only long-term lenders, started to compete for short- and intermediate-term loans.

EXHIBIT 2. Selected financial data — domestic and international operations, 1975–1982

	1975	1976	1977	1978	1979	1980	1981	1982
Income (millions)[a]								
North America	$110	$121	$ 78	$144	$193	$192	$257	$293
Other areas	238	284	303	338	351	315	298	454
Totals	$348	$405	$381	$482	$544	$507	$555	$747
Average assets (billions)								
North America	—	—	$27.8	$29.1	$33.7	$ 41.0	$ 47.9	$ 50.7
Other areas	—	—	40.6	49.9	60.6	66.1	68.0	70.8
Totals	—	—	$68.4	$79.0	$94.3	$107.1	$115.9	$121.5
Average volume — commercial loans (billions)[b]								
Domestic	$14.7	$12.6	$11.9	$11.9	$13.1	$16.2	$18.4	$21.0
International	16.8	19.8	24.0	27.9	32.2	34.8	36.9	38.4
Totals	$31.5	$32.4	$35.9	$39.8	$45.3	$51.0	$55.3	$59.4
Net rate spread (%)[c]								
Domestic	4.11	4.53	4.60	4.94	4.52	4.06	3.56	4.22
International	3.55	3.39	2.98	2.83	2.54	2.17	1.96	2.99
Loans to major multinationals (billions)[d]	—	—	$ 7.3	$ 8.3	$ 9.3	$11.5	$12.2	$15.7

[a]Income before securities transactions.
[b]Domestic figures include Canada.
[c]Net rate of spread is the difference between the average rate earned on interest-yielding assets and the average cost of deposits and other sources of funds.
[d]For 1977–79, as reported. For 1980–82, approximate amounts.
Source: Citicorp annual reports.

4. With the advent of high interest rates in the 1970s, corporate treasurers began to assign high priority to "cash management." Idle balances, once passively left in banks, came to be invested on a daily basis.

5. The boundaries of the commercial banking industry, once clearly defined by federal laws, became progressively more blurred. Competition among different types of financial service institutions was most visible in the consumer sector: Merrill Lynch, a brokerage firm, introduced its highly successful Cash Management Account in 1977, while Sears, Roebuck, the largest retailer in the U.S., acquired a brokerage firm in 1982 and began opening financial service centers in its stores. Industry observers predicted a protracted struggle for supremacy among the "financial conglomerates," with Citibank and American Express listed as entrants along with Merrill Lynch and Sears.[2]

6. Changing technology created new opportunities and problems. The rising cost of providing bank services by traditional, largely manual methods put great pressure on banks to automate their "back room" functions. At the same time, new electronic systems came into use — automatic teller machines for routine consumer transactions and remote terminals for communication with corporate customers.

Outside the United States, competition among banks and other financial institutions also intensified during the 1970s and early 1980s. According to one study, in the early 1960s there was only "modest rivalry in international banking."[3] Banks based in major industrial countries, with some exceptions, did not operate branches in other industrial countries. Even where it was permitted by law, there was very little competition between commercial banks and merchants banks.

During the 1970s, U.S.-based multinational companies continued to expand their activities abroad. At the same time, MNCs based in Europe and Japan grew at an even more rapid rate. One result was growing head-to-head competition among banks based in all of the major industrial countries as these institutions followed their domestic clients abroad. The number of foreign banks with branches in London, for example, grew from 90 in 1961 to 213 in 1972 and 351 in 1980.

Reflecting the increased competition in international banking com-

---

[2]See, for example, "Citibank takes on Merrill Lynch in Battle of the Giants," *Dun's Business Month*, October 1983, pp. 60–63.

[3]Dwight B. Crane and Samuel L. Hayes, III, "The Evolution of International Banking and its Implications for Regulation," *Journal of Bank Research*, Vol. 14 (Spring 1983), pp. 39-53.

petition, interest rate spreads — the average difference between interest revenue and cost for banks — narrowed steadily from 1974 on. The average spread in industrialized countries declined from 1.47 points in 1974 to 0.55 points in 1980.

RELATIONSHIPS WITH CORPORATE CUSTOMERS

Large corporations, including MNCs, typically dealt with a number of commercial banks on a regular basis. One study of larger MNCs showed that, on average, about 20 different banks were used. A corporation did, however, tend to concentrate most of its business among a few banks. Usually, one or two were regarded as "lead banks," and these were given some degree of preferential treatment. For example, if another bank offered better terms in initial bidding on a major financial program, the lead bank(s) might be given a chance to meet those terms. Beyond the 1 or 2 lead banks, another 5 or 6 banks might be viewed by a corporation as "principal" banks. Citibank and its competitors devoted considerable effort to improving their status with major customers, i.e., to converting minor relationships into principal banking relationships and, ultimately, lead relationships.

Corporations' reasons for choosing their banks were varied. *Exhibit 3* summarizes the reasons stated in a 1983 survey of large U.S.- and Canadian-based multinationals. As shown there, the most common single reason was that a company had a "long-term, historical relationship" with the bank. Most of these relationships dated from the time when banking connections were formed through personal acquaintance. Other factors affecting choices included specific facilities or services offered and the quality of personal service provided.

About a third of large MNCs conducted formal, periodic reviews of their banking relationships. A more common approach, used by 60% of MNCs, was to have less formal, ad hoc bank reviews.[4] The factors most commonly considered by these companies in their reviews are listed in *Exhibit 3*. As might be expected, the criteria used in reviewing banks included most of the ones mentioned as reasons for using the bank in the first place. The periodic reviews did, however, seem to put more

---

[4]Greenwich Research Associates, "North American Multinational Banking/Foreign Exchange Services," (Greenwich, CT, 1983), p. 1.

EXHIBIT 3. Factors affecting multinational corporations' choices of banks

Reasons for using principal banks	% mentioning
Long-term historical relationship	75%
Branch network outside N. America	73
Willingness to lend	71
High caliber of account manager	69
Competence in managing global relationships	60
Major domestic bank	59
Competitive loan pricing	56
Factors used in evaluating banks	**% using**
Account officer performance	85%
Credit pricing	83
Pattern of innovative, useful financial ideas	74
Domestic cash management performance	63
Domestic credit facilities provided	51
Foreign exchange quotes	44
International cash management performance	36
Branch network performance	30

Source: Greenwich Research Associates, "North American Multinational Banking/Foreign Exchange Services — 1983" (Greenwich, CT, 1983). The data are based on interviews conducted at 477 North America-based multinational companies. The respondents were directors of international banking (32%), assistant treasurers for international banking (35%), treasurers or controllers (20%), and other financial managers.

emphasis on the quality of service provided by a bank's account manager.

At Citibank, the focal point of a relationship with a corporate customer was the Institutional Banking *account manager.* (Account managers were sometimes called "relationship managers"; customers were variously termed "accounts," "relationships," and "clients.") Account managers generally handled from 5 to 25 corporations, depending on their size and complexity. Between 2 and 5 account managers reported to a *unit head,* and unit heads reported to a department head (in a New York-based unit), a regional office head, or a corporate bank head (in a foreign office).

Citibank's basic approach to organizing its Institutional Banking activities had changed twice since the late 1960s. Prior to that time, the structure was almost completely geographical; accounts were serviced by the country (or region within the U.S.) in which they were located. A few *industry* specialists handled the petroleum, chemical, mining, and airline industries, however, because of their distinctive financing needs.

In the late 1960s, following a study by McKinsey & Company, the bank adopted an organization structure based primarily on customer industries. Account managers were grouped into specialized units serving the automotive industry, retailing, textiles, and so on. This system lasted until the late 1970s when the emphasis shifted to "regionalization" within North America. Thus, in 1984, the IB's organization — for both domestic and international operations — was based primarily on geographic units, each with responsibility for operations in its own area. Some industry specialization had been retained in fields such as petroleum, airlines, and public utilities. Even in these cases, however, regional units were being set up where warranted by geographic concentrations of business.

Citibank's corporate accounts were varied and represented every industry. The Institutional Bank did, however, focus its efforts on medium and large companies. Within the U.S., the bank defined its target market as consisting of the 28,000 companies in the country with sales of $20 million or more. Of these, about one-fourth were already active Citibank customers in early 1984.

At one time, corporate account managers at Citibank (and other banks) would not have viewed their jobs as "sales" or "marketing" positions. In the competitive world of the 1980s, however, they clearly played that role and were even sometimes referred to as the bank's "marketing officers." As such, they were responsible for marketing not only the IB's principal product — credit — but also for developing or coordinating the development of business for other bank services, both within the IB and from other parts of Citibank. These included foreign exchange services, trade financing, electronic banking services, and investment banking. The account manager typically made initial contacts with customers in connection with these services and then brought in a specialist to discuss the customer's needs. For ongoing relationships, the account manager acted as the "quarterback" of an account team that included customer service representatives and, usually, product managers who were responsible for various specialized banking services.

Exhibit 4 summarizes the results of a survey of corporate financial executives' attitudes toward their banks' account managers. A Citibank account manager in the U.K. commented on the subject:

> *Customers always complain most about lack of continuity. The problem is that continuity means staying in the same job for a long time, and this has limited*

EXHIBIT 4. Multinational corporations' attitudes toward account managers

Account manager characteristics	Average importance rating*
Follow up promptly and effectively	4.4
Meet company's credit needs	3.8
Know how to use bank's network	3.7
Know company's worldwide needs	3.7
Experienced, knowledgeable in international finance	3.7
Have backup associates who know company	3.6
Have support from international specialists	3.6
Have single worldwide responsibility for relationship	3.5
Problems companies have with account managers	**% mentioning**
Too much turnover in account managers	35%
Insufficient knowledge of international finance	32
Too few visits to company and its subsidiaries	31
Account managers too inexperienced	30
Account managers can't get cooperation of bank officers abroad	29
Too few account managers handle relationship	23
Insufficient knowledge of bank's international services	19

*Average scale ratings, where 5 = very important, 1 = unimportant.
Source: See *Exhibit 3.*

appeal. The culture here, and in most other banks, is that if you aren't promoted in 3 years, you aren't succeeding. But, there is no question that corporate accounts want to deal with an account manager whom they know well.

ELECTRONIC BANKING

An increasingly important dimension of Citibank's relationship with corporate clients was the provision of services through electronic systems. Citibank had pioneered in the development of electronic banking, beginning with relatively simple systems that permitted customers to access account balance data. *Exhibit 5* lists some of the more important services that the bank offered to corporate customers in early 1984. The

EXHIBIT 5. Partial list of Citibank electronic banking services

CITICASH MANAGER	Access to transaction and balance information (45-day history); funds transfer
CITIDISBURSEMENT	Daily notice of checks cleared against accounts, allowing investment of excess funds
SERPRISE	Reporting and "netting" of intercompany accounts; reporting receivables and payables
CITIINTEGRATOR	Combines personal computer and automatic dialer with proprietary software for automatic daily polling of bank accounts and preparation of consolidated reports
CITITREASURY MANAGER	Reports on securities transactions, commercial paper, debt and investment positions, foreign exchange
CITIRATE®, CITIDATA®	Daily summary of foreign exchange rates, interest rates, gold prices
TREASURY MANAGEMENT SERVICES	Calculates gains and losses on forward foreign exchange contracts
PROSPER, ENTERPRISE	Corporate financial management models for forecasting, sensitivity analysis, etc.
CITIBASE®, CITIQUOTE®, STOCKPORT®, COMPUSTAT®	Data bases covering U.S. economic statistics, securities prices, institutional stock portfolios, financial data on corporations

Source: "Electronic Banking: An Executive's Guide," Citibank, 1983.
COMPUSTAT is a registered trademark of Standard & Poor's, Inc. CITIRATE, CITIDATA, CITIBASE, and CITIQUOTE are registered trademarks of Citibank, N.A.

various specific services were all provided via "CitiNetwork," the bank's proprietary telecommunications system. Citibank owned its own transponders on the Westar 5 satellite, and according to a promotional brochure, the system "links you to more than 500 Citibank offices in 93 countries . . . 24 hours a day, 365 days a year."

Marketing support for electronic banking services within the North American Banking Group was provided by the Marketing Division, headed by Byron Knief. The Marketing Division was organized in a product management structure, which Knief described as "the same, in concept, as that of Procter & Gamble." Each product manager was responsible for preparing and updating marketing plans; continuing product improvements; preparation of promotional materials; attending trade shows and conferences; and internal training activities. In addition, the product managers made presentations to customers, in cooperation with account managers. The Marketing Division staff also included technical consultants who worked with customers in adapting electronic systems to their specific needs.

Knief saw electronic banking as a major strategic direction for Citibank in the 1980s and 1990s. Customer research, he said, showed that cash management was only the "tip of the iceberg." Ultimately, corporate customers wanted to use electronic systems for a wide range of functions including:

> *Collections,* through Lockbox accounts, electronic check presentment, and the automated clearinghouse (a system for handling payments between companies);
>
> *Disbursements,* using checks, funds transfers, and the automated clearinghouse;
>
> *Investments* of surplus funds, using automatic "sweeping" of accounts;
>
> *Reporting* of all transactions.

Beyond the provision of these electronic services *within* a company, Knief saw a potential for the bank's system to handle intercompany transactions:

> *We see the opportunity to connect electronically all of corporate America . . . our electronic highway will post "pages" of information describing a company's goods for sale, current price lists, delivery times, and other information necessary to make a purchase. . . . In addition to exchanging information, buyers will be able to place purchase orders through the system. . . . The basic idea is to capture all information for a stream of transactions by electronically capturing the underlying purchase order.*

COORDINATING MULTINATIONAL RELATIONSHIPS

Multinational corporations shared all of the characteristics of large corporate accounts in general, but also had some distinctive needs. For one thing, major programs such as new overseas plants or acquisitions might require simultaneous, coordinated financial services in two or more countries. An example was described by David Van Pelt, a senior vice-president of the bank:

> *A French corporation needed a total package to provide financing for an export of machinery to the Ivory Coast. Citibank first provided guarantees for the completion of production. Then, the Export Finance Department made a loan which was guaranteed by the French government. Since the export loan did not cover*

the full purchase price, the Merchant Banking Group syndicated a Eurodollar loan for the Ivory Coast buyer. Finally, we provided local banking services for the exporter's Ivory Coast subsidiary.

Apart from the transactions involving services in more than one country, ongoing relationships with MNCs offered opportunities to improve business in one location based on services provided elsewhere. For example, if Citibank's branch in Tokyo provided prompt, efficient foreign exchange services to an American firm's local subsidiary, the bank might gain an edge in the competition for a major transaction in New York. Conversely, poor service in any part of the world could adversely affect a customer's perception of the bank elsewhere.

Prior to 1974, all of Citibank's relationships with U.S.-based MNCs were handled by the Corporate Banking Group, based in New York. The foreign subsidiaries and affiliates of these companies (as well as foreign-based multinationals) were all assigned to Citibank country organizations which reported to an International Banking Group. As the MNCs' international activities grew in the late 1960s and early 1970s, coordination of Citibank's dealings with them became increasingly difficult. Some of the problems were described in a 1975 Harvard Business School case study:

> The most common problem between the CBG and the IBG was that the bank's branch in a foreign country would often prefer to lend money to a local borrower rather than to the foreign subsidiary of a global company. . . . The general belief was that the "spreads," the difference between cost of funds and the percent interest to be charged, was greater when lending to local borrowers. . . . Besides (this) . . ., financing local borrowers would often lead to providing them with other financial services. In contrast, subsidiaries of multinationals were likely to have these services provided by their parent companies.

> Even when local vs. global client preference was not an issue, problems of internal communication existed between the two groups in Citibank. If a U.S. company wanted to build a plant in Argentina, for example, the firm's financial officer might go to the bank's account manager in the CBG. . . . To help his client, the account manager would then make contact with the IBG. "Among other grim realities," recounted one CBG manager, "we didn't know who the bank officer in Argentina was. We were a big bank with hundreds of people, and so you'd write to 'The Manager.' God knows whether he ever got it."

As Citibank's volume of business grew, the problems of dealing with multinational clients through a geographically decentralized organization increased. As early as 1970, there were discussions among senior managers about the possibility of forming a separate organizational unit to service MNCs. It was decided that the first step should be the formation of a staff unit, within the International Banking Group, to explore the subject in detail. Beginning in early 1971, this unit, the World Corporate Division, assembled a data base which would allow management to see the full scope of the bank's dealings with each major multinational client. WCD also provided a mechanism for continuing discussion of possible organizational changes among all concerned — the senior officers in charge of country organizations, account managers in New York, and senior bank management. This process, which continued for more than two years, laid the groundwork for the structural change that was made in 1974.

THE WORLD CORPORATION GROUP

In August 1973, William Spencer, then president, announced that a new unit — The World Corporation Group (WCG) — would be established on January 1, 1974, under the direction of Thomas C. Theobald, executive vice-president. WCG was given line responsibility for a group of 460 major multinational corporate customers which represented about 20% of the bank's total worldwide loan volume. All other accounts remained in either the Corporate Banking Group (domestic) or the International Banking Group (foreign).

The WCG was designed to provide a globally coordinated approach to Citibank's world (multinational) corporate customers. The approach to managing relationships with these accounts, and the systems used to implement them, were collectively designated as the Global Account Management System (GAMS). For each of the companies assigned to WCG, a Parent Account manager (PAM) located in the company's home country was designated to handle relationships with the parent corporation. In each country where a WCG corporation had branches or subsidiaries, a Field Account manager (FAM) handled the local relationship. The same individual might serve as a PAM for accounts in his own country and as a FAM for one or more relationships with companies headquartered elsewhere. Altogether, 460 corporate banking officers located in 26 different countries were assigned to the WCG. An organization chart (as of early 1978) is shown in *Exhibit 6*.

Citibank corporate customers were selected for servicing by WCG on the basis of several criteria:

- having manufacturing facilities in at least four foreign countries;
- exhibiting a strong commitment to international business;

EXHIBIT 6. Partial organization chart — World Corporation Group, 1978

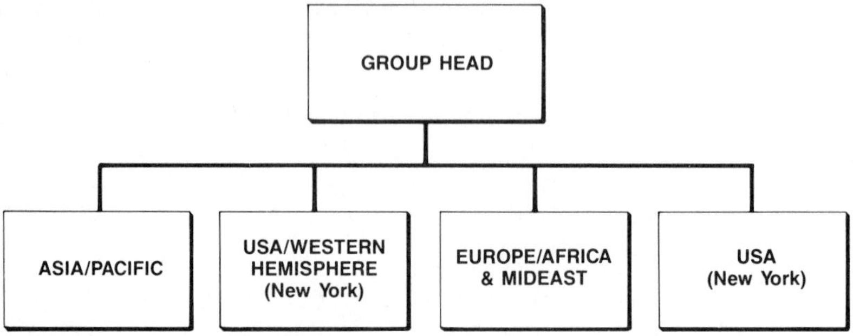

```
                          ┌──────────────────┐
                          │   GROUP HEAD     │
                          └──────────────────┘
          ┌───────────────┬──────────┴──────────┬───────────────┐
┌──────────────┐ ┌──────────────┐ ┌──────────────┐ ┌──────────────┐
│              │ │ USA/WESTERN  │ │              │ │              │
│ ASIA/PACIFIC │ │ HEMISPHERE   │ │ EUROPE/AFRICA│ │    USA       │
│              │ │ (New York)   │ │  & MIDEAST   │ │ (New York)   │
└──────────────┘ └──────────────┘ └──────────────┘ └──────────────┘
```

— Japan/Korea	— Shipping & insurance	— United Kingdom	— Petroleum
— Hong Kong	— Information & consumer products	— Germany	— Capital goods
— Philippines	— Consumer nondurables	— France	— Consumer durables
— Singapore/ Malaysia	— Japanese companies	— Italy	— Metals & mining
— Indonesia	— Canada	— Switzerland	— Chemicals
— India	— Argentina	— Benelux	
— Australia	— Mexico	— South Africa	
— Taiwan	— Venezuela	— Greece	
	— Brazil		
	— Puerto Rico		

Source: Company records.

- utilizing global strategies with regard to manufacturing, marketing, and financial management.

Of the firms thus chosen, about half were U.S.-based; 35% were European; and most of the remainder were Japanese. Among industries strongly represented were consumer products, petroleum, chemicals, mining, and capital goods.

The establishment of WCG as a unit with line responsibility for its designated accounts was a significant change in Citibank's organization.

Traditionally, the bank had put strong emphasis on local autonomy for each country. All activities in a country were directed by a local general manager, then called the senior officer or "SENOF," who had considerable freedom to make decisions, allocate resources, and manage people within the bank's broad policy guidelines. The WCG organization, in contrast, was only partially subject to the SENOF's control.

Walter B. Wriston, chairman, outlined the relationships between the WCG and the existing International Banking Group in a September 1973 memorandum:

1. In each of the designated countries (initially 23 in number) a WCG Department was established, and a department head appointed. (In all other countries, a WCG unit was formed, but functioned as part of the local corporate bank organization.)

2. The SENOF in each country retained "overall direction and responsibility for total country market strategy, funding, and administration of corporate policy and practice." The WCG Department Head was given primary responsibility for market management of his/her assigned accounts, "within the country strategy guidelines established by the SENOF."

3. The SENOF and WCG Department Head were held *jointly* responsible for, and evaluated on, local results with WCG accounts.

4. Country organizations provided premises, administrative services, and MIS to the WCG Department.

5. The WCG Department Head set prices (interest rates and fees) for his/her accounts, consistent with strategies formulated by the PAM responsible for a particular customer. SENOF concurrence was required, however, for "pricing which deviates significantly from established country market practice or policy."

6. Primary evaluation of WCG personnel was done by WCG Department Heads who were, in turn, evaluated by WCG Division Heads. SENOFs also contributed comments to these evaluations.

PLANNING, BUDGETING, AND PERFORMANCE MEASUREMENT

A primary objective of the establishment of WCG was to facilitate planning for global accounts on an integrated, worldwide basis. This was accomplished through the GAMS systems of annual planning, budgeting, and performance measurement.

EXHIBIT 7. GAMS marketing plan

GAMS MARKETING PLAN		
☐ CUSTOMER ☐ PROSPECT		DATE: _____
COMPANY		PARENT
COUNTRY/DEPARTMENT	BUSINESS	REVENUES (U.S. $MM)

CORNERSTONE OBJECTIVE, if any (Include potential annual AP impact, whether or not budgeted)

(AP = Account Profit)

PRODUCT/SERVICE PROFILE (specify services used and/or for which the company is an active prospect, e.g., credit, cash management, treasury, merchant banking, electronic banking, etc.)

CITICORP SERVICE:							
Tier Position if User*;
"P" if prospect							
Importance to customer **							

*"1", LEAD OR SHARED LEAD; "2" MAJOR, "3" MINOR.   **High/Medium/Low

OBJECTIVES/ACTION PLAN FOR CREDIT AND SERVICES MARKETING	POTENTIAL AP IMPACT	TARGET DATE

SIGNIFICANT DEVELOPMENTS WHICH MAY AFFECT RELATIONSHIP, if any

CALL PROGRAM FOR BUDGET PERIOD

CITICORP OFFICERS	FREQUENCY/TIMING
ACCOUNT MANAGER	
COUNTRY/DEPT. MANAGEMENT (SPECIFY)	
SENIOR OFFICERS (SPECIFY)	
OTHER (SPECIFY)	

ACCOUNT MANAGER (PRINT):	APPROVED:
X 9283	**(USE REVERSE SIDE IF NECESSARY)**

EXHIBIT 8. Simplified outline of GAMS account budget format

Company _____ Account manager _____

Country _____ GAMS parent _____

Item	Explanation
1. Total uses*	Amount of funds expected to be used by account
2. Sources:* a. Interest-bearing b. Non-interest bearing	Amount of funds expected to be provided by account in deposits or otherwise
3. Exchange	Expected revenue from foreign exchange services
4. Commissions	Self-explanatory
5. Cost of services	Estimated direct cost of servicing the account (see Appendix A)
6. Matrix earnings	Expected net revenue (revenue less direct cost) from services provided to account by other Citibank divisions, e.g., merchant banking
7. Account profit	Net interest revenue, plus items 3, 4, and 6, minus item 5

*Uses and sources were budgeted and measured separately for local currency and foreign currency amounts.
Source: Excerpted from company budget form.

Under GAMS, the PAM prepared an annual marketing plan for each parent account. Separate plans were developed by the FAMs for each subsidiary that accounted for a significant volume of activity, and these were combined with the parent account plan into a single, global plan. The form used in preparing these plans is reproduced, in part, in *Exhibit 7*.[5]

In conjunction with the marketing plans, the PAM and FAMs prepared annual budgets for each WCG account. The revenue and expense categories covered by these budgets are outlined in *Exhibit 8*, and the procedure used to calculate account profitability is explained (in a simplified fashion) in Appendix A.

Comparison of actual results with budgets allowed PAMs and WCG management to track performance, on a quarterly basis, for each account. Management summaries of these data included compilations for

_____

[5]The term "cornerstone" in *Exhibit 7* refers to goals established by account managers for key transactions with a customer.

all accounts in each country, region, etc. An example of a quarterly Global Account Profitability System (GAPS) report for "ABC, Inc." is given in *Exhibit 9*. In this printout, each component of revenue is shown, by country and in total, and each item is compared with the corresponding budget figure. In the (hypothetical) example given, for instance, worldwide net revenue from funds for ABC, Inc. in the last quarter of 1979 amounted to $252,000 — $122,000 over budget.[6] Additional revenues were earned from exchange ($12,000), commissions ($17,000), and matrix earning ($8,000). Direct costs of services amounted to $2,000, leaving account profitability of $287,000 ($252 + 12 + $17 + $8 − 2 = $287). Actual account profitability can be compared with budget ($132,000 over) and also related to the bank's *risk assets invested*. The last column of the printout shows the APR or Account Profitability Return:

$$\frac{\text{Account Profits}}{\text{Total Risk Assets}} = \frac{\$287}{\$20,776} = \begin{array}{l} 1.38\% \text{ (quarterly) or} \\ 5.5\% \text{ (annual rate)} \end{array}$$

An important feature of the GAPS reporting system was that it enabled management to see and evaluate results for an account in a given country in the context of overall global results. For example, *Exhibit 9* shows that the APR for ABC, Inc. in Argentina was only 1.9%. In isolation, this might have been regarded as unsatisfactory since Citibank's experience had shown that an APR of about 2.5% was needed in order to achieve an overall return on assets of 1%.[7] (As a rule of thumb, 1% was regarded as a very good rate of return on assets in banking.) The results of dealings with ABC, Inc. in Argentina, however, were more than offset by performance elsewhere.

EXPERIENCE WITH THE WCG: 1974–78

According to Citibank managers who had worked in the WCG, it proved to be an effective mechanism for building business with MNCs. The process of adapting to the new structure had not, however, been frictionless. In the early stages, there had been concerns about the relation-

---

[6] In the printout, differences between actual and budgeted amounts are designated as "better" (B) or "worse" (W).

[7] APR was measured before many expenses (see Appendix A). In 1982, Citibank earned $1.3 billion (pretax) on assets of $130 billion — almost exactly a 1% return. Return on equity, after tax, was 16.4%.

EXHIBIT 9. Parent account manager report, global account profitability system

Period QUARTER ENDING DECEMBER 1979   PAM S. Queenslander

Parent Name ABC, INC.

Subsidiaries listed by country	Local uses	Total uses	Non-I.B. sources	Total sources	Net. rev. from funds	Ex-change	Comm.	Cost of services	Total risk assets	Matrix earnings	Account profits	APR
16178 ABC Overseas	0	241	165	453	7	9	2	1	241	0	17	28.0
16190 ABC Manufacturing	0	0	19	19	0	0	11	0	0	0	11	—
18800 DEF Ltd.	6389	6389	5	283	(3)	0	0	0	6389	0	(3)	(.2)
18801 DEF	5296	5791	1351	1761	9	0	0	0	5791	0	9	.6
44026 GHI Ltd.	0	0	982	982	21	0	3	0	0	0	24	—
Total Argentina actual	11685	12421	2522	3498	34	9	16	1	12421	0	58	1.9
B/(W) budget	(1815)	(2579)	1682	(1692)	(33)	(3)	0	(1)	(2579)	0	(35)	(.6)
16175 ABC Export	1747	1747	113	336	190	0	0	0	1747	0	190	43.1
16183 JKL	0	0	11	11	1	0	0	0	0	0	1	—
Total Germany actual	1747	1747	124	347	191	0	0	0	1747	0	191	43.4
B/(W) budget	1102	1223	47	47	128	0	0	(1)	1223	0	129	(3.5)
16170 ABC Southland, S.A.	5077	5077	0	88	27	3	1	1	6608	8	38	2.3
Total Uruguay actual	5077	5077	0	88	27	3	1	1	6608	8	38	2.3
B/(W) budget	5077	5077	0	88	27	3	1	1	6608	8	38	2.3
Total ABC, Inc. actual	18509	19245	2646	3933	252	12	17	2	20776	8	287	5.5
B/(W) budget	4364	3721	1729	(1557)	122	0	1	(1)	5252	8	132	1.5

ship between the WCG departments and the existing country-level organizations. One manager commented on this aspect a year after the change took place:

> *In European countries, like Germany and Italy, WCG was taking something like 80 percent of the profits away from the SENOFs. This was one of the first direct cuts at the geographical responsibility of the SENOFs. . . . Our leading edge has always been geography, but organizing by customer segment or by product line begins to chip away at the authority of the SENOFs.*

The same manager explained how conflicts between WCG and a country organization arose:

> *The problems that came up right away (in Brazil) were characteristic, I think, of WCG in any country with a tight money market. There is one pool of local funds, and it's not unlimited. So how do you divvy them up? . . . We tried doing it by formula, based on amounts of deposits provided by the companies. . . . There were times when a WCG client would need a vast amount of local money. That threw the ratio for the week out of line. But if it was a good deal for the bank as a whole, WCG would get the money and give back something later on. It's horse trading and it worked very well.*

Another kind of friction arose from the perception, by account managers who were *not* assigned to WCG, that the new organization was an "elite group" within the bank. One senior vice-president who had served as a WCG Department head overseas commented,

> *We were viewed as the "Green Berets" within the International Banking Group. Some of my colleagues in the country where I worked spoke about their own accounts as being the "leftovers" after WCG had gotten all the best ones.*

Despite these difficulties, it appeared that WCG had contributed to the growth and profitability of Citibank's international business in the late 1970s. In a presentation to financial analysts in 1978, Executive Vice-President Reuben F. Richards, then head of the WCG, summarized the results achieved by the group between 1974 and 1977:

- Total account profits increased 63%, from $194 million to $317 million;
- Number of relationships (parents and subsidiaries) up from 5,600 to 6,350;
- Total borrowings up from $5.3 billion to $9.8 billion;
- Borrowings by British companies increased by 200%; by French companies, 480%. (Borrowings by U.S. WCG companies rose by 13%.)

THE 1980 REORGANIZATION

In late 1979, Citibank's senior management announced a reorganization to take effect on January 1, 1980. The new organization structure combined three units — the domestic Corporate Banking Group, the International Banking Group, and the WCG — into a single Institutional Banking Group. Thomas C. Theobald, vice-chairman of Citibank, was appointed to head the IB Group.

According to Citicorp's 1979 *Annual Report,* the new IB structure was designed "to simplify the problems of providing overall management to far-flung financial businesses." A simpler structure, it was suggested, would "move decision making closer to the customer" and also "assure that improvements developed in one part (of the organization) spread quickly to the rest."

The new organization structure of the IB is shown in *Exhibit 10.* Within this structure, an IB unit in each country (or region within the U.S.) had full responsibility for all corporate accounts, including MNCs, located in its territory. The account managers formerly assigned to WCG units were reassigned, often in the same location, to country or regional units. Thomas Theobald commented on the reorganization:

> We certainly did not want to reduce our emphasis on global corporations. In fact, at the same time we set up the Institutional Bank, we also decided to extend the Global Account Management System to a larger number of companies. We added almost 1,000 more names to the list for global account planning and profitability reporting. . . . The reorganization was not intended as a repudiation of the global approach which had served us well. It was, instead, an effort to simplify the structure at the top level.

Some Citibank executives who had worked in the WCG felt, in 1984, that the organization might simply have outlived its usefulness. One suggested that the business of lending to MNCs, and large corporations in general, was a mature one by 1980:

> Earnings growth had topped out, and it didn't pay anymore to put a lot of effort into this part of our business. . . . The growth opportunities now are in new products, not in making more loans.

Another executive pointed out that Citibank had, for many years, changed its organization structure from time to time to reflect new priorities. He recalled that at one time, when the bank had decided to develop a leasing business, it had set up an independent subsidiary corporation called Citicorp Leasing. This unit had had its own marketing function as well as a separate accounting system, office staff, and so

EXHIBIT 10. Partial organizational chart as of January 1980

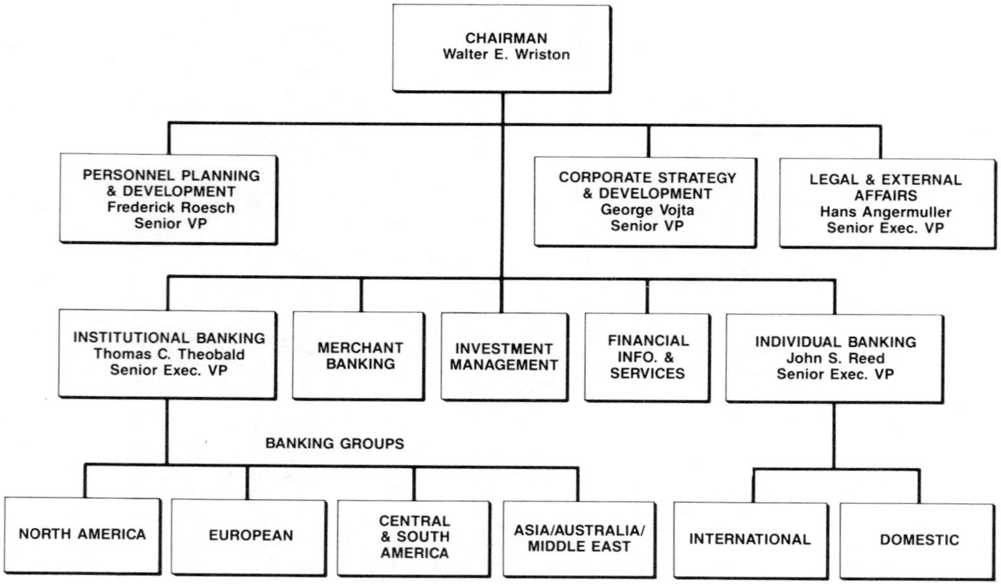

on. Eventually, he recalled, the unit had been dissolved and its activities integrated into the domestic and international corporate banking organizations. The general idea had been summed up by a Citibank executive vice-president in 1975:

> *When you matrix a market or a product line, you do it for a while, until you get the degree of differentiation you want. Then, at some point, you may integrate it. We do a lot of matrixing.*

SUBSEQUENT DEVELOPMENTS

Following the reorganization, the GAMS and GAPS systems continued to operate for the expanded list of around 1,500 accounts. By early 1982, however, there was considerable dissatisfaction with the way the system was working. For instance, many of the former WCG executives felt that the attention being given to planning and budgeting was gradually declining. According to Larry Lee,

> *The system simply lost its momentum. Country managers put more and more emphasis on local profits, and in the review process (i.e., in appraisals of management performance) global account profitability got less and less attention.*

As a result of management discussions, a task force comprised of five senior vice-presidents was appointed to explore the GAMS system and recommend improvements in it. The primary recommendations of the task force, in mid-1982, were as follows:

1. The list of GAMS accounts should be reduced to focus only on "priority clients with real long-term potential." Profitability data for other multinational accounts should still be reported, but marketing plans, budgeting, and institutional reviews should not be required for these accounts.
2. Performance in relation to global profitability goals should be instituted and monitored as part of the regular performance review process. It was recommended, specifically, that AP data from GAPS be included as "notational entries" in quarterly management reports.
3. Steps should be taken to improve the accuracy and timeliness of GAPS data collection and distribution.
4. The electronic capabilities of GAPS should be further developed. This should include, eventually, an electronic customer/account manager directory, monthly compilation and reporting of profit data, and on-line country information about rates, availability, etc.

5. An incentive program should be developed to recognize superior performance by GAMS teams on a global basis.

6. A special module in the IB's account management training program should be devoted to GAMS.

Larry Lee had been appointed to serve as GAMS coordinator, in addition to his own account management responsibilities, to implement the task force recommendations. By the end of 1983, most of the task force recommendations had been implemented or were in process of being implemented. The GAMS list had been cut back to 501 accounts. Of these, about 200 were U.S.-based; 190 were European; and 80 were Japanese. The criteria used for including an account in the revised GAMS system were: annual global account profit potential of at least $300,000; field subsidiaries' profit potential, in aggregate, of at least $150,000; significant operations in at least four countries outside the home country; and a provision that maximizing the account's performance would require "ongoing coordination of (Citibank's) business across the global network." Analysis of trends in the GAMS accounts showed that their profitability had increased by 23% in 1981, by about 4% in 1982, and 12% in 1983.

A second change, instituted in 1982, was the establishment of annual GAMS bonus awards. The first such awards were to be made in April 1983, with individual amounts ranging from $5,000 up to $25,000. Each country or department having responsibility for one or more GAMS parent companies was asked to nominate teams for the awards which were to be based on improvement in global relationship profitability and on "close and effective teamwork among individuals in various geographical and organizational units."

A third change, announced in June 1983, was a clarification of the role of the GAMS coordinators who were responsible for overseeing the operation of the system in each of 70 Citibank units (country organizations and U.S. regional offices). These coordinators were to

> be the focal points for timely dissemination of GAPS reports . . . communicate local needs and problems to other Coordinators . . . [and] coordinate, and ensure compliance with the GAMS Budget/Planning Calendar and other GAMS procedures.

THE SITUATION IN EARLY 1984

Lee felt that the changes made in 1982 and 1983 had strengthened the GAMS system considerably. He was not, however, completely satisfied with the functioning of the system. The problem, as he saw it, was one of getting adequate attention for global accounts from account managers, division heads, and country corporate officers. In late 1983, for example, fewer than half of the countries had submitted their 1984 GAMS budgets on time. Some of the WCG "alumni" felt that the system, without any line authority behind it, "lacked teeth." An account manager in London put it this way:

> *It's a question of how much priority top management assigns to the global accounts. In the last two years or so, the emphasis has been on increasing return on assets . . . global profits (on GAMS accounts) outside your own country don't really count that much.*

Another London account manager said:

> *The value that is attached to international profits depends on your boss. For those that worked in the old WCG, it's no problem. But some others blow hot and cold.*

There was general agreement that for very large MNCs that were profitable accounts, there was relatively little problem in getting local cooperation, at least for major transactions. The London-based account manager for a multinational food processing firm recounted, as an illustration, a recent loan that had been made:

> *We provided the credit at LIBOR plus 1/8% . . . we said "ouch," but we did it.*

Larry Lee suggested that for the 100 largest companies on the GAMS list (in terms of AP) which accounted for about 60% of the total profits, account managers could generally be expected to do what needed to be done, with or without a formal management system. For the remaining GAMS accounts, the picture was not so clear. Among the 500-odd accounts, the 100 that ranked lowest in terms of profitability had yielded, in 1983, an average of about $100,000 of account profits each. The combined profits of this group represented only about 2% of the GAMS accounts' total. Lee wondered if these accounts, or others that were not included in the GAMS planning system, should be treated in a different way.

Opinions varied within the bank on what might be done to improve the GAMS system. The consultant's report, which Lee had recently read, summarized the attitudes of a sample of Citibank executives and account managers. Several of those who had been interviewed commented on the use of global account profit information in performance appraisal:

> *If I tell my boss about a transaction, his first question is "Is it for us or for another country?" If you are $500,000 below on your local earnings goal, and*

$2 million ahead on your global goal, the latter is not going to help you. (An account manager.)

I have domestic and global profit goals. We have talked about (the idea of giving) 50% credit for overseas earnings. (Another account manager.)

Some of the individuals interviewed by the consultant had made specific suggestions for improving GAMS. Some of these suggestions dealt with the mechanics of the system. For example, one FAM urged that communication between PAMs and FAMs, especially personal contacts, be increased:

The only time we hear anything about it (i.e., GAMS) is once a year when the PAMs send out the plan. Everything else we do on our own. There is no discussion, such as "How is it going? Why did you do that?" etc.

Another said:

There should be more interchange across areas . . . increase the use of seminars, have more juniors travel. Have PAM meetings, at least in New York, to talk about common problems.

More basic criticism of GAMS also emerged from the survey. Several respondents expressed the view that the system did not play a sufficiently important role in the day-to-day management of account relationships. One stated, for example, that

it (GAMS) is not really managerial reporting anymore. The system was in the beginning (i.e., under the WCG organization) really used to manage the business. What we do now between FAMs and PAMs is a formal requirement which you fulfill.

Along the same line, a PAM stated that

you've got to keep up awareness that GAMS is still alive. If you don't keep pushing it, it will fade from people's minds . . . FAMs need to be reminded that senior management is paying attention to global earnings.

Lee was also aware that some people in the bank, most of them "alumni" of the old WCG, would like to see that kind of line organizational arrangement reinstituted. One of them had told the consultant a little wistfully,

I think the only way (to improve GAMS) is to reimplement the WCG. I know that's not possible. I don't think the dilution of the system was a consequence of adding more names. It's that the WCG organization isn't there. The solution is to create a separate group since they have a different job, face different markets, and need different approaches. I was a big believer in the WCG system. . . . It was really a management system.

APPENDIX A

Citibank: Marketing to Multinational Customers: Measurement of Account Profitability

The GAPS system called for quarterly reports of revenue, costs, and profitability for each account with budgeted profitability of $25,000 or more. These data were collected from each country in which a corporate customer had dealings with the bank. A similar system was used to measure profitability for large domestic accounts (DAPS). The explanation that follows is a simplified summary of the GAPS system.

REVENUES

Revenues from an account included:

1. Actual interest income from loans and loan-related fees.
2. Fees and commissions for payment services, letters of credit, consulting services, investment management, etc.

DIRECT COSTS

Each account was charged with the direct costs of servicing it, plus an allocated amount of "semi-direct" costs. *Direct* costs included those associated with transaction processing and customer service. *Semi-direct* expenses were those of first-level supervision, support activities such as filing, mailing, communications, data processing, and space. Costs of administration, research and development, and marketing were *not* allocated to individual accounts.

NET EXPENSE/REVENUE FROM FUNDS

Each account was charged (or credited) with the net cost (or income) of providing funds to it. This figure was determined as follows:

1. In each country, a "pool rate" cost of funds was established on a daily basis. This rate represented the marginal cost of funds to the bank from an appropriate external source.
2. Each account was charged or credited with a cost or revenue amount based on its net use (borrowing) or provision (deposit) of funds. Ideally this calculation was made daily, but in practice it could be (and often was)

derived by applying the average pool rate for a monthly period to the account's average net positive or negative balance.

FOREIGN EXCHANGE

Earnings (net of direct costs and taxes) on "matrix products" were credited to each account. These were services provided by Citibank divisions other than the Institutional Bank, e.g., merchant banking, financial advisory asset-based finance, trust, and travellers' checks.

ACCOUNT PROFITABILITY

Account profitability was defined as:

> Income from loans
> + Fees and commissions earned
> + Matrix earnings
> ± Net expense/revenue from funds
> ± Foreign exchange gains/losses
> − Direct cost of services
> − Credit losses (actual write-offs)

RISK ASSETS

The profitability of each account was related to the amount of the bank's "risk assets" invested in it. Risk assets included loans outstanding and amounts at risk via matrix products (e.g., asset-based loans). For each account, a key measure of performance was the Account Profitability Ratio (APR), defined as:

> Account Profitability/Risk Assets

(The same method of calculating account profitability was used for domestic accounts.)

SELECTED BIBLIOGRAPHY

TEXTBOOKS AND READINGS BOOKS

Cateora, Philip R. *International Marketing.* 5th ed. Homewood, IL: Richard D. Irwin, 1983.

Jain, Subhash C. *International Marketing Management.* Boston, MA: Kent Publishing Co., 1984.

Keegan, Warren. *Multinational Marketing Management.* 3rd ed. Englewood Cliffs, NJ: Prentice-Hall, 1984.

Kirpalani, V.H. (ed.). *International Marketing: Managerial Issues, Research and Opportunities.* Chicago, IL: American Marketing Association, 1983.

Leontiades, James C. *Multinational Corporate Strategy.* Lexington, MA: Lexington Books, 1985.

Porter, Michael E. (ed.). *Competition in Global Industries.* Boston, MA: Harvard Business School Press, 1986.

Root, Franklin R. *Foreign Market Entry Strategies.* New York, NY: AMACOM, 1982.

Thorelli, Hans, and Helmut Becker. *International Marketing Strategy.* Revised ed. Elmsford, NY: Pergamon Press, 1980.

ARTICLES

Ayal, Igal. "International Product Life Cycle: A Reassessment and Product Policy Implications." *Journal of Marketing,* Fall 1981, pp. 91–96.

Ayal, Igal, and Jehiel Zif. "Market Expansion Strategies in Multinational Marketing." *Journal of Marketing,* Spring 1979, pp. 84–94.

Barrett, M. Edgar. "Case of the Tangled Transfer Price." *Harvard Business Review,* May-June 1977, pp. 20–25.

Bartlett, Christopher A., and Sumantra Ghoshal. "Tap Your Subsidiaries for Global Reach." *Harvard Business Review,* November-December 1986, pp. 87–94.

Cavusgil, S. Tammer, and John R. Nevin. "State-of-the-Art in International Marketing: An Assessment." *Review of Marketing 1981,* Ben M. Enis, and K.J. Roering, eds. Chicago, IL: American Marketing Association, pp. 195–216.

Colvin, Michael, Roger Heeler, and Jim Thorpe. "Developing International Advertising Strategy." *Journal of Marketing,* Fall 1980, pp. 73–79.

Doz, Yves L. "Strategic Management in Multinational Companies." *Sloan Management Review,* Winter 1980, pp. 27–46.

Doz, Yves, and C.K. Prahalad. "Patterns of Strategic Control within Multinational Corporations." *Journal of International Business Studies,* Fall 1984, pp. 55–72.

Giddy, Ian H. "The Demise of the Product Life Cycle Model in International Business Theory." *Columbia Journal of World Business,* Spring 1978, pp. 90–97.

Hill, John S., and Richard R. Still. "Adapting Products to LDC Tastes." *Harvard Business Review,* March-April 1984, pp. 92–101.

Johansson, Johny K., and Hans B. Thorelli. "International Product Positioning." *Journal of International Business Studies,* Fall 1985, pp. 57–75.

Killough, James. "Improved Payoffs from Transnational Advertising." *Harvard Business Review,* July-August 1978, pp. 102–110.

Kotler, Philip, and Liam Fahey. "The World's Champion Marketers: The Japanese." *Journal of Business Strategy,* Summer 1982, pp. 3–13.

Larreche, Jean-Claude. "The International Product-Market Portfolio." *Readings in Marketing Management,* J. Larreche and E. Strong, eds. Palo Alto, CA: The Scientific Press, 1982, pp. 489–499.

McIntyre, David R. "Your Overseas Distributor Action Plan." *Journal of Marketing,* April 1977, pp. 88–90.

Onkvisit, Sak, and John J. Shaw. "An Examination of the International Product Life Cycle and Its Application Within Marketing." *Columbia Journal of World Business,* Fall 1983, pp. 73–79.

Peebles, Dean M., John K. Ryans, Jr., and Ivan R. Vernon. "Coordinating International Marketing." *Journal of Marketing,* January 1978, pp. 28–34.

Sorenson, Ralph Z., and Ulrich E. Wiechmann. "How Multinationals View Marketing Standardization." *Harvard Business Review,* May-June 1975, pp. 38–45.

Watson, Craig M. "Counter-Competition Abroad to Protect Home Markets." *Harvard Business Review,* January-February 1982, pp. 40–42.

Webber, John A. "Worldwide Strategies for Market Segmentation." *Columbia Journal of World Business,* Winter 1974, pp. 31–38.

Wells, Louis T., Jr. "A Product Life Cycle for International Trade?" *Journal of Marketing,* July 1968, pp. 1–6.

Wiechmann, Ulrich E., and Lewis G. Pringle. "Problems That Plague Multinational Marketers." *Harvard Business Review,* July-August 1979, pp. 118–124.

Wind, Yoram, and Susan P. Douglas. "International Portfolio Analysis and Strategy: The Challenge of the 80s." *Journal of International Business Studies,* Fall 1981, pp. 69–82.